Jana Joachim Klasse 7am 07/08

Gymnasium Bayern

English G

Band 3

für die
7. Jahrgangsstufe
an Gymnasien
in Bayern

Cornelsen

English G
Ausgabe für Bayern – Band 3

Im Auftrag des Verlages herausgegeben von: Prof. Hellmut Schwarz, Mannheim

Erarbeitet von — Laurence Harger; Barbara Derkow Disselbeck; Allen J. Woppert
unter Mitarbeit von — Wolfgang Biederstädt; Joachim Blombach; Dr. Jens-Peter Green; Mervyn Whittaker
in Zusammenarbeit mit der Englischredaktion — Silvia Wiedemann (verantwortliche Redakteurin); Uwe Tröger; Kirsten Bleck (Projektleitung); Susanne Bennetreu
Beratende Mitwirkung — Burkhard Dammann, Nürnberg; Gerhard Finster, Dillingen; Dr. Ursula Mulla, Germering; Esther Obst-Kennedy, Mering; Uwe Schmedemann, München; Susanne Schroeder-Thürauf, Fürth; Norbert Weigler, München; Klaus Weinzierl, München

Grafik/Illustration — David Barnett, Oadby, Leicester; Dr. Volkhard Binder, Berlin; Gabriele Heinisch, Berlin; Eva Muszynski, Berlin; Linda Rogers Associates, London: Tim Benton, Roger Fereday, Jenny Gregory, Tony Morris, Gary Rees; Mark Salwowski, Stanford in the Vale; Constanze Schargan, Berlin; Dick Smolinski/Bookmakers Ltd., Taos, NM; Katharina Wieker, Berlin
Umschlaggestaltung — Katrin Nehm
Layoutkonzept — Gisela Hoffmann
Layout und technische Umsetzung — Petra Eberhard; Gisela Hoffmann

Zusatzmaterialien zum vorliegenden Schülerbuch

Workbook
ISBN 13: 978-3-464-35556-5
ISBN 10: 3-464-35556-X
3 CDs zum Schülerbuch
ISBN 13: 978-3-464-35568-8
ISBN 10: 3-464-35568-3

Auf weitere Bestandteile wird in den Handreichungen für den Unterricht verwiesen.
ISBN 13: 978-3-464-35617-3
ISBN 10: 3-464-35617-5

www.cornelsen.de

1. Auflage, 2. Druck 2006

Alle Drucke dieser Auflage sind inhaltlich unverändert und können im Unterricht nebeneinander verwendet werden.

Druck: CS-Druck CornelsenStürtz, Berlin

ISBN 13: 978-3-464-35550-3
ISBN 10: 3-464-35550-0

Inhalt gedruckt auf säurefreiem Papier,
umweltschonend hergestellt aus chlorfrei gebleichten Faserstoffen.

CONTENTS

Dein Englischbuch enthält folgende Teile:

UNITS	die sechs Kapitel des Buches
TOPICS	Lesens- und Wissenswertes zu weiteren Themen der Unit, z.B. „Hurricanes“
DO-IT-YOURSELF EXERCISES	Aufgaben zum Selbermachen zum selbstständigen Üben
REVISION	Wiederholungsaufgaben
MEDIATION	Übungen zur Sprachmittlung – hier übst du zu dolmetschen, sinngemäß ins Englische zu übertragen und kurze Sätze zu übersetzen
LANGUAGE SUMMARY (S)	eine Zusammenfassung der Grammatik jeder Unit
VOCABULARY (V)	das Wörterverzeichnis zum Lernen der neuen Wörter
DICTIONARY (D)	das alphabetische Wörterverzeichnis zum Nachschlagen
LISTS	Listen: *Names, Countries and Continents, Grammatical Terms, Irregular Verbs, Classroom Phrases*

Die Units bestehen aus diesen Teilen:

LEAD-IN	die erste (Doppel-)Seite einer Unit; Einstieg in das neue Thema
A-SECTION	der neue Lernstoff mit ersten Übungen
PRACTICE	Übungen, Sprachspiele und Aktivitäten
TEXT	Lesetexte, z. B. ein Zeitungsartikel, eine Kurzgeschichte, usw.
HOW TO ...	Übungen und Tipps zum Training der Fertigkeiten *reading, writing, listening* und *speaking*

In den Units findest du diese Überschriften und Symbole:

Now you	Hier kannst du über dich selbst sprechen oder schreiben.
Activity	Aufgaben, bei denen du etwas tust – z.B. eine Collage gestalten
Game	Spiele für zwei, für eine Gruppe oder für die ganze Klasse
Mediation	Übungen zur Sprachmittlung, zum Dolmetschen und Übersetzen
Role-play	Vorschlag für das Spielen einer Szene mit verteilten Rollen
Project	Hier kannst du allein, zu zweit oder in der Gruppe Informationen sammeln und dann anderen vorstellen.
Looking at language	Hier lernst du neue Grammatikstrukturen kennen.
Focus on words	Hier sammelst, ordnest und verwendest du neue Wörter und Ausdrücke.
Word watch	Unter dieser Überschrift geht es immer um Übungen zum Wortschatz.
Listening	Hier gibt es Hörtexte auf CD und dazu Aufgaben im Buch.
Revision	Hier wird wiederholt – damit du nichts vergisst.
◆◆	Partnerarbeit
❖	Gruppenarbeit

UK Calling

1 *UK facts*

The maps below show the five countries England, Wales, Scotland, Northern Ireland and Ireland, and also the British Isles, the United Kingdom and Great Britain.
Which four countries make up the United Kingdom (UK)?
What's the difference between the UK and the British Isles?

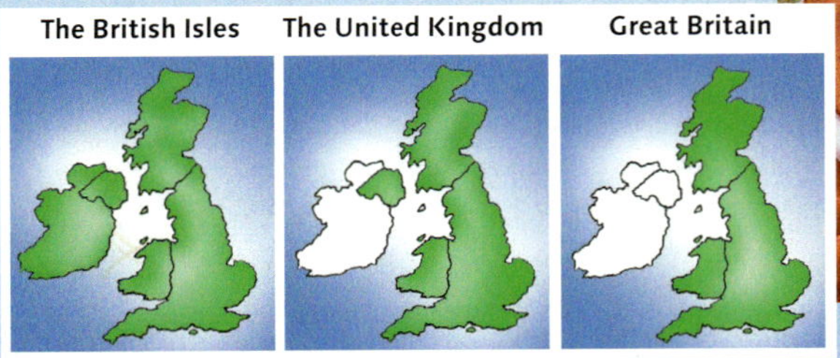

2 *UK quiz*

Match the capitals, flags, populations and highest mountains to the right country in the UK. Look in an atlas, an encyclopedia, on the Internet, … to find out.

The populations
A 49.1 million
B 5.1 million
C 2.9 million
D 1.7 million

The flags

You can easily see which three flags go together to make up the British flag.

The British flag – the Union Jack

The capitals

The highest mountains
A Ben Nevis 4406 ft (1343 m)
B Scafell Pike 3210 ft (978 m)
C Slieve Donard 2796 ft (852 m)
D Snowdon 3560 ft (1085 m)

◆◆ 3 *Activity: Start a UK album*

Choose something like *longest river*, *largest city*, *important tourist sight*, … and find more facts for the four countries of the United Kingdom. Find a photo or two. Write down the facts in your UK album and stick the photos in. Show your album to a partner. Can he/she match the photos/facts to the right countries?
Add more UK photos and captions as you work through the book.

4 *Listening: UK radio*

a Listen to the CD. Try to find all the place names you hear on the map of the United Kingdom at the front of the book.

❖ b Listen again. What are the names of the radio stations? What countries are they in? Write down one thing you remember from each radio station. Compare your information in your group and then in class.

c Now listen a third time. All the people you hear speak English but they've all got different English accents because they come from different countries in the UK. Which radio station was the easiest to understand? Which was most difficult? Give reasons. Can you say anything about the different accents? Tell the class.

5 *UK kids*

For an e-mail project, four schoolchildren from the UK wrote about the areas they come from.

Hello. My name is Pippa. I am 13, and I go to Caistor Grammar School. I do lots of horse riding, and I ride my horse Honey through the beautiful Lincoln Wolds.
Caistor is a very old town at the top of a hill. You can still see the old Roman town wall at St Peter and St Paul's Church.
The Viking Way, a famous walking track, goes right through the town – lots of Vikings lived in this area over a thousand years ago.

My name is Julie and I'm 14. I live in the small village of Laid on Loch Eriboll[3] in Scotland. My dad is a crofter – that's what we call farmers here.
I have to take a taxi and then a bus to my school in Kinlochbervie[4]. This takes about 90 minutes over the small roads. Only about 150 people live in Kinlochbervie and our school is one of the most remote schools in Europe.

Hello, I'm Thomas. I go to the Ysgol Bryn Elian[1] in Colwyn Bay. On a clear day we can look out of the window and see right across the sea to England. Music is very important to us and I am in the school choir. If we practise hard, perhaps we'll be able to sing at the Urdd Eisteddfod[2]. That's the most important festival of Welsh culture for young people and the biggest youth festival in Europe.

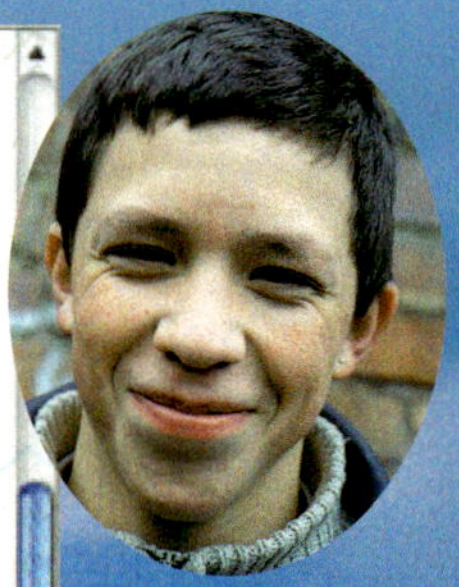

Hi, I'm Steven from Limavady[5] High School in Limavady. It's a small town on the River Roe. The name Limavady comes from the Gaelic 'Leim an Mhadaidh'[6] and means 'Jump of the Dog'. There is an old story about a dog that jumped across the River Roe and warned the town of an enemy attack. Limavady is a good place to see the North West. You can go on day trips to the Sperrin Mountains or to the Atlantic Ocean with Ireland's longest beach, Magilligan Strand.

a Look on the map of the UK at the front of the book and find the places the teenagers are from.

b Imagine you are doing the same e-mail project. Choose one of the teenagers from the UK and write them an e-mail:

- tell them a bit about yourself and your school
- describe the area you live in
- what else would you like to find out about them? Ask questions.

[1] Ysgol Bryn Elian [ˌʌsgɒl brɪn 'elɪən] [2] Urdd Eisteddfod [ˌɪəð‿aɪ'steðvɒd] [3] Loch Eriboll [ˌlɒx‿'erɪɒl]
[4] Kinlochbervie [ˌkɪnlɒx'bɜːvi] [5] Limavady [ˌlɪmə'vædi] [6] Leim an Mhadaidh [ˌleɪm ɒn 'vedɪg]

1

Sports Freak or Couch Potato ...

Which are you?

Write down your answers to the following questions. You can check your score on page 118.

1 *How many hours of sport do you do in a week?*

A Only the PE lessons at school.
B 1 to 3 hours after school.
C More than 3 hours after school.

2 *How many different sports do you do?*

A None.
B 1 sport.
C 2 or more sports.

3 *What would you most like to do on a warm summer day?*

A Go swimming or cycling.
B Go swimming and cycling.
C Sit in a café and eat ice-cream.

4 *What do you most agree with?*

A Sport is only important for boys.
B Sport is important for everyone.
C Too much sport is bad for you.

5 *Imagine you're going to school and the bus is coming. You're 100 metres away from the bus stop. What do you do?*

A Run to the bus stop and take the bus to school.
B Walk to the bus stop and wait for the next bus. It'll come in 15 minutes.
C Go back home and go to bed.

6 *What sport are these Welsh teams playing in the photo?*

A Baseball.
B Rugby.
C Who cares?

7 *At which sport have women called Graf, Navratilova, Seles and Williams all been the best in the world?*

A In-line skating.
B Skiing.
C Tennis.

8 *Which sports can you match to A–D?*

A Air Jordan.
B Kaiser Franz.
C The All Blacks.
D Quarterback.

2 ***Listening: Fitness for couch potatoes***
Listen and move to the music.

WB 1

3

TOPS COMPETITION

Win a bike tour in Wales!

There is no better country for a bike tour than Wales. You can easily keep away from big roads: the many lanes with few cars make it a cyclist's paradise.
It's not just the famous national parks like Snowdonia, Pembrokeshire Coast, and Brecon Beacons which are perfect for a bike tour, but the places in between like the Wye Valley, the Gower and much more.
See river valleys, mountains, coast, moorland, or all four. And Wales is not just beautiful, it is full of history, too.
Happy biking.
Croeso i Gymru – Welcome to Wales

Croeso i Gymru! [ˌkrɔɪsəʊ i ˈgʌmri]

We stay at an old mill

How can you win?

Somewhere in this week's Tops you can find the answers to these three questions:

❖ 4 *Three questions about Wales*

Write three questions about Wales for the Tops Competition. Use a card for each question and write the answer on the back of the card. Number the cards and prepare a quiz in class. Find interesting questions in your library, in a CD-ROM encyclopedia, on the Internet, …

5 *Your diary*

Imagine you have won the bike tour. Choose one of the photos and write your diary for a day on your tour. You can put it in your UK album. Here's some help:

buildings / villages / farms / mill / …
hills / valleys / rocks / cliffs / beaches / …
beautiful / clear / fantastic / empty / …
long / hard / tired / …
weather / sunny / windy / wonderful / …

1 A sports freak

'Rubbish!' said David as he threw the magazine away. 'I like sport, but I'm not a freak!'
'Aren't you? What have you done every evening this week?' his friend Colin asked. 'I'll tell you. You've played rugby or you've trained for your bike race.'
The Aberaeron[1] school rugby team was getting ready for training. They had a big match at the weekend against Llandysul[2]. The big question at both schools was: 'Who will get into the Welsh Schools Championships?'
After training that evening Colin asked, 'Have you made any plans for Sunday after the race? I'm going to Cardigan. Do you want to come?'
'I don't know,' David answered. 'I can only think about the match and the race at the moment.'
'See, you are a sports freak,' laughed Colin.

[1] Aberaeron [ˌæbər'aɪrən] [2] Llandysul [hlæn'dɪsɪl]

SOME OF THE RULES OF RUGBY

- The rugby ball is oval, not round.
- There are 15 players in a team.
- A match lasts 80 minutes.
- Players can kick, carry or throw the ball (but they mustn't throw the ball forward).
- Players can tackle the player with the ball and bring him down. That player must then give up the ball. Another player can then take it.
- A player can put the ball on the ground behind the other team's goal-line. This is a 'try' (5 points).
- There are three types of goal:
  1) After a team gets a try, a player from that team can kick the ball over the crossbar of the other team's goalposts for a 'conversion' (2 points).
  2) A player can also drop-kick the ball over the other team's goalposts when he is running with it. This is a drop goal (3 points).
  3) A penalty goal after a foul also gets 3 points.

The man in white is going to score a 'try'.

What type of goal has the man in white above scored? How many points will he get?

2 *Now you and a group*

Look at the rules of rugby again. What is different from football or other ball games?
Find three things. Example: *In rugby the ball is oval. In football/volleyball/...*
Now try and write some rules for your favourite game or sport.
Read the rules to the class. Can anyone guess the game?

3 Before the big match

Three days before the big match against Llandysul, the Aberaeron coach was talking to the rugby team after training.
'We haven't won against Llandysul for a long time,' he told them, 'but I think we've got a good chance this year. I've been a rugby coach at this school for 10 years and you're the best team I've ever trained.'
'Of course we are,' said David. 'But you know, we've been here since four o'clock and it's getting late …'
'Oh, it's getting late, is it, David Evans? I'm sorry,' the coach said. 'You've been here since four? Well, I've been here since I finished lunch. Since two. But all you can think about is your bike race, isn't it?'
David looked at the ground and said nothing.
'Forget about everything else if you want to win on Saturday,' the coach shouted. 'If you want to win, you must work hard! All right?'
David left quickly and rode home on his bike.
'If I get home by 7.20, I can watch the Champions League,' he thought.

David was watching the news when his dad came home.
'Oh, how long have you been home?' Mr Evans asked.
'Since quarter past seven,' David answered.
'I haven't seen you for days. You've been at training every day this week. How are you?' his dad asked.
'I'm fine, Dad. A bit tired, that's all.'
'I saw your coach at the pub. You're in top form – that's what he said. But it'll be a hard match against Llandysul. Do you think you'll be able to ride a good race on Sunday?'
'Yes, Dad, I'll be OK. I've worked hard for months. I want to beat Llandysul and win the race. Don't worry.'
'OK, David,' Mr Evans said. 'Come on. Turn over. I want to watch the football match.'
'You've missed it, Dad. You'll have to wait for the highlights now.'

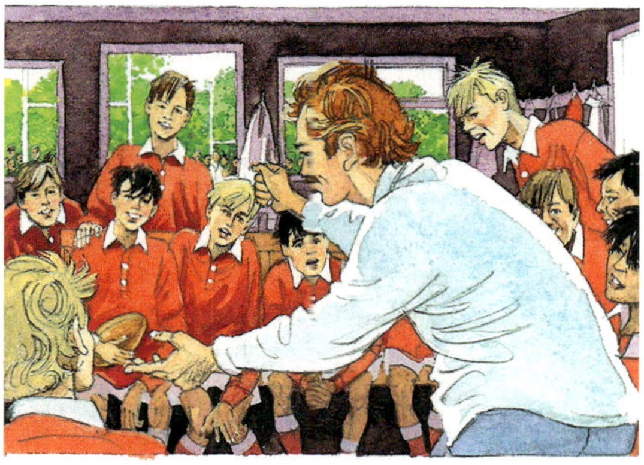

ITV 1 Wales	
7:00	Emmerdale
7:20	Champions League Live
10:00	News at Ten, Weather
10:20	For Love Or Money
11:20	Champions League Highlights

S4C	
7:00	Wedi 7
7:25	Darllediad Etholiadol
7:30	Newyddion
8:05	Pobol y Cwm
8:30	Crwydro
9:05	04 Wal
9:35	Taro Naw

4 *Looking at language*

a Look at A3 and find all the sentences with *since* and *for*. Make a table like this:

Sentences with 'since'	*Sentences with 'for'*
…	…

b What German words do you use for *since* and *for*?

c When do you use *since*, when do you use *for*?

d Look at the sentences again. What tense are they in? What tenses can you use in German?

5 *Now you and a partner*

a Ask your partner
- who his/her best friend is and how long he/she has known him/her,
- who his/her favourite sports star is and how long he/she has been his/her fan.

A Who's your best friend?
B Florian.
A How long have you known him?
B For two years.
A And who's your …?

b Tell the class about your partner.

6 Holiday plans

The evening before the big match David went to his girlfriend's house.
He and Emma wanted to plan their holiday.

Emma Where have you been?
David Sorry, Em. Have you been waiting long?
Emma Yes, I have. I've been sitting here since six-thirty. We agreed on six-thirty. Remember? What have *you* been doing?
David Oh, come on, Em – you know it's the big match tomorrow.
Emma I'll be glad when Monday comes! You've been training for that match and your bike race since the spring. I haven't seen you for a week!
David I know, Em. I'm sorry – but look, I'm here now. Have you asked your grandparents about the caravan in Barmouth? Can we stay there?
Emma Yes, I have. But I've been thinking about that.
David And?
Emma Well, it's a bit boring there, you know, so I've been looking at some stuff on the Internet. Have a look at this …
David Bike tours in Wales? Now that's a good idea!

We'll take care of you

We have been running cycling holidays in Wales for 21 years. So come on a bike tour with us, make new friends, relax and enjoy the beautiful Welsh countryside …

Snowdonia Tour

The north-west corner of Wales has everything – wild beaches, romantic castles, Celtic culture, and beautiful countryside. We cycle along the lanes of the Lleyn[1] Peninsula. We visit Whistling Sands, Hell's Mouth, and the seaside town of Criccieth[2]. We ride into the western side of the Snowdonia National Park, where the views are some of the best in Britain. On your free day you could go up Snowdon, cycle to one of the beaches, or swim in the clear waters of Nantlle[3] Lake.

West Coast Tour

People have been living in the Pembrokeshire[4] Coast National Park for thousands of years. It is an old country full of Celtic history. We ride along quiet lanes to beautiful fishing harbours, sandy beaches where we can swim, huge cliffs and wild seas. We visit the Preseli[5] Hills, where Stonehenge's blue stones came from, and the Gwaun[6] Valley, where people still celebrate New Year on 13 January. On our free day we take a boat trip to Ramsey Island where we see seals and play with dolphins.

[1] Lleyn [hleɪn] [2] Criccieth ['krɪkiəθ] [3] Nantlle ['nænthlə] [4] Pembrokeshire ['pembrʊkʃə] [5] Preseli [prə'seli] [6] Gwaun [gwaɪn]

South Wales Tour

We've only been doing this tour for the last two years, but it's already a favourite. All on cycle tracks, with few hills. We visit the beautiful countryside of Brecon Beacons National Park, ride its Mountain Railway and spend our free day in Cardiff, the exciting Welsh capital.

Wyt ti'n siarad Cymraeg?[1]

Do you speak Welsh? No? About 580,000 of the 2.9 million people in Wales speak Welsh. Most Welsh speakers live in the north and west of the country (Snowdonia and West Coast Tours). But don't worry! Most signs are in English – or in both languages.
And everyone speaks English, too. But why not try and learn a little Welsh?

Croeso i Gymru! –
Welcome to Wales!

[1] Wyt ti'n siarad Cymraeg?
[wɪt tɪn ˈʃəræd ˈkʌmraɪg]

7 *Looking at language*

a Look for examples of *I've/you've/… been* on page 12/13. What type of words come after been?
Have you been waiting …? / I've been sitting …

b This is a new tense. How do you form it? Can you imagine what it is called?

c What can you say about actions in this tense? When did they begin? Are they still going on?

❖ 8 *Now you and a group*

a Where could you go on a bike tour for a weekend in your area? Write an advert for the Internet about your tour.
Describe the places you will visit on the tour, what activities you will do, what the countryside is like, … .
Look at page 12/13 for ideas.

b Swap adverts with another group. Read their advert and then decide which tour you would like to go on.

9 *English and Welsh*

Chwaraeon clwb mwyaf poblogaidd yng Nghymru		Most popular club sports in Wales	
Merched	**Bechgyn**	**Girls**	**Boys**
1 nofio	pêl droed	1 swimming	football
2 dawns	rygbi	2 dancing	rugby
3 pêl rwyd	nofio	3 netball	swimming
4 gymnasteg	criced	4 gymnastics	cricket
5 pêl droed	golff	5 football	golf
6 athletau	tenis	6 athletics	tennis
7 tenis	jiwdo	7 tennis	judo
8 jiwdo	athletau	8 judo	athletics

Are you a good language detective?
In Wales lots of people speak two languages, Welsh and English. Compare the two tables. Can you find the Welsh words for *girls* and *boys*? And for *ball*?

10 *Focus on words*

Different sports have different verbs. For example:

Let's go …	*Let's do …*	*Let's play …*
swimming	*aerobics*	*badminton*
jogging	…	…

Copy the chart into your exercise book and add the names of the sports from A9.

1 *Revision: Where did they go and what did they do?*

1 Liz
Wales / last summer – do / bike tour

2 Eddie
Scotland / a week ago – visit / High-lands

3 Carsten
England / when he was 16 – go / Durham

4 Diana
Northern Ireland / 3 years ago – fly / Belfast

5 Sue
Edinburgh / last August – see / play at the *Edinburgh Festival*

6 Andy
Cardiff / for a week last year – learn some Welsh

1 *Liz went to Wales last summer. She did a bike tour.* 2 *Eddie went ...*

2 *Revision: What has happened?*

a Look at the pictures and say what has just happened.

◆◆ b On a piece of paper, write down two things you've done today, two things you've done this week and two things you've done this year. Then on another piece of paper write down two things you think your partner has done today, this week, this year. Swap the second piece of paper with your partner. How many has he/she got right?

Today
I've made breakfast.
I've fed the cat.
This week
...

Today
I think my partner has checked her e-mails.
I think she has had ...

3 *Revision: They're playing ...*

a What are they doing? Choose phrases from the list below and make sentences.

- cook a meal
- eat Indian food
- play beach volley-ball
- sing in a choir
- watch a play

1 *They're playing ...* 2 ...

◆◆ b Has your partner ever done these things? Did he/she like them? Ask questions.

c Think of more questions.

A Have you ever played beach volleyball?
B Yes, I have.
A When did you play it last?
B When I was in Spain. / In the summer. / ...

4 *The sports news*

There's a virus in the newspaper's computer. It has put ΔΔΔΔΔ where the words *since* and *for* should go. Write the sentences again with the right words.

1 David Evans has been the best cyclist in the area ΔΔΔΔΔ more than a year.
2 Aberaeron has not been in the Welsh Schools Championships ΔΔΔΔΔ 1999.
3 Cardiff has been top of the table ΔΔΔΔΔ the beginning of the year.
4 It could be a great day because Wales has not beaten England at football ΔΔΔΔΔ many years.
5 Ginny Jones has been second in this competition every year ΔΔΔΔΔ it started.
6 Their trainer said: 'This match has only been finished ΔΔΔΔΔ a few minutes but we're already thinking of next week's.'
7 The two teams have not met in a cup match ΔΔΔΔΔ more than twenty years.
8 Hughes has been at the front ΔΔΔΔΔ the start but Thomas has been behind her ΔΔΔΔΔ the last few minutes.
9 She has been the Welsh squash champion ΔΔΔΔΔ 2003 and she hasn't lost a match in Wales ΔΔΔΔΔ a very long time.

❖ 5 *Who is it?*

a Everyone in the group uses some of the verbs below and completes the sentences on a piece of paper.

be • have • know • like • live • see

1 I've … for … years.
2 I haven't … since …
3 I've … for …
4 My favourite sportsman/sportswoman has … since …

b Now work with another group. One of you takes the sentences to another group. Can that group guess who wrote them?

◆◆ 6 *They aren't from Aberaeron*

a Partner B: look at page 118.
Partner A: look at the chart. Not everyone in David's rugby team comes from Aberaeron. Some information about Mark, Colin, Thomas and Craig is missing. Ask your partner 'How long …?' and answer his/her questions.

A How long has Mark lived in Aberaeron?
B For … .
How long has …?
A …

	Mark	Colin	Thomas	Craig
live in Aberaeron	?	last summer	3 years	?
play rugby	10 years old	?	?	first day in Wales
be in the Aberaeron team	a week	?	last winter	?
know his best friend	the summer	a long time	?	?

b Now write about two players in David's rugby team. Example:

Mark has lived in Aberaeron for three months.
He has played rugby since he …

7 *How long?*

How long have they been doing these things?

1 *She has been walking through walls since 1800.*
2 *The earth has been … for …*
3 …

1 
1800

2 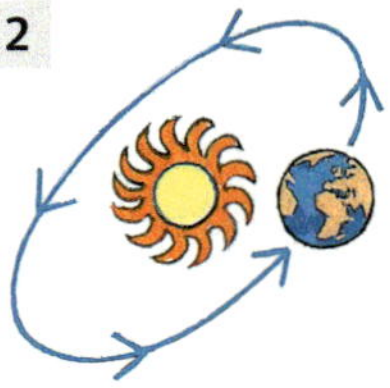
4 billion years

3 
four o'clock

4 
breakfast

5 
ten months

6 
four hours

7 
8.00

8 
half an hour

8 *What have you been doing?*

On Colin's birthday he and his friends go to the Aquadome, a water and sports centre. They all do different things. When they meet again at the café, they talk about what they have been doing. Use the notes and complete the conversation.

Colin	sit in sauna, go down the water chutes
David	swim in the wave pool, use the fitness room
Emma	jump from 10 metre board
Sharon	watch a water polo game, read

Sharon Colin, where have you been? What have you been …?
Colin Oh, I've been …
Sharon In the sauna, all the time?
Colin No, I've … . What about you?
Sharon Oh, I've …, and I've … . Here are David and Emma. Have you two … the same all afternoon? Together?
Emma No we haven't. I've …
Colin What? All the time?
Emma Yes.
Colin What about you, David?
David Oh, I've …

9 *Listening: Radio Sport*

a Have you ever listened to sports on the radio? Listen to these sports reporters and try to guess what sports they are talking about. Choose from:

athletics (running) • basketball
cricket • football • ice-hockey
riding • tennis • volleyball

❖ b Now listen to the reporters again. You want to tell your friends as much as you can about what is happening. Take notes and then check with your group. How much did you find out?

c The words of the song are on the right. When and where do people usually sing it? Have you ever sung it? When?

We are the Champions   Words and music by *Queen*

We are the champions, my friend.
And we'll keep on fighting[1] till the end.
We are the champions. We are the champions.
No time for losers 'cause we are the
champions of the world.

[1] (to) keep on fighting ['faɪtɪŋ] *weiterkämpfen*

Word watch

10 *Word link*

Look at the verbs in the box and say which ones fit in the sentences below.

break • carry • change • cheer • drop
explain • hit • know • listen • lose
make • play • practise • scream • shout
sing • throw • watch • win

1 You can *carry, drop,* … a ball.
2 You can *break,* … a rule.
3 A team can …
4 Fans at a match can …

11 *In the open air*

a Copy this 'open air' network into your exercise book. Draw pictures or write words. Then think of more words and pictures for the network.

b Imagine you are on holiday. Write a card to a friend and tell him/her what the countryside is like and what you are doing.

❖ 12 *Project: Sport or Wales*

In a group, prepare and make a presentation on sport or on Wales. It could be about your favourite sport, sports star or sports team, your sporting week, … . Or you could plan a holiday in Wales with a group of friends, find out more about the Welsh language, … .

1 Where can you get information for your project? The library, a sports club, the Internet, … . What about an e-mail to the Welsh Tourist Board?

Dear Sir or Madam,
…
Thank you for your help. We look forward to hearing from you soon.
<your names>

2 Take notes on the most important information. (Page 19 shows you how.) You could write your notes on cards.

born in … in 19…
has lived in
Chicago since …
has played …
for …

favourite
food: pizza
car: Ferrari
holidays in: Hawaii, Australia

WALES/WELSH
population: 2,903,085 (2001)
No. who speak Welsh: 20%
– understand Welsh: 28%

3 How do you want to make your presentation? Discuss your ideas.

You can talk about it like this:
Let's make a poster/transparency/…
Why don't we make a map/draw …/…?
I think we should do/I'd like to do a PowerPoint presentation …

4 Practise your presentation. Don't forget: check your English. You can use the dictionary and the language summary at the back of this book.

Think about:
- Who is going to present which part?
- How can you make the presentation more interesting?
- What will you need?
- How long can your presentation be?

Remember: speak loudly, clearly and slowly. Ask for questions from the class.

The Race

Answer these questions about the two newspaper articles as quickly as you can:
- What part of the newspaper are they from?
- What is the article below about? And the one on the right?
- What do the two have in common?

Aberaeron will go to championships!

Aberaeron 24 : Llandysul 17

by Barry Masters
They've waited for years but, at last, after their big win against Llandysul on Saturday, our boys are on their way to the Welsh Schools Rugby Championships – and they could even win.

Aberaeron's team captain Steve Phillips scored the first try after only 17 minutes of play. It came after a great pass by team-mate David Evans.
'It was brilliant,' said Phillips. 'The players from the other team were really surprised. David usually goes for the try. But today he threw the ball to me, and I just ran with it.'

Local boy 3rd in cycle race

by Will Roberts
For months, two 16-year-olds, David Evans from Aberaeron and Aled Jones from Bangor, have been favourites for the 60-kilometre race at the Junior Welsh Cycling Championships. But neither of them was the winner. Evans came in third after Tom Porter, 18, from Cilcain, and Nathan Rosser, 17, from Cardiff. Jones did not finish the race.
For a long time Evans and Jones were ahead of the other cyclists. They were together at the 55-kilometre checkpoint, but Jones fell only three kilometres before the finish. An ambulance took him to hospital with a broken leg.
No one knows why Evans did not win after his rival fell. We have been trying to reach him since the end of the race for an interview but have not been able to do so.

1 ***Heads and tails***

a 1 Aberaeron scored the first try …
2 After a pass from David …
… Steve was able to run for the try.
… after 17 minutes of play.

◆◆ b Now make two or three sentences like the ones in 1a. Your partner must match them correctly.

2 ***What happened?***

a Why didn't David win after Aled fell?
Here is an idea:
David didn't win because he was tired after his rugby match on Saturday.
Is this a good explanation? Can you think of a better one?

b Imagine you are David. Use your favourite idea from 2a and tell someone why you didn't win the race. Perhaps make notes first.

3 ***Listening: A radio interview with Aled Jones***
Now listen to the radio interview with Aled and find out what really happened.

WB 10–12

How to ... take notes

1 *Reading: Notes on Wales*

a If you just read or listen to something, you often can't remember it very well. It is easier if you take notes.
Look at these notes on Wales (from pages 9–13). How does the writer make them clear and easy to read? What type of words (nouns, verbs, pronouns, adjectives, prepositions, conjunctions, articles) does he/she mostly use? What type of words doesn't he/she use much?

b What do the symbols in the notes mean? Make a list.
What symbols would you use for the following things? Add them to your list. Add other symbols you know, or your own symbols, too.
– pound(s) – dollar(s) – is more than
– is not the same as – positive – negative

c What do the abbreviations in the notes mean? Make a list.
What are the abbreviations for these words? Add them to your list.
– and so on – disc jockey – electronic mail
– somebody – page – pence
What other abbreviations do you know? Add them to your list, too.

d Some words in the notes are underlined. Why? Can you say how this helps?

2 *Speaking and writing: All about Wales*

◆◆ a Use the notes from 1 and tell your partner about Wales. Don't look at pages 9–13!

b When you take notes on a text, you want to get all the important information out of it. Now look at pages 9–13. Is any important information missing in the notes? Add notes on this information.

WALES: Population – 2.9 m

Sport
– rugby: important sport
– team: 15 players; match: 80 min.
– favourite sports: boys: 1st football, 2nd rugby
girls: 1st swimming, 2nd aerobics

Welsh
– Croeso i Gymru = Welcome to Wales
– c. 580,000 people speak Welsh (most in N and W)
–> 80% don't
– some TV programmes in Welsh; road signs in Engl. + Welsh

Countryside
– coast + sea, hills + mountains

For tourists
– cycling: quiet roads, beautiful countryside
– Cardiff = capital: exciting
– National Parks: Snowdonia, Pembrokeshire Coast, Brecon

3 *Your own notes:*
◆◆ *Practise what you have learned*

a Partner A: Look at Topic 1 on page 21 and take notes on the Welsh language.
Partner B: Look at the text 'Who was the first European in America?' in Topic 1 (page 20) and take notes on 'Madog'.

b Now use your notes and tell your partner what you have found out. Listen to what he/she has to say, too. Then check his/her notes and see if he/she has got the most important information.

Remember

1 Notes help you to remember what you have read or heard.
2 Only write down words and phrases with important information.
3 Give each topic a heading.
4 They are *your* notes, so you must decide which symbols, abbreviations, etc. you want to use.
5 Your notes should be clear and easy to read.
6 Your notes can help you to tell others what you know.

Stories from Wales

Story-telling has a long tradition in Wales, and some 'English' legends really come from Wales – the story of King Arthur and the Round Table, for example.
Read this story about the first European in America. Is it history or legend? What do you think? And why?

Who was the first European in America?

'Christopher Columbus, of course!' will be the answer from an American or English school-child. A few clever ones might say 'Leif Eriksson'. But if you ask a Welsh boy or girl, he or she might give you a different answer: Madog.

Madog's ships leave Wales at the beginning of their great journey

Madog lived in the 12th century. He was the son of Owain, king of Gwynedd in North Wales. When his father died, he and his brothers couldn't agree on what they should do with the king's lands and money. Madog didn't want to fight about this, so he took his men and a ship and sailed to Ireland and then further west. Over a year later, Madog came back to Wales and told stories of a far-away land where people lived in peace. A year after that, he took ten ships, people and cattle, and sailed west again. No one in Wales ever saw Madog or the people who sailed with him again.
300 years later, Columbus sailed to America. As more and more people from Europe came to America, there were reports of 'white Indians' around Louisville, Kentucky. And some of the first Europeans in America said that they met 'Indians' who spoke perfect Welsh! One of them was Morgan Jones, a Welsh missionary. In 1666, Indians caught Jones, but before they could kill him he called loudly to God in Welsh. Then the Indians let him live and Jones found he was able to talk to them in Welsh. How could that be?
The story goes like this: Madog and his followers landed in Alabama. They then sailed on up the great American rivers and became part of the Mandan Indian nation on the Missouri River. And the Mandan Indians have an old story, too: it tells of a 'Lone Man' who came to them in a ship. He brought the tribe spotted cattle and showed them new ways to build and to farm.

Now you
Try to tell a legend from your own country in a few English sentences.
Make notes first on the most important points of the story.

legend ['ledʒənd]   they might [maɪt] say *sie sagen vielleicht*   Gwynedd ['gwɪneð]   (to) fight [faɪt], fought, fought *kämpfen*
further *weiter*   peace [piːs] *Frieden*   cattle (pl) ['kætl] *Vieh, Rinder*   missionary ['mɪʃənri]   nation ['neɪʃn]   lone [ləʊn] *einzeln, einsam*
tribe [traɪb] *(Volks-)Stamm*   spotted ['spɒtɪd] *gefleckt*   (to) farm *Landwirtschaft betreiben; (Land) bebauen*

WB 13

Mae'r Gymraeg yma o hyd

When Gwenllian Ellis tells her great-grandson stories of the fairies in the valleys near their home in the north of Wales, she tells her stories in Welsh – of course.

But things weren't always like that. 'When I was a little girl in school, there was trouble if we spoke Welsh. 'Speak English,' the teachers always told us. And we tried. But sometimes, when we were excited, we forgot. Just one word of Welsh – the language we spoke at home – and we had to wear the Welsh Not.

The teachers tied a piece of wood with the letters 'WN' round our necks, and we had to wear it all day. And everyone knew: that boy or girl spoke Welsh today. It was like something dirty. I only had to wear the Welsh Not once, but it was terrible.'

When Gwen thinks back to those times, she sits very quietly and looks out across the valley towards the sea. But then, slowly, she smiles again. 'When I told my parents about the Not, they were angry. But they didn't go to the teachers and complain. We tried to speak English at home. Imagine, we stopped speaking our own language in our own home!

Later I had children, too, and I never spoke Welsh to them. I remembered the Not, and I didn't want to see my children coming home with stories like mine.'

Gwenllian Ellis

Of course things have changed since then. Gwen's great-grandson will speak Welsh and English at school. Some lessons will be in English, others in Welsh. He will listen not only to the best of English and American rock music, but also to Welsh pop and perhaps to traditional harp music, too.

'The Welsh language is very beautiful,' says Gwen. 'It's very good for poetry. The Welsh people have always been good at poetry and singing.'

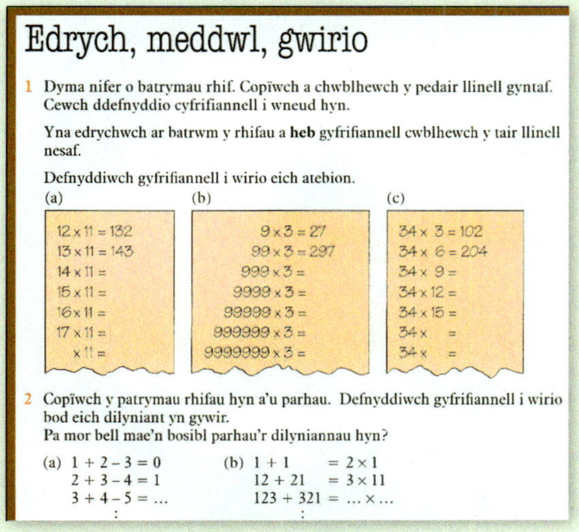

Edrych, meddwl, gwirio

1 Dyma nifer o batrymau rhif. Copïwch a chwblhewch y pedair llinell gyntaf. Cewch ddefnyddio cyfrifiannell i wneud hyn.

Yna edrychwch ar batrwm y rhifau a **heb** gyfrifiannell cwblhewch y tair llinell nesaf.

Defnyddiwch gyfrifiannell i wirio eich atebion.

(a)	(b)	(c)
12 x 11 = 132	9 x 3 = 27	34 x 3 = 102
13 x 11 = 143	99 x 3 = 297	34 x 6 = 204
14 x 11 =	999 x 3 =	34 x 9 =
15 x 11 =	9999 x 3 =	34 x 12 =
16 x 11 =	99999 x 3 =	34 x 15 =
17 x 11 =	999999 x 3 =	34 x =
x 11 =	9999999 x 3 =	34 x =

2 Copïwch y patrymau rhifau hyn a'u parhau. Defnyddiwch gyfrifiannell i wirio bod eich dilyniant yn gywir.
Pa mor bell mae'n bosibl parhau'r dilyniannau hyn?

(a) $1 + 2 - 3 = 0$
$2 + 3 - 4 = 1$
$3 + 4 - 5 = \ldots$
⋮

(b) $1 + 1 = 2 \times 1$
$12 + 21 = 3 \times 11$
$123 + 321 = \ldots \times \ldots$
⋮

Page from a Maths book for pupils in Form 9 in Wales

Today people come from far away to Nant Gwrtheyrn (the National Centre for Language and Culture) to learn Welsh. Many of the people who are learning the old language are Welsh. They don't have to worry about the Welsh Not any more.

Mae'r Gymraeg yma o hyd – Welsh lives on.

Now you

There are about 6500 languages in the world. About half of them have fewer than 10,000 speakers and 1800 have less than 1000 speakers. Many might disappear soon. Do you think we should try to save them?

Mae'r Gymraeg yma o hyd [maɪə 'gʌmraɪg 'ʌmə əʊ hiːd]   great-grandson *Urenkel*   fairy, pl fairies ['feəri] *Fee, Elfe*   (to) tie [taɪ] *binden*   neck [nek] *Hals*   (to) complain [kəm'pleɪn] *sich beschweren*   mine [maɪn] *meine(r, s)*   traditional [trə'dɪʃənl]   harp [hɑːp] *Harfe*   poetry ['pəʊətri]   (to) live on *weiterleben*   Nant Gwrtheyrn [ˌnant 'guːəθeən]

2 London

❖ **1** What do you know about London? Work in groups and write down in a network what you know. Then talk about the city.
Next look at the brochure below and the map. Where do the Thames River Tours start?

Thames River Tours

- ★ See the sights from the river!
- ★ Tours start at Westminster Pier, only two minutes from the Houses of Parliament.

Summer season
(27 May to 1 September)

1100	1130	1200	1225
1300	1325	1400	1430
1455	1530	1600	1630
1700	1730	1800	1830

Fares

Adult	£5.00
Student/ Senior Citizen	£3.60
Child 2–15 yrs	£2.50
Family (Two adults and two children)	£13.50

2

Sir Christopher Wren's most famous building

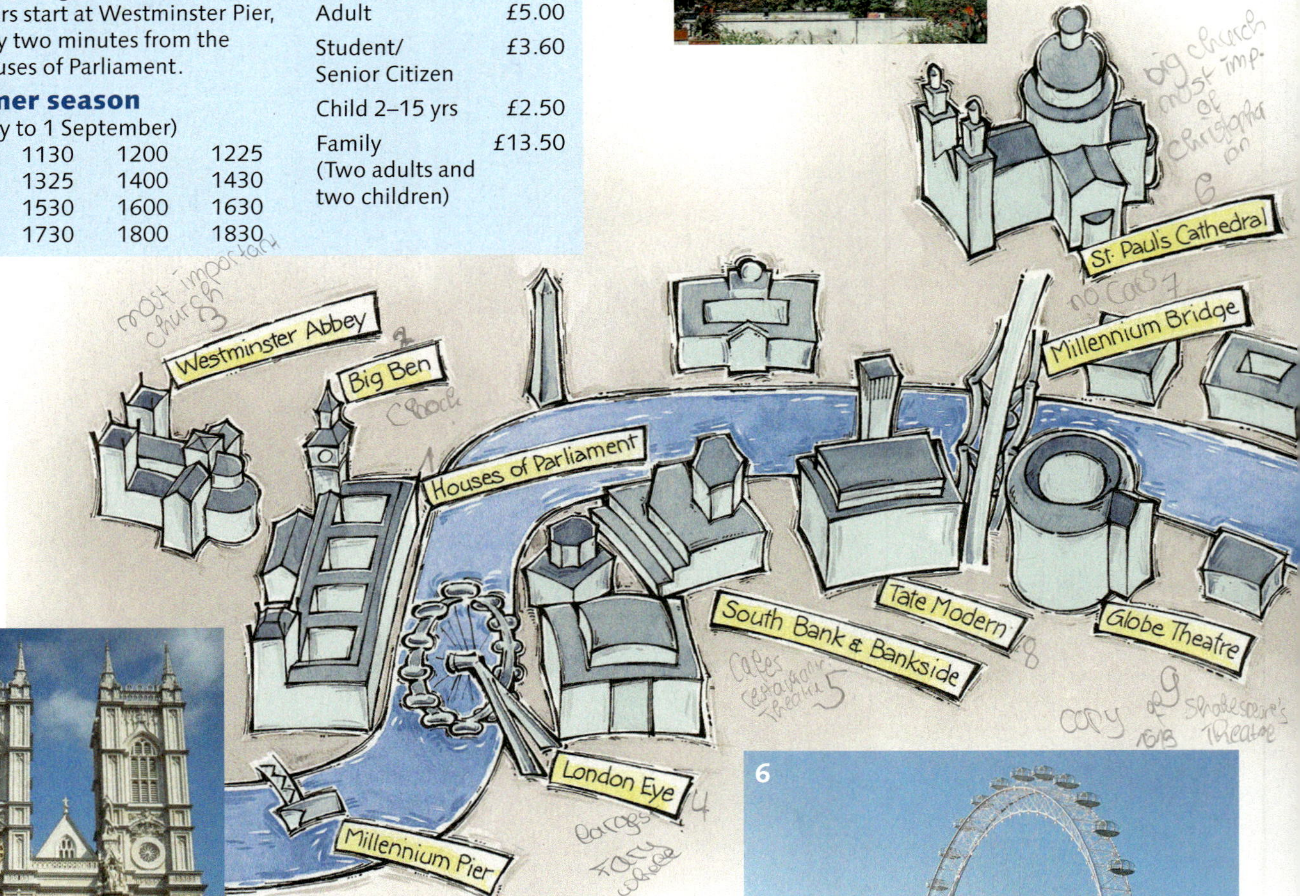

1

An important building for Britain's kings and queens

6

High in the sky for London's best views

Walk across the river
and see all the pictures

The Crown
Jewels

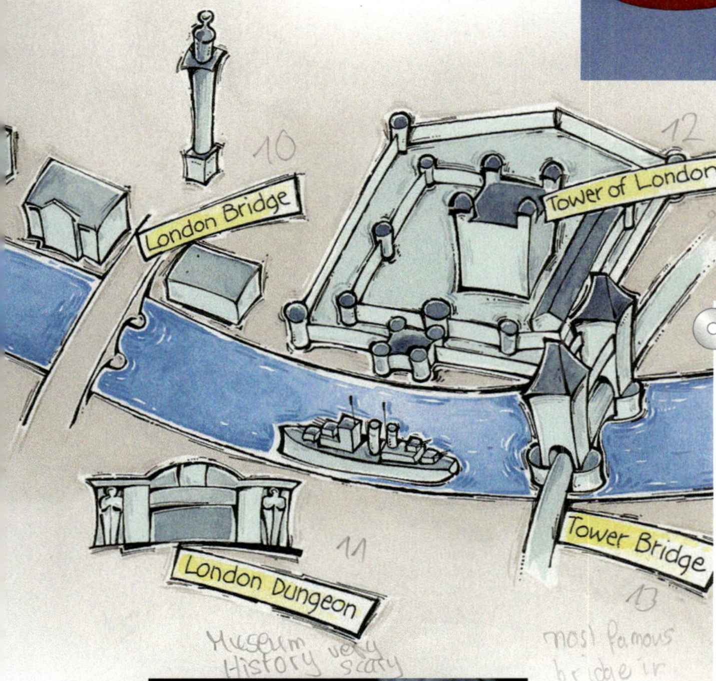

2 *Listening*

a Listen to the guide on a Thames River Tour boat. You can follow the tour on the map. What sights does the guide mention? Which photos show them?
(You can find a list of all these sights in the vocabulary on page 149.)

b Write down the names of two interesting places on the tour. Now listen to the guide again. Write down what you learn about those places. Then compare your information with your partner's.

c Which places would you like to visit? Tell your partner why.

... sounds interesting. I'd like to go there because you can ... there.

Learn about
London's violent
history

1 A school trip to London

The train stopped at Euston Station and a group of children and teachers got off. A lot of the children looked very excited because it was their first trip to London. 'OK, everyone. Please stay together,' said Mrs Martin. She sounded a little nervous. 'We're going to take the underground to our hotel.'
'Yes, that's right,' agreed Mr Martin. 'It's in Bayswater, near Queensway Station.'
'Can I go and fetch tube maps for everyone, Mrs Martin?' Debbie asked.
'Not yet, Debbie,' Mrs Martin told her. 'Please stay with the group. Mr Martin will fetch the maps.'
She looked at her husband.
'I'm on my way, Christine,' he said. 'Now where do they have underground maps?'
Ben pointed to the ticket office and Mr Martin walked off and got the maps. It was his first time back in London for years and he felt very excited, too.

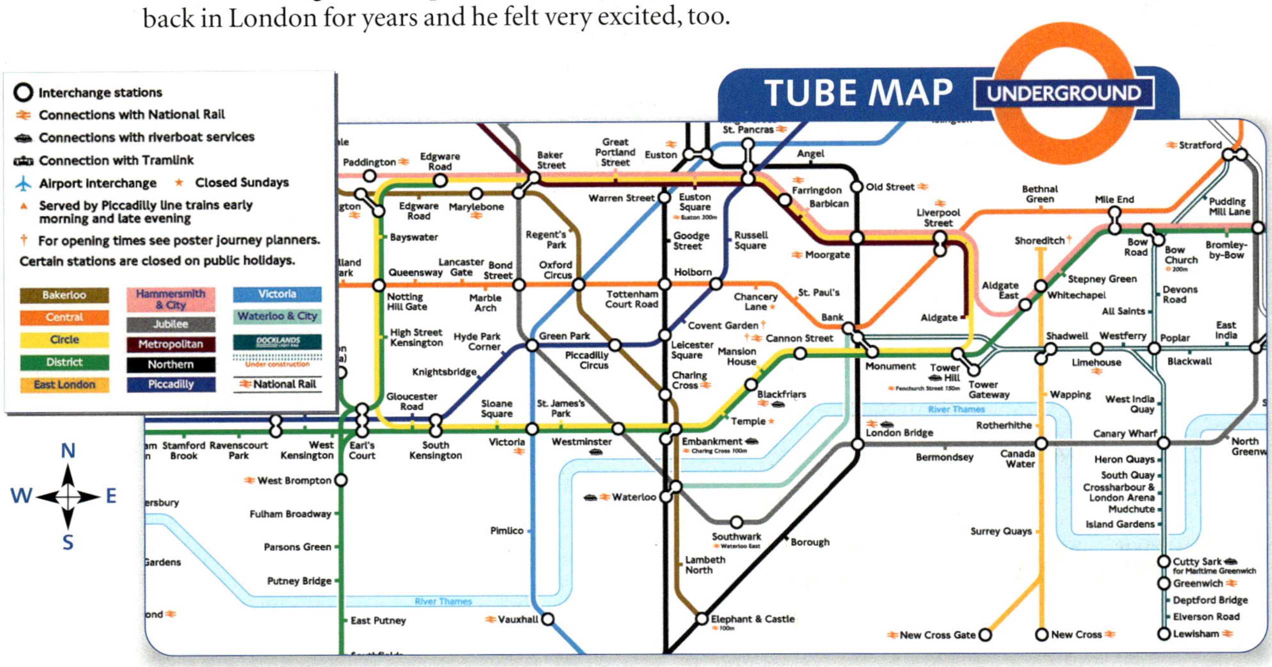

Reg. user No. 03/E/1370

2 *Find the station*

Where is Euston Station on the underground map? *It's on the ... Line and the ... Line.*

Now find Queensway. What is the Kingsway group's best route from Euston to Queensway?

They should take the ... Line southbound to ... There they should change to the ... Line and take a westbound train and get off at Queensway.

3 *Game: What's the best route?*

◆◆ Ask your partner for the best route from one station to another. Don't make it too easy! Then swap.

A What's the best route from ... to ...?
B Well, you should take the ... Line (eastbound) to ....
Change to the ... and get off at ....
Now, what's the best route ...?

4 Famous museums

On their first morning, the Kingsway group went and looked at the Houses of Parliament and then took a bus to the West End. In the afternoon some of the group went with Mrs Martin to Madame Tussaud's wax museum.

Marie Tussaud (1761–1850) made wax figures at a show in Paris for more than 20 years before she became its owner in 1794. She was famous for the masks she made of dead people's heads in the French Revolution.
In 1802 she left France with her two sons and took the wax show to Britain. She became very successful there but never saw France or her husband again.

MADAME TUSSAUDS LONDON

The famous wax show was taken to Britain in 1802. For the next 30 years the wax figures were shown all around the country. Then, in 1835, they were moved to London. A museum was opened not far from the one you can still visit today.
Most of the figures in today's museum (known as 'Madame Tussaud's') are new but there are still some of the old ones that were made last century.
About two million people visit Madame Tussaud's every year.

Henry VIII, king of England (1509–1547), and his six wives as wax figures. Two of Henry's wives were executed.

Mr Martin took the other pupils to the Natural History Museum.

The Natural History Museum is one of the best places in London for kids. The most exciting things are shown in two areas: the Life Galleries, with creepy-crawlies, dinosaurs, etc. and the Earth Galleries, with volcanoes, earthquakes, etc. Everything is wonderfully explained, with lots of interactive displays. Free 45-minute tours are given every hour. Go to one of the live events at the museum's Darwin Centre where new scientific discoveries are brought to life. Meet the scientists and hear about their work. Some events are shown live on the museum's web site.

5 *Now you and a partner*

Complete the four sentences below. Only three of your sentences should give correct information. Now read your sentences to your partner. Can he/she find the sentence which is not correct? If he/she can't, ask someone else.

1 … was born in …
My mother was born in Landshut.

2 … was built in …
3 … is spoken in …
4 … is made of/in …

6 *Looking at language*

a Look at the verb form in this sentence:
The wax show was taken to Britain.
We call this form the passive.
Find more passive forms in A4 and write them down.
was taken, were …, are …, …

b What tenses are the passive forms in?

c How do you form the passive?

S 2: 1a, b (p. 125/126) • P 2, 3 • WB 3, 4

7 London sights

The next morning the Kingsway group was picked up by a tourist guide in front of their hotel. They were taken to all the important sights. In the bus the guide told them everything they wanted to know.

'Buckingham Palace is where the king or queen lives. In the summer tourists can visit some of the rooms. The Changing of the Guard ceremony is watched by hundreds of tourists. But it isn't held every day, so phone for information.

Trafalgar Square is used by Londoners, tourists *and* pigeons. That's the famous Nelson's Column with Admiral Lord Nelson on top. It was built in 1842.'

The group had lunch at Covent Garden, where something really exciting happened. Debbie and Nick told their mum and dad about it in their postcard home.

Dear Mum and Dad,
London is great! We were taken on a bus tour of the city this morning, the best tour I've ever been on. Then we had lunch at Covent Garden. There were lots of people from all over the world there and something really exciting happened!
We were watching a group that was singing 'You've got a friend'. Suddenly one of the boys in the group jumped up and ran to Mrs Martin. He chased away a pickpocket who was trying to rob her. He was a real hero. Love, Debbie

We saw about six different street entertainers at Covent Garden and they were all great. See you tomorrow! Nick

8 *Now you*

Think of a city you have visited or a city you would like to visit. Imagine you are there. Write a postcard for your UK album. Here is some help:

Dear ...,
... is great/fun/interesting/boring/... The weather ...
We've just ...

9 *Looking at language*

a Compare these two sentences:
Londoners, tourists and pigeons use Trafalgar Square.
Trafalgar Square is used by Londoners, tourists and pigeons.
In which sentence does the subject do something?
What is different in the other sentence?

b What do you add to a passive sentence when you want to say who does the action?
Look for more examples in A7.

10 Homelessness

After lunch, the Kingsway group tour continued. The guide talked about the homeless people they saw on the streets.

'There are a lot of homeless people on the streets of London. That young woman stands there every day and sells *The Big Issue*. Some of the magazine is written by homeless people. She gets 70p for each paper she sells.'

THE BIG ISSUE

How much do you know about homelessness? Not many people know about it, but we at *The Big Issue* have all been homeless. We know.
The Big Issue is a magazine which is only sold by homeless people. They buy the magazine for 50p and sell it for £1.20. For a few pence you can help someone to get off the streets. A little money can go a long way.
Please take a little time and talk to us. It's only a few minutes for you, but it means a lot to us.
Thank you.

11 *Now you and a partner*

Why do you think people become homeless? Think of questions you would like to ask one of the homeless people in the photos above. Talk about your ideas. Imagine how the homeless person might answer your questions and write an interview with him/her.

12 *Listening: Another Day in Paradise*

a Listen to the first verse of the song.
Is the homeless person a man or woman? Who does he/she speak to?

b Now listen to the rest of the song.

13 *Focus on words*

Look at pages 22–27 and collect the 'city' words and phrases. Add other words you know and put them in groups (e.g. **transport**: take the underground, get off the bus, …; **buildings**: visit a cathedral, go to the town hall, …; **events**: watch a ceremony, …; **sights**: …). How can you arrange them? Continue to collect these words and phrases for the rest of the unit.

14 In Chinatown

It was Chinese New Year on Sunday and some of the Kingsway group wanted to go to Chinatown and see the parade. On the bus to Piccadilly Circus, Sita and Jenny were reading a brochure about the celebrations.

Chinese New Year

Chinatown will be filled with people on Sunday, when London celebrates Chinese New Year.

London's Chinese community has again been invited by the Mayor of London to hold part of the celebrations in Trafalgar Square.

The streets between Leicester Square and Trafalgar Square will be lined with thousands of visitors for the Children's Fun Parade, which starts at 11.30. Special costumes have been made in China for the 70 children from schools in Soho and East London who will take part in the colourful parade.

Watch out – there's a thief about!

Going to the Chinese New Year parade? The pickpockets are, too! If you are not careful, you will be robbed. Remember, purses can be stolen very easily from jacket pockets. Bags should be kept closed at all times.

More information on pickpockets in London can be found at any police station.

On the train back to Chester, Debbie was talking to Mr Martin. 'There's one thing I don't understand,' she said. 'I was talking to an old Chinese man at the parade. He's a Londoner, he says, because he lives there. But he wasn't born there. You say you're a Londoner because you were born there. But you don't live there. What exactly is a Londoner?'

Mr Martin looked pleased, but Mrs Martin didn't. 'Oh no,' she said. 'He's going to sing now, and it's all your fault …'

15 *Looking at language*

a Find the first four passive forms in A14. What tenses are they in?

b Find the examples of the passive with modal auxiliaries in the text 'Watch out – …'. What form of the verb is used after *can*, *should*, etc.?

c At the parade Sita met a boy who warned her of pickpockets. He said, *'I've been robbed three times this year'*. Could he say the same with an active form?

16 *Activity: A tour of London*

❖ Imagine your class is on a tour of London. Five or six of you are guides – each for one of the famous sights (e.g. Buckingham Palace). When your class arrives at one of the sights, the guide tells you all about it. The tourists can ask questions.

1 *Why do they feel this way?* → Vocabulary p. 152

a Why do the people in the pictures feel angry/…?
What have they been doing?

1 angry 2 hot 3 thirsty 4 happy 5 tired 6 cold

1 *The woman feels angry because she has been waiting for …*
2 *The boy feels … because he has …*

◆◆ b Now draw a picture of yourself and give it to your partner. (You look angry/tired/…) Your partner must say what you have been doing so that you feel this way.

❖ 2 *Places in town*

a Think about three places in town. What things are usually done there? Write down in a list four sentences for each place.

- a railway station
- a theatre
- a school
- a hotel
- a sports centre
- a(n) …

railway station
Tickets are bought.
Information is given.
Trains are cleaned.
Friends are met.

b Swap your lists with another group. Try and add sentences to their lists.
The group that can add most sentences is the winner.

3 *Yesterday's news photos*

a Look at the news photos and say what happened yesterday. Use the simple past passive.

hurt • kill • open • steal

1 *A new bridge was …*

b Look at yesterday's newspaper. Find three or four things that happened to someone or something. Tell the class about them in English. Use the simple past passive.

4 *Revision: A trip to London*

a Match the correct sentence halves and link them with a relative pronoun: *who, which, that.*

1 Who was the boy		– Mr Martin took some of the group to.
2 The Natural History Museum was the place	who	– looks at London's violent history.
3 Covent Garden is the old market		– saved Mrs Martin's handbag?
4 Henry VIII was the king	which	– put two of his six wives in the Tower.
5 The London Dungeon is the museum		– started the famous wax museum.
6 Marie Tussaud was the woman	that	– tourists can watch in front of Buckingham Palace.
7 The Changing of the Guard is the ceremony		– the Kingsway group visited on their bus tour.

b Look at the sentences in a again. In which ones can you leave the relative pronoun out and make contact clauses?

5 *London sights*

Complete the following information about some of London's sights. Use the notes in brackets and the passive of the simple past or simple present.

1 Christopher Wren designed St Paul's Cathedral in 1675.
(building – finish – 1710)
The building was finished in 1710.

2 William I decided to build a castle soon after he became king of England.
(So – Tower of London – begin – 1066)

3 Big Ben is the most famous bell in the world.
(hear – by millions – BBC radio – every day)

4 Tower Bridge is more than 100 years old.
(open – 1894)

5 London has had an underground railway for a very long time.
(first tube line – open – 1863)

6 The Natural History Museum is a favourite with kids.
(Everything – bring to life – in wonderful interactive displays)

7 The Houses of Parliament were built in the 19th century.
(old building – destroy – by fire – 1834)

◆◆ 6 *Revision: After the trip*

Partner B: Look at page 119.
Partner A: You've just been on a school trip to London. Look at the picture of things you brought with you. (Your partner has got a different picture.) Ask about the things in the list on the right. Then answer your partner's questions. Use *a little / a few / a lot / not … any.*

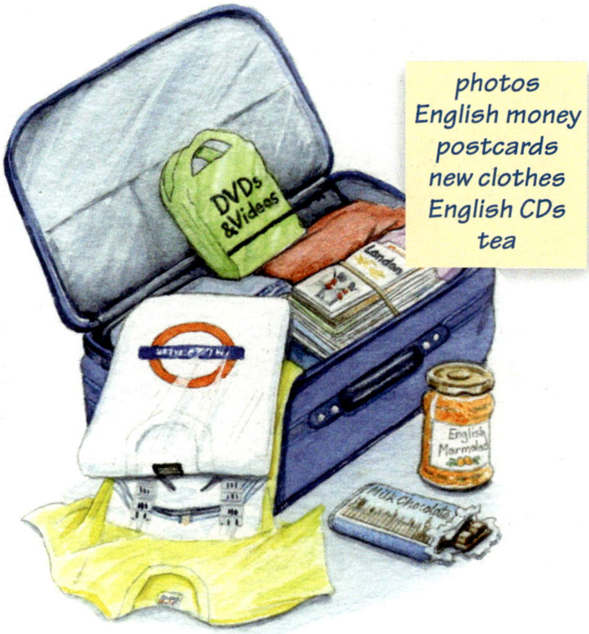

A Did you bring any photos with you?
B Yes, … / No, …

B Did you bring any London T-shirts with you?
A Yes, I brought a few / a lot.
or: No, I didn't bring any.

7 *The Prince's school friend*

Active or passive? Put the verbs in brackets into the right form and tense.

Last week Prince Charles *(visit)* the offices of *The Big Issue*, a magazine that *(write)* and *(sell)* by homeless people, and there he *(meet)* an old friend. One of the magazine's reporters *(say)* to Charles, 'I remember you from school.'
The reporter was Clive Harold – a man who was born rich. He and Prince Charles went to the same school 40 years ago.
Later Harold *(make)* homeless by alcohol problems. At first Prince Charles *(not remember)* him, but later the two *(speak)* happily together about old teachers and football games. Harold *(tell)* his future king, 'We've both had good and bad times. But you were the only one in the school who had bigger ears than I had.'

8 *Listening: Conversations on a London bus*

a The Kingsway kids loved the buses in London and all the conversations people had on them. Listen to these three conversations. What do they tell you about the people who are talking? What do you understand? Copy the chart and fill it in when you listen the second or third time.

Speakers	*Londoner or visitor?*	*Where are they going?*	*What do they discuss?*
1 girl	*Londoner*	*music shop*	*Where can the girl buy a cheap CD for*
boy	*Londoner*	*Don't know.*	*her ...?*
2 ...			

◆◆ b Choose one of the conversations you have heard. Imagine what the people will say when they meet again or get off the bus. Write a short conversation and act it out for the class.

9 *School notice board*

Complete the sentences with the correct passive form of the verbs in brackets.

1 A video of Year 9's trip to London *(show)* in Room 25 after school next Thursday.
2 A mobile phone *(find)* in the canteen yesterday.
3 Tickets for the school play on Saturday *(sell)* at lunch-time tomorrow.
4 Pupils *(invite)* to come with their parents to the parents' evening next Tuesday.
5 A group of visitors from Germany *(welcome)* by the Head on Friday after assembly.
6 The library *(close)* on Monday and Tuesday next week.
7 Photos of today's football match *(put)* on the school's web site tomorrow.

10 *What can be done with it?*

Use *can*, *must* and *should* in the passive and write down three sentences about each of the objects below.

Example:
Ice-cream can be bought in a supermarket.
Ice-cream must be kept cold.
Ice-cream shouldn't be left out in the sun.

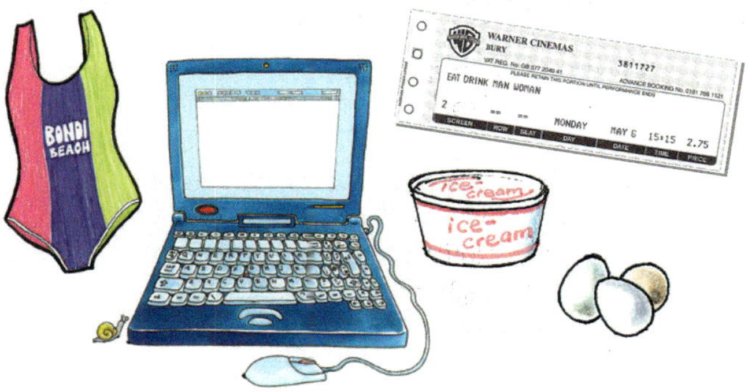

11 *Changes*

a Compare the two maps. Write down what has been changed. Use these verbs:

add • build • make bigger • put in

A garden has been added to ...

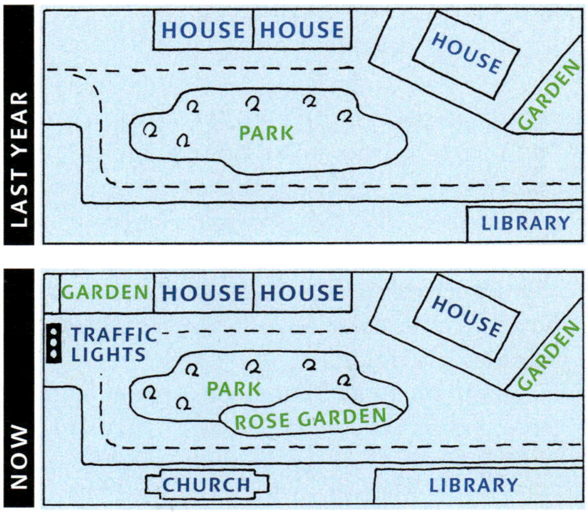

b What has been changed in your area this year? Collect ideas and make a list in class.

c How can your area be made a better place for young people? Make suggestions. Use *could/should/must be* + past participle.

A new swimming-pool should be built.

Word watch

12 *Word building: The suffix* -ness

a You already know the noun *homelessness*. What adjective does it come from?

b Now make new nouns with a *-ness* ending from the adjectives in the box. Be careful with the spelling. For example:
silly + *-ness* = *silliness*

bright • clever • dark • friendly happy • ill • lonely • sad • *silly*

c Use the nouns from 12b in the following sentences.

1 Nick likes to play the clown at school. His *silliness* often gets him into trouble with his teachers.
2 The sun on this white paper is terrible. The … makes it really hard to read.
3 The doctors don't know what's wrong with Sandra. She has got a mystery …
4 Everyone loved the king, so there was great … in the country after he died. The queen died a few months later. People say she died of …
5 I don't want to be an underground train driver. Just imagine: eight hours of … every day!
6 The family's dog brought the newspaper home every day. Other people were surprised at his …
7 Money is nice, but it can't buy you …
8 When I go to Britain, I always like the … of the people.

13 *Word link*

a Find verbs from the box for the groups of words below.

get • have • take • visit

… breakfast, fun, lunch, a party, time, a shower
… friends, a museum, the sights
… off a train, on a bus, pocket money, ready, cold, to Trafalgar Square
… notes, a photo, a seat, the underground

b Now use one phrase from each group and write a short story.

14 *Mediation: English and German are not the same*

How can you put these passive sentences into German? Be careful – a word for word translation of the passive is not always best.

1 German won't be spoken on the tour. *Man spricht …*
2 We'll be picked up at the airport and taken to the Tower by car.
3 The Tower of London was begun by William I in 1066.
4 It is visited by more than 2 million tourists every year.
5 Two of Henry VIII's wives were executed there.

Save the Crown Jewels

The following story is a maze. Don't try to read it like other stories! Just go where it tells you. You are in the story: you are Agent 101, and you must save the Crown Jewels. At each step you and your partner have to agree what you want to do next. Copy the table and write in the numbers of the steps you choose and how long they take. You mustn't go over 300 minutes, or … BOOM!

These phrases and the table will help you:
I think the clue means we should … / Why don't we try …? / That will take too long. / That's too easy. / That isn't hard enough. / I don't think that's the right decision. / No, let's go to …

Step	Time	Total
1	20 mins	20 mins
2	30 mins	50 mins
	+ ?	?
?	?	?

1 You are Agent 101 from the British Secret Service. Your mobile phone rings at 6 o'clock one morning. It's your boss. 'Come to the office at once.'

Half an hour later you're there. '101,' your boss says, 'Max Gladstone has put a bomb in the Tower of London. He says the Crown Jewels will be destroyed at 12 o'clock.'

'Our people can't defuse his bombs – not without the code,' you say. 'What's the game this time?'

'Here, he left this note for you.'

To my old friend, 101
I've got another little game for you, 101. If you can find five clues – and the answers – by 12 o'clock, you'll find the code for the bomb. If not: BOOM! Here's your first clue: When he was alive, he wasn't a tall man. Now he's dead, and he's the tallest man in London. Visit him, and he'll give you your next clue. Yours, Max G.

'What does it mean?' your boss asks.

'Nelson,' you tell her. 'Admiral Lord Nelson was a small man, but his statue was put on top of the column in Trafalgar Square. So now he's the tallest man in London.'

'Brilliant, 101!'

'Yes, I am. … Now, I must get to Trafalgar Square at once.'

'A car and driver are waiting for you, 101. You have five hours – 300 minutes.'

▶ *Go to 2*, Trafalgar Square. This takes **20 minutes**.
Remember: you must add your time at each step!

2 You're at Trafalgar Square. But where's the clue? Then you remember: 'The clue is about Nelson, not Trafalgar Square!'

'Get me a rope,' you say to your driver, and you climb the 44 metres up to the statue. Nelson is holding the next note from Gladstone in his hand: 'That was too easy, 101. Try this one: Everyone knows, "To be or not to be." But do you? Put that in your pipe and smoke it.'

▶ **30 minutes** have passed. What's next?

a You know that 'To be or not to be' is from a play by William Shakespeare, so you drive to Shakespeare's Globe Theatre on the Thames. **40 minutes**. *Go to 7*.

b Suddenly you see something in the note: 'Every<u>one</u> knows, "<u>To</u> <u>be</u> or not <u>to</u> <u>be</u>."' 'One' = 1; 'to' = 2; 'be' = B; 'to' = 2; 'be' = B. 12B2B. 'Of course! The numbers and letters are in the wrong order!' you shout. '<u>2</u> <u>2</u> <u>1</u> <u>B</u> <u>B</u>aker Street! Sherlock Holmes's address.' You drive to Baker Street. **20 minutes**. *Go to 6*.

3 Why are you reading this?
▶ Go back to 2 and follow the directions. Add 10 minutes to your time.

4 You get off the train in Oxford and walk to the taxis outside. Before you get there, you hear your name. At the information desk a message has been left for you: 'A clown like you should be in a circus. Max G.'

▶ **55 minutes** have passed. What's next?

a You decide that Oxford was a mistake, so you catch the next train back to London. When you arrive at Paddington Station, you take the tube to Oxford Circus. This takes **150 minutes**. *Go to 13*.

b You decide that you must be in the right place because Max has left a message for you. You take a taxi around the university. *Go to 16*.

5 The man at the London Dungeon tells you that they *have* got figures of Henry and his wives, that the figures *are* having dinner and that one of them *is* a ghost.
You say you're going to drive there and look at it, but he says you needn't come because they've turned off the power. 'The ghost of Anne Boleyn is a hologram,' he explains. 'She doesn't usually talk. But today she was talking.'
'What was she saying? Can you remember?'
'Yes, of course. She said: "Where did you go to university, you clown?"'
▶ This has taken **10 minutes**. What now?
a You went to university in Oxford, so you take the tube to Paddington Station. The trains to Oxford leave from there. *Go to 8*.
b 'Oxford, you clown!' you think. Then: 'Clown – circus – Oxford Circus!' You take the underground to Oxford Circus. This takes **6 minutes**. *Go to 13*.

6 You're at the Sherlock Holmes Museum, but where's the clue? Then you remember: 'Put that in your pipe and smoke it.' Of course, Holmes's famous pipe! Max's note has been hidden inside the pipe: 'He was married to three Catherines, two Annes and a Jane. Two lost their heads – poor things! Now they're all together for dinner, but one of them is a ghost.'
'He means Henry VIII and his wives,' says your driver.
'But where are they together for dinner?' you ask.
▶ This has taken **10 minutes**. What now?
a You remember that Madame Tussaud's has figures of Henry VIII and his wives. You're very near there, so you decide to send your driver away and walk. This takes **15 minutes**. *Go to 17.*
b You think there are figures of Henry VIII and his wives in the London Dungeon, but you aren't sure. You decide to phone there. *Go to 5*.

7 You don't find anything at the Globe. Then you think, 'That was too easy! Max isn't going to make things easy for me.'
▶ **45 minutes** have passed. What now?
a You remember your other choice and go there. The journey takes **60 minutes**.
b You can't remember your other choice and must *go back to 2* and look again. This takes **50 minutes**.

8 You arrive at Paddington Station by tube and buy a train ticket. You're waiting on the platform for the train to Oxford when you suddenly hear: 'The next train to Oxford will be 45 minutes late. We are very sorry ... '
▶ **35 minutes** have passed. Now what?
a You wait for the next train to Oxford. This takes **45 minutes**. *Go to 4*.
b You decide that Oxford Circus wasn't a bad idea and go there. This takes **17 minutes**. *Go to 13*.

9 You run from Tower Hill underground station to the Tower of London, then to the Jewel House.
▶ This has taken **10 minutes**. *Go to 10*.

10 The microchip fits into a hole in the bomb. You put it in, a small door opens and a figure jumps up. It looks like Max Gladstone. Then you hear Max's voice: 'Very good, 101. You're better than I thought. You've saved the Crown Jewels.'
'Yes, I have! That's enough games, Max!'
'Maybe ... but you'll hear from me again, 101. Our little games are really fun!'

11 You take a Central Line train to Liverpool Street, change there to a southbound Circle Line train and get off at Tower Hill.
▶ This takes **29 minutes**. *Go to 9*.

12 You quickly find the figures of Henry VIII and his wives and know you've made a mistake. (Look at the picture on page 25.)
▶ This has taken **25 minutes**. If you still have time, you can phone the London Dungeon. *Go to 5*.

13 You're at the tube station at Oxford Circus, but you can't find the clue. Then you see the sign which usually tells you when the next train will be there. But today it says 'Fish and chips – that great British invention.' This means nothing to you. But then you see a poster for the London Aquarium with a big picture of a fish. You look at it carefully and see that something has been stuck onto the eye of the fish. It's a microchip – fish and chips! You take the microchip and decide that you have to get to the Tower of London at once.
▶ This has taken **15 minutes**. *Go to 11*.

14 You're looking around Madame Tussaud's when the police come. They take you to the police station and keep you there until your boss phones. The Crown Jewels have been destroyed. You can look for a new job.
▶ This is the end of the story for you.

15 You get into Madame Tussaud's and find the figures of King Henry VIII and his wives. They aren't having dinner. (Look at the picture on page 25.)
▶ This has taken **115 minutes**. If you still have time, you can phone the London Dungeon.
Go to 5.

16 You drive around the university but find nothing. Oxford was a mistake, so you drive to Oxford Circus in London.
▶ This has taken **60 minutes**, and the drive into London takes **90 minutes**.
Go to 13.

17 About 500 people are waiting in front of Madame Tussaud's, so you go to the door and tell them you're from the Secret Service. They say you have to wait like everyone else.
▶ What do you do now?
a You show them your gun and tell them that you can't wait. You have to see Henry VIII and his wives now. They open the door for you. *Go to 14.*
b You wait like everyone else. *Go to 15.*
c You ask the people at the door to phone their boss. You explain everything; then you can go inside. *Go to 12.*

1 *Max Gladstone's next game*

Look at Max Gladstone's note for Agent 101 in Step 1 on page 33. Imagine you are Max Gladstone and you have a new 'game' in London for Agent 101. Write another note to Agent 101 about your new game.

2 *How to scan a text*

a Sometimes you want to find some specific words or information in a text quickly. How do you do it? Close your eyes and try to see the words as a picture in your head.

b Try to find the words 'Trafalgar Square' in the text on page 33. Just move your eyes very quickly along the text. You should still have a picture of the two words in your head. When you move your eyes past the words, they will suddenly be clear.
Try it now. Find the steps the two words are in and take notes on what you find out about Trafalgar Square.
Now use the same technique and scan pages 33–35 quickly for these:
Sherlock Holmes, Madame Tussaud's. Write down all the information about them.

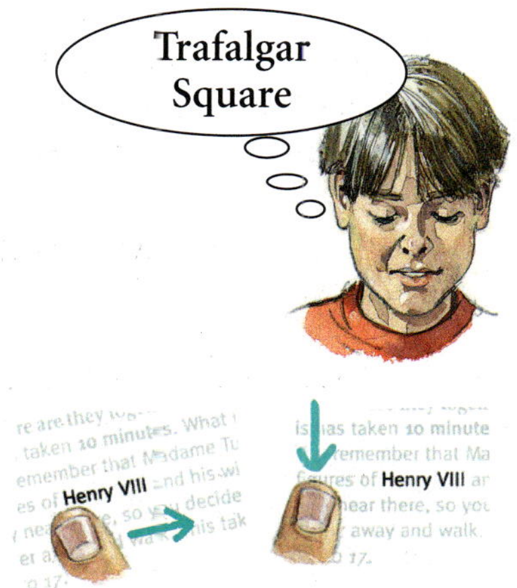

c Now try different ways to scan: move your finger in wavy lines or move your finger along the edge of the text.
Scan for and take notes on:
Henry VIII, Max (Gladstone).

❖ 3 ***Role-play: At Madame Tussaud's***

In groups of three, act out the scene at Madame Tussaud's (Step 17). One of you plays Agent 101, another plays the person at the ticket office, a third plays the manager of Madame Tussaud's.

a Before you start, read your role card carefully and try to imagine the situation. Make sure you 'know' your character well. Think of a favourite phrase that makes him/her real. Write down some of the things that your character might say. Try and use the expressions on your role card.

b Now do the role-play in your group. Perhaps you can act it out for the class later.

Role Card 1

You are **Agent 101**. You have to find Henry VIII and his six wives at Madame Tussaud's but there are about 500 people waiting there. You explain to the person at the ticket office that you are from the Secret Service and that they should let you in at once. When the person says you have to wait like everybody else, you ask for the manager. Explain everything and try hard so that the manager believes you.

Useful expressions:

If I don't find … then …
I haven't got time …
You have to listen to me.
Listen, I must …

Role Card 2

You **work at the ticket office** at Madame Tussaud's. A person you don't know tells you a story about the Secret Service and that he/she has to go in at once and find Henry VIII. You think the person is crazy and tell him/her quietly to wait like everybody else. The person asks you to phone your manager. At first you do not want to but the person won't take 'no' for an answer. So, in the end, you agree and you call the manager.

Useful expressions:

Just wait here, please.
Well, I'm sorry but …
I'm afraid the manager is …
Well, all right.
Excuse me, Sir, but there's somebody …
I think he's crazy, but …

Role Card 3

You are the **new manager of Madame Tussaud's**. You are working in your office on a very busy day when the phone rings. Somebody from the ticket office tells you there is an 'agent' who wants to talk to you. At first you say 'no'. But the person won't go away. So in the end you go to the ticket office and talk to him/her. Then you decide what to do.

Useful expressions:

Who does he say he is?
I'm very busy at the moment.
I don't believe that for a moment!
So, you're the person from …

How to ... find and use information

1 *Collecting information*

For a project in English on London, you have collected the following information about Greenwich. Where do you think the texts come from? An encyclopedia, ...? Where else could you look for information?

You can stand on the Prime Meridian, or Greenwich Meridian, with one foot in the east and one foot in the west.

... arrived in Greenwich on the boat from Westminster. That seemed like just the right thing to do because Maritime Greenwich is a World Heritage Site. There was so much to see and we spent the whole day there. We started at the Cutty Sark, then visited the National Maritime Museum and ...

Der **Nullmeridian** ist ein senkrecht zum Äquator stehender und von Nord- zu Südpol verlaufender Halbkreis, von dem aus die geographische Länge gerechnet wird. Seit einer Konferenz im Oktober 1884 in Washington, D.C. mit Vertretern aus 25 Nationen verläuft er durch die Sternwarte in Greenwich.

Vgl. Royal Observatory, Greenwich.

National Maritime Museum

The world's greatest museum of seafaring.
Some of the topics that are explored: Passengers, Nelson, the Future of the Sea and Explorers.
A special All Hands Gallery for children also has storytelling and live interpretation.
Tel: 020 8858 4422
Web site: www.nmm.ac.uk

2 *Making the best of the information*

a Two pupils have used the material in 1 and written about Greenwich. Which text do you think is better? Why?

Greenwich is a World Heritage Site on the River Thames in London. A nice way to arrive there is by boat from Westminster.
Some of the important sights in Greenwich are:
- The National Maritime Museum (very good for children)
- The Royal Observatory (stand on the Prime Meridian)

The Prime Meridian runs through Greenwich. It has been there since there was a conference in Washington, D.C., in 1884 when 25 countries decided this. In Greenwich there is also the Cutty Sark and a museum and you can arrive there on the boat from Westminster. The museum is the ...

b When you write your own reports, first decide what the most important information is. Then underline or mark it or take notes on it. Next you have to arrange the information – which ideas go together? When you write, give every new topic a new paragraph.

3 *Do-it-yourself*

Choose a London sight you like. Collect information about it from different sources. (Use a dictionary if you need one.) Then write about your sight.

- London Eye
- Tate Modern
- The Monument
- Westminster Abbey
- Natural History Museum
- Houses of Parliament
- ...

Remember

1 Use different sources of information, e.g. books, newspaper articles, encyclopedias, the Internet, maps, statistics, ...
2 Underline or mark important facts or take notes (see page 19).
3 Plan what you write carefully. Don't just copy or translate one text.

Virtual London

You want to go to London, but you don't have the cash?

You want to go to London now, but you have to be at school tomorrow morning?

You want to go to London, but your parents are against it?

No more excuses!

Through the magic of Cyberspace, you can visit Virtual London. Turn on your computer and get ready for a WWW trip to the capital.

What's out there? – We show you the best places in town.

Number 10 Downing Street
The home of the British Prime Minister!
www.number-10.gov.uk

The British Monarchy Website
The Queen online!
www.royal.gov.uk

The London Aquarium
Meet the fish!
www.london aquarium.co.uk

The Tower of London The virtual tour!
www.toweroflondontour.com/kids

Arsenal Football Club
Find out all the latest news from one of London's top Premier League football clubs.
www.arsenal.com

The British Museum
One of the great museums of the world!
www.british-museum.ac.uk

Camden Markets
Watch the people, eat and drink or buy some great stuff at the wonderful markets in Camden Town
www.camdenlock.net

virtual ['vɜːtʃuəl] prime minister [ˌpraɪm 'mɪnɪstə] monarchy ['mɒnəki] latest *neueste(r, s)*
the Premier League [ˌpremiə 'liːg] *die Erste Liga*

WB 12

And what's behind the homepages?

The Tower of London Kids Tour

Do the quiz on the kids' Tower of London Web site!

Enjoy the underwater world at the London Aquarium!

CORAL REEF

Visit the stunning world of the coral reef, inhabited by some of the world's most colourful fish. Its residents include the picasso triggerfish, deadly lionfish, tangs, moray eels and batfish. Don't miss the elegant seahorses – the only species in the world where the males give birth!

And the OTHERS?

You'll have to GO there yourself.

Enjoy your TRIP to Virtual London!

coral reef [ˌkɒrəl ˈriːf] *Korallenriff* stunning [ˈstʌnɪŋ] (infml) *umwerfend* inhabited by [ɪnˈhæbɪtɪd] *bewohnt von*
resident [ˈrezɪdənt] *Bewohner/in* (to) include [ɪnˈkluːd] *(mit) einschließen* species, pl species [ˈspiːʃiːz] *Art, Spezies*
deadly [ˈdedli] *tödlich* lionfish *Rotfeuerfisch* tang [tæŋ] *Doktorfisch* moray eel [ˌmɒreɪ ˈiːl] *Muräne*
batfish [ˈbætfɪʃ] *Fledermausfisch* male [meɪl] *männlich* picasso triggerfish [pɪˌkæsəʊ ˈtrɪgəfɪʃ] *Picasso Drückerfisch*

Internet

3 When the Romans Ruled Britannia

1 Match these words to the photos of the objects.

amphora • board game • comb • hairpins
knives and spoons • oil-lamp • Roman coin

2 Maybe you already know something about the Romans from your History lessons. Imagine that the objects on this page all belonged to a family in Roman Britain. What do the objects tell you about their lives? Try and describe some of them.

The objects tell us that people in Roman Britain used/had/cut/played/liked/lit/kept/ ...

Archaeologists in the 'hot room' of some Roman baths in London. The baths were built about 70 AD. Remains like these can tell us a lot about everyday life in Roman Britain.

1

2

3

4

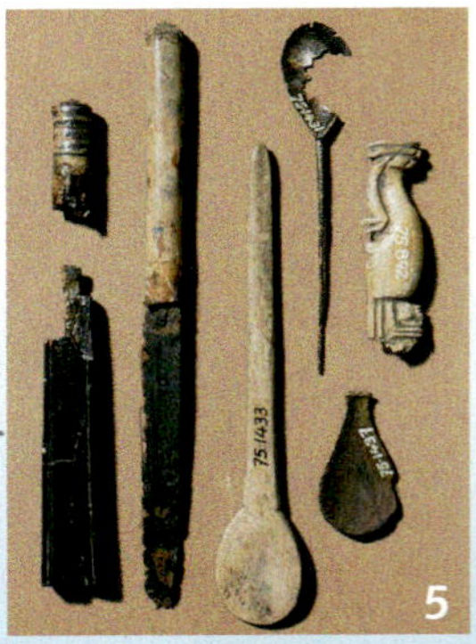
5

7

6

1 Time is running out for Roman site

Time has almost run out for archaeologists at a Roman site on the new B2011 road near Dover. Work was stopped there when the grave of a young girl from Roman Britain was dug up. If more remains are not found today, the bulldozers will return tomorrow.
'Unfortunately we didn't have much time. But we hope we got everything valuable,' said Dr Trisha Willis from the Dover Museum.

Melissa pointed at the B2011. 'Isn't that the old Roman site your mum is working on?' she asked.
'Yes,' Mark answered. 'But they didn't find much there. Just an old grave.'
Melissa loved old things. 'My mum hasn't got a very interesting job. You're lucky. Your mum has got a really exciting one.'
'She just looks through 1000-year-old rubbish dumps all day long,' said Mark. 'That may be your idea of what's exciting, but I think it's boring.'
They continued without a word until Melissa suddenly said, 'Maybe they didn't find everything.' Then, before Mark could stop her, she climbed over the fence and soon came back with something she found on the ground.

Melissa I've found something.
Mark Oh, it's a tile, isn't it? Mum has got some tiles like that on the wall – big ones I mean, not little ones like this.
Melissa Look at the letters on it. This one is a 'B'. The tile looks really old, doesn't it? If you ask your mum, she'll know if it's valuable, won't she? Yes, Mark, please show it to your mum. Please!
Mark OK. Or, no, you show it to her. She'll be at the museum tomorrow.

The next morning, Melissa showed her tile to a woman at the Dover Museum.
Woman Well, it looks like one from the *Classis Britannica.*
Melissa CLBR, of course! The Roman fleet in Britain. It was in Dover, wasn't it?
Woman Yes, it was. But I'm not an expert. I don't know if this one is genuine.
Melissa Dr Willis is here today, isn't she?
Woman No, she's at the Roman Painted House in New Street. Why don't you go over there? I'll phone and tell her you're coming.

2 *The Roman rap*

This tile is grey, this one is brown,
In a Roman house in a Roman town.
This one is big, that one is small,
A Roman tile on a Roman wall.
A blue one here and a white one there,
On a Roman door and a Roman chair.

This comb is ..., this ...

3 *Looking at language*

Find sentences with *one/ones*. What words do *one/ones* stand for? Can you guess why you use these words?

4 *Game: What are we talking about?*

First one pupil goes out. The other pupils choose a word, e.g. 'magazine' or 'spoon'. Then the pupil comes in again. He or she must guess what the others are talking about.

I buy one every week. – Is it a ticket? – No, it isn't. I'm reading a really interesting one at the moment. – A magazine? – Yes, that's right.

S 3: 1 (p. 128) • P 1–4 • WB 1–3

5 Life in Roman Britain

Before she left, Melissa looked at some books about life in Roman Britain in the museum shop.

What are the modern names of the Roman towns on the map?

ROMAN ROADS

The Romans were famous for their roads. While they were in Britannia (from 43 AD to 410 AD), they built over 6000 miles of them from the south right up to Hadrian's Wall, where the Roman Empire ended. Soldiers could move quickly along these roads when there was trouble with the Celtic tribes. Roman roads were built so well that they lasted for a very long time. Many modern roads still follow the same routes today.

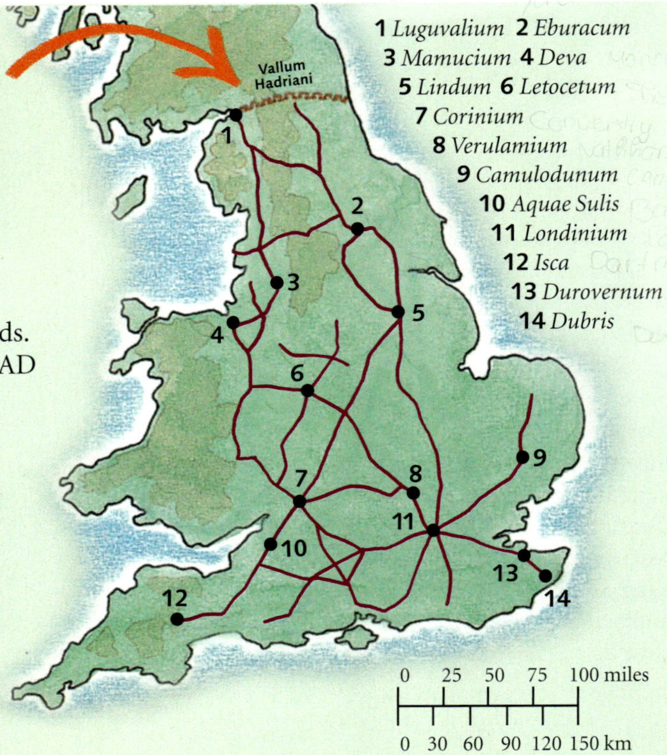

WHAT'S COOKING?

Roman Britons cooked food in pots over charcoal fires. Other food like bread was baked in charcoal ovens.
From the south of France and Spain, the Romans brought fish sauce and olive oil to Britain. These were used a lot and were kept in amphoras.

A ROMAN KITCHEN

AT THE BATHS

Visitors met friends and after exercise sat or took a bath in the 'warm room'. Next came the 'hot room' where they cleaned themselves and relaxed in the hot bath. After that they jumped into the cold bath. At the end of their visit oils and perfumes were rubbed into their skin.

THE ROMAN BATHS AT AQUAE SULIS (BATH)

6 What the remains can tell us

The Roman Painted House was only a few minutes from the museum. When Melissa arrived, a class of schoolchildren was on a visit and an archaeologist was talking to them.

'In 1970 they wanted to build a car park here. So it's lucky we dug a hole and found the remains of some painted walls, the painted walls you can see down there in Room 2. More interesting than a car park, isn't it? The rooms you can see were part of a much larger building 1800 years ago. It was a mansio – a sort of hotel. It had about 96 rooms. And there were paintings on the walls – paintings of Roman gods, e.g. Bacchus, the god of wine. Just right for the travellers who arrived here in Dubris from Londinium or from Portus Itius in France. They enjoyed the food and wine and got a good night's sleep. And they were comfortable even if it was cold. Do you know why? Well, because this hotel had central heating. You can still see where hot air went through the walls and under the floors.
Now, in a moment, you're all going to get a bowl of real archaeological remains that were found here. These remains tell us a lot more about everyday life in Roman Dover. We'll work with those and then after that you'll be able to make a real Roman mosaic.'

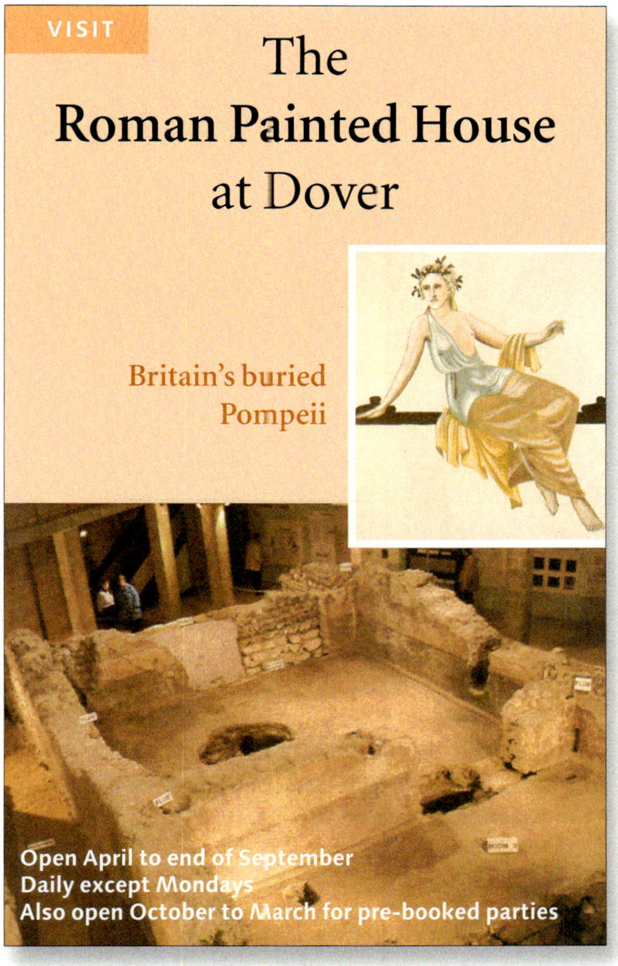

7 *A conversation in the mansio*

Write a short dialogue that takes place in the mansio back in 150 AD: two guests are talking about where they are from, why they are here and what they are going to do this evening (eat, play a game ...).

8 *Focus on words*

Collect words and phrases from pages 40–43 that can help you to talk about everyday life in Roman times and today. Put them in groups, e.g.

- **eating and drinking:** bake bread in charcoal ovens, ...
- **free time:** meet at the baths, ...
- **travel:** stay in a mansio, ...

You can add more words and phrases later in the unit.

9 *Now you*

Imagine a 14-year-old boy from Roman Britain is visiting you in his time machine. Compare your everyday lives. Talk about what is the same/different/better/worse/more exciting/ ...

10 More time for the archaeologists

Melissa was still listening to the archaeologist when Dr Willis found her. 'Melissa! So you brought this tile! Listen, it's genuine. If I drove you to the site, would you show me exactly where you found it?' 'Yes, of course.'

They were soon in Dr Willis's car on the way to the site. 'Work on the road would stop again if we found something valuable. Right?' Melissa asked.

'It wouldn't be so easy, I'm afraid,' Dr Willis replied.

'But if they gave you more time, you'd find more remains, I know you would.'

'Yes, maybe we would. But that new road would get more and more expensive if the workers had to stop again now. Their manager wouldn't agree, even if we found something really unusual. OK, here we are. Now, where did you find it?'

Four more weeks at Roman site

'I found an old Roman tile at the site of a new road,' said Melissa Wells. 'When I heard it was genuine, I wanted to help. I talked to my friend Mark and he said: "If we held a demonstration, then they'd listen."'

When road workers arrived at the site on Monday, a hundred children and their teachers were already there. The workers' manager was very unhappy, but after some long discussions she gave the archaeologists four more weeks at the site.

11 *Looking at language*

a Find all the sentences with *if* in A10 and the article on the left and make a table like this:

If-clause	*Main clause*
If I drove you to the site,	*would you show me ...?*
...	...

b What verb forms appear in the two clauses? What time does the *if*-clause refer to – past, present or future? What verb forms do you use in this sort of sentence in German?

c Compare these two sentences:
A If they give me more time, I'll find more.
B If they gave me more time, I'd find more.

Who is more of an optimist, who is more of a pessimist?

12

The next day Dr Willis thanked Melissa's class for the demonstration with a book about the Romans for their class library.

GIRLS HAD IT HARDER!

A Roman girl was ready to get married when she was 14. Who said so? Her father. But imagine she didn't want to get married. Bad luck! A husband was chosen for her. Who by? Her father. She didn't like the man? Nobody cared. She had to marry him anyway.

ROMAN MATHS

The Romans didn't have the number 0. That made maths really difficult. If you aren't very good at doing sums, just look at this Roman sum: LXXXVIII + XII = C. Now do you see how lucky you are!?

13 *Role-play: History lesson*

❖ Melissa's classmates and teacher didn't want to hear about her old tile. How did that change? With your group, act out their conversation. You can use role cards for this activity.

1 *Revision: Roman remains*

Complete the sentences about the discovery of some Roman remains. The beginning of each sentence is given. Some sentences are active and some are passive. Be careful with the tenses.

1 discover – Roman remains – at – farm – near Cirencester
Roman remains have been discovered ...
2 farmer – take – archaeologists – to – site
Archaeologists were ...
3 farmer – take – some Roman coins – to – Corinium Museum – last week
The farmer ...
4 children – dig up – coins – in – potato field
The coins ...
5 archaeologists – work – in – field – all weekend
The archaeologists ...
6 find – 15 more objects
15 ...
7 put – objects – in – child's grave – in about 150 AD
The objects ...
8 archaeologists – now – believe – remains – part of – small Roman hotel
The archaeologists ...
9 build – hotel – in about 120 AD
The hotel ...

2 *Revision: At the Roman site*

Complete the conversation. Add the right question tags.

Melissa Your mum is a real expert, ...?
Mark I suppose she is.
Melissa She'll know how valuable the tile is, ...?
Mark Maybe.
Melissa It could be *very* valuable, ...?
Mark Maybe.
Melissa You aren't very interested in history, ...? And you don't like talking about your mum's job, ...?
Mark You think you know a lot about me, ...?

3 *Mark's diary*

Write the text again. Don't use the same nouns twice but put in *one*/*ones*.

Melissa was looking for Roman tiles at mum's site. And she found a tile. It was an interesting tile with letters on it. The colour was like some of the tiles in our kitchen. Mum usually finds every object, but this time she missed an object. She found some coins last week, but they're not as good as the coins they've already got in the museum. But the tile is good news. The archaeologists wanted a reason to stop the bulldozers, and now they've got a reason. But I'm not really interested. I like new coins better than old coins.

4 *After the party*

It's 100 AD. There was a party at a house in Roman Dover last night. The children are tidying up. Complete their conversation.

Helena Is this ... lamp, Falco?
Falco No, I think that ... belongs to Marcus. And there's ... on the table, too. I think ... Justina's.
Marcus Olivia, ... a board game here. It isn't the ... we ... with us.
Olivia Maybe ... belongs to Helena. She brought ... with ..., didn't ...?
Justina These are my hairpins, but whose are ... ones ... the chair there?
Helena The green ... are Olivia's. I don't know ... the red ... belong ... .
Falco ... is this comb?
Olivia Is it ... old broken ...? I think that ... belongs to Marcus.
Justina ... be silly. Marcus ... never used a comb in his ...!

5 *Listening: At Dubris harbour*

a In the museum Melissa watched a video about some people at Dubris harbour in 150 AD. Listen to the CD and match the names to the jobs and problems.

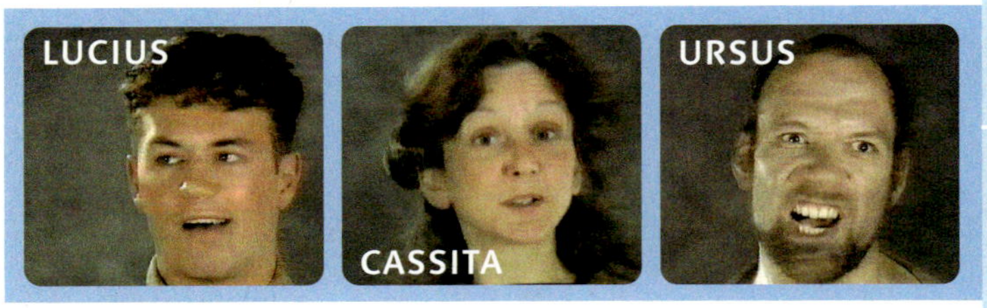

Jobs	*Problems*
soldier	*Life is hard.*
slave	*The old life is disappearing.*
farmer	*Life is boring.*

b Listen again. What do Lucius, Cassita and Ursus think or feel about the following?

LUCIUS	– the party tonight – Dubris – the game 'Soldiers' – the kid at the baths
CASSITA	– the village – the future of Celtic life and the Celtic language – young people
URSUS	– the mines – his brother – his life now – his future

6 *Revision: If the archaeologists …*

Use the phrases a–h and complete the sentences.

1 If work on the road starts again, the archaeologists …
2 We'll never finish the road if the archaeologists …
3 If we always have to ask the archaeologists first, we …
4 If Melissa's tile is really very old, Mark's mother …
5 If you like looking at Roman remains, you …
6 You'll know a lot more about life in Roman Britain if you …
7 You should try and find work on an old Roman site if you …
8 If we can't dig up archeological remains, we …

a be allowed to work as long as they can
b be interested in it
c love the Dover Museum
d never be able to build anything
e not be able to find any more remains
f not know very much about the past
g spend a few hours at the Dover Museum
h want to become an archaeologist

7 *Suggestions*

When Melissa told the class about her Roman tile, a lot of people had suggestions. What did they say?

1 *Robert* we (write) to the mayor – he (have to) do something about it

If we wrote to the mayor, he would have to do something about it.

2 *Julie* Melissa (bring) the tile to school – I (find) it more interesting
3 *Teacher* we (go on) with our history lesson – we (learn) a lot more about Roman Dover
4 *Mark* we (hold) a demonstration – they (have to) listen
5 *Natalie* we all (go) to the site very early in the morning – the road workers (not be able to) start work
6 *Melissa* we (tell) the newspaper – they (send) a reporter
7 *Jane* they really (build) the new road – the city (be) a lot safer for kids
8 *Mark* everyone (think) like that – we never (know) anything about the past
9 *Jane* we (not think) about the past all the time – we (make) the present better for everyone

8 *A poem*

a Read the poem on the right.

b What would you do if you were:
- a teacher?
- an archaeologist?
- an animal?
- a pop star?
- …?

c Write a short poem (2–4 lines). You could put it in your UK album and draw or find a picture for it. Read all the poems in your class.

9 *Just imagine!*

◆◆ a Partner B: Look at page 119.
Partner A: Ask your partner these questions and write down what he/she answers. Answer your partner's questions and give reasons for your answers.

1. If you could meet a famous person from history, who would you like to meet?
2. If you could buy just one thing, what would you buy?
3. If you could have any job in the world, which job would you like to have?

b Now think of one more question for your partner.

10 *Well, but if …*

❖ Work in groups of four.
Partner A: Start and ask a question like this:
What would you do if …
– you saw a house on fire?
– you found an old gold coin in the park?
– …

Partner B: Answer the question.
I'd call the fire brigade. / I'd …

Partner C: Ask a 'Well, but if …'-question.
Well, but if you couldn't find your mobile, what would you do then? / …

Partner B: Answer the question.
Partner D: Ask a 'Well, but if …'-question.

How long can you make your discussion? Present it to the class. Make notes for your presentation.

11 *Project: Signs of the past*

❖ Many remains from the past have been found in Britain.
What remains have been found in your part of Germany? Find out who lived there, how they lived, etc.
Look at page 17, P12 again and present information in English for visitors who are interested in the history of your area. Don't forget photos, pictures, maps, etc. Here are some ideas:

History

BC/AD	What happened?
…	…
…	…

A museum
- where?
- opening times
- price
- what can you see?
- what can you do?
- …

An old site
- what?
- where?
- opening times
- how old?
- when discovered?
- …

Everyday life
- houses
- food and cooking
- farms
- festivals
- religion
- language
- …

Remains
- art
- graves
- personal objects
- walls and stones
- objects from houses

Word watch

12 *Word building: The prefix* un-

a You have already learned about some suffixes like *-er*, *-ness*, *-tion*. English also makes new words with prefixes like *un-*, e.g. *unhappy*, *unusual*. How does *un-* change the meaning of *happy* and *usual*?

Now say what the following words mean (in English or German).

unfriendly • untidy • unpack • unlucky
unimportant • unload • unhealthy

b Complete the sentences with the right words from a.

1 Slaves in Britain often had an … life, with bad food, too much work and cold rooms.
2 They had to … the ships at Dubris harbour.
3 Richborough was a big fort in Roman times but it's an … little place now.
4 The first Romans in Britain got an … welcome from the Celtic tribes.
5 The Romans liked board games, even if they were … and didn't win.

13 *Say it differently*

Replace the underlined expressions with words that mean the same.

1 When will the bulldozers <u>come back</u>?
2 Real objects from Roman times <u>cost a lot of money</u>.
3 The museum? Just <u>drive on</u> along this road.
4 Dr Willis <u>knows everything about</u> the Classis Britannica.
5 This amphora was <u>found in the ground</u> near Hadrian's Wall.
6 It <u>was Ortho's</u>, a Roman soldier from Spain.

❖ 14 *Things from another world*

a Work in groups of four. Imagine you are going to send a spaceship to another planet. Which five objects will you put in the spaceship to tell aliens about the everyday life of young people today? Draw your objects on cards and give the cards to another group.

b Now you are the aliens. You have just found the spaceship. What do the objects on the cards tell you? Talk about them in your group and then write your ideas down.

Useful expressions:
I think we should put a … in, because …
… are very important to me, so let's …
Everyone uses … so we need …
If …, that won't tell the aliens much.
If we put … in, it will tell …

Useful expressions:
This thing looks like …
This object has got … so I think it is …
How can it be a … when there is …?
I think this is a … because …
The … shows/tells us that they use/have …
People on Earth might … because …
If they have …, then they must/will …
Only people who can … could … a …
They may … if they …

A funny look at history

Invaders

Britain was last invaded a long time ago – in 1066. But for 1000 years before 1066 it was a favourite with invaders. And they all brought their own languages to Britain – and gave the world English!

The Britons

When the Romans invaded Britain in 43 AD, Celtic tribes were living peacefully all over the country. Peacefully? Well, maybe not quite ... The tribes liked fighting and they did it all the time. That made things easy for the Roman invaders.

Life for the Britons wasn't very exciting. Most of them lived in round farmhouses, often in small forts at the top of hills. Like the Romans, they had many gods. Their most important ones were the gods of nature. These farmers didn't go on holiday very much, so they didn't have real roads – just tracks across the countryside. Because they were Celts, the language they spoke is called Celtic. There are almost no Celtic words in English today. Most of them are place names like 'the Thames, Dover, Kent'.

PLACES TO VISIT Chysauster, Cornwall
Here are the beautiful remains of a Celtic village. People lived and farmed here for 400 years between about 100 BC and 300 AD. When you walk around the site, you have the feeling that the Britons only left a few days ago.

The Romans

ruled Britannia from 43 AD until 410 AD. If you learned Latin, you could do well in Roman Britain because the Romans brought their language with them. That's why words like 'wine' and 'wall' are now English.

The Romans loved building. They built good straight roads with forts and towns along them. So their soldiers were able to move around the country quickly when there was any trouble (and there often was!). The Romans also built villas in the countryside and temples to their gods. And the Emperor Hadrian built Hadrian's Wall so that Celtic tribes from the north couldn't invade Roman Britain.

PLACES TO VISIT Hadrian's Wall, Cumbria and Northumberland
The best part is the 12 miles (19 km) between Banina and Vergovicium. Walk along next to the wall. Imagine it's night and you're a Roman soldier who is hoping the Celtic tribes from the north aren't going to attack.
Visit the Roman Army Museum at Vindolanda. Become a Roman soldier, buy Roman goods with Roman coins, and find out how Romans and Britons lived at the time.

The Anglo-Saxons

The Angles and Saxons began their invasions of Britain when it was still part of the Roman Empire. When the Romans left, more and more Angles and Saxons came. They went up and down the long, straight Roman roads and burned and pillaged. Then they went back home to the north-west of Germany again. But around 430 AD they thought, 'This place isn't so bad, is it? If we got rid of the Britons, we could stay.'
So the Angles and Saxons pushed the Celtic Britons into Cornwall, Wales and Scotland. At first they lived just like the Britons before the Romans came – they were farmers, and the different tribes loved a good fight. But after about 450 years there was only one tribe left and the country it ruled was called England, 'Land of the Angles'. Because this was a long time ago, the language they spoke is called Old English. Of course, they couldn't spell very well and always wrote Englisc. Almost all the most common words in Modern English come from Old English. For example, the 20 most common – 'the, of, to, and, a, in, is, it, you, that, he, was, for, on, are, with, as, I, his, they' – all come from Old English, except the last – 'they' comes from Old Norse.

PLACES TO VISIT Dover Castle, Kent
The wonderful Anglo-Saxon church, St Mary-in-Castro, is inside the grounds of the Norman castle. You can also see the remains of the pharos (a Roman lighthouse) here.

The Vikings

– or Danes or Norsemen, as some people called them – burned and pillaged just like the Anglo-Saxons before them. But they were even better at it. They loved travelling, so they sailed across the North Sea from their homes in Scandinavia and 'visited' all of Europe. They even went to Iceland, Greenland and North America. The east of England was one of the places they liked, so in the ninth century they started to settle there. 'If there were more of us Vikings than Anglo-Saxons here,' they thought, 'we could give it a new name.' That is just what happened and that part of England was called Danelaw (no, not Vikinglaw or Norsemanlaw). But they did not speak Danish in Danelaw. No, they were Norsemen, so they spoke Old Norse. About 2000 English words come from Old Norse, words like 'skin, leg, sky' and 'window'.

PLACES TO VISIT York, Yorkshire
Go back in time to Viking York (Jorvik). At the Jorvik Viking Centre you can see, hear and smell what life was like in Viking York in 948 AD. In York, you can also visit the remains of the Roman city (Eburacum).

The Normans were the last invaders and gave us the most famous date in English history – 1066. They came from France under William the Conqueror and beat the English at the Battle of Hastings.

But who were the Normans? (This is where it gets hard!) Well, they were really Vikings who went to the north of France in about 900 AD and became French. That's why they spoke French when, 150 years later, they decided to become English, too. So they got in their ships and invaded. The Normans liked building almost as much as the Romans and they built castles all over England, like the Tower of London.

The castles were full of Norman soldiers so that the Anglo-Saxons would know whose country it was now.

The Normans didn't want to learn English and they spoke French for a long time after they arrived. And when they learned to speak English two or three hundred years later, there were already a lot of their own French words in it, like 'action, blue, chair, close, lesson, mirror' or 'music'.

PLACES TO VISIT London

The most famous Norman place in London is, of course, the Tower of London. But you can also go and see the Domesday Book. In 1086 King William I ordered a survey of Norman England. This survey, called the Domesday Book, gave details of the people, animals, buildings and land in every village in the country. If you were a Roman you would be able to read the Domesday Book easily. It was written in Latin.

1 ***Peoples of Britain***

a What different peoples lived in Britain between 0 and 1100 AD?
Copy and complete this chart:

Name of people	*Time*
...	...

b Choose <u>one</u> of the following headings and make notes on the different peoples:

- what they did and built
- where and how they lived
- their language and influence on modern English

❖ c Find partners who have made notes under the other headings. In your group, use your chart from a and your notes from b and make a timeline of the invaders of Britain from 0 to 1100 AD. Show when they came, where they came from, how they lived, … and anything else you think is important.

2 *The English language*

a What do you think these Old English and Old Norse words mean in modern English?

aron • cyning • earm • helpan • skinn
ic • thæt • the • thei • wæs • vindauga

b Which English words come from the Latin words *vallum* and *vinum*?
What about *facies, punctum, schola, tabula*?

c Which English words come from these Old French words?
bleu, clos, chaiere, dangier, leson, mireor, sillabe
Find out how you spell these words in modern French.

3 *History book*

a Read this history book extract about the Anglo-Saxons. Which information about the Anglo-Saxons is the same as on page 50? Which is different? Take notes in a table like this:

Same	*New*
...	...

b What makes the extract of the history book on the right and the text 'Invaders' (pages 49–51) different?
Think about:
– how long the sentences are
– direct speech
– fun
– ...

c Choose one of the other invaders from pages 49–51. Check the facts in an encyclopedia, on the Internet or in a history book and find out more information. Report to the class.

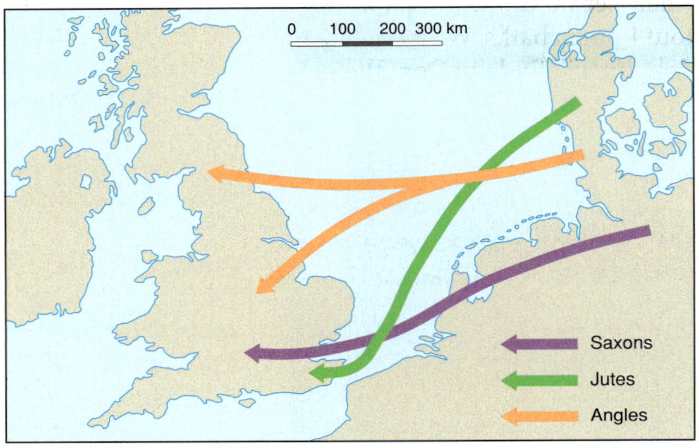

THE INVADERS

At first Germanic tribes only pillaged in Britain, but after 430 AD they began to settle. The newcomers could not read or write and what we know about them comes mainly from an English monk called Bede who lived three centuries later.

Bede tells us that the invaders were from three Germanic tribes, the Saxons, Angles and Jutes. The Jutes settled mainly in Kent and along the south coast. The Angles settled in the east and the north Midlands. The Saxons settled between the Jutes and the Angles. The Anglo-Saxon invaders gave the larger part of Britain its new name, England, 'The Land of the Angles'.

The British Celts fought the Germanic invaders as well as they could. However, in the next hundred years they were slowly pushed west into the mountains the Saxons called 'Wealas', or 'Wales', the 'Land of Foreigners'. Some Celts were driven into Cornwall, others in the north into Scotland. Some Celts stayed behind and many became slaves of the Saxons. Almost no Celtic language or culture is left in England, just the names of some rivers, e.g. Thames, Mersey, Severn and Avon, and two large cities, London and Leeds.

Adapted from: **An Illustrated History of Britain,** ***David McDowall***

4 *Places to visit*

What would be a good place to visit in your area for somebody who is interested in history? Find a picture and write a short text about the place like the ones on pages 49–51. Put it in your UK album. Or put all the texts on the classroom wall.

WB 10–11

How to ... listen for information

1 ***Before you listen***
When you visit an old Roman site, you can often get audio tours about the place. You are going to listen to an audio tour of the Roman baths at **Wall**, or **Letocetum**, as the Romans called it.
You will find it easier to follow the tour if you prepare for listening. Look at the picture on the right. Remember what you already know about Roman baths. What do you think you will find out from the tour? Collect ideas in class.

Inside the Letocetum bathhouse (in about 200 AD)

Plan of the Letocetum bathhouse

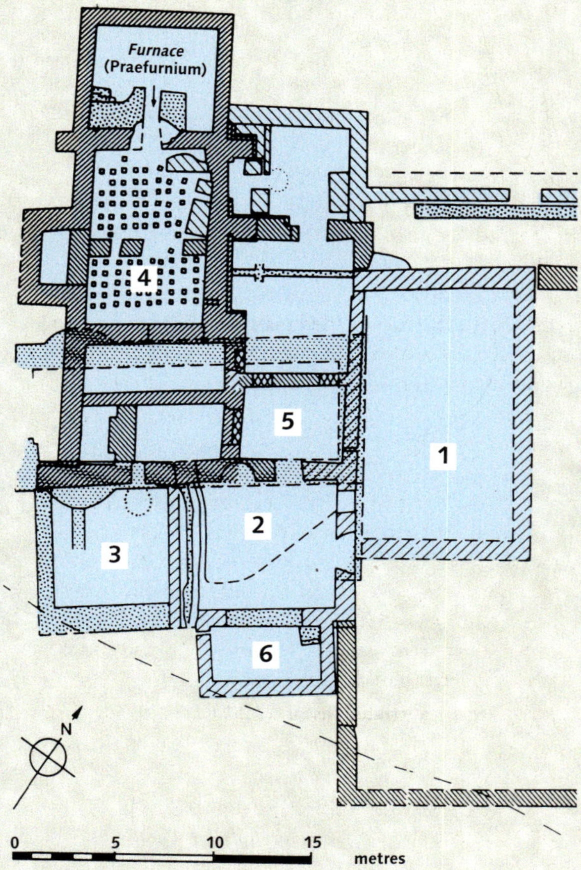

2 ***Listening: An audio tour***

a First look at the plan of the bathhouse and follow the route of the audio tour. Then close your eyes and try to 'see' the baths. What rooms do you hear about? Don't worry if you don't understand everything.
Were the ideas that you collected in 1 correct?

b Listen again, for details this time. What does the Roman soldier Gallus say about the different parts of the bathhouse? Take short notes.

exercise room – ball games, ...
changing room – ...
furnaces – ...
...

3 ***Writing: A brochure about Wall Roman Site***
Write part of a brochure (in easy English for foreign visitors) about the baths at Letocetum. Use your notes from 2b and write about two of the rooms. Copy the plan of the building and show where your rooms are.

Remember
1 Before you listen for information, prepare if you can.
2 Listen for the main information and don't worry if there are things you don't understand.
3 Listen again for details that you missed, if you can.
4 Short notes help you to remember what you heard and to tell others about it.

ROMANS RETURN

A play to read, act and write

Characters

LAVINIA – a Roman girl from Aquae Sulis
QUINTUS – her father, a Roman businessman
OLIVER – a boy from modern Bath
CHRISSIE – Oliver's sister
WOMAN – sells fruit in the market
MOTHER – Oliver and Chrissie's mother
POLICEMAN

The Bath Chroni

Price: 70 pence — 1 April 200

BATHS SENSATION

– Two Romans asleep for 2000 years? –

BATH. Archaeologists were trying to find out yesterday if two people really 'slept' in the baths for 2000 years. A tourist who saw the man and girl in Roman clothes said, 'They were talking English but seemed very lost.'

Dr Sulis, the TV expert who worked on the 'Ötzi' mummy from the Alps, told our reporter: 'We know that the water here is very special. If it's true, maybe the water put them into a coma.'

Bath Museum guide Liz Croaker added, 'I suppose they heard us and the tourists while they were asleep and learned the language like that.'

LON and but whe their did t sund Prin Que we

Scene 1

In the market

(Lavinia and her father, Quintus Lavinius Timidus, are walking through the market in Bath.)

LAVINIA Pater, come along now. We must find the road to Londinium.

QUINTUS Oh, oh, poor me. Where is my villa? Where are my slaves? Lavinia, dear, run over to Maximus. I want to talk to him.

LAVINIA Pater, his house is gone.

QUINTUS Oh, what's wrong with this town? Lavinia, where is my TABERNA, … er, shop? It can't be far.

LAVINIA Pater, we are out of our time. Everything has changed. And it's all because you slept too long again.

QUINTUS That's it! Perhaps we're still dreaming! I had such a funny dream. I dreamed of carts that moved without horses, imagine!

LAVINIA But that's real! That's now! All the Romans we knew have gone and we're alone.

QUINTUS Now, don't you worry, my dear. Remember you're the daughter of Quintus Lavinius Timidus, *Import and Export to all Four Corners of the Empire*, the richest man in Aquae Sulis. Remember that and hold your head high! – Oooh, ESURIO!

LAVINIA You're hungry? Here's some fruit.

(Not far away, Oliver and Chrissie are looking at the newspapers outside a shop.)

OLIVER See this, Chrissie? Two Romans woke up in the baths yesterday.

CHRISSIE What? You mean Romans from thousands of years ago?

OLIVER Yeah, here, look. There's a picture. The girl is nice.

CHRISSIE Stop it, Ollie. Let me see. – Oh I bet they feel stupid in those clothes …

(Chrissie and Oliver are interrupted by Quintus' loud voice.)

QUINTUS And why can't I take the MALUM, I mean apple, my good woman? You should know that I am Quintus Lavinius Timidus, *Import and Export to all Four Corners of the Empire*, and I'm testing this apple.

WOMAN Well, you can buy it before you test it, Mr Caesar.

LAVINIA Pater, here's our last denarius, give her that.

QUINTUS Well, I'm not an unfair man. Here is a silver denarius. I'll have four pounds of apples for that, woman.

WOMAN You can keep your toy money, sir. And your silly Roman clothes. Some kind of show for the tourists again, is it?

QUINTUS By Jupiter!

WOMAN No bad language, here, thank you! In front of his daughter, too!

OLIVER Excuse me, er, can we help you? Are you in trouble?

QUINTUS My daughter is already married – go away!

LAVINIA Pater!

CHRISSIE Ollie, let me do this – ESURITISNE? MALUMNE EDERE VULTIS? ECCE 50 pence.

QUINTUS How can I thank you, my dear child? Two apples, please.

(The woman gives them the apples, Quintus eats.)

LAVINIA Kind people, we are lost. We can't find our villa or the temple. We want to go home to Rome. We've got nowhere to stay here.

OLIVER Look, why don't you come home with us? You can have some real food. Then we can help you.

LAVINIA Kind sir, I thank you.

CHRISSIE Mum won't like it …

QUINTUS Did he say food?

(They leave the stage.)

mummy ['mʌmi] *Mumie* the Alps [ælps] coma ['kəʊmə] such a [sʌtʃ] *so ein/e* cart [kɑːt] *Karren, Wagen* import ['ɪmpɔːt] export ['ekspɔːt] denarius [dɪ'neəriəs] Denar silver ['sɪlvə] *Silber* some kind of show *irgend so eine Show* Jupiter ['dʒuːpɪtə] We've got nowhere to stay. *Wir haben keine Bleibe.* stage [steɪdʒ] *Bühne*

Scene 2

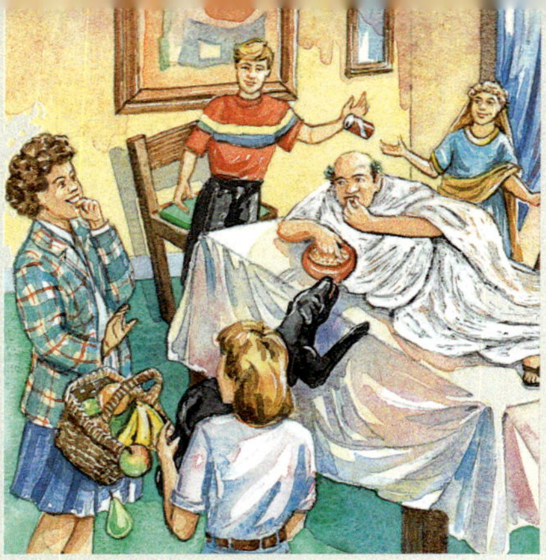

At Oliver and Chrissie's house in the dining-room

(Oliver, Chrissie, Quintus and Lavinia enter.)

CHRISSIE Now, this is the TRICLINIUM.

OLIVER No, it isn't. It's the dining-room.

CHRISSIE That is 'dining-room' in Latin, stupid!

OLIVER Well, please sit down, and we'll look for some lunch.

QUINTUS Food, eh? Well, I'm ready for it! *(climbs onto table and lies down on it)* Your sofas are very high. *(starts eating peanuts)*

MOTHER *(enters)* Oh my … What's going on in here?

LAVINIA SALVE, lady of the house. Your kind children have invited us to lunch. We're Romans out of our time.

MOTHER Yes, er, hello, dear. Oliver, why is that old man lying on the table?

OLIVER Well, it's a long story, Mum. I'll tell you in the kitchen. – Er, so what would you like to eat? Oh I know: pizza. You're from Italy, aren't you? You'll love pizza. *(pushes his mother out of the room)*

CHRISSIE I expect you want a drink. Is cola OK for you?

QUINTUS Is that your name for VINUM … er, wine?

CHRISSIE Er, well, some people like it more than wine. Here, try it. *(gives him a glass of cola)*

QUINTUS Bah! *(claps hands and calls out into kitchen)* Slave woman! Bring me some wine!

MOTHER *(in the kitchen)* Well, really! That's enough! I don't care if he's the Emperor himself. He's rude and macho and I want him out of my house!

OLIVER OK, OK.

(re-enters dining-room) Here we are – Pizza Furiosa!

QUINTUS Where's the slave woman with my wine?

MOTHER *(in the kitchen)* Oooh! *(looks angry, makes a phone call)* Police? Two crazy people have come into my house … I don't know. They're 2000 years old … No, *I'm* not crazy, *they* are! … Yes, but hurry! … 23 Augustan Way.

(In the dining-room)

LAVINIA Oliver, you are so kind to us, …

OLIVER Oh, that's all right, we …

LAVINIA … but we must get back to Rome. It's our real home.

OLIVER Well, Rome is different today, too.

LAVINIA We must start at once. It is many weeks' journey and we must be home before winter starts.

CHRISSIE Don't be silly – you can fly from London.

QUINTUS *(mouth full)* Haha, fly like Daedalus, you mean?

CHRISSIE No, you take a plane, well, a flying machine.

QUINTUS No! Not for me. I'm too, er, I don't like being higher than on a horse.

OLIVER Well, there are other ways to get to …

(A policeman is pushed into the room.)

MOTHER They're in there. Be careful, the man is crazy.

POLICEMAN Oh, it's you again. I remember you. You called that Scotsman a barbarian in the pub last night, didn't you?

QUINTUS SALVE. You must be a soldier.

CHRISSIE *(whispers)* Lavinia, he's a policeman. This means trouble.

POLICEMAN Have you got a passport, sir? Or a driving-licence?

QUINTUS Sir, I am Quintus Lavinius Timidus, *Import and Export to all Four Corners of the Empire.* How can I help you?

POLICEMAN That's enough of that. Would you come along to the police station, sir?

OLIVER Officer, we were just having a snack. Would you like a piece of Pizza Furiosa with us? *(gives him a plate with pizza on it)*

POLICEMAN Well, that's very kind, …

LAVINIA *(whispers)* Pater, do you want to go to prison or to Rome? Then move fast, please!

CHRISSIE Quick, out of the back door. Here's £20 from Ollie and me. It's all we've got.

(The pizza is too spicy for the policeman. Oliver gives him a drink.)

POLICEMAN Thanks, I needed that.

LAVINIA Chrissie, give my love to Oliver …

QUINTUS *(finishes his cola)* Hey, don't hurry me.

LAVINIA Out here. Chrissie, take this hairpin so that you remember me.

(Quintus and Lavinia leave the stage.)

What happens next?
It's over to you:
What do Lavinia and Quintus do?
What do they see?
Where do they go?
How do they go?
Who do they meet?
What do they think?
Write scene 3 of the play and act it in class.

WB 12

(to) enter ['entə] *eintreten* (to) lie (*-ing form:* lying), lay, lain [laɪ, leɪ, leɪn] *liegen;* (to) lie down *sich (hin)legen* the Emperor himself *der Kaiser selbst* rude [ruːd] *unhöflich, unverschämt* (to) hurry ['hʌri] *sich beeilen; (jn.) antreiben, drängen* barbarian [bɑːˈbeəriən] driving-licence ['draɪvɪŋ ˌlaɪsəns] *Führerschein* prison ['prɪzn] *Gefängnis* spicy ['spaɪsi] *scharf* It's over to you. *Jetzt bist du dran.*

Welcome

TO THE UNITED STATES OF AMERICA!

What do you think of when you hear the words 'United States of America'? Famous people and places, Hollywood films, hamburgers, crime, ...? Collect ideas on the board and talk about them.

1

2

3

4

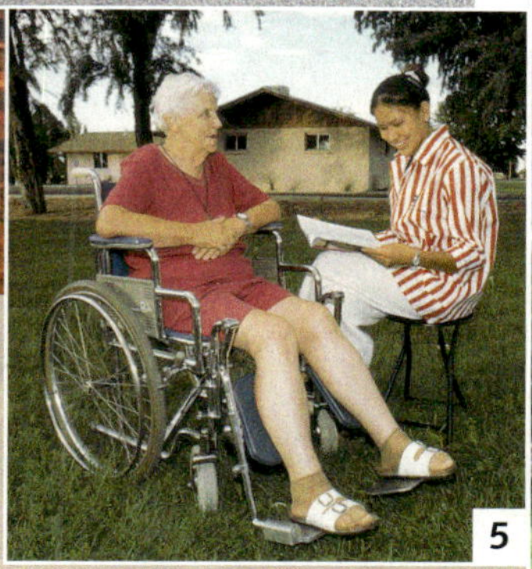
5

6

1 An American girl chose the seven photos on these two pages. She thinks they give a good idea of life in the USA. Match these captions to the photos.

a) Supermarkets often stay open 24 hours.
b) It's about 5000 kilometres from the east coast to the west coast.
c) Family barbecues are very popular.
d) Lots of kids in cities play streetball.
e) Religion is important for most Americans in their everyday lives.
f) Kids from high schools often do volunteer work in hospitals.
g) Some Americans think it's boring to live in one place and prefer the life of a traveller .

How are your ideas about the USA different from the American girl's?

2 ***Listening***

Listen to the song on the CD.
- Write down as many place names from the song as you can. Look for them on the US map at the back of the book.
- Say how the singers feel about the USA.

3 ***Activity***

Now start a US album. Collect photos, post-cards or maybe souvenirs from the USA. Stick them into your album. You can add more as you go through this book.

mdl. Schulaufgabe

4 Florida, Space and Sunshine State

1 Have you ever thought about a trip into space? These kids have because they met during Astronaut Training Experience at Kennedy Space Center in Florida. Find the places they are from on the maps of the USA and the UK. Which kid is not American?

Margo Blair, 14
Carlisle,
Cumbria

Glen Oktollik, 14
Anchorage,
Alaska

Conchita Gonzales,
14, Chicago,
Illinois

Scott Truong, 14,
San Francisco,
California

Your Mission. Your Crew.

ATX™

ASTRONAUT TRAINING EXPERIENCE

NEW AT KENNEDY SPACE CENTER

TRAIN LIKE AN ASTRONAUT

Move in ways you've never felt before on the training simulators.
Go on a Space Shuttle mission with your ATX crew.

Get a briefing from a real NASA Astronaut.

"WE HAVE LIFTOFF!"

With those words, your crew is on their way to the International Space Station where you'll do critical repairs and drop off supplies.

YOUR DAY OF ATX

10 am – 4:30 pm
Crew: Must be 14 or older

Space is infinite. But ATX is not. ATX crews are small so you should book early.
Call 321-449-4400 or look for ATX on our web site at www.KennedySpaceCenter.com

2

About Florida

After your program at Kennedy Space Center, why not explore Florida, the Sunshine State? There's so much to see and fall in love with: the sunny beaches of Miami, the Everglades, where the alligators swim through the water, and the beautiful fruit farms which produce oranges and grapefruit for the whole world! Don't miss a visit to one of Orlando's many fantastic theme parks – Epcot for science fans and Sea World for dolphin lovers are just two of many and are both in Orlando.

Oh, and you'll find lots of great places where you can eat. Many of them offer wonderful Hispanic food because about three million Hispanics live here in Florida.

◆◆ **3** Work with a partner. Collect all the technical words in the ATX brochure on page 58. Can you explain what they mean? Compare your ideas with other groups'.

4 Make notes about Florida. Use what you already know and the information on pages 58/59. Use headings like: *cities, weather, tourist attractions, …*

5 ***Activity***
Collect photos and other material about Florida for your US album.

1 Conchita and Margo

Conchita Gonzales was crazy about space. Ever since she could remember, she had wanted to be an astronaut. Her dream came true when she won a scholarship to Space Camp and an extra day of ATX at Kennedy Space Center.
Before she travelled to Florida for her day of ATX, she had spent five days at Space Camp, in Huntsville, Alabama. When she had checked in and put her stuff in her room, Conchita took the elevator down to the hotel café. She looked for an empty table but couldn't see one.
'That's too bad,' she thought. 'I'll just go back up to my room and have some ice water. Cheaper anyway.' As she turned around a girl with red hair spoke to her, 'Do you want to sit here with me?'
Conchita knew at once the girl couldn't be American. She had a funny accent, and Americans usually like to have their own table in a café.
'Hi, I'm Margo,' the girl went on. Conchita smiled at her and sat down.
Margo Blair had already been in Florida for a week with her parents. She had just started a postcard to her grandparents and her older brother in England when Conchita came into the café. She only finished it after Conchita had left an hour later.

Cocoa Beach on Florida's Space Coast

Dear Grandma, Grandpa and Rob,
How are you all back home in 'little old England'? When we landed here, we weren't sure whether we had come to the right country – all the signs were in Spanish! (And English, of course.) Tomorrow I'm doing a day of astronaut training at Kennedy Space Center. And I've just met a really nice girl who is doing it, too. Her family is from Mexico. She's coming to dinner with us tonight. She might come to Orlando with us. I hope mum and dad say it's OK. See you soon.
Love, Margo xxxxx

2 *Different from Britain*

What has Margo found out about Florida and the USA that is different from her own country? Start a list and add to it during this unit:

Different in Florida/the USA

A lot of people speak ...

...

3 *Looking at language*

a Look for examples of a new tense in A1: *had wanted, ...* How do you form this tense? What do you think it is called?

b Look at the sentence in A1 that begins *'When she had checked in ...'* What happened first? What happened next? When do you use this tense?

c How are the examples of the new tense in the cartoon different? When do you use this form of the new tense? What do you think it is called?

Mr Jones had been waiting for half an hour when the bus came, but Mr Smith had been waiting much longer.

S 4: 1, 2 (p. 130/131) • P 2–5, 12 • WB 3–5

4 A short break

At 10.15 the next morning, the NASA astronaut came to the end of his briefing: 'OK, you'll be able to start work on the training simulators in a few minutes. Now, they're pretty safe – but some of you might want to talk to your family and loved ones first … . So we'll let you take a short break now. But you ought to be back here at 10.30 with your team leader, Bill Wade. 10.30. Not one or two minutes after. Don't make Bill wait. He'll just make you work harder if you do.'

Glen Oktollik ran to the café where he had already seen the computers with Internet access. A few minutes later he had sent this message back home.

Subject: space walk

Attachments:

Stationery

Hi Dad, hi Amy,
You should look at this photo of a kid in a space-walk simulator. I'm sending it because you may never see me again. In about an hour, at 11.15 am Eastern Time, I'll be in it!
:-) Glen

Conchita ran quickly to the phones. There was one free. Scott was right behind her.

'Can you let me use the phone first, Conchita?' asked Scott. 'I need to talk with mom before she goes to work at seven-thirty.'

'Sorry, Scott,' Conchita smiled at him, 'it's already ringing, and anyway, if my watch is right, it's ten-twenty.'

'Not in San Francisco!' he laughed.

'So, you're from Cali… Oh, hi Mamá! Sí, estoy bien … I'm fine … Oye, Mamá. Listen. There is a real nice English girl here … Sí, inglesa, and her parents are here, too, and they're all driving to Orlando later. She says I can go with them in their car. Is that OK? Then I won't need to take the bus. … Great! Mil gracias, Mamá. … No, I must go now, or I'll be late and make the others wait. … Sí, I'll call again. Hasta pronto, Mamá, bye!'

◆◆ 5 *Time zones*

It's 10.30 and training on the simulators has just begun. What time is it in LA (Los Angeles), Denver, Milwaukee, Phoenix, Seattle? (Look at the map at the back of the book.)
Then choose another city and ask your partner what time it is there.

6 *Now you*

Finish these sentences to write a *Make me – Let me* poem:

Make me learn and I'll …
Let me learn and I'll …
Make me play and I'll …
Let me play and I'll …

◆◆ 7 *Activity*

Imagine you are on holiday with your family in Florida. You have made a new American friend and want to do something with him/her without your parents. Look at the box for ideas.
Will your parents let you go? Make notes first, then phone your friend and explain why you cannot go – or talk about your plans.

Everglades
alligators
ATX
space-walk simulator
Cocoa Beach
surfing
…

8 Conchita's diary

After the ATX program, Conchita went to Orlando with Margo and her parents. That evening she wrote in her diary.

FRIDAY, SEPTEMBER 12

ATX was even better than Space Camp because it wasn't just for kids. The VIP tour of Kennedy Space Center at the end was out of this world. I could listen to those Kennedy guides talk about space all day and all night. Except when they try to be funny. Here's one of our guide's corny jokes: "If you're staying in Florida this week we have got some good and some bad news for you. The good news is: you're real lucky. You can see us launch a satellite on Thursday. The bad news is: it's at 5 am!"
I had a great time on the ATX team with Margo, Glen and Scott – especially Scott! He's going to send me a letter or call me every week – well, I'm sure I heard him say that. We were all a little sad at the end of the day. On the bus after the tour we watched KSC disappear behind us and listened to Glen tell us how cold and dark Alaska winters are.

And we swapped addresses and phone numbers. On the way to Orlando, we stopped at a Mexican restaurant. The waiter talked Spanish to us and I had to help the Blairs. Mr. and Mrs. Blair were surprised that Spanish is my first language. In the end we all had chicken tacos with rice. I think the other stuff on the menu was just too strange for them.
I wonder what they eat in England! The people at the restaurant were real nice. Mrs. Blair asked how tacos are made – so we all went into the kitchen and watched the cook make them. Then he gave me the menu for my diary.

9 *Looking at language*

a Look at A8 again and find the sentences with these verbs of perception:
watch, listen to, see, hear.
Write them down in a table like this:

	Verb of perception	Object	
I	could listen	to those KSC guides	talk about ...

b How would you say these sentences in German?

c What is the form of the verb after the object?

10 *Now you*

Think of a time when you had to say goodbye to a group of friends – the end of a class trip, a change of school, etc. Write your diary for that day and describe how you felt.

Our class trip ended this afternoon. When we got back to ..., I was very ... . We ...

11 *Focus on words: Florida*

a Collect words and phrases about some of the Florida word fields in this unit.
Make a network with them.

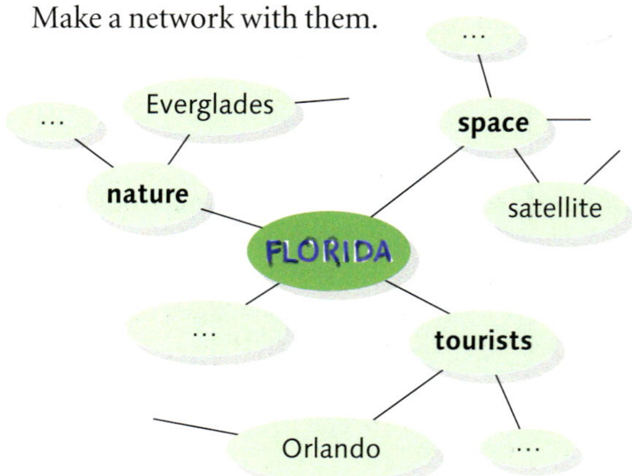

◆◆ b Where would you like to go and what would you like to do and see if you went to Florida? Use your network and tell your partner.

If I went to Florida, I'd like to go to Kennedy Space Center and see them launch a satellite. I'd also ...

1 *Florida and the USA*

◆◆ Partner B: Look at page 120.

a Partner A: Look at the table on the right. The Florida information is missing, but your partner has it. Ask your partner questions about Florida and answer his/her questions about the USA.

A What's the capital of Florida?
B It's …
What's the capital of the USA?
A It's …
How big is …?
B It's …

	USA	Florida
capital	Washington, D.C.	?
size	9.5 million square km	?
population	290.8 million	?
Hispanics	39.8 million (= 13.7%)	?
national bird	bald eagle 	?

b Write down what you have found out about Florida. You can put the information about the USA and Florida in your US album.

c Make a table like this for Germany. Compare the facts for Germany with the facts you have for the USA.

2 *Revision: Have they been to Orlando yet?*

Mrs Blair phoned Margo's grandmother back in Carlisle. Margo's grandfather wanted to know how the Blairs' holiday was going. Use the notes to form his questions and his wife's answers. Be careful with your tenses.

1 be to Orlando/yet?
yes/arrive there/yesterday evening
– *Have they been to Orlando yet?*
– *Yes, they have. They arrived there yesterday evening.*
2 see a space shuttle liftoff?
yes/see one/at Kennedy Space Center
3 Margo/go surfing?
no/not have time/at Cocoa Beach/but want to go/after leave Orlando
4 what/weather/be like?
good/most of the time/but a storm/blow over the coast/a few days ago
5 meet/anyone interesting?
yes/Margo/meet a girl from Chicago/at ATX training
6 like/ATX?
yes/love it
7 how long/stay in Orlando?
stay/for 3 days
8 fly back home/from Orlando/too?
no/fly from Miami

3 *They had been busy*

a Margo wasn't very happy when she returned home from Florida. It seemed everything was different. Try and guess who had done what. Use the past perfect.

1 Margo wasn't able to find anything in her bedroom.
Maybe her brother Rob had taken her stuff. Or perhaps …
2 Her computer was turned on.
3 Her favourite CD was in her brother's player.
4 Her pencil case was empty.
5 There was a fax with a party invitation for yesterday.
6 Her room looked all tidy and clean.
7 She couldn't find her mobile phone.

b Describe a situation where you were angry because somebody had done something you didn't like.

4 *When Conchita had returned to her room*

a Read the pairs of sentences below and decide what happened first and what second. Then link the two sentences with words like *after, because, but, so, when,* etc. Always use the simple past and the past perfect.

1 Conchita returned to her room. She phoned her mother.
When Conchita had returned ..., she phoned ...
2 Conchita slept for an hour. She met Margo's parents downstairs.
3 Mr and Mrs Blair already knew about Conchita. Margo told them about her.
4 The Blairs stayed in the same hotel a few years ago. They knew a nice restaurant.
5 Margo came down. They called a taxi.

b Now try to finish these sentences.

1 I was only allowed to watch TV after ...
2 My brother couldn't come on the trip because ...
3 My sister had already tried on eight sweat-shirts before ...
4 ... because he had seen the film before.
5 ... after I had learned to swim.
6 ... I bought the group's new CD.
7 When I had heard the news, ...
8 All my friends had arrived before I ...

◆◆ c Write sentence halves like the ones in 4b for your partner. He/She has to finish them.

5 *What had they been doing when ...?*

Use the past perfect progressive and say what these people had been doing when something happened.

1 Joe/play computer game/lights go out
Joe had been playing a computer game when the lights went out.
2 Margo/write postcard/Conchita come in
3 Jack/dig in the garden/since 9 o' clock/ his wife came home from work
4 Todd/ride his bike along road/man open car door in front of him
5 Bettina/dream she was an astronaut/ mother/wake her for school
6 Gordon/travel for three months/break his leg in an accident

6 *Mediation: Interpreting*

An English visitor who is interested in space travel finds this German-language web site about cosmonaut training in Moscow. They want to know what it is about. Can you help them? Don't try and translate word for word – just put the main points into easy English.

Kosmonautentraining in Star City/Moskau

- Sie können an einem echten Kosmonauten-training im Gagarin Cosmonaut Training Center des russischen Sternenstädtchens teilnehmen.
- Sie müssen fit sein und Abenteuer lieben.
- Sie können Teile des Trainingsprogramms buchen oder sich für das gesamte Programm entscheiden – aber Sie sollten früh buchen.
- Sie müssen sich keine Sorgen wegen der Sprache machen – Dolmetscher übersetzen alles ins Englische.
- Bringen Sie bequemes Schuhwerk mit. Während des Trainings müssen Sie Raumanzüge tragen.

7 *Scott's phone call* → Vocabulary, p. 160

a When Scott phoned his mother from Kennedy Space Center, she was already out. So he left a message. Complete what he said with the right form of *let* or *make*.

'Hi, Mom. Sorry I didn't call earlier. They … us work hard this morning and they didn't … us have a break till now. They're going to … us try one of the simulators after break. It looks scary and they (not/…) anyone go in it until the doctor says everything's OK. They're so careful. They … us check everything three times before we do anything. And they (not/…) us do anything alone. One of the team leaders is always there. But they … us talk to a real NASA astronaut. That was cool! Bye, Mom!'

◆◆ b What do your parents make you do at home? What do they let you do? Tell your partner and listen to what he/she says. Who has an easier time at home?

c Now imagine you could tell your parents what they should do at home. What would you make or let them do?

"I would make my parents go out every evening."

8 *Voyager*

Two spaceships, called Voyager 1 and Voyager 2, were launched in 1977 to collect information about Jupiter, Saturn, Uranus and Neptune. They left our solar system in 1990. They both carried gold discs with sounds and pictures of the Earth.

Jupiter ['dʒu:pɪtə] Saturn ['sætɜ:n]
Uranus ['jʊərənəs] Neptune ['neptju:n]

Imagine Voyager 1 entered another solar system and arrived at Planet X. Complete this story about what happened. Use the correct verbs from the box.

arrive • bring • call • play (2x) say • sing • speak

The pilot of the spaceship Unik couldn't believe his three eyes when he saw *Voyager arrive* in the Xian solar system. He caught this strange ship and sent a message to Planet X. Later a large crowd watched Unik … *Voyager* down to the ground. When Xian scientists looked in the spaceship, they found a gold disc. They listened to the disc … sounds from another world. They heard strange voices … songs and orchestras from another planet … music. Pictures showed these strange people from another solar system. They listened to the people … to them in a strange language. They heard them … hello and … their planet 'Earth'.

9 *Revision: ATX information line*

On the right there are some of the answers people got when they called the ATX information line one day. You can see that the line was bad. Use the right form of the verbs in the box and complete the answers.

not be able to • must
can (2x) • not have to
ought to • should

10 *America*

Read this poem about America. Then choose a word from pages 58–62 *(Florida, space, ...)* and write your own poem. You can put it in your US album.

A MERICA SITS TO THE LEFT ON THE
M AP OF THE WORLD,
E UROPE SITS TO THE
R IGHT.
I N THE MIDDLE, THE
C OOL, BLUE WATER OF THE
A TLANTIC.

11 *Listening: Telephone calls*

a Work with a partner. Think of as many telephone words and phrases as you can and write them down: *(to) phone, phone call, (to) leave a message, ...*

b Amy, Glen Oktollik's sister back in Alaska, is trying to phone her friend Tina Jenkins. Listen to the five telephone calls on the CD. Then match these descriptions to the calls:

3 1 Tina is at home – she'll come to the phone in a minute.
2 2 Amy has got the wrong number.
1 3 Amy leaves a message with Mrs Jenkins.
5 4 Mrs Jenkins tells Tina that she should go to her phone.
4 5 The answering machine is on.

c What can you say when you hear these questions or statements on the phone?

1 'Hello?'
2 'Who is this, please?'
3 'Can I give him/her a message?'
4 'You've got the wrong number.'
5 'Please leave a message after the beep.'

Listen again to the phone calls and add the phrases to your list from a.

d Everyone writes a message for an answering machine. Swap messages with another group. Choose one message. What would you say if you heard it on an answering machine? Record your messages and answers on cassette or read them out to your class.

Word watch

12 *The astronaut's report*

a Choose the correct words from the box and complete the astronaut's report below.

at • off • on • out (2x) through • to • up (2x)

When we were in space, I looked … and saw the Earth. Then I got … from my seat to start work. I took … my helmet and went … the radio. At first we couldn't get … to NASA but we heard Mission Control after about a minute. I put … my hand so that everyone would be quiet.
"Turn … the computer," they told us, "and look … your mission instructions." That's when we found … why we were up there.

b What happened next? Finish the story. Use some of these verbs:

land on • talk to • put on look for • take off …

13 *Not nice*

Can you make this letter about a holiday in Florida sound better? It's OK to use nice once or twice – but not 6 times! What other words could you use here? Find four different ones.

> Dear Auntie,
> We had a very nice holiday in Florida. We stayed at a nice hotel on a nice beach not far from Orlando. We went to Disney World and that was really nice.
> The weather in Florida was so nice – it didn't rain once. All in all it was the nicest trip we've ever had.

14 *Mixed-up phrases*

These mixed-up phrases are all used in this unit. Can you correct them?

llaf ni evol htiw	ryzac tabou
odn't smis	mared moce retu
devol seno	tuo fo hist rowld

15 *Listening: British English and American English* → Vocabulary, p. 161

Book 3 of English G has three units about the USA, so it uses a lot of American English (AE), not just British English (BE). For example, AE vocabulary like *elevator*, *sidewalk* and *fall*. It also uses AE spelling – like *favorite*, *center* and *program*. And the speakers on the CD speak, of course, with their own American accents.

a Listen to the speakers on the CD. Do you think they're British? Hold up your right hand. Do you think they're American? Hold up your left hand.

b Listen to the song on the CD. Who do you think is British – the woman or the man? Do you think British and American speakers find it hard to understand each other?

c American spelling and British spelling are sometimes different. Can you write these sentences with British spellings?

1 My favorite color is gray.
2 I traveled a thousand miles to summer camp last year.
3 There's a new theater at the Madison Center. It's great!
4 In Germany you have kilometers and meters. In the USA we have miles and feet.

What's Conchita's Problem?
know about the story

Little Miss Astronaut

What do you think Conchita's first day back at school was like? Why? Now read the story.

My plane from Orlando arrived late at O'Hare Airport. Papá got time off at the factory to meet me and he, Mamá and the little ones had been waiting for me at the airport for two hours when I arrived. It was great to see them all. It's like I've been away much longer than a week and my whole life has changed.

When we got on the bus, I remembered what Margo had said: "All Americans have cars, don't they?" Why hadn't I answered, "Well, we don't have enough money"? On the way home I told Paco and María all about Camp. They both asked lots of questions.

Before María went to bed, I had to tell her about Orlando, too. When I'm an astronaut and have lots of money, I'll take her there.

The wind is cold tonight. I missed it in Florida, but now I'm back home and I miss the warm sun! Here fall has really begun – lots of trees are already red and yellow. I talked to Linda on the phone. I tried to tell her all about Camp and KSC, but she wasn't interested. She just said, "See you tomorrow" and told me some boring stuff about what Mike Donovan and the other guys on the football team had done.

I wonder: will Scott really write?

School tomorrow. Must sleep … can't sleep …

"Look, here comes little Miss Astronaut!" whispered Rita.

"Hi, Linda! Hi, Rita!" called Conchita to her friends.

"Oh, hi, Conchita," said Linda.

"Well, are you ready for your talk tomorrow?" asked Rita. "Remember, we 'ordinary' kids have to learn all about the great US space program from you!"

"Here's the bus. Come on!" said Linda.

"Space Camp was real exciting," Conchita told her friends as she sat down behind them on the bus.

"Yeah? Well then your talk will be 'real exciting', won't it?" smiled Rita. She got out her magazine and started to read. "Hey, Linda, did you see, there's another competition this week … you can win a weekend in San Francisco. Maybe one of us can win that – more fun than a week at a Space Camp, huh?"

"I met this real nice guy from San Francisco at Kennedy Space Center. If you really went there, maybe he could show you the city …"

"Sure, Conchita. I couldn't go on a trip to California without your help!" said Rita.

Conchita was quiet the rest of the journey.

At Roberto Clemente High School it was the usual loud Monday morning. José saw the three girls come into the class and called: "Hey, guys – look who's here! It's little Miss Astronaut …"

At recess Conchita didn't go outside with the others. She sat alone in the classroom and began to cry. She had been so happy and proud when she won the scholarship to Space Camp and the chance to come back with an extra Science credit. It had all seemed so great, but now …

Ms Morrison looked in. "Why aren't you outside?" she asked Conchita. Then she saw that Conchita had been crying. "Hey, what's wrong?"

"It's like I've come back and no one wants to know me any more," said Conchita. "They call me stupid names and …"

Ms Morrison smiled and sat down.

"It's like this, kid!" she started. "You can be like everyone else – that's cool, you're one of the clique. Or you can try to do something different. That's cool, too, but the clique may be J - E - A - L - O - U - S."

"Jealous? You think the others are jealous of me?"

"Sure they are, Conchita! I was real popular on our block down on the South Side – you know: all poor blacks together – till I was the first girl who went to college. Suddenly the sidewalk was empty when I walked down it! But here I am today with a crowd of new friends and I do what I want to do. So, hang in there, kid!"

Conchita started to smile.

"I'll try, Ms Morrison, thanks."

Next day, in Science class, it was time for Conchita's talk.

"I know you are all very excited!" said Ms Morrison. "Here's 'little Miss Astronaut'! She's going to tell us all about the glamor of life in space."

The kids all watched Conchita walk to the board. She smiled.

"Yeah, that's what I thought: one week of glamor as an astronaut. Here's the suit – neat, huh?" Conchita showed the class her spacesuit from Space Camp. "Until you want to go to the bathroom!"

Conchita laughed. A few of the kids began to laugh, too. Even Rita laughed, but then she saw José. He was in the Fireball Gang on her block. He was looking at the ceiling and yawning. "Ha, ha, ha!" he said loudly. Rita and Linda began to yawn, too.

Conchita looked across to Ms Morrison. Then she went on, "Not so glamorous – right? And just wait till you try a freeze-dried space meal! Here, 'hamburgers' – I brought one back for each of you."

Conchita gave everyone in her class some freeze-dried food. When Mike Donovan had read the instructions, he said, "Hey, Ms Morrison, we need hot water for this. Can I go and get some when Conchita finishes her talk?"

"Yeah!" shouted some of the other kids.

"Come on!" shouted José. "Who wants to eat this sh…?"

"What do you know?" shouted Mike. "Why don't you just shut up and listen?"

Linda and Rita looked at each other again. José was really angry. He started to shout, "Boring, boring …"

"OK," said Ms Morrison. "Who thinks Conchita's talk is boring? Hands up!"

Rita watched José and his friend Pedro put their hands up – then she put her hand up, too.

"Put your hand up," she whispered to Linda.

But Linda didn't put her hand up.

"OK," said Ms Morrison. "Twenty-eight kids want to hear Conchita, so you three can be quiet!"

After school, Conchita met Linda at the bus stop.

"That was nice of you, Linda," she said.

"Yeah, well, I'm glad not everyone is scared of José. He's a jerk. Great talk. And wasn't it funny when Mike Donovan showed us how to catch a hamburger in the air and eat it when you're at zero gravity?"

"Yes, even José and Pedro had to laugh!"

1 Spot the mistakes

a Look at these pictures. Put them in the right order. Can you find the mistakes in two of them?

1

2

3

4

b Can you say which page and lines go with each picture? *Lines ... to ... on page ... go with picture 1. ...*

2 What people felt

a Read 'Little Miss Astronaut' again. Make a list of the people and their different feelings during the story. (The adjectives are not all in the text.) Complete the notes.

Conchita – happy, proud, excited; sad, ...
Rita – ...
Linda – not interested in Space Camp; jealous, ...
Ms Morrison – ...
... – ...

◆◆ b Now choose one of the characters in the story and tell your partner the feelings that character has. Your partner has to say when that was in the story.

A Conchita was happy and proud.
B I think Conchita was happy and proud when she met her family at the airport.

3 How you feel

How do you feel about the way José, Pedro and Rita acted during Conchita's talk?
Why did Linda act differently?
How do you feel about her?

4 Beyond the text

Are there cliques at your school? Do they always stick together or have the same opinions about everything? Is that 'cool'? Could something like this story happen in your class?

5 First day at school

Write Conchita's diary for her first two days at school after Space Camp and ATX.

◆◆ 6 Role-play: 'Hi, Conchita, how was school?'

Imagine that Scott calls Conchita and they talk about their first day back at school. What do they say? With a partner, record the conversation on cassette and play it to the class. You can write your own role cards or use the ones your teacher has.

P 15 • WB 12, 13

How to ... tell a story

1 ***Reading: Accident in space***

People often tell stories about something that has happened to them or to someone else.
Look at how Astronaut Jim told the story of the day that changed his life. This will help you when you want to tell stories about other exciting situations.

I'll never forget that day – April 13. Fred, Jack and I were traveling in space, 55 hours from Earth on our way to the moon. We had just finished a TV broadcast about our comfortable life in space when suddenly an oxygen tank exploded. Soon we knew we had lost our normal supply of power, oxygen and water. We were about 200,000 miles from Earth so the big question was, "How do we get back home safely?"

We had to save power, oxygen and water, so Fred and I quickly moved into the Moon Lander while Jack stayed at the controls in the main ship. Someone had to and he was the best pilot. We only joined him again just before we entered the atmosphere. Jack was glad to see us because he hadn't slept for 36 hours.
When we came down in the blue Pacific Ocean, we were all tired, hungry, thirsty, wet and cold – but we were alive.

a When you tell a story, you usually answer the following questions: *Who? What? Where? When? How? Why?*
Find this information in Astronaut Jim's story.

b How does Jim start and finish the story?

c Find all the time expressions in the story, like *April 13, suddenly*, etc.

d Which linking words like *and, when*, etc. can you find?

2 ***Speaking: Fred's story***

Fred's grandchildren often ask him about the accident in space. How does Fred tell his story? Make notes first. You can look at the *Remember box* for help.

3 ***Writing: Can you tell this story?***

a Look at the pictures and write the story. Use the *Remember box* for help.

b Write your own story about an exciting situation. Make notes first and look at the *Remember box* for help.

Remember

1 In your story, answer the questions *Who? What? Where? When? How? Why?*.
2 Think about how you can start and finish the story.
3 Use time expressions like *now, suddenly, then, at first, after that, later, the next moment*, etc.
4 Don't forget linking words like *after, and, because, before, but, or, so, when*, etc.
5 Check your story (or ask your partner to check it).
Are the grammar, spelling, vocabulary correct?

Hurricanes in Florida

Sunshine State? Space State? Yes, but Florida is also a Hurricane State. About five Atlantic hurricanes hit the United States every three years and kill between 50 and 100 people.

What are hurricanes?

Hurricanes are strong tropical storms that form over the ocean. They usually start in the Caribbean or off the west coast of Africa.
As the storms move slowly westward, they gather heat and energy from the warm ocean waters. Evaporation from the sea makes them even stronger.
Warm, wet air moves toward the center of the storm and spirals upward. Hurricanes turn around a calm center called the eye. The most violent part of a hurricane is at the edges of its eye, called the eye wall.
Hurricanes have winds of 74 miles per hour (118 kph) and more. They get stronger until they pass over land or cooler water. When they come onto land, hurricane winds do a lot of damage, but most people who die in a hurricane are drowned. Hurricanes cause storm surges – these are huge waves and tides which may be 25 feet or more above normal. A storm surge is very dangerous so you MUST stay away from the ocean during a hurricane.

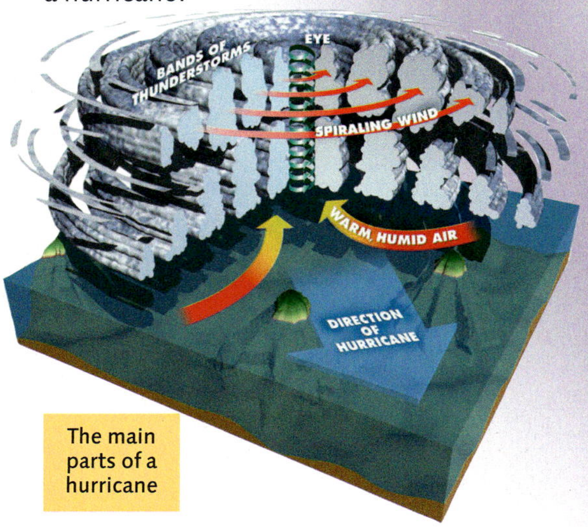

The main parts of a hurricane

Hurricane Andrew, the most expensive natural disaster in US history, passes over the Florida coast in August 1992.

Saffir-Simpson Hurricane Scale

Category	Wind Speed	Effects
1	74–95 mph (119–153 kph)	• Storm surge 4–5 ft (1.2–1.5 m) • Some flooding • Little or no damage to buildings
2	96–110 mph (154–177 kph)	• Storm surge 6–8 ft (1.8–2.4 m) • Trees down • Road damage
3	111–130 mph (178–209 kph)	• Storm surge 9–12 ft (2.7–3.7 m) • Damage to houses • Mobile homes destroyed • Severe flooding
4	131–155 mph (210–249 kph)	• Storm surge 13–18 ft (4–5.5 m) • Severe flooding inland • Some roofs destroyed • Major damage to buildings
5	> 155 mph (> 249 kph)	• Storm surge over 18 ft (5.5 m) • Severe flooding further inland • Severe damage to most wooden buildings

1 Use the picture *(The main parts of a hurricane)* and information from the text and describe how a hurricane works. These words might help you:

form • gather heat • evaporation
move toward • spiral upward
turn around • violent • calm

❖ 2 If there is something you don't understand, write down your question on a card.
Then work in groups and try to answer each other's questions.

3 Look for more information about hurricanes on the Internet. These web sites might be useful, but there are many more. You could find out how hurricanes get their names, which countries they hit, how to prepare for a hurricane, …

http://teacher.scholastic.com/activities/wwatch/hurricanes/
http://hurricanes.noaa.gov/
http://www.howstuffworks.com/hurricane.htm

strong *stark, kräftig* the Caribbean [ˌkærɪ'bi:ən] *die Karibik* off the west coast *vor der Westküste* (to) gather heat ['gæðə hi:t] *an Hitze gewinnen* evaporation [ɪˌvæpə'reɪʃn] *Verdunstung* (to) spiral upward ['spaɪrəl 'ʌpwəd] *spiralförmig aufsteigen* calm [kɑ:m] *ruhig, still* per hour *pro Stunde* damage ['dæmɪdʒ] *Schaden* (to) be drowned ['draʊnd] *ertrinken* storm surge [sɜ:dʒ] *Sturmflut* tide [taɪd] *Flut, Woge* disaster [dɪ'zɑ:stə] severe [sɪ'vɪə(r)] *schwer, erheblich* further inland ['fɜ:ðə(r)] *weiter landeinwärts*

Hurricane Andrew survivor

I was sleeping at about 5:00 a.m. when I was woken by a thundering crash. I looked out my window and suddenly a mailbox flew by. Houses were being destroyed right before my eyes.
I decided to run to my basement. As I was leaving the room, the roof of my bedroom fell in. I was not seriously hurt, so I climbed out of the wreckage and walked as fast as I could to my basement. I couldn't run because I had hurt my leg.
When I got to the basement, my house suddenly fell down on me. I couldn't move my neck and I thought it was broken. After six long hours, I was dug out by a rescue team.
I was one of the two million people who were evacuated from their homes. I was also lucky because I didn't die. My friend Shane wasn't so lucky. He was one of the 60 people that were killed.

Six people survived Hurricane Andrew in this Florida home

There were one hundred and twenty-five thousand homes destroyed and my house was one of them
Now, I live in Jacksonville and after one year, I'm still scared of what Hurricane Andrew did to me and my family and friends.

Have you ever seen stories on TV about hurricanes or storms? Have you had an exciting, scary or funny time with the weather? Write about what happened. Look at page 71 again for tips.

Storm poems

Read the two poems and choose *two* of the following activities:

Hurricane Night
By Eve C.

Leaves, trees, branches
Fall.
Rain, thunder, lightning
Call.
Every house is closed up
Tight.
As if today was actually
Night.

Windy Nights *By Robert Louis Stevenson*

WHENEVER the moon and stars are set,
Whenever the wind is high,
All night long in the dark and wet,
A man goes riding by.
Late in the night when the fires are out,
Why does he gallop and gallop about?
Whenever the trees are crying aloud,
And ships are tossed at sea,
By, on the highway, low and loud,
By at the gallop goes he.
By at the gallop he goes, and then
By he comes back at the gallop again.

- Make a song or rap of them (sing lines twice, have a chorus, …) or find some music that fits them.
- Write a poem like *Hurricane Night* about another time of the year, e.g. 'Summer Day'.
- Find new titles for the two poems.
- Look for photos in magazines and make a collage to show the atmosphere of one of the poems. Explain your choice to a partner.
- Make a network for *Windy Nights*.

survivor [sə'vaɪvə] *Überlebende(r)* thundering ['θʌndərɪŋ] *donnernd, dröhnend* crash *Krachen* mailbox ['meɪlbɒks] (AE) *Briefkasten* basement ['beɪsmənt] *Keller(geschoss)* seriously hurt ['sɪəriəsli] *schwer verletzt* wreckage ['rekɪdʒ] *Trümmer* neck [nek] *Hals* (to) evacuate [ɪ'vækjueɪt] leaf [li:f] pl leaves *Blatt* branch [brɑ:ntʃ] *Zweig, Ast* lightning (no pl) ['laɪtnɪŋ] *Blitz(e)* closed up tight [taɪt] *fest verschlossen* (to) be set [set] *am Himmel stehen* (to) gallop (about) ['gæləp] *(umher)galoppieren* (to) be tossed [tɒst] *hin und her geworfen werden* low [ləʊ] *hier: tief gebeugt* chorus ['kɔ:rəs]

5 Alaska – the Great Land

Listening

Look at the photo for a minute.

Then close your eyes and try to remember as much as you can about the photo. Listen to the CD and take an imaginary journey to the Brooks Range, some mountains in the north of Alaska.

WB 1

1 Glen Oktollik's sister Amy wrote this article for her high school newspaper, Igaramkin.

A City Girl Goes Whaling

Dimond's own Amy Oktollik writes about her adventures in Barrow

Amy and an "umiak" near Barrow last spring

As you can probably guess from my name, I'm an Inuit, one of the "blubbers" you see at school. (I've learned to laugh at that word now – but you really shouldn't use it.)

Last spring I visited my grandmother in Barrow. More than half of the 4,100 people there are Inupiat Eskimos. That's what the Inuit there are called. It was good to be with my own people and hear them speak their language, Inupiaq. And I was able to learn more about Inupiat traditions. Barrow is great in the spring: everybody is excited to see the sun again after 67 days of endless darkness.

When I was there, we went whaling: yes, we Inuit are allowed to kill some whales – about 60 every year! I know a lot of people are against whaling. But if you want to understand Inuit culture, you have to know how important whaling is for us.

Everyone has a job to do at whaling time. Holes in the ice are the best place to find whales, and the men know where to look for them. The women cover the "umiaks", the boats we use, with seal skins.

We use snowmobiles to pull our tents and umiaks to an ice-hole. Then the men wait, often for days, for a whale. When a whale comes, they use harpoons to kill it and pull it onto the ice. It takes a day to cut up a whale. We use every part of the animal.

In June we go out on the tundra in our all-terrain vehicles in order to celebrate *Nalukataq*, the whaling festival, with family and friends. We eat the whale meat, talk, sing, dance and do Inupiat sports. We Inuit were the first to come to Alaska 8,000 years ago and we had to learn how to live in this cold climate. We have been doing things this way since then.

2 *Listening: Inuit whaling – for and against*

a How would you start a discussion about whaling? Write one or two statements as an introduction, read them to the class and pin them on the wall in your classroom.

b Dave, a new boy at Amy's school, saw her article and was shocked. So the class talked about Inuit whaling. Here are two of Dave and Amy's arguments:
– Whaling is an old Inuit tradition.
– Modern Inuit don't need whale meat to live.
Think of more arguments for or against whaling and write them down in two lists.

c Now listen to the CD and find out if any of your arguments are used. Then listen again and add more arguments to your lists.

d Who do you agree with – Amy or Dave? Find others in your class with your opinion and discuss your ideas. Write a statement as a conclusion and read it to your class. Pin the statement on the wall.

INUIT WHALING – FOR AND AGAINST

Introduction	*Arguments for*	*Arguments against*	*Conclusion*
...	...	...	...

Now write to Amy's newspaper about Inuit whaling. Use the outline and ideas from your classroom wall. Remember to give reasons and examples.

3 Glen versus Amy

The day Amy's article appeared, Glen was alone at home after school.
Beep, beep, beep.
Glen Oktollik opened the door of the microwave and took out his supper. When his father and his sister came in, he had just started his meal.
'How can you eat that stuff?' Amy asked.
'It's easy, Amy. You just open your mouth and put it in. I know you prefer whale blubber, but the butchers don't have it here in Anchorage.'
'Oh, you're so stupid! Our science teacher says fresh food is better for you than microwave food.'
Later, while they were all watching TV, Amy suddenly asked, 'Dad, can I go up to Barrow for Christmas? Grandma says I should come.'
'How do you plan to get there?' Glen asked.
'I'm going to fly. What else?'
'What about the timeless old traditions of the Inuit, Amy? Real Eskimos would go by dog sled!'
'Don't be stupid, Glen. We can combine old ways and new. Grandma always says that.'

'Grandma also thinks the weather in Barrow is OK,' Glen told his sister, 'but that doesn't mean she's right.'
'That's enough, you two,' said their father.
'If you can't be quiet, go to your rooms.'

In her room, Amy complained about her brother in a letter to her grandma.

... Glen has really changed since he came back from Florida. We're arguing a lot. He's only interested in his silly science projects. He makes fun of our Inuit traditions all the time. I think he's jealous because I visited you in Barrow in April.
Now, about Christmas: Dad says that I can come – if I can pay for half of my flight. I hope I have enough money!
I really need to practice my Inupiaq – there are lots of Inupiat here in Anchorage, but the language isn't spoken much.
Write back soon!

Lots of love,
Amy

At the same time, Glen called a friend and complained about his sister.
'You can't talk to Amy about anything ordinary any more. Only Eskimos. She isn't interested in anything else. I know they say Inupiaq is a difficult language, but she's been learning it for months and she still can't speak it. At least my science projects aren't useless.'

4 *Now you*

Imagine you are talking to Glen on the phone. Do you agree or disagree with what he says? Make notes first. Then use your notes to react to what Glen says.

5 *Distances in Alaska*

Look at the map of Alaska on pages 88/89. Find the town where Glen and Amy live, and their grandmother's town. How far is it between them?

6 Dating in Alaska

When Amy visited Barrow last April, her grandmother took her to a big festival with song and dance.

Amy I can't understand what's happening.
Grandma That's because you only hear Inupiaq when you're here. You'll understand more of the festival tomorrow.
Amy You think so? I really want to speak Inupiaq better. I even dated an Inupiat guy in Anchorage once, but his Inupiaq was terrible!
Grandma There are lots of Inupiat boys here. You'll speak Inupiaq better – if you visit me more often.
… …

The next day, Amy spoke to Glen on the phone. When Mr Oktollik came home, Glen told him about the call.
'Grandma took her to an Inuit festival. Amy said she couldn't understand what was happening. Grandma said that was because she only heard Inupiaq when she was there.'
'There?' Mr Oktollik asked.
'In Barrow, Dad. But she said Amy would understand more of the festival today. Hey, Amy said she had dated an Inupiat guy in Anchorage once. To learn more Inupiaq. Did you know that?'

'No, I did not. What did she say about him?'
'Not much,' Glen answered. 'She just told me that his Inupiaq had been terrible. And that Grandma thought Amy would speak Inupiaq better if she visited her more often. Oh, yes, then she said she had met a cute guy at the festival. But Grandma told her she couldn't ask him for a date because it might embarrass him. Weird!'
'Things are different in Barrow, Glen,' Mr Oktollik told his son. 'Boys there aren't like the boys in Anchorage.'
'Right, Dad. Grandma told Amy if she just sat next to this guy she'd soon know if he was interested. Boy,' Glen laughed, 'dating sure is easier in the city!'

7 *Looking at language*

a Look at Amy's conversation with her grandmother in A6 and how Glen reports what they said. Make two lists like this:

Direct speech	*Indirect speech*
Amy: 'I can't understand ….'	*Amy said she couldn't understand …*

What tense are the reporting verbs (*say, tell, think*) in?

b Compare the direct and indirect speech. What happens to the tenses in indirect speech?

c Find more examples of indirect speech in what Glen says. Write down what Amy and her grandmother said in direct speech.

8 *Focus on words: Old and new*

a On pages 76–78 find examples of words and phrases for old ways and new in Alaska.

old ways	*new ways*
prefer whale blubber/ fresh food	*eat microwave food*
speak Inupiaq	*…*

b Write a few sentences about old and new ways in Alaska. You could write about: *food, language, transport, dating, …*

A long time ago the Inuit in Alaska only travelled by dog sled or boat. Now they use snowmobiles, all-terrain vehicles and planes.

9 Denali National Park Alaska

Denali, the "High One", is the name the Indians gave North America's highest mountain, Mount McKinley. Denali is also the name of the huge national park around the mountain. With its 9,420 square miles (24,395 square kilometers), Denali National Park is larger than the state of Massachusetts.

How big is Bavaria? Compare it with Denali National Park.
Find out about a national park in Germany. Look for information like its name, where it is, what animals you can see there, etc. Then tell your class about it.

10 *Activity*

◆◆ Partner B: Look at page 120.
Partner A: Read your information about the caribou in Denali National Park. Close your book and tell your partner what you know about it. Then listen to what your partner tells you about the caribou and take notes.
Exchange your information on the other three animals, too.
Use your information and notes and write about one of the animals in your US album.

Some animals of Denali

Caribou

Moose

Grizzly bear

Wolf

Caribou travel in groups and move a long way from south of the Alaska Range and northwest of Mount McKinley to the northern parts of the park in winter. Caribou may be seen from the park road.

Moose, the deer family's largest members, are not herd animals. The young are born in May and will stay with the mother one or two years. In spring, the mother and young eat young plants.

Grizzly bears eat plants, small animals, and young, old, or sick moose, sheep and caribou.

Wolves are not seen often, but they play an important role in the park. They keep Denali healthy because they catch the weak, old and very young animals. And only a healthy park can support wolves.

1 *Revision: What Amy was able to do in Barrow*

a Fill in the right verb forms from the list on the right.

was able to (2x)
are allowed to
was allowed to (2x)
have been allowed to
had to (2x)
didn't have to

1 When Amy was in Barrow, she … learn a lot about Inupiat life.
2 She … go whaling with some people from the town.
3 The Inuit … pull their tents and umiaks by dog sled – they had snowmobiles.
4 For many years Inuit … kill some whales.
5 In the old days they … kill whales to live.
6 Now they … do it because it is part of their culture.
7 When Amy returned to Anchorage, she … write about her trip for the school newspaper.
8 She … write anything she wanted.
9 She didn't know if she … make Inuit whaling sound OK.

b Write four or five sentences about what Glen was able to/was allowed to/had to do during his ATX training at Kennedy Space Center.

2 *Here's what to do!*

a When Rob has got a problem, he always turns to other people for help. But they are fed up with him and tell him he should find out for himself. What do they say to Rob?

dictionary			
instructions			
manual	can	show	how to …
street map	should	tell	what to …
teacher	will	…	…
timetable			
Yellow Pages			

1 My computer has crashed! What shall I do now?
Don't ask me! Why don't you look in the manual? It will tell you what to do.
2 Where's the town library?
3 Where can I get a new watch?
4 How do I go on with my project?
5 Where's the Maths lesson?
6 How do I say this silly word?
7 What do I push for 'record'?

◆◆ b What do you do when you have a problem at school? Tell your partner.

A When I …, I often use/ask/look at/ … He/She/It tells me where to …/how to …/…
B Oh, I usually … He/…

3 *The place to live*

a Amy loves Barrow but Glen prefers the Anchorage area. Here is part of a brochure he sent to the friends he made in Florida. Add the verbs from the box in the right places.

come • do • explore • live • see
look at • miss • *come to* • visit

If you want a change of address, ANCHORAGE is the city *to come to*. For tourists, it's a great place …, and for its population of 250,000, a beautiful place … . There are thousands of things … and endless sights … . The Aviation Museum is the place … old planes. And a trip into the beautiful Chugach Mountains is one of the best ways … the countryside. Portage Glacier is not a place … on your trip. You can watch ice fall from the end of the glacier into the lake below. March is the only time … if you want to see the famous Anchorage-to-Nome Dog Sled Race. See you in Anchorage, everybody!

b Now write about your own area. Explain why it is a great place to live (or not). Try to use infinitive constructions.

4 *Revision: Amy's letter*

a Here is some more of Amy's letter to her grandmother. Complete what she wrote. Put the verbs in brackets into the simple past, past progressive or past perfect.

b Write about something that happened in your family after school one day last week. It could be something unusual or just an ordinary afternoon or evening. Remember: *who – what – when – where – why*, and be careful with your tenses.

... Dad (finish) work early today, so he (give) me a call and (pick) me up from school. I (wait) for him outside school when Kelly Redding (come) along. She works on the student newspaper. She (talk) to somebody on her cellphone but she (make) a sign to me. When she (finish) her call she said, "Congratulations Amy! We (like) your article a lot. So we're putting it in the paper."
In the car on the way home I (try) to talk to dad about Barrow, but he (have) a very busy day and just (want) to relax and listen to the radio. When we (come) home, Glen (eat) one of those microwave dinners again. I (tell) him how unhealthy that stuff is but he (not listen).
Glen has really changed since he (come) back from Florida. We're arguing a lot ...

5 *Who said what?*

Look at the speech bubbles. Decide who said what and then report what they said. Be careful with tenses and pronouns.

Real Inuit don't travel by plane. They use dog sleds and umiaks.

I'm sure that Inupiat boy likes you. But he was too embarrassed to tell you.

If you sit next to him in a group, it will be fine. That's how I met your grandfather.

You can't compare boys in Barrow to boys in Anchorage. They live completely different lives.

Glen Amy Grandma Mr Oktollik	told Amy said explained added ...	that	...

I wanted to speak Inupiaq better, so I went out with an Inupiat boy. But he spoke worse than I did.

My culture is very important to me. That's why I'll be in Barrow again at Christmas.

Glen told Amy that real Inuit didn't travel ...

6 *What did they say?*

What did the woman say to her husband before they left? (Begin: '*If we* ...')

What did the little penguin really say to the bear? (Begin: '*I* ...')

7 *But you told me …*

Complete the answers with the words in brackets. Be careful with the tenses. It might help you if you find out first what was said in direct speech.

1 'I didn't see you at Jane's party on Friday.' – 'But you told me … (be on Saturday).'
(Direct speech: 'Jane's party is on Saturday.') 'But you told me it was on Saturday.'
2 'Suzy has fallen in love with Mark.' – 'Oh, I thought … (hate him).' she ~~had~~ hated him
3 'Mom and dad are going to the movies tonight.' – 'But they said … (help me with my homework).' they woued help me with the homework
4 'I played tennis here with Joe once.' – 'You told me … (never come to this part of town before).' he had never come to this part of town before
5 'Shall we both pay half?' – 'Didn't you say … (going to buy me dinner)?' you woued go to buy me dinner
6 'I'll meet you after the game at 8 pm.' – 'But you said … (finish before seven).' it woued finish before seven
7 'I won't have time next weekend. My grandparents are coming.' – 'I thought … (only come at Christmas).' they only came at Christmas

8 *June said …*

Often when you report what someone has said, you do not remember the exact words. So you just report the meaning. Match the sentences on the left to the statements on the right.

1 June said she was going to Spain in the summer.
2 Jim told me he'd seen – oh, what's her name?
3 Dad said it would take longer by car.
4 Did you hear about that terrible accident on the east coast? At first they thought over 200 people had died.
5 She said she'd come early.
6 He explained that there were no ferries at the weekend.

a) 'Guess who I met at the club yesterday. Lisa. You remember her, don't you?'
b) 'I'll be there no later than 8 am.'
c) 'My next holiday is going to be in Mallorca.'
d) 'There aren't enough customers on Saturdays and Sundays for a big boat like this.'
e) 'You'll get there faster by train, you know. Much faster.'
f) 'The ship hit the rocks and people jumped into the sea. First reports spoke of over 200 deaths.'

9 *Alaska information*

A tourist from California phoned an Alaskan tourist information office. She listened to a recorded message and then spoke to a tourist guide. The next day she reported what she had heard to her family. What did she say? Be careful with the words in green. How do you need to change them?

1 This message will help you to plan your visit to Alaska.
It was a recorded message. It said it would help us to plan our visit to Alaska.
2 Alaska is very big! When you plan your trip you should make sure you have enough time for the places you want to see and the things you want to do.
It said that Alaska …
3 It's quite warm here in Alaska during the summer, between 60° F and 80° F. It's cooler at night and in the mornings.
4 It's nice and sunny here in Anchorage today. We're expecting a high of 69.
The tourist guide told me …
5 Yes, I can send you the *State Vacation Planner*. There are lots of hotels and motels in there. But you might want to look at our web site, too.
6 Yes, you can travel to Denali National Park by train. The summer schedule started yesterday.
7 I'm alone in the office today so I can't find out about tickets now. But I'll be able to help you if you call back tomorrow. Of course, you can buy tickets online.
8 I hope you have a great day. And I hope we'll see you in Alaska soon.

Word watch

10 *Word building: The suffix* -less

The suffix *-less* usually means 'without something'. Add *-less* to the nouns in the box to make adjectives, e.g. *homeless*. Then put the adjectives in sentences 1–8.

end • head • *home* • hope • job • life sleep • time

1 It's so cold, I wouldn't want to be *homeless* in this weather.
2 It's .... We'll never find the place without the right address.
3 Barrow is OK in summer but it's quite a ... place in winter. Just dead.
4 I'm so worried It's giving me ... nights.
5 If they don't open new oilfields, thousands of people will be ...
6 Please stop, you two! I'm fed up with your ... arguments.
7 You like the ... traditions of the Inuit, but I think their time is over.
8 What's the problem? You're running around like a ... chicken.

11 *Words and phrases: Arguments*

a Describe the situation in the photo. The words on the right can help you. What do you think the boy and the girl might say to each other? You can use the list below.

angry • argue • complain • fight • hate have an argument • love • jealous • shout unhappy • ...

Useful expressions:
At least I/my ...
Don't think you can ...
Have you ever thought about ...?
How can you ...?
If you could only ...
The difference is ...
Why can't you ...?
You'll just have to ...
You may not believe this, but ...

◆◆ ***Role-play***

b What do you argue about with other people? Think of a situation that made you feel angry. Write a role card and act out the situation. Or take a role card from your teacher.

Here is a suggestion:
You think you have made a good friend on holiday until you find out he/she has organized a party but hasn't invited you.

12 *Mediation: English and German are not the same*

How would you translate 'man' into English in these sentences? Try different translations. The box on page 164 can help you.

1 Man sollte sich nicht über die Traditionen der Inuit lustig machen.
2 Man kann die Fahrkarten nach Anchorage online kaufen.
3 Man sagt, Inupiaq sei eine schwierige Sprache.
4 Man kann Barrow nicht mit Anchorage vergleichen.

13 *Word link*

Choose a verb from the box for each group of words below.

get • give • have • hurt • spend • teach

... an argument, breakfast, tea, time
... History, a lesson, someone
... someone's feelings, one's leg, a friend
... angry, cold, a letter, ready, help
... reasons, sb. a message, up, sb. your love
... money, time, one's holidays

Imagine you are going on a walking trip in the cold north of Alaska. Decide what the five most important things are that you will take with you.

Alone on the North Slope

Lester Swenson was woken up by the sound of an all-terrain vehicle. He heard the ATV move away and he felt cold – but he didn't know where he was.
He closed his eyes again and thought about it. Of course! He and his friend Henry Serkoak had come here on a camping and hunting trip. 'Here' was on the North Slope of Alaska, 45 miles from Atqasuk.
Why had he gone on this trip with Henry? 'I could be in my big office back in Barrow now – all nice and warm,' he said to no one. Henry had wanted to show Lester this place – 'before you destroy it,' Henry had said.
But Lester had told Henry the project wouldn't destroy anything. The pipeline hadn't hurt the environment and the new oil wells wouldn't hurt it either. But Henry never listened.

* * *

Lester and Henry had always been good friends. They had grown up together in Atqasuk, both the youngest sons of poor Inupiat families. Lester had been more interested in school than Henry. So when the Native Regional Corporation got all that money from the oil companies and decided to send young Inuit to college with it, Lester went to college in Seattle. Henry stayed at home. Lester had come back to Barrow and started work with the Corporation. He had worked hard, and now, at 39, he was president.
As president, Lester helped to make a lot of decisions for the Inuit people:
Who gets money to go to college? Which towns or villages can kill a whale this year? Should a new hospital be built? And now: Can the oil companies build their new oil wells on Native land?
Meanwhile, Henry had become a guide: he took groups of city people out to hunt or fish and led a life that was completely different from Lester's. '*My* office is the North Slope,' Henry often joked. But Lester and Henry had stayed friends.

* * *

'Where's Henry now?' Lester thought. 'And why did he take the ATV? Why did he leave me alone out here?'
There was only one way to find out. Still in his sleeping-bag, Lester put on his new super-warm jacket and trousers. This wasn't easy: it took almost five minutes. Then he got up. 'Man, that's cold!'
Lester opened the tent and went outside. He looked around: no Henry, no ATV, no equipment, nothing. Henry had taken everything! Three hours later, Lester understood that Henry wasn't coming back. He had thought about it the whole time: Was Henry trying to kill him? Was he trying to teach him a lesson? Or had he just gone for a ride when something happened to him?
Lester knew it didn't matter. He knew he was a dead man. If the cold didn't kill him, the bears would.
Lester was hungry – and cold – and 45 miles from the nearest town. He had to walk the whole way. But not today. The sun had risen three hours before. He had only two more hours of light.

The next morning Lester woke up a little before the sun. His whole body was cold. 'Got to make a fire,' he said and looked around. There was still some oil in the lamp in the tent, but he had no matches to light it. Then he remembered that the early Inuit knew how to make fires: they hit two stones together to make sparks. Lester found some paper, some dry leaves and some wood. Then he poured a little oil from the lamp on them. It didn't take long until he had a nice fire. He sat down next to it and waited until he felt a little warmer. Then he tied the tent and sleeping-bag together and threw them over his back. He put the lamp over his arm and started to walk.

'Got to go east. Sun's in the south. I must keep the sun to my right,' he said again and again. When he couldn't walk any more, Lester began to look for a new campsite. He stopped on some flat ground near a frozen stream because he needed water. 'Starting to think like a real Inuit,' he laughed.

He put up the tent quickly, then looked for wood. When his fire was burning nicely, he thought about water. As a boy he had read that the Inuit had melted snow in their hands to get water, but that was in a white man's book. His grandmother had laughed when he had told her that. 'If you used your hands, you would freeze,' his grandmother had said. She had told him they had made little bottles out of animal skins, put snow in them and hung them near the fire.

But Lester didn't know how to make little bottles, and the idea of animal skins only made him hungrier than he already was. 'What about the tent?' he said loudly. The sound of his voice made him feel less alone. He tried to tear off a piece of material from the tent, but the nylon was too strong for him. 'Need a knife. No knife … . What did the early Inuit do? – They had knives, stupid!'

Lester sat down on the cold ground. He wanted to cry. Then he remembered something his grandfather had told him. 'We used what we could find. And the right tool is always there. Always.'

'That's where you're wrong, Grandpa!' But when Lester looked around, he found the right tool: fire. He took a piece of wood from the fire and blew out the flame. The wood was still very hot – hot enough to melt the nylon of the tent! Lester used his fire-knife to cut a round piece of nylon. He pulled the edges together and tied his little bottle with a piece of rope from the tent. It was easy to find a tool to break the ice: a large stone worked well, and soon Lester had his first bottle of water. He drank five bottles before the thirst went away. He felt stronger, but he needed food to survive.

Lester remembered that he had seen animal tracks in the snow: some were bear tracks, but there had been smaller ones, too. 'Probably rabbit,' he thought. 'But without a gun …?'

The right tool is always there.

Lester went back to where he had seen the tracks. When he found them, he followed them to a hole in the ground. The animal's warm body had melted some of the snow around the hole.

Slowly Lester moved towards the hole. But what could he use to catch the rabbit? He looked down at his hands and knew that they – and his brain – were his best tools.

With one quick movement Lester had the rabbit in his hands. The animal was frightened and fought hard. Lester didn't want to kill it, but he knew that one of them had to die.

And Lester didn't want to die. He had to stay strong. He had to survive and get back to Atqasuk. He had to find Henry.

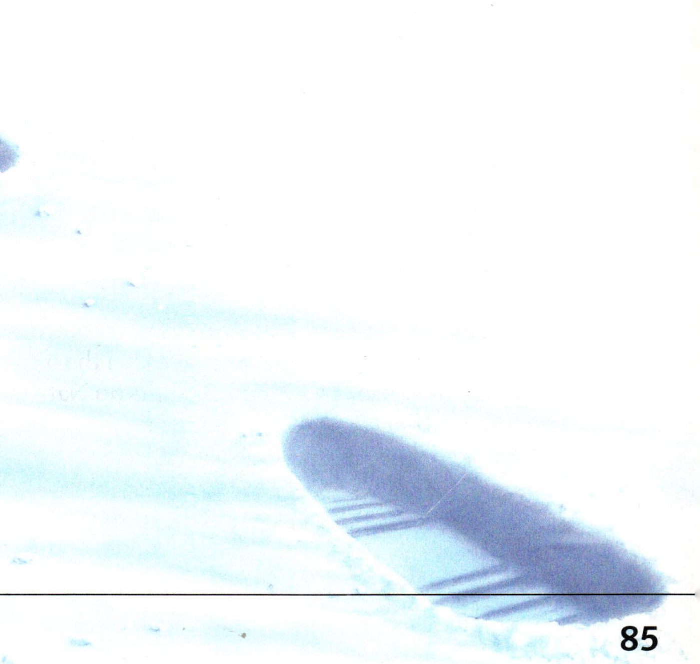

1 *What is the story about?*

a The story has four parts (p. 84, ll. 1–18; p. 84, ll. 19–41; p. 84, ll. 42–67; p. 85). Choose one sentence from each part that you think is most important. Write down what each part is about.

b Now, in no more than three sentences, write what the whole story *Alone on the North Slope* is about. Use the present tense. Your three sentences should answer the questions *Who? Where? What? When? Why?*

◆◆ c Swap your work with a partner. Correct anything that you think is not right. Make notes on anything you think your partner has done better than you. Then give back your partner's work. Use your partner's corrections and the notes you took and rewrite what you wrote in 1b.

2 *Lester and Henry*

Copy and complete this table about Lester and Henry's lives. What's the same? What's different?

	families	*education*	*jobs*	*where they work*
Lester				
Henry				

3 *The old ways to survive*

How did old Inuit traditions help Lester to survive? Copy this network and complete it.

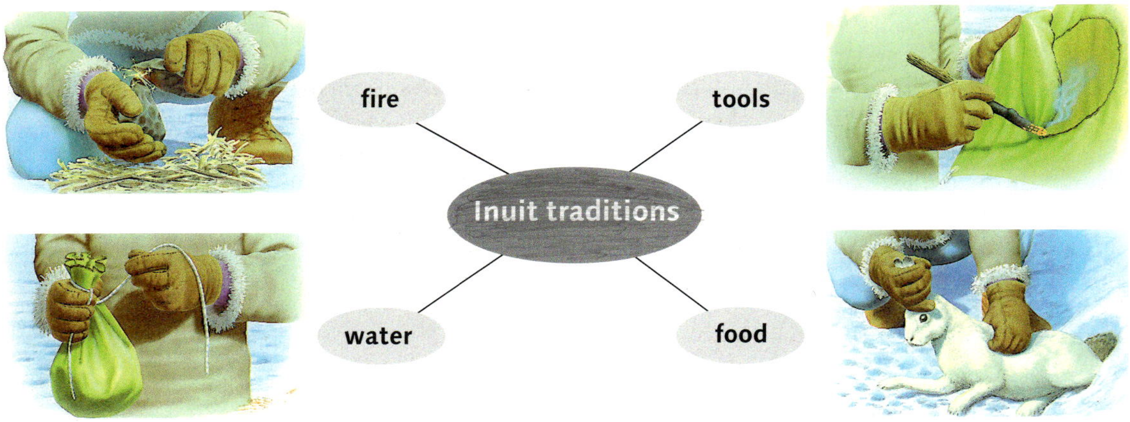

❖ 4 *Beyond the text*

Why do you think Henry left his friend alone on the North Slope without any food or equipment? Does one of Lester's ideas (p. 84, ll. 56–59) seem right to you? Discuss this in your group and then report back to the class.

◆◆ 5 *Role-play: 'Where were you, Henry?'*

a If Lester survives and finds Henry, what will their meeting be like? With your partner, write role cards for their conversation. Your ideas from 4 might help you. Or look again at exercise 11 on page 83. Don't forget to make a list of useful phrases.

b Now use your role cards and act out the conversation. Or swap your role cards with another pair and act out the conversation with their role cards.

WB 14, 15

How to ... use a dictionary – Part 1: German-English

1 *Looking up a word*

a When you do a project or a writing task, you'll probably need some words that you don't know yet in English. Imagine you want to look up the English word for *Kern* in a dictionary. How does the dictionary help you to find the page the word is on? Would you look at page 616 or page 617?

b If you want to find words faster, try this: Write down ten German words that start with different letters and see how quickly you can find them all in a dictionary. Write down the page numbers.

617 **Ketschup**

Kehre *Kurve* sharp bend

...icken ge- ...im; ***in sich*** ... be* an in-

Kellnerin waitress
Kenia Kenya
kennen know* [nəʊ]; ***wir ~ uns schon*** we've already met; ***kennst du mich denn etwa nicht mehr?*** do you mean to tell me you don't recognize me any more?; ***kennst du schon die neue CD***

Karton 616

Karton *Material* cardboard; *Schachtel* cardboard box
Karussell roundabout, *AE* car(r)ousel
Karwoche: ***die ~*** Holy Week (⚠ *ohne* ~~the~~)
Kaschmir cashmere ['kæʃmɪə]
Kathedrale cathedral [kə'θi:drəl]
Katholik(in) Catholic ['kæθəlɪk]
katholisch Catholic ['kæθəlɪk]
Kätzchen *junge Katze* kitten; *Katze* pussy ['pʊsi]; *Blüte* catkin

2 *The entry*

Look at this dictionary entry for *Kern* and find out what it tells you. What help does your dictionary give you when you look up *Kern*?

Kern *von Obst* pip, *AE* seed; *von Kirsche, Pfirsich o.Ä.* stone; *von Nuss* kernel; TECH core (*auch Reaktorkern*); PHYS nucleus ['nju:kliəs] (*auch Atomkern*); *übertragen* core, heart [hɑ:t]

- the headword
- the correct translation for your context
- how to pronounce the word

3 *Test yourself*

a Find the correct English words for the underlined German words in these sentences:

1 Das Lager am Fluss war gut geschützt.
2 Im Lager hatten sie viele verschiedene Schlafsäcke.
3 Die Wolken jagten über den Himmel.
4 Es ist illegal, Tiere im Nationalpark zu jagen.
5 Der Rat beschloss, den Parkplatz zu vergrößern.
6 Die Touristen befolgten den Rat des einheimischen Bergführers.

Lager camp (*auch übertragen: Partei*), *Vorrat* stock; *Lagerstätte* bed; *Geologie* deposit; TECH bearing; ***etwas auf ~ haben*** *Waren* have* sth. in stock; *Witze, Tricks* have* sth. at the ready

jagen hunt; *übertragen*: *rasen* race; *verfolgen* hunt; ***jn. aus dem Haus*** *o.Ä.* ~ drive* *od.* chase sb. out of the house *o.Ä.*; ***etwas in die Luft ~*** blow* sth. up; ***jm. eine Kugel in den Kopf ~*** shoot sb. in the head

Rat advice; *Ratschlag* piece of advice; *Versammlung* council; ***jn. um ~ fragen*** ask sb.'s advice, ask sb. for advice; ***jn. zu Rate ziehen*** consult sb.

b ◆◆ Find German words with two or more meanings, e.g. *Karte, handeln, faul.* Then write at least two sentences with each of the German words. Let your partner find the correct English words. If you aren't sure which translation is right, check the English words in the English-German part of your dictionary.

Remember

1 Use the words at the top of the page to find the entry faster.
2 Study the entry carefully and find the meaning you need for the context of your word. Notes in italics will help you.
3 Example sentences and phrases show you what constructions the word is used in.
4 If you aren't sure, check the translation in the English-German part of your dictionary.

WB p. 48

Alaska

Alaska Quiz

Everybody knows that Alaska is really cool, right? Well, not just cool, it's freezing! Back in 1867, U.S. politician William Seward paid Russia $7.2 million for 586,000 square miles (1.7 million square km). That's only $12 per square mile or $4 per square km!
But a lot of people laughed at "Seward's ice-box" and wondered what could be done with this huge, cold place in the middle of nowhere.
Today Alaska is one of the richest states in the USA. But what do you know about it? Get all the answers to the quiz right and find the magic word.

The numbers in brackets tell you which letter of your answers you should use. The magic word is the town near Anchorage where the dog sled race starts.

1 the northernmost town in the state (6)
2 the capital of Alaska (5)
3 the old Russian capital of Alaska (1)
4 the language most Europeans in Alaska spoke at the beginning of the 19th century (5)
5 where a tanker lost millions of liters of oil in 1989 (9)
6 Indian name for the "High One" (5)
7 the most famous dog sled race in the world (5)

In Alaska, there are lots of places you can't get to by road – the capital, Juneau, for example. So you often have to fly. That's why one of every 60 Alaskans has a plane. That's more planes per person than in any other U.S. state. Most of the 560 "airports" in Alaska are small airstrips. Of course, you don't always need an airport – with the right plane you can just land on the nearest lake!

How about a short walk with your dog? The Iditarod Dog Sled Race is 1,049 miles (1,688 km) long through some of the coldest and unfriendliest country in the world. But if that's too much for you, there is a junior race for kids, and it's only 130 miles (210 km) long!

Only stuff for tough guys? Not true! Susan Butcher has been the champion of the race four times.

politician [ˌpɒlə'tɪʃn] nowhere *nirgendwo* (to) get sth. right *etwas richtig machen* per *pro* airstrip *Start- und Landebahn*
tough [tʌf] *hart, zäh*

– THE LAST FRONTIER

Oil's good side: Oil and gas have brought a lot of money into the state. Oil is carried through the Trans-Alaska pipeline from the oilfields in Prudhoe Bay to the harbor at Valdez. Over half of the 800 miles (1,300 km) of pipeline was built above ground so that the heat from the pipeline does not hurt the environment.

What!? There are Indians in Alaska? Not just Inuit? That's right. And it's only the Natives of the northwest coast of North America that make totem-poles. If you know how to read these poles, they will tell you stories of a family's history.

Oil's bad side: There are about 400 spills a year in Prudhoe Bay and on the Trans-Alaska pipeline, of 40 different substances from acid to oil. After an accident in March, 1989, over 40 million liters of oil from the Supertanker Exxon Valdez covered hundreds of kilometers of the Alaskan coast. It was a tragedy for the wildlife of Prince William Sound.

Russia, Alaska's neighbor in the west, is only 51 miles (82 km) away – much nearer than any US state. The Russians were the first Europeans in Alaska. St. Michael's Cathedral is in Sitka, the old Russian capital of Alaska.

heat [hiːt] *Hitze* pole [pəʊl] *Stange, Pfahl, Mast* oil spill *Ölteppich, Unfall, bei dem Öl austritt* to spill *ausschütten*) substance ['sʌbstəns] acid ['æsɪd] *Säure* wildlife *die Tier- und Pflanzenwelt* sound [saʊnd] *Sund, Meerenge, Bucht*

6 Dreamland California

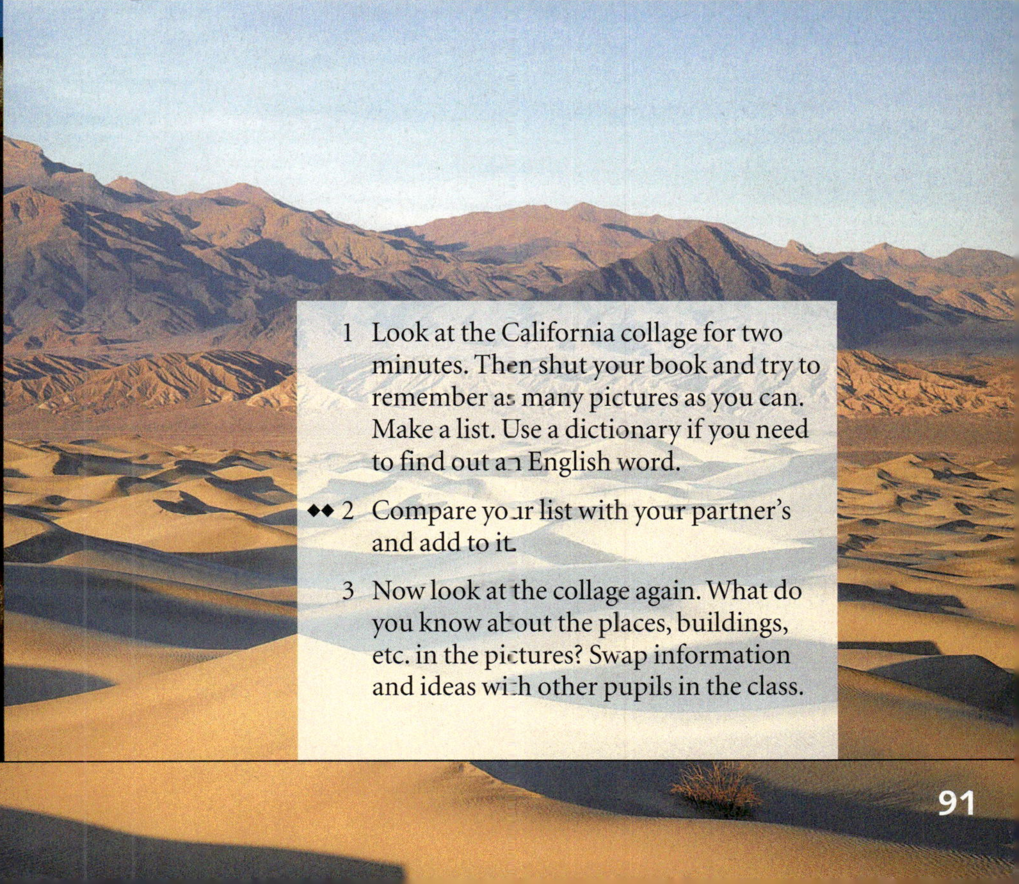

1 Look at the California collage for two minutes. Then shut your book and try to remember as many pictures as you can. Make a list. Use a dictionary if you need to find out an English word.

◆◆ 2 Compare your list with your partner's and add to it.

3 Now look at the collage again. What do you know about the places, buildings, etc. in the pictures? Swap information and ideas with other pupils in the class.

1 California places: Sights to see

DEATH VALLEY

"Tomesha", the Native Americans' name for Death Valley, means "land where the ground is on fire". That's a good name for this desert where temperatures can reach 130 °F (54 °C) in the summer! If you want to find out more about the hottest place on earth but keep yourself cool, there is a video twice an hour at the visitor center.

SEQUOIA NATIONAL PARK

Sequoia has been a national park since 1890. It is famous for the largest trees on earth: the giant sequoias or redwoods. The biggest is the 3000-year-old General Sherman tree. It is 275 ft (84 m) tall and still grows about half an inch (1 cm) every ten years.

THE GOLDEN GATE BRIDGE

Joseph Strauss from Chicago designed the bridge. Work started on it in 1933 and finished in 1937. The bridge is 1.7 miles (2.7 km) long, and the road on it is 220 ft (67 m) above the water. 120,000 vehicles a day use the bridge. Cars pay $5 to cross the bridge and enter San Francisco.

Prepare yourself for the most fantastic adventure in 65 million years on *Jurassic Park – The Ride*. Deep in the forest, on the most awesome water ride of all time, T-Rex is waiting for you!

Watch as Peter Parker changes from high-school zero into superhero to fight the Green Goblin in *Spider-Man Rocks.*

Take the greatest rides through the biggest movies. See how a real movie studio works. Enjoy yourself like nowhere else on earth on all the rides and adventures at Universal Studios Hollywood!

2 *Now you*

a Match pictures from pages 90/91 to the four texts.

b Imagine you've won a trip to California and can go to four different places. Choose three from the brochure above and one more from pages 90/91. Find other pupils with the same places and then tell your class the reasons for your choices.

3 *Activity*

◆◆ a Partner B: Look at page 121.
Partner A: You and your partner have got different information about Bodie State Historic Park. Ask your partner these questions and take notes on the answers. (Then your partner will ask you.)

1 Who first found gold in California?
2 When did people first find gold in Bodie?
3 Why can't you see all of the town's old buildings any more?
4 How long has Bodie been a state park?

b Now use all the information you have and write a short German text for a brochure on Bodie.

Bodie State Historic Park

The discovery of gold in California on January 24, 1848, started the gold rush that brought hundreds of thousands of people to California. Most came in 1849 and they called themselves Forty-Niners. Bodie became a busy gold-mining town of 8,000 people. In 1882 there was no more gold and everybody left. Bodie is now California's largest ghost town and still has 170 of the old buildings.

P 1, 2

4 California people: Zero to hero

ARNOLD SCHWARZENEGGER

was born in a small village in Austria in 1947. In 1968 he arrived in the USA to do bodybuilding competitions and became Mr Universe in 1970. He wanted to be an actor and had his first big success when he played himself in the bodybuilding documentary film *Pumping Iron*. Later films like *Terminator* made him one of the biggest names in Hollywood. He next turned to politics, and the bodybuilding and film legend became a political star when he was elected Governor of California in 2003.

DINA MOHAJER

was just another cool, young student in Southern California when she decided she needed blue nail polish that would go with her blue shoes. So she made some herself. Her friends were crazy about it, so she borrowed $50,000 from her parents to start her own company, "Hard Candy". Soon Hollywood stars like Drew Barrymore, Cher and Antonio Banderas (yes, boys wear it, too!) were buying her nail polish.

JERRY YANG AND DAVID FILO

met each other when they were students at Stanford in California. They both enjoyed themselves more on the World Wide Web than at their studies, and in 1994 the two of them started to send each other lists of the web sites they had visited. They put their lists on the Internet as "Jerry and David's Guide to the World Wide Web". It became wildly popular. They changed its name to "Yahoo!" and that's how one of the Internet's favorite search engines started.

5 *Looking at language*

a Look at A1, A3 and A4 and collect sentences with reflexive pronouns. Then complete the following sentences with reflexive pronouns.

Before our trip to Death Valley I asked *myself*: 'Have you prepared … well enough?' My sister was looking at … in the mirror and my brother was keeping … busy with a map of California. 'Forget the map,' I thought. 'We'll have to find out for … what we can do there.' Mum warned us: 'You must keep … cool and drink a lot of water.' But dad said: 'They can take care of … .'

b Find the sentences with the words *themselves* and *each other* in the 'Jerry Yang'-text above. Then match these sentences to the pictures below.

Jack and Jill are looking at themselves.
Jack and Jill are looking at each other.

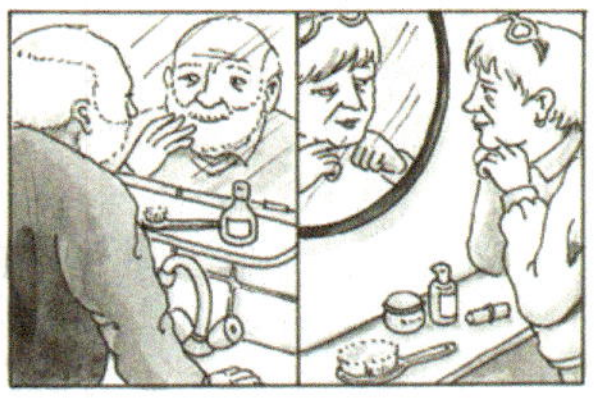

c How can you translate *themselves* and *each other* into German to show the difference?

6 *Focus on words: Famous sights, famous people*

Collect words and phrases from A1–A4 for what you can do or see at tourist sights and for what people have done to become successful or famous. Can you think of more ideas?

Universal Studios
- take a ride
- …

Arnold Schwarzenegger
- do bodybuilding
- …

7 Meet the Truongs

One day, after Scott Truong had returned from ATX in Florida to San Francisco, a reporter interviewed his family for an article.
Here is what he wanted to know:

Later, a friend asked Scott about the interview.

Scott Oh, this reporter just had a lot of questions for dad. He hardly talked to me and mom.

Friend What did he ask?

Scott A lot of stuff about Vietnam. Like, he wanted to know whether dad still thought about Vietnam a lot and what life had been like there after the war.

Friend Gee, nothing about now?

Scott No, and then he asked when my parents had come to the USA and if my dad had found work easily. Stuff like that. At the end he told us to smile for the camera and took a photo of us. You can read the article in the paper next week.

San Francisco Vietnamese Community News

Meet the Family: This Week – the Truongs

"I was very sad when I left Vietnam so I think about it a lot," says Nguyen Duc Truong quietly. "After the war, life in Vietnam was very difficult. I tried really hard to help my family. But then in 1976 they put me in a work camp. That was the most terrible time of my life. So I am glad I came here to the U.S."

Truong met his wife, Hoa, on the boat to America in 1981. First he worked on a farm in the Central Valley. Then the family moved to the city and he got a job in a laundry. But he lost that job last year.

"I haven't been able to find another job yet because I don't speak English very well. All my friends are Vietnamese immigrants, too, so I don't often talk to Americans."

Hoa Truong works full-time as an office cleaner and sometimes in the evenings in the kitchen of a Vietnamese restaurant. Their son, Scott, 14, is in high school and would like to study math and computer science in college. This year Scott won a trip to Kennedy Space Center, Florida. "I had a great time. I met people from all over the U.S. and even from Europe," he says. "It was fantastic!"

8 *Looking at language*

a Scott tells his friend what the reporter asked. Write down all the examples:
He wanted to know whether dad still thought ...
Then he asked when ...
...

b Now look at the reporter's questions again.
Do you still think ... ?
...

How does Scott report the questions?
What happens ... ... to the word order?
... to the question words?
... in *yes/no* questions?

c At the end of the interview the reporter said, 'Smile for the camera, please.' How did Scott report it? How would you translate what Scott said into German?

9 New ways and old

Scott loves visiting his Aunt Phuong and his cousin Jennifer at their modern West Hollywood apartment in Los Angeles. It is so different from his home in San Francisco. Here's what he wrote to Conchita, his friend from ATX, about his last visit.

> *Hi Conchita,*
>
> *Just back from Venice Beach with an L.A. story for you. I went there with my cousin this morning. We were about three blocks from the beach when we heard police sirens. The sirens got louder and then two police cars drove past us. Seconds later we heard an explosion. We ran round a corner and saw the police cars in front of a store. There was a big crowd outside and a police officer shouted, "This is the police. Come out with your hands in the air – real slow."*

◆◆ *Listening*

What do you think happened next? Discuss it with your partner. Then listen to the CD and find out.

* * *

'This is your last chance. Throw down your gun and come out with your hands up,' the police officer on TV shouted. Scott laughed at the scene he had seen months ago in L.A.
Then his father came into the room and told Scott to go to the bus stop and meet his mother. 'I don't want her to walk home alone with all the gangs in this area. Why do they expect your mother to work on Tet? It isn't fair. Our New Year should be a holiday here – like Christmas.'
On the way home from the bus stop Mrs Truong said with a smile: 'I'm so much looking forward to Tet.'
Scott asked why they couldn't just celebrate Christmas, like other Americans. Her smile disappeared. 'We don't celebrate Christmas,' she replied. 'We're Buddhists.'
She told Scott that he was learning too much of his aunt's and cousin's western ways. Mrs Truong loved all 'that old Vietnamese stuff', as Phuong and her daughter rudely called their traditions. She still made her own banh chung pastries for Tet. She was so excited when the children got money in red envelopes for good luck. She even liked the firecrackers that kept evil spirits away.
'But this is America, Mom,' Scott said. 'We're not in Vietnam now. I'd like to be a good American.'
'And I'd like you to be a good American, Scott,' his mother answered. 'But always remember where you come from.'

10 *Immigrants*

Mr and Mrs Truong are first-generation immigrants. What is life like for them in the USA? Scott is a second-generation immigrant. How is he different from his parents?
Do you know any immigrants in Germany? What do you know about their life?

11 *Activity: The American in me*

You like watching Hollywood movies, don't you? But there are probably lots of other things from California and the USA that play a role in your life. Think of

- what you wear,
- what you eat and drink,
- what sports you like,
- what music you listen to.

Make a collage in your US album.

1 *California or Germany – which is bigger?*

a Compare California to Germany and write down what you think.

1 Which is bigger?
I think ... is bigger than ...
2 Which is farther north?
3 Which has more people?
4 Which has more kilometres of coast?
5 Which has higher mountains?
6 Which makes more movies?

◆◆ b Swap your answers with your partner. Then look at the statistics on page 121 and check your partner's answers. There is one point for each correct answer. Who is the winner?

Tomales Point, Point Reyes National Seashore

Point Reyes Lighthouse

2 *Listening: Tourist information*

a Imagine you're travelling in California and you see these two photos in a brochure. What do you think you can do or see at Point Reyes?

b In your car you hear some tourist information on the radio. Listen to the CD. Which of your ideas were correct?

c Listen again for the answers to these questions. Take notes on what you find out.
1 Where is the main entrance?
2 When is the visitor centre open?
3 Who were the Miwok Indians?
4 What happened in 1906?
5 When are the lighthouse steps open?
6 In what weather are they closed?
7 When can you see whales?

d Use your notes and write some short information for a Point Reyes brochure on the visitor centre, the lighthouse or some other interesting part of the park.

3 *Jenna goes to California*

Complete these sentences about a teenager's trip to California. Use reflexive pronouns.

1 'I can take care of *myself*, Dad,' Jenna said as she said goodbye to her parents at the airport in Boston.
2 'Well, enjoy … and call us as soon as you arrive,' Jenna's mother told her.
3 'I will, Mom, – and you and Dad enjoy …, too. Don't worry about me.'
4 On the plane, Jenna sat next to a young guy with a walkman – he was listening to music and singing to … .
5 Jenna had been teaching … Spanish for six months. So she got out her Spanish book and cassette.
6 To practise her pronunciation, Jenna had recorded … onto a cassette. She listened to … and thought, 'Not bad!'
7 Jenna's Uncle Bob met her at San Jose airport. 'We've bought … a lovely new house since you were here last,' he told Jenna in the car.
8 Aunt Sheree welcomed Jenna to their Silicon Valley home. 'You just get … some cookies from that jar, Jenna,' she said, 'and I'll make some tea.'
9 The next morning Jenna slept until 11, so her aunt and uncle cooked … a big breakfast and ate without her.

4 *Jenna's e-mail* ➜ Vocabulary, p. 169

Complete Jenna's e-mail to her parents. Be careful: with some verbs you need reflexive pronouns, with others you don't.

Subject: news from SF

Hi Mom, hi Dad!
I felt ... real tired the day before yesterday and didn't want to do anything special, so Aunt Sheree and I just stayed at home and relaxed ... . Then yesterday we decided ... to drive to San Francisco. The city has changed ... a lot but the view from the Golden Gate Bridge is still out of this world! I remembered ... lots of places, although I was only a kid the last time I was here. Some friends of Sheree's and Bob's wanted to have lunch with us, so we met ... at a Vietnamese restaurant. Their son, Jake, was with them. He hurt ... at football last week and can't move ... very well. So we just sat in a café all afternoon and really enjoyed ... . He's teaching ... Spanish, too! Can you imagine ... that? Jake is cool (and cute!). Jenna :-)))

◆◆ 5 *Each other or themselves?*

Partner B: Look at page 121.
Partner A: Look at these pictures. You and your partner have the same pictures, but in a different order. Tell your partner about your pictures and write down the order of your partner's pictures.

A In my picture 1, two kids are taking photos of each other.
B Oh, that's my picture 6. In *my* picture 1, a girl and a boy ...

1

take photos of

2

think about

3

laugh at

4

think about

5

laugh at

6

take photos of

6 *Mediation: English and German are not the same*

How would you write these sentences in English? Be careful with *sich*, *sie* and *selbst*.

1 Sie waren sehr überrascht, als sie sich im Spiegel anschauten.
2 Sie sahen sich durch das Fenster an und lächelten sich zu.
3 Ich sah sie durchs Fenster, als sie sich am nächsten Morgen im Café trafen.
4 Der Garten sieht toll aus! Habt ihr alles selbst gemacht?
5 Es tut mir Leid, ich weiß den Weg zum Bahnhof nicht. Ich bin selbst Tourist hier.

7 Revision: As a tourist in L.A.

What questions might you need to ask in these situations?

1 You've just bought some postcards in a shop. *(Do you ...?)*
Do you sell stamps, too?
2 You've just decided to go on a tour by coach. *(Where can ...?)*
3 You would like to go to a show but it's 7 pm already. *(When does ...?)*
4 You'd like to buy a map to the stars' homes. *(How much ...?)*
5 You want to find Julia Roberts's house but you don't know the way. *(Where ...?)*
6 You want to see Tom Hanks's house, too. *(How far ...?)*
7 You don't know the price of the cassette tour to the stars' homes. *(How much ...?)*
8 You need 75 cents for a cold drink from the machine. *(Have ...?)*

☆☆☆ **STAR ADDRESSES** ☆☆☆

TOM HANKS 23414 Malibu Colony Drive, Malibu	JULIA ROBERTS 6220 Del Valle Drive, West Hollywood

8 Revision: California immigrants

a The adverbs and adverbial phrases on the right are all from A7, p. 94. Put them under the right headings. Then try and add more adverbs to each list.

after the war • *full-time* • hard • *here*
in 1976 • in a work camp • in college
in the evenings • in Vietnam • last year
often • on the boat • quietly • *really (hard)*
sometimes • then • this year • to the U.S.
to the city • very • well

Frequency (how often?)	Time (when?)	Place (where?)	Manner (how?)	Degree (how big/hard/...?)
often	*after the war*	*here*	*full-time*	*really (hard)*

b Read what a student from Scott's class has written about California immigrants. Add the adverbs and adverbial phrases in brackets to the sentences. Be careful with the word order.

1 For over 150 years, California has welcomed immigrants. (from all over the world)
2 More immigrants live in California than in any other state. (here)
3 Asian immigrants have been coming to this state. (since 1849)
4 They have worked in their new home country. (always – hard – very)
5 They come from many different Asian countries. (today)
6 California's culture is becoming more and more Asian. (slowly)
7 In parts of San Francisco, it's easy to think that you are in an Asian city. (often – really)
8 Some Chinese who have lived there all their lives don't speak English. (still – very – well)

CALIFORNIAN BUG

Simple past → past perfect
was → had been

9 *What Conchita wanted to know*

When Scott phoned Conchita she asked him a lot of questions. Read the speech bubbles and report what she asked. Remember how tenses change in indirect speech!

1 *How was your first day back at school?*
2 *Did you give a report on your Florida trip?*
3 *Were your friends at school happy to see you?*
4 *Do you know where the Chabot Space and Science Center is?*
5 *Have you ever been there?*
6 *What's the weather like in San Francisco?*
7 *What are you going to do at the weekend?*
8 *Where does your cousin live in L.A.?*
9 *Do you visit her often?*
10 *When are you going there next?*

1 Conchita asked Scott how …
2 She wanted to know if …
3 She asked him if …
4 Conchita asked Scott if …
5 She wanted to …
6 …

10 *Difficult questions*

Questions sometimes make Joe think that life is very hard. Report what these people asked him.
His girlfriend asked him …

girlfriend: *Where were you when I phoned last night?*

father: *Have you tidied up your room yet?*

best friend: *Why don't you talk to me when your girlfriend is around?*

little brother: *Can I come to the party with you on Saturday?*

teacher: *Where's your homework?*

mother: *When are you going to throw that old jacket away?*

11 *Smile for the camera, please!*

Report what the reporter asked or told the Truongs to do.

1 *The reporter told the Truongs to smile for the camera.*
2 'Can you answer a few questions for me, Mr Truong?'
He asked Mr Truong to …
3 'Could you speak a little louder, please?'
4 'Please translate my questions for your husband, Mrs Truong.'
5 'Now, tell me some more about the work camp.'
6 'Would you answer some questions, too, Mrs Truong?'
7 'Can you just give me five minutes more?'
8 'Can we go outside for the photo, please?'

❖ 12 *Game: On TV or at the movies*

Write a description of your favourite film or TV show. Give the same sort of information as in the TV magazine on the right, but don't give the name of the film or show. Read your description to the class. Can anybody guess the name of the film or the show?

> **This week's movies on TV**
>
> **Hostages[1] in L.A. ★★★** (drama) Cheryl Mann, Rod Silver. Cheryl Mann is great as a police officer from the country in this action drama. Gangster Silver has 20 hostages in an L.A. store. When some of the hostages escape[2], the showdown[3] begins.

1 hostage ['hɒstɪdʒ] *Geisel*
2 escape [ɪ'skeɪp] *fliehen, entkommen*
3 showdown ['ʃəʊdaʊn] *Entscheidungskampf*

13 *Things to do*

a Scott arrived home one day from school and found a message from his mother. What does she want/tell/ask him to do?

> *Hi, Scott!*
> *Your father and I won't be home until late tonight. Your dinner is in the fridge. Could you do it in the microwave yourself, please? And take the noodles in the fridge round to Mrs Nguyen. She's ill. Call her first. Don't forget to call your aunt. Do your homework before you watch TV! See you about 9:30.*
> *Mom*

You can use

She asks Scott to ...
She tells him to ...
She wants him to ...
She would like him to ...

◆◆ b Think of three or four things you would like people in your family to do for you. Write them a message. Swap messages with a partner. Report what they want their family members to do.

14 *The UK, the USA: A quiz on the whole book*

a You've learned a lot about the UK and the USA in this book. But what can you remember? Answer these questions as quickly as you can. All the answers are somewhere in this book.

- *Which three oceans border on the USA?*
- *At what London station do trains from Chester arrive?*
- *What are the main languages of Miami, Florida?*
- *What's the capital of Wales?*
- *Whose statue can you see in Trafalgar Square?*
- *What did the Romans call Dover?*
- *What is the biggest airport in Chicago?*
- *What is a sequoia?*
- *How many points do you get for a try in rugby?*
- *In what national park can you see the highest mountain in the USA?*

❖ b Make your own UK/USA quiz in a group. On each of 24 cards, write down a question about the UK or the USA on one side and the answer on the other. Make four cards for each of these topics:

⚀ history
⚁ geography
⚂ cities
⚃ nature
⚄ people
⚅ 'mixed bag'

Now swap your cards with another group and play their quiz. You need a dice. Player A throws the dice for a topic. Player B takes a card and asks A the question. A tries to answer it:
– correct answer = 1 point for A, and A may throw the dice again
– wrong answer = B may now throw the dice, player C takes a card, etc.
Use all the cards. Who has got the most points at the end?

Word watch

15 *Word link*

a Choose a verb from the box for each group of words below.

dream • have • make • start
visit • win • write

write … a book, an e-mail, software, a story, songs
visit … your aunt, California, a museum, a web site
win … a prize, a race, a scholarship, a battle
start ~~have~~ … a company, to cry, a family, a race
make … a decision, a film, money, someone cry, fun of sb./sth.
~~have~~ … a break, dinner, a dream, a look, something in common
dream … a lot, about your best friend, that you can fly, you're as rich as …

b Write seven sentences about the people or things below.
For each sentence use a different verb (and phrase) from a. Also use as many different tenses for your sentences as you can.

1 Arnold Schwarzenegger
2 Hollywood star
3 my mother/father
4 ATX
5 high school newspaper
6 film
7 the Internet

Examples:

1 *Arnold Schwarzenegger has made a lot of films.*
2 *I dreamt I was as rich as a Hollywood star.*

16 *Word building: Compound nouns*

a Match the words from the two boxes and make nine compound nouns. Be careful whether you spell the new words as one word, with a hyphen (-) or as two words. Check in a dictionary.

	+	
ghost		bag
high		ball
oil		call
phone		engine
search		kilometre
side		school
sleeping		*town*
square		walk
street		well

ghost town, …

b How many compound nouns can you make with these words?

phone + … • post + … • school + …

phone number, …

… + ball • … + board • … + room

football, …

17 *Listening: Weak forms*

a Some English words don't always have the same pronunciation. Listen to the CD. How is *from* pronounced in these three sentences – [frəm] or [frɒm]?
This letter is from Megan, not for Megan.
This letter is from Scott.
Who is this letter from?

The strong form [frɒm] is only used when *from* is stressed or comes at the end of a sentence. Usually the weak form [frəm] is used.

b Decide which of the underlined words use the weak [ə]-sound. Then listen to the CD and check if you were right.

1 I'll tell you what I'm thinking of. A lovely cup of tea.
2 Can I have an English breakfast? – Yes, you can.
3 Bacon and eggs, please. Oh, and coffee.
4 There's some cola in the fridge. Do you want some?
5 Where's your dad from? – My dad? From Canada.

c Listen again and try to say the sentences with the right pronunciation.

Look at the title of the story and the picture. In your opinion:

- what is the text about?
- what is a 'high school talent night'?
- what are the relationships between the three people in the background of the picture?

Next Month … Hollywood

"This is your last chance, Rodney," I said to myself as I looked at the poster on the wall. Today was May 19 and the activity office closed in two minutes. I went into the office and signed my name … Rodney Suyama.

I want to be one of the first great Asian rappers – totally new, full of hope, maybe a few lines about the earth, stuff like that. I've written a lot of raps but I just haven't known what to call myself. A rapper needs to have the right name. The name *Rodney Suyama* just doesn't work as a rap name.

Actually, I should mention that I'm not all Asian. I'm half Asian and half Polish. But like a lot of kids who are half white, I don't think of myself as white. Anyway, most people think that my sister Suzanne and I are totally Asian. But Suzanne says an Asian guy can't be a rapper.

"Why the hell not?"

"You have to be black; they're the only guys that are cool rappers."

But my girlfriend wants to help me. Well, she's not exactly my girlfriend. I've been sitting next to Ivy Ramos all year in language class. She always talks to me and we've become good friends. Ivy's dad is Filipino and her mom is black and Ivy is beautiful. And nice, too.

Ivy was the girlfriend of the famous Lavell Tyler, the greatest footballer to play at Franklin High. Guys like Lavell Tyler don't breathe the same air as guys like me. All year Ivy told me about her and Lavell Tyler. Then last month it all changed.

When Ivy came into class, she looked like someone had died and she was crying.

"Ivy … what's wrong?" I whispered.

"That bitch!" she said.

After class she sat there while everyone else left. Then she asked me if I would take her to the pizza place.

Music, that was what those words were. As we walked out of the building, I put my arm around her.

At the pizza place the whole story came out. She had seen Lavell Tyler in Deleisha Johnson's car. He was kissing Deleisha Johnson.

"I felt like a total idiot! He was kissing that girl in front of everyone. That bitch!"

"That's terrible," I said.

"Then when I saw him before class and told him I'd seen them, he asked why I couldn't try to understand him and said that he just wanted to see us *both*! I told him what he could do with that idea!"

"So you finished it?" I tried not to sound too happy.

"Of course! I want a guy to be reliable – you hear what I'm saying, Rodney?"

Reliable Rodney, that's what they call me.

From then on, Ivy and I were together all the time. We were more than friends, although I don't think she thought of me exactly as her boyfriend. She got closest to me when Lavell was in sight. When she saw him, she took my hand and looked into my eyes and smiled as if we were the only two people in the world. The one time she kissed me was when we were walking past him. Ivy stopped, put her lovely brown arms around my neck, lifted her face, and kissed me. Did I worry that this was all a show for Lavell Tyler? No, I did not. I'm not a proud person and I wanted Ivy.

Ivy wanted to help me to find a good rapper name. "What about Havana Banana?" she asked.

"I don't know – sounds like I'm Hispanic. Anyway, banana means you aren't really Asian. Remember?"

"Yeah … Asian on the outside but white on the inside," Ivy said. "I'm telling you, Rodney, if I was worried about stuff like that, it would make me crazy."

I thought about this for a minute. "It would be cooler if I was Hispanic and not half Japanese and half Polish." But then I had an idea. "Ivy, why not something with *happa*?"

"*Happa*? Like people who are half Asian?"

"Sure. I think it came from Hawaii, from *happa haole*."

"*Happa haole* means half white, right?"

"Yeah, what do you think? MC Happa? Or DJ Happa? I know – I've got it! Ice Happa."

"That's not bad, Rodney. In fact, it's cool."

"OK, Ice Happa it is."

Back at my house, Ivy and I were in the kitchen with Mom when I had another idea. I asked Ivy if she wanted to be in the act with me.

"I thought you had a drum machine."

"I do, I do." I was getting excited. "I'll do the rap and you'll walk up and down with a big drum –"

Ivy was getting interested.

"Yeah, and you'll walk up and down, and there'll be the Japanese flag on one side of the drum and a picture of the earth on the other side."

Ivy got excited. "I'll be like the model in the TV ad! The one in that cute outfit who beats the drum for those veggie burgers! You'll do the rap and I'll carry the drum! We have to do it in front of people before Talent Night," Ivy said, "because we *have* to be good."

"You can." Mom jumped up and looked for something by the kitchen phone. "Look, this came yesterday." AN EVENING OF MUSIC AT THE ASIAN AMERICAN THEATER it said.

"It's a talent show and it's open to everyone," Mom said.

Ivy and I practiced every night for the next two weeks in my garage until we were perfect. And she looked sexy. Very sexy. "This week the AAT, next week FRANKLIN, next month HOLLYWOOD … then LONDON! … TOKYO … THE WORLD!" Ivy had big plans for us.

The night of the AAT show, we were the fourth act. The presenter was Philip Omori, a local weather guy on TV. He introduced the first act.

"We are proud to present Eric Lew. He will play Max Reger's Cello Suite Number One."

His parents probably gave him a cello when he was a baby – the guy was fantastic. The audience clapped for five minutes. Next Julie Muramoto played Paganini. She was awesome on the violin. The audience went crazy. I turned to Ivy.

"They're all playing classical stuff."

"Be cool, Rodney," whispered Ivy.
After that Martin Wong played a Chopin piece on the piano and everyone clapped for a million years. Then the weather guy said, "Ladies and gentlemen, we are happy to present Ice Happa." I went up on to the stage, turned on the drum machine and started to rap. Then Ivy came out with the drum with the Japanese flag and the earth. There was a lot of noise from the audience when they saw her. As Ivy walked up and down, she held her head high. I went on rapping:
Don't hurt the earth / you gotta love this planet / don't break it, we can make it.

Then Ivy fell over a cable. Splat! Her drum flew through the air and hit me in the stomach. *Bam!* Ice Happa and the veggie queen are on the floor. The audience goes wild, everyone is laughing. Later, on the way to the car, the Franklin kids want to know if we're going to do the act for Talent Night.
"That was the funniest thing I've ever seen," says Julie Muramoto. "Great act, you two."

Ivy and I sat in the car after the show.
"Damn."
"What's the matter, Rodney?"
"I wanted to be cool."
"So? No one has to know that."
"Damn, I really wanted to be cool."
Then Ivy came close to me. "It's good if you can make people laugh, Rodney. I like going out with someone who can do that."
Then she started to kiss me but stopped suddenly. "You stay reliable, you hear what I'm saying, Rodney?"
Then I kissed her and we stayed in the car in the dark for a long time.
Lavell Tyler was nowhere in sight.

Adapted from: Jean Davies Okimoto, Next Month … Hollywood

◆◆ 1 *What is the story about?*

a Finish these sentence beginnings.
  1 Rodney Suyama went into the school activity office because he …
  2 Rodney wanted to be a great rapper but he couldn't find a …
  3 A month before, Ivy Ramos had been very sad because …

b Write three or four more sentence beginnings (like the ones in a) about the end of the story. Can your partner finish them?

c In no more than three sentences, explain what the story is about.

2 *Who are Rodney and Ivy?*

a *"But like a lot of kids who are half white, I don't think of myself as white."* (p. 102, ll. 14–16)
Why do you think Rodney calls himself Asian, although he is half white?
b What do Rodney and Ivy have in common?
c Explain why Rodney doesn't like the name *Havana Banana.*
d *"It would be cooler if I was Hispanic and not half Japanese and half Polish."* (p. 103, ll. 46–48)
Why does Rodney say this? Can you give any reasons?
e Explain why Rodney and Ivy think that *Ice Happa* is a good name for him.

3 *Beyond the text*

a Why do you think American high schools have talent nights? How might they help students? If your school had a talent night, what act could you do for it?
b Rodney says, *"I wanted to be cool"* (p. 104, l. 27). Ivy says, *"It's good if you can make people laugh"* (p. 104, ll. 30/31).
And you? Do you like 'cool people' or 'people who make other people laugh'? Say why.
c Find Rodney's rap in the text. Can you write a few more lines? What does your rap sound like?
d Imagine what will happen when Rodney and Ivy do their act at their school's talent night. Write a report about the act for the Franklin High School newspaper.

WB 8–9

How to ... use a dictionary – Part 2: English-German

1 *Understanding new words*

When you are working on a project, you may find information (in English) with words you don't know. You can often guess the meanings of these words from the context or because you know part of a new word, or the word is like a German word, or even like a word you know in another language (French, Latin, ...). Pictures might also help.

Located 3.5 miles from San Francisco, Angel Island was where thousands of Asians commenced their new lives in the USA. For those of Asian nationality it was often not the life of freedom they had hoped for.

2 *Looking up the meaning of words*

a If you can't guess the meaning or want to check if you guessed right, you will need a dictionary. On page 87, you learned about some of the information that dictionaries give. What information do the entries below give?

> **primary** ['praɪməri] Haupt-
> **primary colour**, *AE* **primary color** [ˌpraɪməri'kʌlə] Primärfarbe
> **primary school** ['praɪmərisku:l] Grundschule

> **detention** [dɪ'tenʃn] *in Gefängnis* Haft; *in Schule* Nachsitzen; ***get*** ~ nachsitzen müssen; ***be in*** ~ nachsitzen

b Look at the dictionary entries again and decide what *primary* and *detention* mean in these sentences.

1 Immigrants were kept in <u>detention</u> on Angel Island. The <u>primary</u> worry there was that the immigrants might bring dangerous illnesses into the country, so doctors screened them all. Many immigrants were then not admitted to the USA.

2 Which school does your brother attend? – He's only 8, he's still at <u>primary</u>. It's a strict school: he's in <u>detention</u> today because he was late.

c Your dictionary might use abbreviations like *bes.*, *Obj*, *Sg*, *umg.*, MIL, POL or symbols and colours like ◆ or **primary school** to give you extra information about grammar, style and meaning. Find the list of abbreviations in your dictionary.

3 *Test yourself*

a Look at the dictionary entries for *admit*, *attend* and *screen* and find the correct translations of these words in 2b (sentences 1 + 2) on the left.

> **admit** [əd'mɪt] (**-tt-**) *Schuld, Fehler* (ein)gestehen, zugeben; *akzeptieren* zugeben; *in Schule, Verein* aufnehmen (***to*** in); *zur Universität* zulassen (***to*** zu); *in Disco, Museum* hineinlassen (***to*** in); ***be admitted to hospital*** ins Krankenhaus eingeliefert werden

> **attend** [ə'tend] *Hochzeit, Schule, Kurs* besuchen; *Treffen, Seminar* teilnehmen an
> ◆ **attend to** sich kümmern um

> **screen** [skri:n] **1** *Nomen; von Fernseher, Computer* Bildschirm; *in Kino* Leinwand; *als Trennung* Trennwand; *beweglich* Stellwand; ***on the*** ~ *im Film* auf der Leinwand; ***on*** (***the***) ~ COMPUT auf dem Bildschirm **2** *Verb mit Obj; schützen, verstecken* abschirmen; *Film* zeigen, vorführen; *Bewerber, Gepäck* überprüfen

b Find the best translation for the underlined words from the context or in a dictionary:

The gold rush <u>attracted</u> the first Chinese to California in 1848. Later, they <u>laid tracks</u> for the new railroads and <u>provided</u> cheap <u>labour</u> for all the jobs that nobody else wanted. A new <u>law</u> in 1882 made life even more difficult for them and <u>excluded</u> many Chinese from the country.

Remember

1 Don't look up every word. Whenever possible, use the context to guess the meaning.
2 Read the whole dictionary entry. Don't just use the first word you see.
3 Use all the information that is given in the entry (abbreviations, symbols, colours, ...) to decide which meaning is right or best.

WB p. 54

California
Where the Earth Is Always Moving

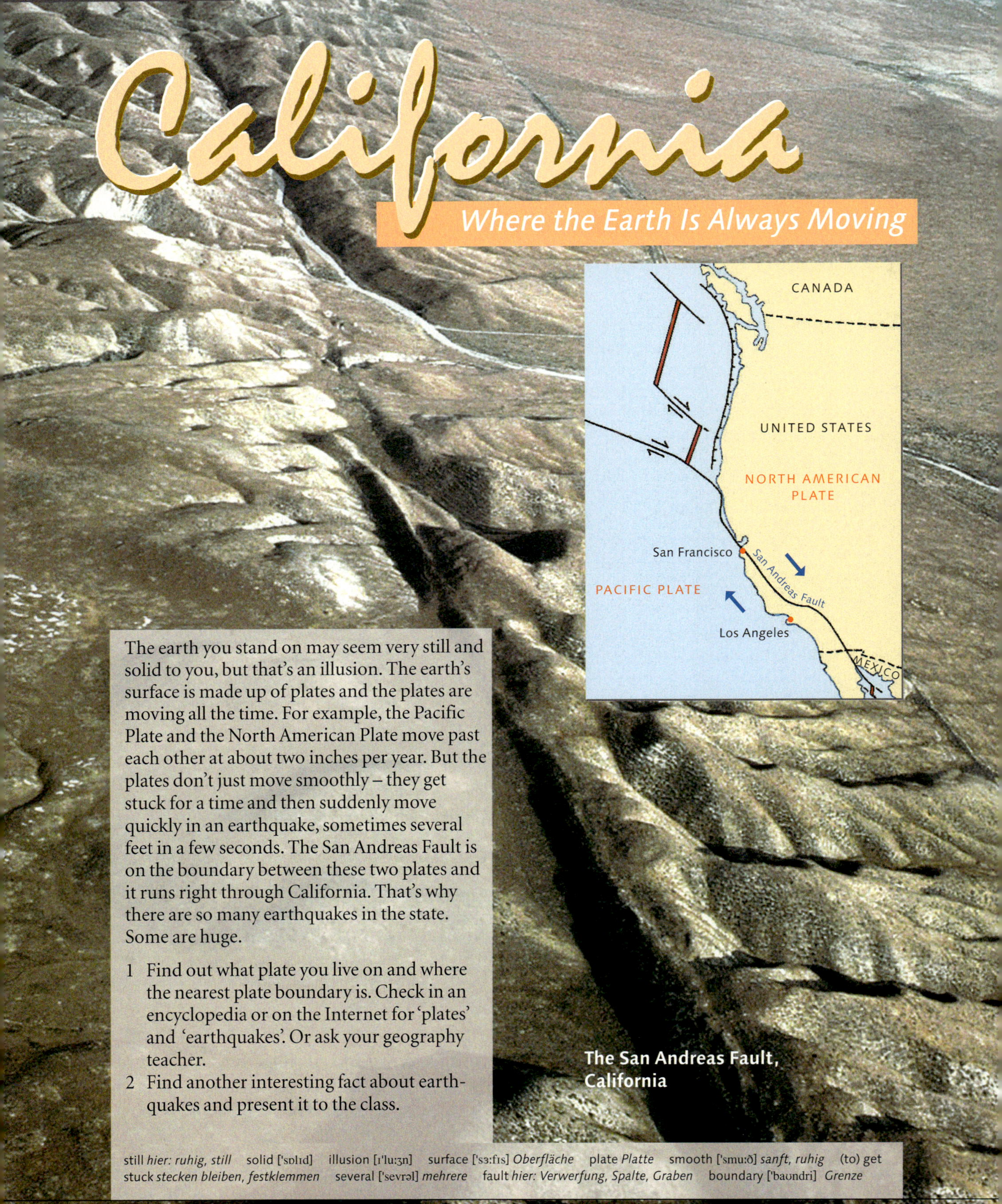

The earth you stand on may seem very still and solid to you, but that's an illusion. The earth's surface is made up of plates and the plates are moving all the time. For example, the Pacific Plate and the North American Plate move past each other at about two inches per year. But the plates don't just move smoothly – they get stuck for a time and then suddenly move quickly in an earthquake, sometimes several feet in a few seconds. The San Andreas Fault is on the boundary between these two plates and it runs right through California. That's why there are so many earthquakes in the state. Some are huge.

1 Find out what plate you live on and where the nearest plate boundary is. Check in an encyclopedia or on the Internet for 'plates' and 'earthquakes'. Or ask your geography teacher.
2 Find another interesting fact about earthquakes and present it to the class.

The San Andreas Fault, California

still *hier: ruhig, still* solid ['sɒlɪd] illusion [ɪ'lu:ʒn] surface ['sɜ:fɪs] *Oberfläche* plate *Platte* smooth [smu:ð] *sanft, ruhig* (to) get stuck *stecken bleiben, festklemmen* several ['sevrəl] *mehrere* fault *hier: Verwerfung, Spalte, Graben* boundary ['baʊndri] *Grenze*

This January, as every year, Brian Watson remembers January 17, 1994, when the earth below Northridge in Los Angeles moved. "It felt like Godzilla picked our building up, shook it, didn't like his new toy and threw it back down on the ground." The 6.7-magnitude earthquake killed 60 people and caused damage of more than $20 billion.

An even bigger earthquake hit the San Francisco Bay area in October 1989, and 62 people died. These were just two of the thousands of earthquakes in California every year. Most are small and nobody notices them. All over the state people are waiting for the 'Big One', like the earthquake that destroyed San Francisco and killed 3000 in April 1906.

San Francisco after the earthquake in 1906

If you're going to California this year, here's what you can do to protect yourself in an earthquake. Match the texts to the right pictures.

HOLD

If you take cover under a desk or table, HOLD on to it and move with it until the earthquake stops.

DUCK

DUCK down to the floor.

COVER

Take COVER under a desk or table. If you can't do that, take COVER by an inside wall and protect your head with your arms.

Try this simple experiment and see what can happen to land with a lot of water in it in an earthquake.

1 Fill a pan with sand: the deeper the better.
2 Pour in water to just below the surface of the sand.
3 Put the end of a brick down into the wet sand so it stands up like a building.
4 Now, very gently, tap the side of the pan with a hammer and see what happens to the sand and the brick.

Put 'Earthquakes for kids' into an Internet search engine and see what you find.

magnitude ['mægnɪtjuːd] *Stärke, Größe* damage ['dæmɪdʒ] *Schaden* (to) take cover *Schutz suchen, sich unterstellen*
pan [pæn] *Topf, Pfanne* the deeper the better *je tiefer desto besser* (to) pour [pɔː] *gießen* brick [brɪk] *Ziegelstein*
gently ['dʒentli] *sachte, sanft* (to) tap [tæp] *(leicht) schlagen an*

Only in L.A.

Does something about this L.A. school bus tell you the school can't be very good?

A True Story

Since he was a boy, Larry Waters had always wanted to fly a plane, but he couldn't because his eyes were too bad. Then he had an idea:
"I bought 45 weather balloons. I tied the balloons to a chair and the chair to my jeep. Then I put helium into the balloons and got some sandwiches, beer and my gun.
I thought I'd float up fifty feet or so, look around for an hour, and then shoot a few balloons and come slowly back to earth.
Things happened a little differently. When I cut the rope to the jeep, the chair went straight up very fast to 11,000 feet. It was cold and I was too scared to shoot the balloons. Then after 14 hours things got worse because I moved close to Los Angeles International Airport. They saw me on their radar and sent a helicopter up. They rescued me. When they pulled me out, the chair went up higher and I never saw it again. Then, would you believe it, when I got back to earth, the police arrested me and asked me why I'd done it. Well, it's a hobby, isn't it?"

Do you know any funny or strange 'true stories'? Write one down in English. You can put it in your US Album.

Dream of Being Stars

Since the 1920s Hollywood has been a magnet for people with one thought in their heads: I want to be a star! A few made it, most didn't. Here are two songs about the subject. Dionne Warwick's was a hit in the sixties; Neil Young's is a seventies song.

Dionne Warwick

Do you know the way to San Jose?

...
L.A. is a great big freeway.
Put a hundred down and buy a car.
In a week, maybe two, they'll make you a star.
Weeks turn into years. How quick they pass!
And all the stars that never were
Are parking cars and pumping gas.
...
Fame and fortune is a magnet.
It can pull you far away from home.
With a dream in your heart, you're never alone.
Dreams turn into dust and blow away,
And there you are without a friend.
You pack your car and ride away.
I've got lots of friends in San Jose.
Do you know the way to San Jose?
Can't wait to get back to San Jose.

Don't be denied

...
Well, pretty soon I met a friend,
He played guitar.
We used to sit on the steps at school
And dream of being stars.
We started a band,
We played all night.

Don't be denied, don't be denied
...
The businessmen crowded around.
They came to hear the golden sound.
There we were on the Sunset Strip,
Playing our songs for the highest bid.
We played all night,
The price was right.
...

Neil Young

Do you know any other songs about Hollywood, California or people who want to be stars? Maybe Madonna's *Hollywood*, or *Californication* by the Red Hot Chili Peppers? Bring them to school and present them to the class.

balloon [bə'lu:n] helium ['hi:liəm] (to) shoot [ʃu:t] *schießen* radar ['reɪdɑ:] (to) arrest [ə'rest] *verhaften* magnet ['mægnət] subject *hier: Thema* freeway *AE Autobahn* (to) put a hundred down *100 Dollar anzahlen* (to) turn into *werden zu* (to) pump gas [ˌpʌmp 'gæs] *AE Benzin zapfen* fame [feɪm] *Ruhm* fortune ['fɔ:tʃu:n] *Reichtum* dust [dʌst] *Staub* Don't be denied. [dɪ'naɪd] *Lass dich nicht unterkriegen.* the highest bid *das höchste Gebot*

English Songs

You can hear songs in English like the ones on page 108 everywhere. But how can you understand them better and talk about them? Here are some ideas.

1 You all know some English or American songs. What is your favourite one at the moment? How could you describe it? Think about:
- the sort of music it is,
- how slow/fast it is,
- who the singer/group is,
- where the singer/group is from,
- what the song is about,
- why you like it.

You can use these expressions:

It's a pop/rock/folk/rap/jazz/… song.
It's fast, very slow, … / It changes a lot.
It's by a singer/group/band called …
He's/She's/They're from …
It's a love song. / It's about life in … / …
I like this song because …
 it's beautiful.
 the singer has got a great voice.
 it makes me feel sad/happy/…
 it's great for dancing.

2 Do you remember Nick and Debbie's trip to London in Unit 2? At Covent Garden they heard a group sing the song *You've got a friend*. Look at the parts of the song below – they are in the wrong order. Try and write the letters (A–F) in the correct order in your exercise book. Now listen to the song. Did you get it right?

A You just call out my name,
and you know wherever I am,
I'll come running to see you again.

B When you're down and troubled
and you need some loving care,
and nothing, nothing is going right,

C Keep your head together,
and call my name out loud.
Soon you'll hear me
knocking at your door.

D Close your eyes and think of me
and soon I will be there
to brighten up even your darkest night.

E If the sky above you
grows dark and full of clouds
and that old north wind begins to blow,

F Winter, spring, summer or fall,
all you have to do is call,
and I'll be there.
You've got a friend.

3 Here is part of another song. The last word of every line is missing. Try and complete the lines. Check with your group and with other groups. What do they think? Now give the song a title. Then listen to the song and check. Did you get any of the real words? Is 'your' song or the real song better?

I miss …
but I haven't met you … .
So … –
but it hasn't happened … .
You are …
but I haven't met you … .
I …
but it hasn't happened … .

And if you believe in …
or, what is more …,
that a dream can come …,
I will meet … .

4 Bring some English-language songs to school and listen to them. How can you describe the songs? (Look at 1 for help.) What are the songs about? How do you know? How does each song make you feel? Why does it make you feel like that? Say why you like or don't like the song.

loving care *etwa: liebevolle Zuwendung* Keep your head together. *Versuche, ruhig zu bleiben.* (to) knock [nɒk] *klopfen* (to) brighten up [ˌbraɪtn_ˈʌp] *erhellen* (to) grow *werden*

Do-it-yourself exercises

You don't know all the words on these four pages. But you'll find them in the dictionary (pp. 171–198).

◆◆ *Find your problem areas*

a What problems do you have with English? Look at the chart and make a list.

Vocabulary	Grammar
– Spelling – Prepositions (*at, behind, …*) – How to find the right words – How to explain words – …	– Tenses and verb forms (*goes, went, has gone*) – Word order (*to the big city in July,* etc.) – …

b Swap lists with your partner. Help your partner with his/her problems. Choose exercises from below. Read the instructions, make the exercises and give them to your partner.

1 *Vocabulary: Spelling*

Find an easy text of 50–60 words that you can understand. (You can find one in your book, on the Internet, …) Read it to your partner. Your partner has to write down the text. You can give punctuation in English like this:

.	=	full stop [ˌfʊl 'stɒp]
,	=	comma ['kɒmə]
?	=	question mark ['kwestʃən mɑːk]
!	=	exclamation mark [ˌekskləˈmeɪʃn mɑːk]
‘	=	Open quotation marks. [kwəʊ'teɪʃn mɑːks]
’	=	Close quotation marks.
:	=	colon ['kəʊlən]
;	=	semicolon [ˌsemiˈkəʊlən]

–	=	dash [dæʃ] *Gedankenstrich*
-	=	hyphen ['haɪfn] *Bindestrich*
…	=	three dots *or* dot – dot – dot [dɒt]

Internet & E-mail addresses:

@	=	‘at’-sign ['æt saɪn]
.	=	dot [dɒt]
/	=	forward slash [ˌfɔːwəd 'slæʃ]

Read a group of words, then wait a few seconds (//) before you read the next group:

Most signs are in English – or in both languages. And everyone speaks English, too. → *Most signs are in English (dash) // or in both languages (full stop) // And everyone speaks English (comma) // too (full stop)*

Your partner checks his/her work. Then you read the text again: he/she checks again.

2 *Vocabulary: Explain the words*

Make a list of five things. How many can your partner explain to you in English?
Example: *answering machine* *It's a thing that records phone messages when you are not at home.*

3 *Vocabulary: Spelling/Find the words*

Find words that belong together, for example, *places in town*. Write them down as on the right. Can your partner find all the words?

B	R	H	O	U	S	E	B	U	S	M	A	R	K	E	T
A	C	A	T	H	E	D	R	A	L	H	O	T	E	L	E
N	S	A	P	O	I	W	E	L	Y	T	O	K	H	I	P
K	D	O	G	S	M	U	S	E	U	M	V	P	E	Y	B
F	A	R	M	P	O	P	C	I	T	Y	W	A	L	L	S

4 *Vocabulary/Grammar: Find the words/Grammatical forms*

Find and arrange pairs of words as in the examples below. Leave one word out. Can your partner find it? You can ask for words or for grammatical forms.

fast	slow
good	?

man	men
mouse	?

→

fast	slow
good	*bad*

man	men
mouse	*mice*

5 *Vocabulary/Grammar: Find the words*

a Copy a short text from this book, but leave out some of the words, for example, verb forms or prepositions. You can write these words next to the text – but in the wrong order. Can your partner put them in the right places?

after • against
before • to

Three days … the big match … Llandysul, the Aberaeron coach was talking … the rugby team … training. → Three days *before* the big match *against* Llandysul, the Aberaeron coach was talking *to* the rugby team *after* training.

b You can also take out every fourth or fifth word. Can your partner fill in the missing words?

Three days before … big match against …, the Aberaeron coach … talking to the … team after training. → Three days before *the* big match against *Llandysul*, the Aberaeron coach *was* talking to the *rugby* team after training.

6 *Grammar: Verb forms*

Copy a short text from this book. For each verb, write the infinitive of that verb in brackets. Can your partner fill in the right verb forms? The list of irregular verbs on pages 203/203 will help you.

'Rubbish!'(say) David as he (throw) the magazine away. 'I (like) sport, but I (not be) a freak!'

↓

'Rubbish!' *said* David as he *threw* the magazine away. 'I *like* sport, but *I'm not* a freak!'

'Somewhere with no irregular verbs.'

7 *Grammar: Word order*

Find sentences and write them with words and phrases in the wrong order. Can your partner write down the sentences correctly?

everything else / forget about / on Saturday / if you want to win → *Forget about everything else if you want to win on Saturday.*

and play with dolphins / on our free day / to Ramsey Island / we take a boat trip / where we see seals → *On our free day we take a boat trip to Ramsey Island where we see seals and play with dolphins.*

and / speaks English / too / everyone → *And everyone speaks English, too.*

8 *Grammar: Word order*

Copy the chart. Can your partner add five sentences like this?

subject	*adverb*	*verb*	*object*	*place*	*time*
I	*often*	*play*	*football*	*at school*	*on Mondays.*
…	…	…	…	…	…

Practise your tenses → S 1: 1 (p. 122)

1 ***Keypals?*** *Simple present* **(After Unit 1)**

a These kids are looking for e-mail penfriends – keypals. Choose the right forms of the verbs from the list in the middle and complete their messages.

Samantha USA
Hi!! I ... 13. I ... a lot of things. I ... soccer, ... my bike, and ... to the mall. I ... a keypal who ... sports and ... from a different country. See ya all!

Jake U.K.
Hi I ... Jake, I would like to be friends with someone who ... Harry Potter and books like that. But I ... my eye on a special girl at school, so I ... a girlfriend. See ya Jake!!!!

be (4x)
come (2x)
do
go
have
like
live
love
(not) need
play
read
ride
speak
want (4x)
write

Fabienne GERMANY
Hey!!! I ... a crazy girl from Germany and I ... some new friends from all over the world. I ... 3 languages: German, French and English, and I ... to practise them all. Please ... to me!!! xxx Fab

Urs CANADA
I ... from Switzerland but I ... in Canada. I ... tall with brown hair and blue eyes. I ... sports and I ... a nice girl as a keypal. Luv Ya Urs

b Write your own keypal message.

2 ***A letter from London***
Mixed tenses **(After Unit 2)**
Complete this Australian girl's letter with the right verbs from the list in the correct tenses.

arrive • be (4x) • call • go (2x)
have (2x) • hope • live • love • say • see
stay • take (2x) • visit • wear

Dear Grandma,
We ... a great flight from Sydney and ... in London three days ago. I already ... the place. We ... at a lovely hotel in Kensington. My room ... a view over a beautiful square of really old houses. The guy downstairs ... they ... more than 200 years old.
Yesterday we ... to a lot of the famous sights.
We ... Buckingham Palace where the Queen ... .
I ... Lord Nelson at Trafalgar Square and we ... the tube – that ... what they ... the underground in London – to the Tower of London. It ... a castle full of guys who ... red uniforms.
Tomorrow we ... the bus to Hyde Park and ... to a show in the evening.
I ... you and grandpa ... fine.
Love, Cindy

3 ***Say it in English***
Mixed tenses **(After Unit 2)**
Now imagine you are in London. You want to write a letter or an e-mail to an American keypal. Here is what you want to say – how can you say it in English?

Dear ...
Schreibe, dass du seit drei Tagen in London bist und dass die Stadt dir sehr gut gefällt. Du hast schon viel gesehen und bleibst noch zwei weitere Tage.
Sage, dass du am Samstag nach München zurückfliegst.
Schreibe, dass du gerade den Tower of London besucht hast. Es war sehr spannend.
Erkläre, dass du mit dem Boot dort hingefahren bist, die Themse entlang. Die Fahrt dauerte 40 Minuten.
Sage, dass du heute Abend ins Theater gehst – ein Musical. Deine Eltern haben die Karten heute am Leicester Square gekauft. Sie waren dort sehr billig.

Verabschiede dich und beende den Brief.

4 *What were the Watts doing …?* *Past progressive/Simple past* **(After Unit 3)**

a The lights went out at the Watts' house last night. What were they doing when it happened?

Mrs Watts

Dale Watts

Macie Watts

Mr Watts

Grandma Watts

b Say what you were doing yesterday:
– when the street lights came on – when the news on TV started – at 10 pm – …

5 *Michael's plans*

The going to*-future* **(After Unit 4)**

a What's Michael *going to* do on Saturday?

b What about you? What are your plans?

6 *The weather* *The* will*-future* **(After Unit 5)**

Explain what the weather will be like in Anchorage in the next few days.
Here's some help:

It will be (partly) cloudy …
There will be …
Temperatures will be between …

Anchorage, Alaska, Vereinigte Staaten		Max (C)	Min (C)
Fr 16 Jan	Leicht bewölkt	-4 °C	-11 °C
Sa 17 Jan	Bewölkt	-1 °C	-9 °C
So 18 Jan	Bewölkt	1 °C	-6 °C
Mo 19 Jan	Regen/Schneeschauer	-4 °C	-11 °C

7 *Holidays*

Present perfect/Simple past **(After Unit 6)**

a What did these people write about their holidays? Choose the right tenses.

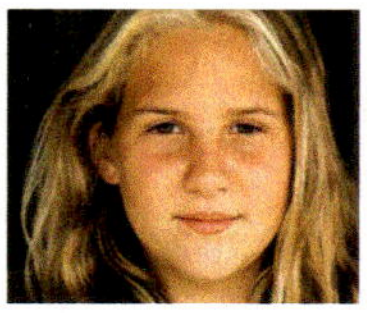

We *have arrived/arrived* in Los Angeles ten hours ago after a 12-hour flight. I'm still up, so it *has been/was* a very long day. We *have checked/checked* in to our motel quickly and then *have taken/took* a taxi to Hollywood and *have walked/walked* along Hollywood Boulevard. We *have seen/saw* all the stars' names. I *have never been/never was* so excited in my life. After dinner we *have been/went* for a walk on the beach and I *have swum/swam* in the Pacific Ocean. The water *has been/was* quite cold. Mum and Dad *have already gone/already went* to bed and Tori *has fallen/fell* asleep an hour ago. Time for bed for me now, too.

I *have hated/hated* every minute of this trip and it still *hasn't finished/didn't finish.* This is the 8th time we *have stayed/stayed* in this old Welsh farmhouse. As usual, we *have visited/visited* Mum's crazy aunt as soon as we *have arrived/arrived*. She *has given/gave* us leek and potato pie for dinner – that is the only thing she *has ever cooked/ever cooked* for us. Last year the weather *has been/was* beautiful so we *have been/were* able to go to the beach every day. But this year it *has rained/rained* almost every day so we *have stayed/stayed* at home all the time, without a TV, without a computer. Ugh!

b Write about your last holiday.

After Unit 1

Erinnere dich an die Sätze und Wendungen aus deinem Englischbuch, wenn du dich auf Englisch unterhältst. Versuche, „Englisch zu denken", anstatt im Kopf vom Deutschen ins Englische zu übersetzen.

1 Say it in English: An interview with Lance Armstrong

a Imagine you are doing an interview with the famous cyclist Lance Armstrong. Find the questions. Be careful with the tenses. Here's what you want to know:

1 Wann hat er sein erstes internationales Rennen gewonnen?
When did you win ... ?
2 Wie lange ist er schon beim USPS team (United States Postal Service)?
3 Wie viele Kilometer trainiert er jeden Tag?
4 Wie oft hat er die Tour de France gewonnen?
5 Was macht die *Lance Armstrong Foundation*?
6 Wie vielen Menschen hat die *Lance Armstrong Foundation* geholfen?
7 Was sind seine Pläne für die Zukunft?

b Try and find the answers to your questions on the Internet. Report back to the class.

2 Interpreting: A bike tour

You're planning a bike tour in Wales with your parents. On the phone you get the following information about the tour. What do you tell your parents?

Beim Dolmetschen kommt es darauf an, das Wichtigste in die andere Sprache zu übertragen. Du solltest nicht versuchen, Wort für Wort zu übersetzen.

1 'Most people bring their own bikes, but you can get one from us if you let us know before the tour starts.'
2 'If you can ride 30 miles a day, you'll be all right.'
3 'Yes, it is cheaper if you're 12 or under. Then you get a 20% discount.'
4 'All the food is vegetarian. Breakfast and dinner are in the price of the tour, but you have to buy your own lunch.'
5 'No, we're not doing a Snowdonia trip in August. Only in July and September.'

3 Say it in German: Holiday Cottages[1] in West Wales

Your parents are also thinking of booking a holiday apartment and doing day trips. You have found this advert on the Internet. Tell your parents about it. Don't worry about unknown words but just give the most important information in German.

Get away from it all at Holiday Cottages in West Wales

- Coastal location near Cardigan in West Wales, just five minutes from the beach.
- Magnificent countryside, some of the finest beaches and Britain's only Marine Heritage Coast, providing a haven for dolphins, seabirds and seals.
- The cottages are well placed to explore the local area of west Wales, Cardigan Bay, the Pembrokeshire Coastal Path and National Park – ideal for active visitors to explore Wales by bike.
- The holiday cottages are at the end of a road where there is no through traffic making it ideal for children to play safely.
- Five cottages available, sleeping two, four, six and eight.
- The cottages are very modern, of a high standard and with everything you need.
- Every cottage has a large decking area with seating to enjoy the fresh air and sunshine.

[1] cottage ['kɒtɪdʒ] *kleines Landhaus*

After Unit 3

1 *Say it in English: A little bit of history*

a A tour guide in Regensburg is showing some visitors the *Steinerne Brücke* across the Danube River. Listen to what she tells them and take notes on the important facts.

b Imagine the guide had to show the *Steinerne Brücke* to some foreign visitors. How could she tell them about it in English? Use your notes from a and write the English tour. You might want to look up[1] these words in a dictionary first:

Baumeister • Bischof • Hahn • Henne
jagen • Kurve • Legende • Seele
Steinfigur • Teufel • (Wasser-)Strudel

c Think of a historic[2] place in your area. What could you tell English-speaking visitors about it?

2 *Interpreting: Vindolanda*

a You're on a visit to Vindolanda at Hadrian's Wall. Your sister has lots of questions. How can you ask the guide in English? Here's what your sister wants to know:

1 Kannst du ihn fragen, wie die Römer das kalte Wetter in Großbritannien ertragen haben?
2 Und frag ihn, wie lang Hadrians Wall war.
3 Und warum Hadrian ihn gebaut hat.
4 Und ob die Soldaten auf dem Wall nicht unheimlich einsam waren.
5 Frag ihn auch mal, was man Wichtiges in Vindolanda gefunden hat.

b Listen to the guide's answers. Take notes. Now use your notes and interpret the answers for your sister.

c You're looking at one of the writing tablets. Can you tell your sister what it is about?

To Sulpicia Lepidina, wife of Cerialis, from Severa.

Greetings, Lepidina, from Claudia Severa.
On 11 September, sister, for the day of the celebration of my birthday, I give you a warm invitation to make sure that you come to us, to make the day more enjoyable for me by your arrival, if you are present. Give my greetings to your Cerialis. My Aelius and my little son send him their greetings. I shall expect you, sister. Farewell, sister, my dearest soul.

3 *English and German are not the same: Hadrian's Wall*

Can you express this in English?

A An deiner Stelle würde ich zum Hadrians Wall fahren.
B Wenn er nicht so weit weg wäre, würde ich gern Hadrians Wall besuchen. Aber wenn ich das auch noch machen würde, hätte ich keine Zeit mehr für London.
A Das stimmt, ich würde auch mehr Zeit in London verbringen wollen.

[1] (to) look up *nachschlagen* [2] historic [hɪˈstɒrɪk] [3] (to) catch [kætʃ], caught, caught [kɔːt] *(ein)fangen*

After Unit 5

1 Say it in English: Chat on whales

In a chat room, some kids are talking about whales and whaling. You want to say these things in English – how do you do it? Don't try to translate word for word. Just put the main points into English.

- Hab im letzten Jahr zum ersten Mal in Kalifornien Wale gesehen.
  Es waren Blauwale, Grauwale und Tausende von Delfinen.
  Die Delfine sprangen in die Luft and schwammen um, unter und vor das Boot.
  Das war genial, das Schönste, was ich je gesehen habe.
- Welche Länder machen noch Walfang?
  Wie kann man bloß Wale töten? Das finde ich absolut schrecklich.
  Wir sollten alle E-Mails an ihre Regierungen[1] schicken und schreiben, dass wir das furchtbar finden.
- Wisst ihr, wo man mehr über Wale erfahren kann? Coole Webseiten?

2 Interpreting: Whale stranding

Look at this report. How could you tell someone who doesn't understand much English what the main points are? Here's some help:

- Wie viele Wale strandeten und wo?
- Wie viele starben, wie viele wurden gerettet?
- Rettungsmaßnahmen?
- Wie oft passiert so etwas? Aus welchem Grund?

***159 pilot whales** were stranded on Stewart Island, New Zealand yesterday. By nightfall half of them were dead.*

About 30 volunteers and 20 Department of Conservation (DOC) workers tried to keep the whales alive. The whales were covered in sheets and kept wet. Volunteer Shirley Whyte said last night 39 whales had been rescued and had swum out to sea.

DOC manager Andy Cox said strandings were common for pilot whales and that there were two main reasons. "A lot of strandings happen when the whales have navigation problems. Or a sick whale will strand and the rest will follow it in."

3 English and German are not the same: Whale Rider

Listen to this extract from the film *Whale Rider* and translate it into German. You can use a dictionary. Be careful with the underlined phrases. Then listen to the German film version on the CD and compare it with your version. Where is it different? Why?

Paikea Everyone was waiting for the first-born boy to lead us. But he died. And I didn't.

(After Paikea's birth at the hospital)

Koro Where's the boy? Son. What's done is done. Come home.
Come home. Start again.
Koro's son What do you mean? Pretend it didn't happen?
Koro That's not what I'm saying.
Koro's son You didn't even look at her, dad.
She died.
Koro Son …
Koro's son No. No. No. No, all you want is your boy.

The film tells the story of Paikea, a young girl from New Zealand. She was named after a famous hero of her people, who rode on the back of a whale a thousand years ago. When Paikea was born, her mother and her twin brother died. Her grandfather Koro had wanted a boy as a future leader.

Koro It's all right.
Koro's son That's all you want, isn't it?
Koro You can start again.
Koro's son No, I've got a child. Her name's Paikea.
Koro What?
Koro's son You heard me.
Koro No. Not that name.
Koro's son It's Paikea.
Koro No!
…
Paikea My Koro wished in his heart that I had never been born. But he changed his mind.

[1] governments ['gʌvənmənts]

After Unit 6

1 *Interpreting: Hearst Castle to Monterey*

You're going on a bus tour in California with your parents and grandmother. Your grandmother has some questions for the bus tour guide. Can you help her?

Grandmother	Wohin fahren wir heute?
You	Where are we …
Tour Guide	We're going to visit Hearst Castle first.
You	Wir besuchen zuerst …
Grandmother	Castle? Das ist ein Schloss, oder? Gibt's denn Schlösser hier?
You	…
Tour Guide	Sure is a castle and really beautiful, too. Up on a hill. You'll see.
You	…
Grandmother	Klingt schön!
Tour Guide	Then we'll drive on up Highway One to Big Sur, where we'll take a walk to a waterfall in Julia Pfeiffer Burns State Park.
You	…
Grandmother	Wie weit müssen wir da laufen?
You	…
Tour Guide	Oh, just five or ten minutes. And it's all on the flat. No hills.
You	…
Tour Guide	Then we have a break and a meal at Nepenthe Restaurant. It has the most spectacular views of the ocean.
You	…
Grandmother	Ja, davon habe ich gelesen.
Tour Guide	And after that we continue on to Monterey. That's where we're staying tonight, at the Doubletree Hotel right in the centre of Old Monterey.
You	…
Grandmother	Das wird aber ein langer Tag!

2 *Say it in German: Julia Pfeiffer Burns State Park*

Your guide has given you this leaflet. Tell your grandmother about the park. Don't worry about unknown words but just give the most important facts in German: Where it is, what it is like, what you can do there, when it is open and what weather you can expect.

California State Parks

This state park is named after Julia Pfeiffer Burns, a well respected pioneer woman in the Big Sur country. The park stretches from the Big Sur coastline into nearby 3,000-foot mountains. Its main attraction is an 80-foot waterfall that drops from granite cliffs into the ocean. A panoramic view of the ocean and miles of rugged coastline is available from the higher elevations along the trails east of Highway 1.

Activities

Whale Watching: In December and January the bench at the end of the Overlook trail is an excellent place to watch for gray whales migrating southward to their breeding grounds. In March and April, they can be seen returning north to their summer feeding grounds in the North Pacific.
Sea otters can sometimes be seen, too, and harbor seals and California sea lions are occasional visitors. Many sea and shore birds – black cormorants, seagulls, brown pelicans, and black oystercatchers – also make an appearance.
Underwater Area: Between Partington Point and McWay Creek is the Julia Pfeiffer Burns Underwater Area, which was established in 1970 and is now a scuba diving area.

Location-Directions

The park is 37 miles south of Carmel on Highway 1, and 12 miles south of Pfeiffer Big Sur.

Climate/Recommended Clothing

The weather can be changeable. Warm clothing is advised.

Operating Hours

Open 1/2 hour before sunrise to 1/2 hour after sunset.

Unit 1

Sports Freak or Couch Potato – Which Are You? (p. 8)

Your score

1 A = 1; B = 3; C = 5
2 A = 0; B = 3; C = 5
3 A = 3; B = 5; C = 0
4 A = 0; B = 5; C = 0
5 A = 5; B = 3; C = 0
6 A = 0; B = 5; C = 0
7 A = 0; B = 0; C = 5
8 1 point for each correct answer:
A = Basketball;
B = Football;
C = Rugby;
D = American football

10 points or less
You're a couch potato. You spend too much time at home in front of the TV. Go out and do some sport. It's healthy, and you'll feel better, too.

11 to 29 points
You have a healthy attitude towards sport and exercise.

30 points or more
You're a real sports freak. But too much sport isn't always good for you. You should relax sometimes, too – it's healthier!

6 *They aren't from Aberaeron* (p. 15)

a Look at the chart. Not everyone in David's rugby team comes from Aberaeron. Some information about Mark, Colin, Thomas and Craig is missing. Ask your partner 'How long ...?' and answer his/her questions.

A How long has Mark lived in Aberaeron?
B For three months.
How long has Colin ...?
A ...

	Mark	Colin	Thomas	Craig
live in Aberaeron	3 months	?	?	6 years
play rugby	?	2 years	4 years ago	?
be in the Aberaeron team	?	last year	?	5 years
know his/her best friend	?	?	3 years	half a year

b Now write about two players in David's rugby team. Example:

Mark has lived in Aberaeron for three months.
He has played rugby since ...

Unit 2

6 *Revision: After the trip* (p. 30)

You've just been on a school trip to London. Look at the picture of things you brought with you and answer your partner's questions. Use *a little / a few / a lot / not … any*. Then ask your partner about the things in the list on the right. (Your partner has got a different picture.)

London T-shirts
marmalade
English DVDs
brochures
posters
English chocolate

A Did you bring any London T-shirts with you?
B Yes, … / No, …

B Did you bring any photos with you?
A Yes, I brought a few / a lot.
or: No, I didn't bring any.

Unit 3

9 *Just imagine!* (p. 47)

a Answer your partner's questions and give reasons for your answers. Then ask your partner these questions and write down what he/she answers.

1. If you could be anywhere in the world tomorrow, where would you like to be?
2. If you could be a famous person for a day, who would you like to be?
3. If you could live at another time in history, when would you like to live?

b Now think of one more question for your partner.

Unit 4

1 *Florida and the USA* (p. 63)

a Look at the table below. The USA information is missing, but your partner has it. Answer your partner's questions about Florida and ask him/her questions about the USA.

	Florida	USA
capital	Tallahassee	?
size	140,000 square km	?
population	17 million	?
Hispanics	c. 3 million (= 18%)	?
national bird	mockingbird 	?

A What's the capital of Florida?
A It's …
What's the capital of the USA?
A It's …
How big is …?
A It's …
How big is …?

b Write down what you have found out about the USA. You can put the information about the USA and Florida in your US album.

c Make a table like this for Germany. Compare the facts for Germany with the facts you have for the USA.

Unit 5

10 *Activity* (p. 79)

Listen to what your partner tells you about the caribou in Denali National Park and take notes. Then read your information about the caribou, close your book and tell your partner what you know about it. Exchange your information on the other three animals, too.
Use your information and notes and write about one of the animals in your US album.

Some animals of **Denali**

Caribou

Moose

Grizzly bear

Wolf

Caribou travel in groups, but the numbers of the Denali herd have changed a lot in the last 30 years. Today groups of 20 or more may be seen from the park road. Years ago it was thousands.

Moose are not herd animals. Bulls may live alone or in groups of three or four. The young are born in spring. At this time of year, be careful. A moose that is protecting its young can be very dangerous.

Grizzly bears are seen all over the park. Mothers usually have two young, sometimes one or three. They are very dangerous when they are protecting their young.

Wolves are not seen often. In winter, they usually hunt in packs but they can be seen alone, too. If you see a wolf, you're a very lucky person.

Unit 6

3 *Activity* (p. 92)

a You and your partner have got different information about Bodie State Historic Park. Answer your partner's questions. Then ask him/her these questions and take notes on the answers.

1 What was the exact date of the discovery of gold in California?
2 What was the special name for the people who came to California in 1849?
3 How many people lived in Bodie?
4 How many of the town's old buildings are still there?

b Now use all the information you have and write a short German text for a brochure on Bodie.

Bodie State Historic Park

When James Marshall found gold in California in 1848, he started the gold rush. The greatest numbers of people came in 1849. It was ten years later that somebody found gold in Bodie, and it soon became a busy gold-mining town. In 1882, when there was no more gold, everybody left. Fires destroyed a lot of the town. Then Bodie was left to itself until it became a State Historic Park in 1962.

1 *California or Germany – which is bigger?* (p. 96)

	California	Germany
size	411,060 square km	356,733 square km
position[1]	c. 32°– 42° N[2]	c. 47°–55° N
population	c. 35.5 million	c. 82.5 million
kilometres of coast	2222 km	1975 km
highest mountain	Mount Whitney (4418 m)	Zugspitze (2962 m)
movies made per year	440	84

[1] position [pəˈzɪʃn] *Lage* [2] 32°– 42° N = 32 to 42 degrees north *32 bis 42 Grad nördlicher Breite*

5 *Each other or themselves?* (p. 97)

Look at these pictures. You and your partner have the same pictures, but in a different order. Tell your partner about your pictures and write down the order of your partner's pictures.

A In my picture 1, two kids are taking photos of each other.
B Oh, that's my picture 6. In *my* picture 1, a girl and a boy are thinking …

1

think about

2

think about

3

laugh at

4

take photos of

5

laugh at

6

take photos of

▮ Die folgenden *LANGUAGE SUMMARY*-Seiten geben einen Überblick über das, was du in den Units dieses Buches gelernt oder wiederholt hast.

▮ Links stehen grammatische Regeln und Hinweise sowie Lerntipps und Merkkästen. Rechts stehen Beispiele und Übersichten. Warndreiecke (⚠) weisen auf Fehlerquellen und wichtige Regeln hin.

▮ Ein Hinweis wie → **P 1–3 (p. 14)** bedeutet, dass zu diesem Abschnitt die Übungen 1–3 von Seite 14 gehören.

▮ Die mit **REMEMBER** gekennzeichneten Stellen enthalten Stoff, den du bereits kennst und an den du dich erinnern solltest.

▮ Zwischendurch findest du immer wieder kurze englische Zusammenfassungen der wichtigsten Regeln, damit du auch auf Englisch über die neue Grammatik sprechen kannst.

▮ Am Ende jeder Unit zeigt eine kleine Übersicht, was du schon auf Englisch ausdrücken kannst („In Unit 1 hast du gelernt …“).

▮ Und wenn du Probleme mit grammatischen Begriffen hast, kannst du in der Liste auf den Seiten 200–201 nachschauen.

WICHTIG! LERNEN! 

Unit 1

1 *Wiederholung: Die Zeitformen der Verben*	***Revision: The tenses of the verbs***
Die einfache Form der Gegenwart Wenn etwas **regelmäßig**, immer, oft oder nie geschieht.	***The simple present*** My parents **watch** TV every evening. **Does** it often **rain** here in the summer?
Die Verlaufsform der Gegenwart – Wenn etwas gerade **im Verlauf** und noch nicht abgeschlossen ist. – Wenn etwas für die Zukunft **fest geplant** oder **verabredet** ist.	***The present progressive*** What **are** the Porters **doing**? – They**'re watching** TV. Look, we can't play outside. It**'s raining**. What **are** you **doing** tomorrow? – I**'m visiting** my aunt. We**'re flying** to Spain on Saturday.
Das present perfect Wenn man sagen will, **dass** (nicht: wann!) etwas geschehen ist. Oft hat das Geschehen Auswirkungen auf die Gegenwart.	***The present perfect*** Sue **has broken** her leg. She can't go to the disco. **Have** you **listened** to your new CDs yet? David **has** just **gone** shopping.
Die einfache Form der Vergangenheit Wenn man sagt, **wann** etwas geschah.	***The simple past*** Sue **broke** her leg when she **fell** off her bike yesterday. **Did** you **listen** to your new CDs last night? David has gone shopping. He **left** five minutes ago.
Die Verlaufsform der Vergangenheit Wenn etwas zu einer bestimmten Zeit in der Vergangenheit gerade **im Verlauf** war.	***The past progressive*** What **were** you **doing** at 10 o'clock last night? Tom **was watching** TV when suddenly the lights went out.
***Das Futur mit* will** Wenn man **Vermutungen** über die Zukunft äußert oder **Vorhersagen** macht.	***The will-future*** The weather **will be** fine tomorrow. I don't think you**'ll like** it at Tony's party.
***Das Futur mit* going to** Wenn man **Absichten** oder **Pläne** beschreibt.	***The going to-future*** We**'re going to have** a party next weekend. What **are** you **going to do** tonight? → **P 1–3 (p. 14)**

2 *Das present perfect mit* since *und* for

a Das *present perfect* kann verwendet werden, um über **Zustände** zu sprechen, die in der Vergangenheit begonnen haben und in der Gegenwart noch andauern.

⚠ Im Deutschen wird in diesen Fällen meist das Präsens verwendet. Aber in den englischen Sätzen muss das *present perfect* stehen.

The present perfect with since and for

They**'ve lived** in Wales since last summer.
Sie leben seit dem letzten Sommer in Wales.

Tim's mother **has been** out of work since May last year.
Tims Mutter ist seit Mai letzten Jahres arbeitslos.

We**'ve had** this car for six years.
Wir haben dieses Auto seit sechs Jahren.

Wales **has not won** a football match against England for many years.
Wales hat seit vielen Jahren kein Fußballspiel mehr gegen England gewonnen.

Es gibt zwei Möglichkeiten zu sagen, seit wann oder wie lange ein Zustand schon andauert:

– Man verwendet ***since*** mit dem *present perfect*, wenn man sagen will, **wann** der Zustand begonnen hat, wenn man also einen **Zeitpunkt** nennt *(since 1996, since April, since last year)*.

***since* + Zeitpunkt**

My mother **has been** a teacher | **since 1996.** / **since April.** / **since last year.**

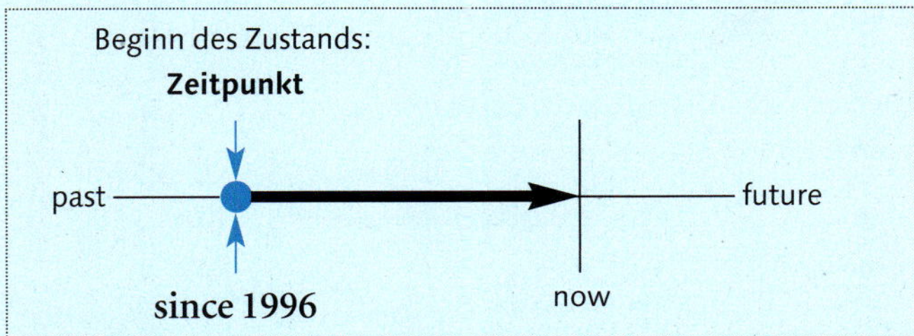

– Man verwendet ***for*** mit dem *present perfect*, wenn man sagen will, **wie lange** der Zustand schon andauert, wenn man also einen **Zeitraum** nennt *(for three months, for years, for a long time)*.

***for* + Zeitraum**

My mother **has been** a teacher | **for three months.** / **for years.** / **for a long time.**

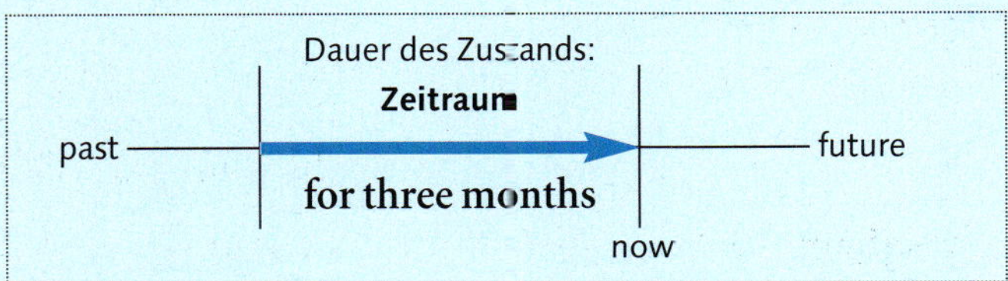

Wenn man danach fragen will, seit wann oder wie lange ein Zustand schon andauert, lautet die Frage ***How long ...?*** + *present perfect*. Darauf kann man mit *since* + Zeitpunkt oder *for* + Zeitraum antworten.

How long have they **lived** in Wales?
– Since last month. / – For a few weeks.
Wie lange / Seit wann wohnen sie (schon) in Wales?
– Seit letztem Monat. / – Seit ein paar Wochen.

b since + *Nebensatz*

Zur Angabe des Zeitpunktes kann nach *since* entweder ein **Nomen** *(Sunday; 1998)* oder ein **Satz im *simple past*** *(he left; I was a child)* stehen.

since + *sub-clause*

We haven't seen Mark	since Sunday.	seit Sonntag
	since he left.	seit er gegangen ist
I've lived here	since 1998.	seit 1998
	since I was a child.	seit ich ein Kind war

→ P 4–6 (p. 15)

In English:
***The present perfect with* since *and* for**

[1]state *Zustand* [2]up to the present *bis in die Gegenwart* [3](to) last *(an)dauern*

1 We use the present perfect to describe a state[1] or situation that started in the past and has gone on up to the present[2].
2 We use ***since*** with the present perfect to say **when** the situation started (= a point of time).
3 We use ***for*** with the present perfect to say **how long** the situation has lasted[3] (= a period of time).

3 *Die Verlaufsform des present perfect*

a *Gebrauch*

Mit dem *present perfect progressive* drückt man aus, dass eine **Handlung** oder ein **Vorgang** in der Vergangenheit begonnen hat und bis (oder fast bis) in die Gegenwart andauert.

⚠ Auch in diesen Fällen benutzt man im Deutschen meist das Präsens. Aber in den englischen Sätzen muss das *present perfect progressive* stehen.

The present perfect progressive

Use

The kids have been playing football since two o'clock.
Die Kinder spielen (schon) seit zwei Uhr Fußball.
(Die Kinder haben um zwei Uhr mit dem Fußballspielen begonnen und spielen jetzt, d.h. zum Zeitpunkt des Sprechens, immer noch.)

You've been driving for three hours. Shall I drive now?
Du fährst schon seit drei Stunden. …
How long has it been raining? – Since lunch.
Wie lange regnet es schon? – Seit dem Mittagessen.

What have you been doing, dear? – I've been making lunch, Mum.
Was hast du gemacht, Schatz? – Ich habe das Mittagessen gekocht, Mama.

b *Form*

Das *present perfect progressive* wird mit *have/has been* + *-ing*-Form gebildet.

Form

Statements:	I/You/We/They have been / He/She has been	reading all day.
	I/You/We/They haven't been / He/She hasn't been	playing.
Questions:	Have I/you/we/they been / Has he/she been	watching TV?

c Verben, die **Zustände** beschreiben, können nicht in der *progressive form* verwendet werden. Solche Verben sind z.B. *know, like, need*.

How long have you known David?

Nicht: How long ~~have you been knowing~~ David?

→ P 7, 8 (p. 16)

In English:
The present perfect progressive

1 We form the present perfect progressive with *have/has been* + *-ing* form.
2 We use the present perfect progressive to say that an action began in the past and is still going on (or has only just ended).

In Unit 1 hast du gelernt ...

- über Spielregeln zu sprechen.
  ▶ Players must kick the ball over the goalposts.
- Landschaften zu beschreiben.
  ▶ My part of Germany has lots of small lakes.
- zu sagen, ob und wann jemand etwas getan hat.
  ▶ I've been to Florida. We went there last summer.
- zu sagen, seit wann oder wie lange ein Zustand oder ein Vorgang bereits andauert.
  ▶ I've known Jennifer since 1999.
  Marie and I have been friends for many years.
  I've been watching television since I came home.
  Mr Porter has been waiting for two hours.

Unit 2

1 *Das Passiv*

a *Aktiv und Passiv*

Man kann einen Vorgang oder eine Handlung mit einem Aktivsatz oder mit einem Passivsatz beschreiben:

Mit einem **Aktivsatz** sagt man, wer oder was etwas **tut**.

The passive
Active and passive

Active: In 1802, Marie Tussaud took her wax figures to Great Britain.
Im Aktivsatz führt das Subjekt die Handlung aus:
Im Jahre 1802 brachte Marie Tussaud ihre Wachsfiguren nach Großbritannien.

Bei einem **Passivsatz** liegt die Betonung darauf, mit wem oder womit etwas **getan wird**.

Passive: The famous wax show was taken to Great Britain in 1802.
Im Passivsatz wird mit dem Subjekt etwas getan:
Die berühmte Wachsausstellung wurde 1802 nach Großbritannien gebracht.

b *Form*
Man bildet das Passiv mit einer **Form von *be* + Partizip Perfekt** *(past participle)*.
Also:

- ***Simple present passive:***
  am/is/are + Partizip Perfekt
- ***Simple past passive:***
  was/were + past participle
- ***Present perfect passive:***
  have been/has been + past participle

Passiv: Form von *be* + *past participle*

Für die Verwendung der Zeitformen im Passiv gelten dieselben Regeln wie im Aktiv.

Form

		Form of *be*	Past participle	
Simple present:	Our dog	is	fed	at six.
	Unser Hund wird um sechs gefüttert.			
	Lots of bikes	are	stolen	here.
	Hier werden viele Räder gestohlen.			
Simple past:	The match	was	shown	on TV.
	Das Spiel wurde im Fernsehen gezeigt.			
Present perfect:	The money	has not been	found	yet.
	Das Geld ist noch nicht gefunden worden. / Man hat das Geld noch nicht gefunden.			

→ P 2, 3 (p. 29)

⚠ Eine zum Verb gehörende Präposition steht an derselben Stelle wie im Aktivsatz, d.h. **hinter dem Verb**.

This problem was talked about all night.
Über dieses Problem wurde die ganze Nacht geredet.
Vergleiche: We talked about this problem. (Aktiv)

c *Das Passiv nach* will *und nach modalen Hilfsverben*
In Passivsätzen mit Hilfsverben (z.B. *will, can, must, should*) folgt auf das Hilfsverb der **Infinitiv *be* + Partizip Perfekt** *(be built, be bought, be left)*.

The passive after* will *and modal auxiliaries

***will*-future:** A new road will be built soon.
Bald wird eine neue Straße gebaut (werden).

Modal auxiliaries: Stamps cannot be bought here.
Briefmarken können hier nicht gekauft werden. / Man kann hier keine Briefmarken kaufen.
Hats and coats should be left at the door.
Hüte und Mäntel sollten am Eingang abgegeben werden. / ... sollte man am Eingang abgeben.

→ P 9–11 (pp. 31/32)

d *Gebrauch*
Mit einem Passivsatz kann man eine Handlung beschreiben, ohne zu sagen, wer sie ausführt. Das Passiv steht daher z.B. oft in Berichten über Unfälle oder Verbrechen sowie in historischen Berichten oder technischen Beschreibungen.

Use
Two men were killed in a road accident near Chester. Seven people were badly hurt and had to be taken to hospital.
Some of the masks at Madame Tussaud's were made in the French Revolution.
Covent Garden was planned and built without a roof. The metal and glass roofs were added 45 years later.

Wenn man in einem Passivsatz hervorheben will, **von wem** etwas getan wird oder **wodurch** etwas geschieht, verwendet man die Präposition *by*.

The Kingsway pupils **were picked up** by a tourist guide.
... von einem Fremdenführer ...

The restaurant **was destroyed** by fire.
... durch einen Brand ...

→ P 5, 7 (pp. 30/31)

In English:
The passive

1 The passive is formed with a form of *be* + past participle.
2 The passive is used to say what is done to people or things. Often we do not say who does the action.
3 In a passive sentence, *by* is used when we want to say who does the action.

2 *Wiederholung: Mengenbezeichnungen mit zählbaren und nicht zählbaren Nomen*

Revision:
Quantifiers with countable and uncountable nouns

- ***much*** („viel") + nicht zählbares Nomen; ***many*** („viele") + zählbares Nomen im Plural.
- ***a little*** („ein bisschen, (ein) wenig") + nicht zählbares Nomen; ***a few*** („ein paar, einige") + zählbares Nomen im Plural.
- ***lots of / a lot of / some / any*** + nicht zählbares Nomen oder + zählbares Nomen im Plural.

Nicht zählbare Nomen	Plural von zählbaren Nomen
How much **money** have you got? – Not much.	How many **T-shirts** did you buy? – Not many.
I've got a little **money**. I've got a little **time**. I've got a little **homework**.	I've got a few **pounds**. I've got a few **minutes**. I've got to do a few **exercises**.
Tim has got a lot of **money**. Debbie hasn't got any **homework**.	Tim has got a lot of **pounds**. Debbie hasn't got to do any **exercises**.

→ P 6 (p. 30)

In Unit 2 hast du gelernt ...

- über öffentliche Verkehrsmittel und Verkehrsverbindungen zu sprechen.
  ▶ What's the best route to Eaton Square?
  – Take the number 4 bus to Oak Street, then get off and change to the number 19.
- zu sagen, was gemacht wird oder wurde oder was jemandem passiert ist.
  ▶ I'm driven to school every day.
  The school was built last year.
  I've been robbed.
- zu sagen, von wem etwas gemacht wird oder wurde.
  ▶ Madame Tussaud's is visited by two million people every year.
  Tom Sawyer was written by Mark Twain.
- Empfehlungen zu geben.
  ▶ A new swimming-pool should be built.

Unit 3

1 *Das Stützwort* one/ones

Wenn man ein schon genanntes (zählbares) Nomen nicht wiederholen will, verwendet man die „Stützwörter" *one* (Singular) bzw. *ones* (Plural).

Man nennt *one/ones* „Stützwörter", weil im Englischen Adjektive (z.B. *white*) und der bestimmte Artikel ohne diese „Stützen" nicht allein stehen können.

⚠ Also nicht:

I like those horses – ~~the browns~~ look nice.

Sondern:

I like those horses – the brown ones look nice.

(… – die braunen sehen nett aus.)

The prop-word one/ones

I've got two rabbits – **a white** one and **a brown** one.
… ein weißes und ein braunes.

I like all dogs, but I like **little** ones best.
… mir gefallen kleine am besten.

This boutique isn't as good as **the** one in our street.
… wie die in unserer Straße.

→ P 3, 4 (p. 45)

In English:
The prop-word one/ones

1 If you don't want to say the same noun twice, you can use the prop-word *one* (plural: *ones*).
2 In German, you can use an adjective or the definite article without a noun. In English you can't. You need *one* or *ones*.

2 *Bedingungssätze*

a Ein Bedingungssatz besteht aus einem **Nebensatz mit *if*** *(if-clause)* und einem **Hauptsatz** *(main clause)*.
Der Nebensatz nennt eine Bedingung.
Im Hauptsatz steht, was geschieht, wenn diese Bedingung erfüllt wird.
Wenn der Hauptsatz vor dem *if*-Satz steht, verwendet man im Englischen kein Komma.

⚠ *if* leitet einen Nebensatz der **Bedingung** ein.

when leitet einen Nebensatz der **Zeit** ein.

Conditional sentences

REMEMBER

***if*-clause**	**main clause**
If it rains, Wenn (= Falls) es regnet,	we'll stay at home. bleiben wir daheim.
main clause	***if*-clause**
We'll stay at home	if it rains.

I'll tell her if I see her. **wenn (= falls)** ich sie sehe
(Ich bin nicht sicher, ob ich sie sehen werde.)

I'll tell her when I see her. **wenn (= sobald)** ich sie sehe
(Ich bin sicher, dass ich sie sehen werde.)

b *Bedingungssätze (Typ I)*

Bedingungssätze des Typs I drücken aus, dass die **Bedingung offen, d.h. erfüllbar** ist. Es ist gut möglich, dass das im *if*-Satz Gesagte eintritt.

Typ I: „Was ist, wenn, …"-Sätze

Conditional sentences (type I)

If this tile **is** genuine, I **will get** a lot of money for it.
Wenn diese Fliese echt ist, bekomme ich viel Geld dafür.
(Es ist durchaus möglich, dass die Fliese echt ist, und ich bringe zum Ausdruck, was dann der Fall ist.)

Im *if*-Satz steht das ***simple present***.
Im Hauptsatz stehen häufig
- das ***will-future***,
- ein ***Modalverb*** (z.B. *can, must, should*) + Infinitiv,
- ein **Imperativ**.

REMEMBER

If we **don't find** more tiles, the bulldozers **will return**.
If you **like** Roman remains you **should visit** the Dover Museum.
If you **find** another tile, **phone** Mark's mother.

In allgemein gültigen Aussagen steht auch im Hauptsatz das ***simple present***.

If I **miss** the last bus home, I always **take** a taxi.
(if heißt hier „jedes Mal, wenn … ", „immer dann, wenn …")

→ **P 6 (p. 46)**

c *Bedingungssätze (Typ II)*

Bedingungssätze des Typs II drücken aus, dass man es für **unwahrscheinlich (oder unmöglich)** hält, dass das im *if*-Satz Gesagte eintritt.

Typ II: „Was wäre, wenn, …"-Sätze

Conditional sentences (type II)

If this tile **was** genuine, I **would get** a lot of money for it.
Wenn diese Fliese echt wäre, würde ich viel Geld dafür bekommen.
(Ich halte es für eher unwahrscheinlich dass die Fliese echt ist. Ich bringe nur zum Ausdruck, was der Fall wäre, wenn sie echt wäre.)

If I **won** £100,000, I'**d** (= I **would**) **fly** round the world.
Wenn ich 100.000 Pfund gewänne/gewinnen würde, …

Im *if*-Satz des Typs II steht das ***simple past***. (Der *if*-Satz bezieht sich aber trotzdem auf die Zukunft oder die Gegenwart!)
Im Hauptsatz steht ***would/could/might*** + Infinitiv.

Kein *would* im *if*-Satz!

If we **held** a demonstration, they **would have to** listen.
Wenn wir demonstrieren würden, müssten sie uns anhören.
If you **drove** me to the site, I **could show** you the tiles.
Wenn Sie mich zur Ausgrabungsstätte fahren würden/führen, könnte ich Ihnen die Fliesen zeigen.
If we **had** more time, we **might find** more objects.
Wenn wir mehr Zeit hätten, würden wir vielleicht … finden.

Statt *was* steht im *if*-Satz manchmal *were*.

If Grandma **were** 30 years younger, …

Um Ratschläge zu erteilen, wird die Wendung ***If I were you, …*** benutzt.

If I **were** you, I'd take the job.
Wenn ich du wäre, würde ich … / Ich an deiner Stelle würde …

Statt des *simple past* kann im *if*-Satz auch ***could*** + Infinitiv stehen.

If you **could meet** a film star, who **would** you **like** to meet?
Wenn du einen Filmstar treffen könntest, …?

→ **P 7–10 (pp. 46/47)**

In English:
Conditional sentences (type II)
[1]condition [kən'dɪʃn] *Bedingung*
[2](to) come true *wahr werden, eintreten*

1 We use conditional sentences (type II) if we think the condition[1] won't or can't come true[2].
2 We use the simple past in the *if*-clause and *would/could/might* in the main clause.

In Unit 3 hast du gelernt ...

- zu sagen, was vielleicht der Fall ist oder vielleicht geschehen könnte.
  ▶ You may be right. They say it might rain tomorrow.
- zu sagen, was unter bestimmten Bedingungen geschehen würde oder geschehen könnte.
  ▶ If I won £100,000, I'd fly round the world. I'm sure we could stop the bulldozers if we found more remains.

Unit 4

1 *Das past perfect*

a *Gebrauch*

Wie du weißt, drückt das *simple past* aus, dass Handlungen oder Ereignisse zu einem bestimmten Zeitpunkt in der Vergangenheit stattfanden.

The past perfect
Use

REMEMBER
Conchita **went** to Space Camp two weeks ago.
In the afternoon, Margo **wrote** a postcard to her grandparents.

Wenn man über zwei vergangene Ereignisse redet, kann man das *past perfect* (Plusquamperfekt oder **Vor**vergangenheit) verwenden, um zu sagen, welches Ereignis **zuerst** geschah.

Before Conchita **arrived** in Florida, she had spent five days at Space Camp.
Bevor Conchita in Florida eintraf, hatte sie fünf Tage im Space Camp verbracht.

When Sue **got** to the platform, the train had just left.

Auch für Zustände (vor einem vergangenen Ereignis) wird das *past perfect* verwendet.

When I came back home, one of my friends had been in hospital for ten days.
Als ich wieder nach Hause kam, lag einer meiner Freunde schon seit zehn Tagen im Krankenhaus.

⚠ Je nachdem ob man das *past perfect* oder das *simple past* verwendet, verändert sich die Bedeutung.

The lesson had started when we arrived.
Der Unterricht hatte (schon) begonnen, als wir kamen.
The lesson started when we arrived.
Der Unterricht begann (erst), als wir kamen.

⚠ Wenn die Reihenfolge der Ereignisse klar ist, steht oft das *simple past* anstelle des *past perfect*, z.B. nach *after* (= „nachdem").

After I **had left** school, I went to America.
oder: After I **left** school, I went to America.

b ***Form***

Das *past perfect* wird mit *had* (Kurzform *'d*) + Partizip Perfekt gebildet.

⚠ Im Deutschen wird für das Plusquamperfekt „hatte" oder „war" verwendet. Im Englischen steht immer *had* (oder *'d*).

Form

When I **had saved** enough money, I bought a CD player.
Als ich genug Geld gespart hatte, …
Tom was sad because the letter from Sue **hadn't arrived**.
…, weil der Brief von Sue nicht angekommen war.
Had he **known** her for a long time before they got married?

→ **P 3, 4 (pp. 63/64)**

In English:
The past perfect

1 We form the past perfect with *had* + past participle.
2 We use the past perfect to show that one thing in the past happened before another thing in the past.

2 *Die Verlaufsform des past perfect*

a ***Gebrauch***

Mit dem *past perfect progressive* drückt man aus, dass eine Handlung oder ein Vorgang vor einem Zeitpunkt in der Vergangenheit begonnen hatte und bis (oder fast bis) zu diesem Zeitpunkt andauerte.

The past perfect progressive

Use

The postcard came on Friday. Margo's grandparents **had been waiting** for it since Monday.
… *Margos Großeltern hatten schon seit Montag darauf gewartet.*
It was 6 o'clock. Mr Brown was tired. He **had been working** in the garden since 2 o'clock.
… Er hatte seit 2 Uhr im Garten gearbeitet.

b ***Form***

Das *past perfect progressive* wird mit *had been* + *-ing*-Form gebildet.

Form

Statements:
I/You/He/She/We/They **had been playing** all day.
I/You/He/She/We/They **hadn't been watching** TV.

Questions:
Had I/you/he/she/we/they **been watching** TV?

→ **P 5 (p. 64)**

In English:
The past perfect progressive

1 We form the past perfect progressive with *had been* + *-ing* form.
2 We use the past perfect progressive to say that an action had begun before a point of time in the past and continued up to[1] (or almost up to) that time.

[1]up to *bis zu*

3 *Wiederholung: Modale Hilfsverben und ihre Ersatzverben*

Revision: Modal auxiliaries and their substitutes

a *Fähigkeit:*
can/could – be able to

Ability:
can/could – be able to

– ***Present:*** *can – be able to*

My mother can **speak** / is able to **speak** English but she can't **speak** / isn't able to **speak** French.

– ***Past:*** *could – was/were able to*

Could you **swim** when you were five? – No, I couldn't.
The shop was open. So I was able to **get** some bread.

– **Andere Zeiten:** *have/has been able to, will be able to*

I've always been able to **sing** well.
Soon you'll be able to **speak** English well.

---

b *Erlaubnis:*
can/could, may ▸◂ mustn't – be allowed to

Permission:
can/could, may ▸◂ mustn't – be allowed to

– **Bitte um Erlaubnis:** *can, may, could*

Can/May/Could we **use** your phone, please?

– **Ausdrückliches Verbot:** *mustn't*

You mustn't **leave** your bike here.

– ***Present:*** *can – be allowed to*

My friend can always **do** what she likes.
We can't **go** / aren't allowed to **go** out. It's raining.

– ***Past:*** *could, was/were allowed to*

When we were children, we could **watch** / were allowed to **watch** TV until 9 o'clock.

– **Andere Zeiten:** *have/has been allowed to, will be allowed to*

Our dog has always been allowed to **sleep** on the sofa.
Will you be allowed to **go** to the disco next week?

---

c *Notwendigkeit, Zwang:*
must ▸◂ needn't – have (got) to

Necessity, strong obligation:
must ▸◂ needn't – have (got) to

– ***Present:*** *must, needn't – have (got) to*

I must **leave** / have to **leave** now. I don't want to be late.
You needn't **do** / don't have to **do** your homework now.

– ***Past*, andere Zeiten:** *had to, have/has had to, will have to*

Did you have to **wait** long? – No, I didn't.
Emma has always had to **help** her parents.
I'm sure people won't have to **work** all day in the future.

→ P 9 (p. 66)

---

4 *Verben der Wahrnehmung + Objekt + Infinitiv*

Verbs of perception + object + infinitive

Nach Verben der Wahrnehmung wie *see, watch, hear, listen to, feel* kann ein **Objekt + Infinitiv** (⚠ ohne *to*) stehen.

I didn't see **anyone** leave the house.
Ich habe nicht gesehen, ob/dass jemand das Haus verlassen hat.
I woke up because I heard **the phone** ring.
Ich bin aufgewacht, weil ich das Telefon klingeln hörte.
Sue felt **something wet** touch her feet in the dark.
Sue fühlte, wie in der Dunkelheit etwas Nasses ihre Füße berührte.
We watched **the cook** make tacos.
Wir sahen zu, wie der Koch Tacos machte.

→ P 8 (p. 65)

In English:
Verbs of perception + object + infinitive

After verbs of perception *(see, watch, hear, listen to, feel)* we can use an object + infinitive without *to*.

In Unit 4 hast du gelernt ...

- zu sagen, dass etwas vor etwas anderem geschah. ▶ I arrived at the station after the train had left.
- zu sagen, seit wann oder wie lange eine Handlung in der Vergangenheit andauerte. ▶ I had been working for two hours when the computer crashed.
- zu sagen, was jemand hört, sieht oder fühlt. ▶ I saw a space shuttle take off from Cape Canaveral. I heard Conchita talk to her parents in Spanish.
- zu sagen, dass jemand einem anderen erlaubt, etwas zu tun. ▶ Mum often lets us stay up late at the weekend.
- zu sagen, dass jemand einen anderen veranlasst, etwas zu tun. ▶ Dad always makes me wash the dishes on Sundays.

Unit 5

1 *Der Infinitiv mit* to

a *Verben + to-Infinitiv*

Der *to*-Infinitiv kann nach bestimmten Verben (z.B. *decide, forget, learn, plan, start*) stehen. Er entspricht einem deutschen Infinitiv mit „zu".

⚠ Beachte aber die deutschen Entsprechungen für:

want to do	„tun wollen"
would like to do	„tun mögen"
be able to do	„tun können"
be allowed to do	„tun dürfen"
have to do	„tun müssen"

The to-infinitive
Verbs + to-infinitive

We **decided** to phone the police.
Wir beschlossen, die Polizei anzurufen.
Mark **forgot** to do his homework last night.
Gestern Abend vergaß Mark, seine Hausaufgaben zu machen.

He wants to go home.
Er will nach Hause gehen.
She would like to stay.
Sie würde gern noch bleiben.
Julia wasn't able to answer the questions.
Julia konnte die Fragen nicht beantworten.
You aren't allowed to leave your car here.
Sie dürfen ihr Auto hier nicht abstellen.
When do you have to get up on a school day?
Wann musst du ... aufstehen?

b *Adjektive und Nomen + to-Infinitiv*

Der *to*-Infinitiv kann auch nach bestimmten Adjektiven (z.B. *good, easy, nice*) und nach bestimmten Nomen (z.B. *decision, plan*) stehen.

Adjectives and nouns + to-infinitive

It was **nice** to meet you.
Es war schön, Sie kennen zu lernen.
Our **decision** to help him was right.
Unsere Entscheidung, ihm zu helfen, war richtig.

c *Der* to-*Infinitiv zum Ausdruck eines Zwecks*

Der *to*-Infinitiv kann zum Ausdruck eines **Zwecks** oder einer **Absicht** verwendet werden.
Die Form *in order to* ist etwas förmlicher als *to*, bedeutet aber dasselbe.
Im Deutschen steht meist „um zu".

The* to-*infinitive to express purpose

Amy visited her grandmother **to find out** more about Inuit traditions.
…, um mehr über die Traditionen der Inuit herauszufinden.
Janet went to Paris **in order to learn** French.
…, um Französisch zu lernen.

d *Fragewörter* + to-*Infinitiv*

Der *to*-Infinitiv kann nach Fragewörtern (z.B. *how, what, where, when*) stehen.
Er entspricht einem Nebensatz mit modalem Hilfsverb („sollen", „können" usw.).

Question words* + to-*infinitive

Can you tell me **how** | **to get** to the library? / I can get to the library?
Können Sie mir sagen, wie ich zur Bücherei komme(n kann)?
Rob didn't know **what to say**.
Rob wusste nicht, was er sagen sollte. → P 2 (p. 80)

e a place to visit

Nach bestimmten Nomen und nach *something, anybody* usw. entspricht der *to*-Infinitiv einem Relativsatz mit modalem Hilfsverb.

a place to visit

Barrow is **a place** | **to visit** in the summer. / that you must/should visit …
…, den man im Sommer besuchen sollte.

Mr Oktollik is **the man** | **to help** us. / who can/could/will help us.
…, der uns helfen kann/könnte/wird.

I don't know **anybody** | **to talk** to. / who I could/might talk to.
…, mit dem ich sprechen kann/könnte.

What's the best **place** | **to find** whales? / where you can find whales?
…, wo man Wale finden kann.

→ P 3 (p. 80)

f the first / the last / the next / the only + to-*Infinitiv*

Der *to*-Infinitiv kann nach *the first, the last, the next, the only* sowie nach Superlativen verwendet werden.
Er entspricht einem Relativsatz.

the first / the last / the next / the only + to-*infinitive*

Armstrong was **the first (person)** | **to walk** on the moon. / who walked …
Armstrong war der erste Mensch/der Erste, der den Mond betrat.

The captain is **the last (one)** | **to leave** the ship. / who leaves the ship.
Der Kapitän verlässt als Letzter das Schiff.

Who was **the youngest kid** | **to go** to Space Camp? / who went to …?
Wer war der jüngste Teilnehmer am Space Camp?

⚠ Nach *the only* **muss** immer ein Nomen oder *one/ones* stehen.

Jane was **the only person to say** what she thought.
Jane was **the only one to say** what she thought.
Jane war die Einzige, die sagte, was sie dachte.

In English:
The to-infinitive

We can use the *to*-infinitive
- to express purpose[1] (= German 'um zu'),
- after question words instead of[2] a sub-clause *(what to say = what I/you/he/she/... should say)*,
- after nouns instead of a relative clause *(a book to read = a book that I can read/that you should read)*,
- after *the first/the last/the next/the only* and superlatives *(the oldest)* instead of a relative clause *(the first to arrive = the first who arrived)*.

[1]purpose ['pɜːpəs] *Zweck*
[2]instead of *statt, anstelle*

2 *Die indirekte Rede (I)*

a *Direkte und indirekte Rede*

Indirect speech (I)
Direct and indirect speech

Man kann das, was jemand sagt oder gesagt hat, auf zweifache Art und Weise wiedergeben:
- In der **direkten Rede** *(direct speech)* wird **wörtlich wiedergegeben**, was jemand sagt, schreibt oder denkt (oder gesagt, geschrieben, gedacht hat). Die direkte Rede steht wie im Deutschen in Anführungsstrichen.

Amy's teacher: 'Fresh food is better than microwave food.'
Glen: 'Inupiaq is a difficult language.'
Grandma said, 'You should come to Barrow.'

- In der **indirekten Rede** *(indirect speech)* wird **berichtet**, was jemand sagt, schreibt oder denkt (oder gesagt, geschrieben, gedacht hat). Häufige Verben, die die indirekte Rede einleiten, sind: *say, tell sb., answer, explain, mention, reply, write, believe, know, think, ask, want to know, wonder*.

Amy's teacher **says** (that) fresh food is better than microwave food.
Amys Lehrer sagt, dass frische Lebensmittel besser sind als Lebensmittel aus der Mikrowelle.
Glen thinks (that) Inupiaq is a difficult language.
Glen meint, dass Inupiaq eine schwierige Sprache ist.
Grandma **told Amy** (that) she should come to Barrow.
Oma sagte Amy, dass sie nach Barrow kommen sollte.

⚠ Im Englischen steht vor der indirekten Rede **kein Komma**, und *that* („dass") wird oft weggelassen, besonders nach *say, tell sb.* und *think*.

b *Veränderungen der Zeitform*

Tense change

Wenn das **einleitende Verb im *simple past*** steht (z.B. *said*), werden die Zeitformen der direkten Rede meist verändert. Sie werden um eine Zeitstufe in die Vergangenheit „zurückverschoben" *(backshift of tenses)*:

	Direct speech		Indirect speech
present ▶ ***past***	'I play chess on Fridays.'	▶	Liz said she played chess on Fridays.
	'I'm enjoying my holiday in France.'	▶	Pete wrote that he was enjoying his holiday in France.

	Direct speech	Indirect speech
past ▶ *past perfect* (In der Umgangssprache werden *past tense*-Formen der direkten Rede manchmal beibehalten, d.h. nicht ins *past perfect* verändert.)	'I **met** the others at the club.' ▶	Cheryl **replied** that she **had met** the others at the club.
	'We **were watching** a football match on TV.' ▶	Bob **said** they **had been watching** a football match on TV.
present perfect ▶ ***past perfect***	'My parents **have been** to the USA once.' ▶	Colin **explained** that his parents **had been** to the USA once.
will-future ▶ ***would* + Infinitiv**	'I'm sure Tom **won't be** late.' ▶	Sue **was sure** that Tom **wouldn't be** late.
going to-future ▶ ***was/were going to* + Infinitiv**	'I think Sally **is going to work** hard.' ▶	David **thought** Sally **was going to work** hard.
can ▶ ***could***	'I'm sorry we **can't come**.' ▶	Eric **mentioned** that they **couldn't come**.
may ▶ ***might***	'Mum and Dad **may be** late.' ▶	Jean **told** us that her parents **might be** late.

⚠ Ein Verb im *past perfect* sowie *would, could, should, might, must, needn't* bleiben unverändert.

'The bus **had** already **left**.' ▶ John **said** the bus **had** already **left**.'
'I **would** like to go to Space Camp.' ▶ Marie **said** that she **would** like to go to Space Camp.

⚠ Anders als im Deutschen gibt es in der indirekten Rede im Englischen keinen Konjunktiv *(sei, habe)*.

She **told** us that her husband **had** a job at Chester Zoo.
Sie sagte uns, dass ihr Mann eine Stelle im Zoo von Chester habe.

⚠ Wenn das einleitende Verb im *simple present* steht, bleibt die Zeitform der direkten Rede unverändert.

'I**'ve lived** in Florida since 1983.' ▶ Julie **says** that she **has lived** in Florida since 1983.

→ P 5–8 (pp. 81/82)

c Veränderungen der Pronomen und der Orts- und Zeitangaben

Changes of pronouns and place and time phrases

Auch im Englischen werden in der indirekten Rede Pronomen und Orts- und Zeitangaben aus der Sicht des Berichtenden gewählt. Sie werden, je nach Situation, in der indirekten Rede verändert:

– **Pronomen**

Direct speech		Indirect speech
Tina: 'I'll help **you** with **your** homework, Scott.'	▶	*Scott (to his parents):* 'Tina said **she** would help **me** with **my** homework.'
	▶	*Tina (to her brother):* '**I** told Scott **I** would help **him** with **his** homework.'

Direct speech | Indirect speech

– **Ortsangaben**

– **Zeitangaben**

now	▶ *then, at that time*
today	▶ *(on) that day, yesterday, on Monday, …*
yesterday	▶ *the day before, on Monday, last Monday, …*
last night	▶ *the night before, on Monday night, …*
two days ago	▶ *two days before, two days earlier*
tomorrow	▶ *the next/following day, today, …*

→ P 9 (p. 82)

In English: Indirect speech

If the reporting verb (*say, tell, answer,* etc.) is in the past tense, there is usually a change of tenses ('backshift'):

present	▶ past
present perfect	▶ past perfect
past	▶ past perfect
going to-future	▶ *was/were going to* + infinitive
will-future	▶ *would* + infinitive
can, may	▶ *could, might.*

In Unit 5 hast du gelernt …

– über Absichten zu sprechen.

▶ Amy went to Barrow to learn Inupiaq.

– wie man deutsche Nebensätze im Englischen kürzer wiedergeben kann.

▶ He didn't know what to do.
Can you tell me how to get to the station?
Alaska is a great state to visit.
Amy's teacher is the person to ask.

– wiederzugeben, was jemand gesagt, geschrieben oder gedacht hat.

▶ Glen said his sister was only interested in Eskimos.
Amy wrote that she felt great in Barrow.
Grandma thought that Amy would soon speak Inupiaq better.

Unit 6

1 Das Reflexivpronomen

a Formen und Gebrauch

Das Reflexivpronomen (*myself, yourself, himself* usw.) ist „rückbezüglich“: Es bezieht sich auf das Subjekt des Satzes und bezeichnet dieselbe Person oder Sache wie das Subjekt (*I, you, Scott* usw.).

⚠ Betonung auf der zweiten Silbe:
myself [maɪ'self]
themselves [ðəm'selvz]

The reflexive pronoun

Forms and use

I taught **myself** French.	mir/mich (selbst)
Be careful or **you**'ll hurt **yourself**.	dir/dich (selbst)
Scott can take care of **himself**.	sich (selbst)
She often talks to **herself**.	sich (selbst)
The cat is clean. **It** washes **itself** all day.	sich (selbst)
We can see **ourselves** in the window.	uns (selbst)
Did **you** listen to **yourselves** on cassette?	euch (selbst)
They can take care of **themselves**.	sich (selbst)

⚠ Beachte den Unterschied zwischen Reflexivpronomen *(myself)* und Personalpronomen *(me)*.

Merke dir die Wendungen:

Enjoy yourself. „Viel Spaß!“ („Amüsier dich gut!“)
Help yourself. „Greif zu!“ („Bedien dich!“)

Did you **enjoy yourselves** at the party?
Habt ihr Spaß gehabt auf der Party?
The food is on the table – just **help yourself**.
Das Essen steht auf dem Tisch – bedien dich einfach.

⚠ Viele Verben, die im Deutschen reflexiv sind, werden im Englischen ohne Reflexivpronomen verwendet. (Im *vocabulary* auf S.169 findest du eine Übersicht über solche Verben.)

Julie **felt** horrible after the accident.
Julie fühlte sich schrecklich nach dem Unfall.
Mrs Donovan and I **met** at the station.
Frau Donovan und ich haben uns am Bahnhof getroffen.
Can you **remember** when we first met?
Kannst du dich daran erinnern, …?

(to) buy kann mit Reflexivpronomen verwendet werden. Häufiger steht es jedoch ohne.

I'**ve bought myself** a new computer.
oder: I'**ve bought** a new computer.

→ P 3, 4 (pp. 96/97)

b Reflexivpronomen oder each other?

- **Reflexivpronomen:**
  „sich“ (= sich selbst).
- ***each other:***
  „sich“ (= sich gegenseitig, einander). Statt *each other* kann man auch *one another* verwenden.

*-**self**/-**sel**ves* = „sich **sel**bst“
each other = „**ein**ander“, „sich gegenseitig“

Reflexive pronoun or each other?

Ann and Dan are looking at **themselves**.

Ann and Dan are looking at **each other** / at **one another**.

→ P 5 (p. 97)

In English:
Reflexive pronouns and each other

1 The reflexive pronoun *(myself, ourselves, ...)* refers to the subject.
2 There are some verbs that are reflexive in German, but not reflexive in English (e.g. *imagine, meet, worry*).
3 *-selves* means 'sich selbst', *each other* means 'sich gegenseitig'.

2 *Das verstärkende Pronomen*

Man kann *myself, yourself, himself* usw. auch verwenden, um ein Nomen oder Pronomen hervorzuheben. Im Deutschen verwenden wir dafür „selbst" oder „selber".
Wenn das Subjekt hervorgehoben werden soll, rückt das verstärkende *-self*-Pronomen oft an das Satzende.

The emphasizing pronoun

The house itself is quite small, but the garden is fantastic.
Das Haus selbst ist ziemlich klein, ...
I rang the number and spoke to **Madonna herself**.
Ich habe die Nummer gewählt und mit Madonna selbst gesprochen.

We're going to build the garage ourselves.
Wir haben vor, die Garage selbst zu bauen.
Sorry, but I can't help you. I'm a tourist myself.
... Ich bin selbst Tourist.

→ P 6 (p. 97)

In English:
Emphasizing pronouns

Myself, yourself, etc. can be used to emphasize[1] a noun or pronoun. Their meaning is 'selbst', 'selber'.

[1](to) emphasize ['emfəsaɪz] *hervorheben, betonen*

3 *Wiederholung: Fragen im Englischen*

Englische Fragen werden mit einem Hilfsverb gebildet. Wenn der entsprechende Aussagesatz kein Hilfsverb enthält, wird *do/does/did* verwendet.

Revision: Questions in English

	auxiliary (in questions)	subject	auxiliary (in statements)	main verb	
Modal auxiliaries		*Pete*	*can*	*eat*	*meat.*
	Can	Pete		eat	meat?
Present/Past progressive		*Steve*	*is/was*	*leaving*	*Eve.*
	Is/Was	Steve		leaving	Eve?
Simple present		*Trish*		*likes*	*fish.*
	Does	Trish		like	fish?
Simple past		*Kate*		*came*	*late.*
	Did	Kate		come	late?
Present/Past perfect		*Kurt*	*has/had*	*hurt*	*Bert.*
	Has/Had	Kurt		hurt	Bert?
Present/Past perfect progressive		*Rory*	*has/had* been	*reading*	*stories.*
	Has/Had	Rory	been	reading	stories?
will-future		*Keith*	*will*	*clean*	*his teeth.*
	Will	Keith		clean	his teeth?

⚠ Vorsicht bei **Fragen nach dem Subjekt** („Wer oder was tut etwas bzw. hat etwas getan?"): Sie werden **ohne *do/does/did*** gebildet.

Who likes fish?	– Trish (likes fish).	Wer mag Fisch?
Who came late?	– Kate (came late).	Wer kam zu spät?
What happened?	– Nothing (happened).	Was ist passiert?

⚠ **Subject question:** Who asked you? **Wer** hat dich gefragt?
Object question: Who did you ask? **Wen** hast du gefragt?

→ P 7 (p. 98)

4 *Wiederholung: Stellung der Adverbien*

Revision: Position of adverbs

Es gibt drei mögliche Stellungen für Adverbien:

- **vor dem Subjekt** *(front-position)***:** Hier stehen gewöhnlich **Satzadverbien** wie *maybe, suddenly, of course, in fact, at first, then*.

Suddenly the lights went out.

- **zwischen Subjekt und Vollverb** bzw. **nach dem (ersten) Hilfsverb** *(mid-position)***:** Hier stehen gewöhnlich **Adverbien der unbestimmten Zeit oder Häufigkeit** wie *ever, always, often, never*.

My sister always walks to school.
This story will never be forgotten.

- **nach dem Vollverb** bzw. **nach dem Objekt** *(end-position)***:** Hier stehen gewöhnlich
  - **Adverbien der Art und Weise** *(carefully, hard, well)*,
  - **Adverbien des Ortes** *(here, everywhere, in/to London)* und
  - **Adverbien der Zeit** *(yesterday, next week, in 1998)*.

You should always drive carefully.

My parents are visiting friends in London.

We're going to buy a new car next week.

Treten mehrere dieser Adverbien in einem Satz auf, gilt die Reihenfolge **Art und Weise – Ort – Zeit**.

	manner	place	time
I hope I'll do	well	in the test	tomorrow.
Mike can't go		to school	today.

Gradadverbien – z.B. *very, quite, really, too* (= „zu") – stehen meist direkt vor dem Wort, das sie verstärken oder abschwächen.

Our new French teacher is quite/really/very/too **nervous**.
Do you really **believe** that?
Dave walked really/very **slowly**.

→ P 8 (p. 98)

5 *Die indirekte Rede (II)*

a *Fragen in der indirekten Rede*

Auch bei indirekten Fragen verändern sich die Zeitformen bei einleitendem Verb im *simple past* (vgl. Unit 5, **2b**, S. 135/136).

- Wenn die direkte Frage mit einem **Fragewort** (*how, what, when, where* usw.) beginnt, wird das Fragewort in der indirekten Rede beibehalten.
- Ist in der direkten Rede **kein Fragewort** vorhanden (Entscheidungsfrage), wird die indirekte Frage mit *if* oder *whether* (= „ob") eingeleitet.

⚠ Die Wortstellung in indirekten Fragen ist wie in Aussagesätzen, nämlich ***subject – verb – …*** . Es gibt keine Umschreibung mit *do*.

Indirect speech (II)

Questions in indirect speech

'How do you like San Francisco, Scott?' ▶ The reporter **asked** Scott how he liked San Francisco.

'When did you leave home, Jake?' ▶ Margo **asked** Jake **when** he had left home.

'Are you coming to the party on Saturday, David?' ▶ Anne **wanted to know** if/whether David was coming to the party on Saturday.

		Subject	Verb	
Statement:		Kate	likes	dogs.
Indirect question: I wondered	if whether why	Kate	liked	dogs.

→ P 9, 10 (p. 99)

b *Aufforderungen und Bitten in der indirekten Rede*

Aufforderungen und Bitten werden in der indirekten Rede meist mit *tell sb. to do sth.* bzw. *ask sb. to do sth.* wiedergegeben.

Commands and requests in indirect speech

'You shouldn't work at night.' ▶ The doctor told me not to work at night.
Der Arzt sagte mir, ich solle nachts nicht arbeiten. / …, dass ich nachts nicht arbeiten soll.

'Close the window, please.' ▶ Miss Evans told Linda to close the window.
Miss Evans forderte Linda auf, das Fenster zu schließen.

'Smile for the camera, please.' ▶ The reporter asked the Truongs to smile for the camera.
Der Reporter bat die Truongs, für die Kamera zu lächeln.

→ P 11 (p. 99)

In English:
Indirect speech (II)

1 The word order in indirect questions is subject – verb.
2 You use *tell sb. to do sth.* or *ask sb. to do sth.* to report commands[1] and requests.

[1]command [kə'mɑːnd] *Befehl(ssatz)*

6 *Verb + Objekt +* to-*Infinitiv*

Nach bestimmten Verben (z.B. *ask, help, invite, teach*) kann ein **Objekt + *to*-Infinitiv** stehen. Im Deutschen steht meist ein Infinitiv mit „zu".

Verb + object + to-*infinitive*

REMEMBER

My dad **asked** me to help him.
Mein Vater bat mich, ihm zu helfen.
Who **taught** you to play the piano?
Wer hat dir beigebracht, Klavier zu spielen?

Auch nach *cause, expect, tell, want, would like, would love* kann ein **Objekt + *to*-Infinitiv** stehen. Nach den entsprechenden deutschen Verben steht jedoch meist ein Nebensatz mit „dass".

I **expect** you to be home by ten.
Ich erwarte, dass du bis 10 Uhr zu Hause bist.
I **would like** you to clean the board.
⚠ *Nicht:* ~~I would like that you~~ …
Ich möchte, dass du die Tafel abwischst.
I **want** you to tidy up your room.
⚠ *Nicht:* ~~I want that you~~ …
Ich möchte, dass du dein Zimmer aufräumst.

⚠ Beachte die unterschiedliche Bedeutung der zwei *want*-Sätze.

Sue **wants** to help John. — Sue will John helfen.
Sue **wants** me to help John. — Sue will, dass ich John helfe.

→ P 13 (p. 100)

In English:
Verb + object +* to-*infinitive

The *to*-infinitive can be used after some verbs + object:
expect/want/would like somebody to do something.
In German we usually use a sub-clause with 'dass':
'erwarten/wollen, dass jemand etwas tut'.

In Unit 6 hast du gelernt …

- zu sagen, dass jemand sich verletzt hat, sich etwas beigebracht hat usw. ▶ I've hurt myself with a knife. My sister taught herself to play the piano.
- zu sagen, dass jemand etwas selbst gemacht hat. ▶ I made this dress myself.
- wiederzugeben, was jemand gefragt hat. ▶ The reporter asked Scott how he liked San Francisco. Julie wanted to know if Alex was coming to the party.
- wiederzugeben, worum jemand gebeten hat. ▶ They asked their grandfather to help them.
- wiederzugeben, wozu jemand aufgefordert hat. ▶ The teacher told them to wait outside.
- Wünsche und Erwartungen an andere auszudrücken. ▶ I want you to come home at once.

- Das ***vocabulary*** (Vokabelverzeichnis, S. 143–170) enthält nur die neuen Wörter und Wendungen, die du lernen sollst, und zwar in der Reihenfolge, in der sie in den Units vorkommen.
- Im ***dictionary*** (S. 171–198) – der alphabetischen Wörterliste – kannst du nachschlagen, wenn du nur schnell die Bedeutung oder Aussprache eines Wortes oder einer Wendung wissen möchtest. Das *dictionary* enthält den Wortschatz der Bände 1 und 2 sowie alle neuen Wörter und Wendungen aus den sechs Units des Bandes 3.
- *Grammatische Fachbegriffe* stehen gesammelt auf den Seiten 200/201.
- Die Seiten 202/203 enthalten eine *Liste der unregelmäßigen Verben*.
- *Personen- und Ortsnamen* stehen auf den Seiten 204/205. *Ländernamen* (und zugehörige Adjektive) findest du auf Seite 206.
- Außerdem findest du auf den Seiten 207/208 zwei Listen mit Ausdrücken für Gespräche und Diskussionen im Klassenzimmer *(Classroom phrases* und *Discussions and presentations)*.

Der folgende Ausschnitt zeigt dir, wie das ***vocabulary*** aufgebaut ist:

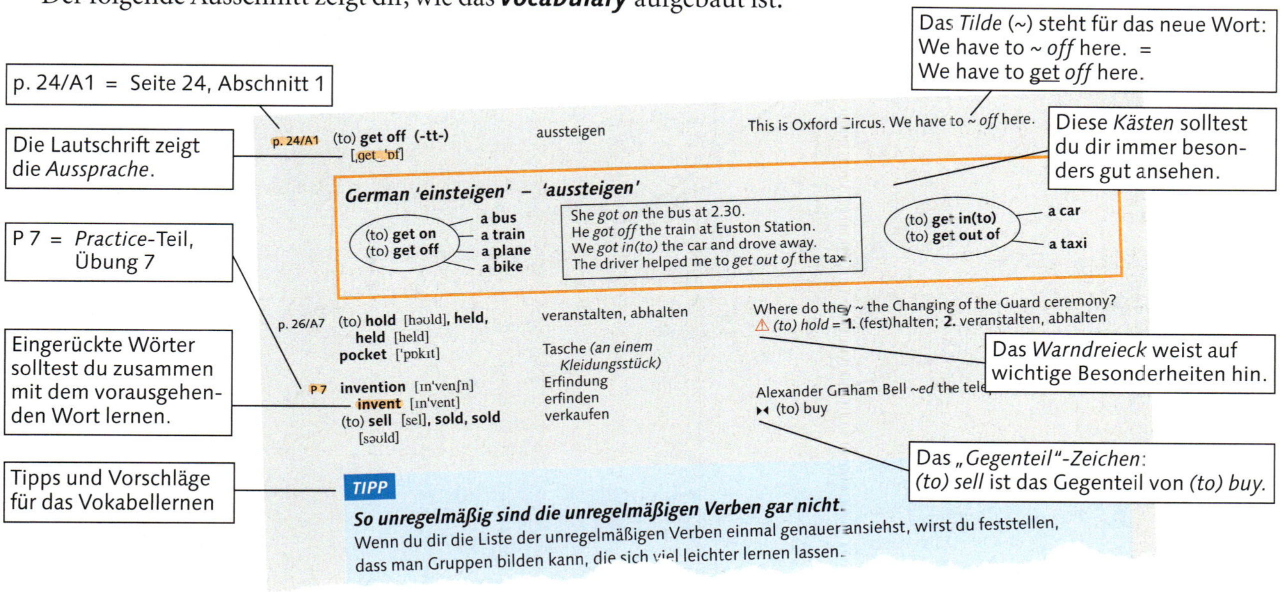

Abkürzungen:

adj = *adjective*	*adv* = *adverb*	sb. = somebody/someone	*AE* = *American English*
conj = *conjunction*	*n* = *noun*	sth. = something	*BE* = *British English*
prep = *preposition*	*v* = *verb*	jd. = jemand	*lat.* = lateinisch
p. = page	pp. = pages	jm. = jemandem	*frz.* = französisch
no pl = *no plural*	*pl* = *plural*	jn. = jemanden	*infml* = *informal* (umgangssprachlich)

TIPP

Das Wichtigste zuerst …

- Nimm dir beim Vokabellernen nicht zu viel vor! 10 bis 15 neue Vokabeln auf einmal genügen – dann solltest du eine Pause machen.
- Lerne nicht zu lange, aber regelmäßig! Beim Lernen sind 6 mal 10 Minuten mehr als eine Stunde.
- Lerne nicht nur mündlich! Wenn du die Vokabeln aufschreibst, behältst du sie besser.
- Wiederholung ist wichtig! Sieh dir regelmäßig auch die „alten" Wörter wieder an.

UK Calling

p. 6	**the UK (the United Kingdom)** [ˌjuːˈkeɪ, juˌnaɪtɪd ˈkɪŋdəm]	das Vereinigte Königreich *(Großbritannien und Nordirland)*	
	isle [aɪl]	Insel, Eiland	⚠ *isle* (statt *island*) wird in Gedichten u. Eigennamen verwendet: *the British Isles; the Isle of Skye.* *frz.* l'île *(f)*
	(to) **make** sth. **up** [ˌmeɪk‿ˈʌp]	etwas bilden	11 players *make* ~ a football team.
	population [ˌpɒpjuˈleɪʃn]	Bevölkerung, Einwohner(zahl)	the number of people who live in a country or city: Wales has got a ~ of about three million people. *lat.* populus, *frz.* la population
	encyclopedia [⚠ ɪnˌsaɪkləˈpiːdɪə]	Enzyklopädie, Lexikon	

Numbers

⚠ **11.4**	= eleven *point* four	(*deutsch:* 11,4 – elf *Komma* vier)	
1.3 million	= one *point* three million	(*deutsch:* 1,3 Millionen)	
⚠ **11,400**	= eleven thousand four hundred	(*deutsch:* 11.400)	Im Englischen steht oft ein Komma
1,300,000	= one million three hundred thousand	(*deutsch:* 1.300.000)	in Zahlen, die größer als 1.000 sind.

	flag [flæg]	Flagge, Fahne	The British ~ is called 'the Union Jack'.
	album [ˈælbəm]	Album	*lat.* album, *frz.* l'album *(m)*
p. 7	**accent** [⚠ ˈæksənt]	Akzent; Betonung, Aussprache	accent – Akzent *lat.* accentus, *frz.* l'accent *(m)*
	grammar school [ˈgræmə skuːl]	(GB) *heute eher seltene, etwa dem Gymnasium entsprechende Schulform*	
	honey [ˈhʌni]	Honig	
	right *(adv)*	direkt, gerade(wegs), genau	They live ~ at the end of the street, in the last house. The accident happened ~ in front of the hotel.
	bay [beɪ]	Bucht	*a bay*  *frz.* la baie
	choir [⚠ ˈkwaɪə]	Chor	*lat.* chorus
	Welsh [welʃ]	walisisch; Walisisch	
	culture [⚠ ˈkʌltʃə]	Kultur	*lat.* cultus, *frz.* la culture
	youth [juːθ]	Jugend	the time when you are young ⚠ *die Jugend(lichen) = young people, teenagers*
	(to) **take, took, taken**	dauern, *(Zeit)* brauchen	It ~s about 20 minutes to do this exercise. How long *does* it ~ to get from Euston to Victoria?
	remote [rɪˈməʊt]	abgelegen, entlegen, weit entfernt	far away in space or time
	(to) **warn** sb. **(about/of** sth.**)** [wɔːn]	jn. (vor etwas) warnen	⚠ *jn. davor warnen, etwas zu tun = (to) warn sb. not to do sth.:* My parents *~ed me not to walk* home alone.
	enemy [ˈenəmi]	Feind/in	▸◂ friend *lat.* inimicus, *frz.* l'ennemi *(m)*
	attack [əˈtæk]	Angriff	noun: *attack* – *frz.* l'attaque *(f)*
	(to) **attack** [əˈtæk]	angreifen	verb: *(to) attack*
	about yourself [jəˈself, *betont:* jɔːˈself]	über dich selbst	

they = he or she

Manchmal wird *they* (bzw. *them, their*) benutzt, um das umständliche *he or she (him or her, his or her)* zu vermeiden.
Dabei handelt es sich oft um Sätze mit *someone, anyone* usw., in denen es nicht wichtig oder nicht bekannt ist, ob ein Mann oder eine Frau gemeint ist.

Choose *one of the teenagers* and write *them (= him or her)* an e-mail.
There's *somebody* at the door. What could *they (= he or she)* want?
If *anyone* phones, tell *them (= him or her)* I'll be back at 7.
Someone has parked *their* car *(= his or her car)* in front of our garage.

Unit 1: On the Move in Wales

p. 8	**score** [skɔː]	Spielstand, (Spiel-)Ergebnis, Punktestand	The English team lost the match. The ~ was Italy 3, England 1. / The ~ was 3–1 to Italy.
	none [nʌn]	keine(r, s)	I read three books last month but ~ of them were good.
	Who cares? [keəz]	Wen interessiert das? / Ist doch egal!	Her parents have got a lot of money! – *Who ~?* Money isn't everything.

Sports

aerobics [eə'rəʊbɪks]	Aerobic	**in-line skating**	*(das)* Inline-Skaten
American football	Football	**jogging** ['dʒɒgɪŋ]	*(das)* Joggen, Jogging
athletics [æθ'letɪks]	Leichtathletik	**netball**	Korbball
baseball	Baseball	**riding**	*(das)* Reiten, Reitsport
biking/cycling	*(das)* Radfahren	**rugby** ['rʌgbi]	Rugby
cricket ['krɪkɪt]	Kricket	**running**	*(das)* Laufen
dancing	*(das)* Tanzen	**sailing**	*(das)* Segeln
gymnastics [dʒɪm'næstɪks]	Gymnastik, Turnen	**skiing**	*(das)* Skilaufen, Skisport
ice-hockey	Eishockey	**squash** [skwɒʃ]	Squash
ice skating	*(das)* Eislaufen	**windsurfing**	*(das)* Windsurfen

⚠ Remember: You do aerobics/judo/… • You go cycling/jogging/… • You play baseball/cricket/…

p. 118	**Your score**		
	less [les]	weniger	▸◂ more
	(to) **spend** time/money **(on)** [spend], **spent, spent** [spent]	Zeit verbringen (mit) / Geld ausgeben (für)	I *spent* three hours at the chess club yesterday. My brother *~s* a lot of money *on* clothes.
	healthy ['helθɪ]	gesund	It's very ~ to do sports.
	attitude (towards) ['ætɪtjuːd]	Haltung (gegenüber), Einstellung (zu)	What's your ~ *towards* alternative energy?
	exercise *(no pl)* ['eksəsaɪz]	(körperliche) Bewegung, Training, Gymnastik	⚠ **1.** *exercise (no pl, no article)* = Bewegung: My parents say I need more *exercise.* **2.** *exercise(s)* = Übung(en): Which *exercises* have we got for homework?
	(to) **relax** [rɪ'læks]	(sich) entspannen, sich ausruhen	*lat.* relaxare 
p. 9	**lane** [leɪn]	(schmale Land-)Straße; Gasse	
	paradise [⚠ 'pærədaɪs]	Paradies	*lat.* paradisum, *frz.* le paradis
	perfect [⚠ 'pɜːfɪkt]	perfekt, einwandfrei, vollkommen; ideal	This park is the ~ place for a picnic. *lat.* perfectus,a,um
	in between [ˌɪn bɪ'twiːn]	dazwischen	I like London and Oxford and the area *in* ~.
	valley ['væli]	Tal	the land between two mountains or hills *lat.* vallis, *frz.* la vallée
	mill [mɪl]	Mühle	
	(to) **number**	nummerieren	Now ~ the sentences from one to ten. *frz.* numéroter
	(to) **prepare (for)** [prɪ'peə]	(sich) vorbereiten (auf); *(Mahlzeit)* zubereiten	I got a bad mark in the test because I didn't ~ *for* it. Where's Dad? – He's *preparing* lunch. *lat.* praeparare, *frz.* préparer
	empty ['empti]	leer	▸◂ full
p. 10/A1	**section** ['sekʃn]	Abschnitt, Teil	*frz.* la section
	rubbish ['rʌbɪʃ] *(infml)*	Quatsch, Blödsinn	⚠ *rubbish* = **1.** Abfall, Müll; **2.** Quatsch, Blödsinn
	(to) **get ready** ['redi]	sich bereitmachen, sich fertig machen	It's half past eight. You must *get* ~ for school now.
	championship ['tʃæmpiənʃɪp]	Meisterschaft	
	oval [⚠ 'əʊvl]	oval	*frz.* ovale 
	round [raʊnd]	rund	
	(to) **last** [lɑːst]	(an-, fort)dauern	A football match *~s* 90 minutes. ⚠ *(to) take* = dauern (Zeit in Anspruch nehmen) *(to) last* = andauern, fortdauern (im Gang sein)
	(to) **kick** [kɪk]	treten (gegen)	The football player *~ed* the ball.
	forward(s) ['fɔːwəd(z)]	vorwärts, nach vorn	
	(to) **give** sth. **up**	etwas aufgeben	I had to ~ *up* football. I didn't have the time.

	type (of) [taɪp]	Art, Sorte, Typ	What ~ of person is he? Noisy? Quiet? Funny?
p. 11/A3	**coach** [kəʊtʃ]	Trainer, Trainerin	⚠ *coach* = **1.** (Reise-)Bus; **2.** Trainer/in
	chance [tʃɑːns]	Chance, Gelegenheit	You have one ~ to guess the right answer. *frz.* la chance
	for 10 years	seit 10 Jahren	Ron has lived (⚠ *nicht:* ~~lives~~) in Ulm ~ two years.
	since four o'clock [sɪns]	seit vier Uhr	Alison has lived (⚠ *nicht:* ~~lives~~) in Ulm ~ 1999.

since

Zeitangaben mit *since* (= „seit") geben immer einen **Zeitpunkt** an. Das kann auf zweierlei Weise geschehen:

- durch ein **Nomen** *(since this morning* – seit heute Morgen*)*
- durch einen **Satz im *simple past*** *(since she left* – seit sie ging/gegangen ist*)*.

We haven't seen her	*since this morning.*	*since (prep)* + ***noun phrase***
	since she left.	*since (conj)* + ***simple past clause***
I've been here	*since two o'clock.*	*since (prep)* + ***noun phrase***
	since I finished lunch.	*since (conj)* + ***simple past clause***

everything/everyone **else** [els]	alles andere/alle anderen	Have you got the drinks? I've got *everything* ~. Have you finished? *Everyone* ~ has finished.

... else

Let's go to the park. We've been *everywhere else.*	... Wir sind *überall sonst schon* gewesen.
I met Jo at the party. – Did you meet *anyone else*?	... – Hast du *sonst noch jemanden* getroffen?
Do you need *anything else* from the shop?	Brauchst du *sonst noch etwas* ...?
So you went to Paris. Did you go *anywhere else*?	... Bist du *sonst noch irgendwo* hingefahren?
I'm tired. *Someone else* will have to tidy up.	... *Jemand anders* muss aufräumen.
Let's play football. – Can't we do *something else*?	... – Können wir nicht *etwas anderes* machen?
We always go there. Let's go *somewhere else.*	... Lasst uns *woanders* hingehen.
Who else did you meet?	*Wen* hast du *(sonst) noch* getroffen?
What else do you know about Scotland?	*Was* weißt du *(sonst) noch* über Schottland?

by 7.20	bis (spätestens) 7.20	We need your report ~ (= not later than) next Monday.

till – by

till *(prep; conj)* = **„bis"**

(prep) I'll have to work *till* 5 o'clock today.
Ich muss heute bis 5 Uhr arbeiten.

(conj) John lived in Wales *till* he was 13.
John lebte in Wales, bis er 13 war.

by *(prep)* = **„bis spätestens", „nicht später als"**

We needed your report *by* Friday (= *on or before Friday*). Now it's too late.
Wir brauchten Ihren Bericht bis Freitag.

All letters must be with us *by* 31st May.
Alle Briefe müssen bis zum 31. Mai bei uns sein.

	pub [pʌb] *(BE)*	Kneipe, Lokal	where people go to drink and talk
	(to) **beat** [biːt], **beat, beaten** ['biːtn]	schlagen; besiegen	I *beat* my brother at tennis last Sunday.
	(to) **turn over** *(BE)*	umschalten *(Fernsehen)*	(to) change to another TV channel
	highlight ['haɪlaɪt]	Höhepunkt	
A4	**table** ['teɪbl]	Tabelle	a sort of chart *lat.* tabula, *frz.* la table
p. 12/A6	(to) **agree on** sth. [ə'griː]	etwas vereinbaren, sich auf etwas einigen	Yes, I'm free on Wednesday. Can we ~ *on* 9 o'clock? How much? £20? Could we ~ *on* £18?
	(to) **be glad (about)** [glæd]	froh sein, sich freuen (über)	(to) be happy, (to) be pleased
	spring [sprɪŋ]	Frühling	
	autumn ['ɔːtəm]	Herbst	

spring *summer* *autumn* *winter*

	caravan ['kærəvæn] *(BE)*	Wohnwagen	
	(to) **take care of** sb./sth. [keə]	sich um jn./etwas kümmern	We're going on holiday. Can you *take ~ of* our dog?
	(to) **run** sth. **(-nn-), ran, run**	etwas durchführen, veranstalten, betreiben, leiten	My uncle ~*s* surfing holidays in Spain. Catherine's parents ~ a hotel by the sea.
	countryside ['kʌntrɪsaɪd]	Landschaft; (ländliche) Gegend	Last year we went cycling in the most beautiful Welsh ~.
	romantic [rəʊ'mæntɪk]	romantisch	*frz.* romantique
	peninsula [pə'nɪnsjələ]	Halbinsel	*lat.* paeninsula
	sand [sænd]	Sand	noun: *sand* – adjective: *sandy*

'of' in place phrases

the *city of* Glasgow *die Stadt Glasgow* • the *town of* Criccieth *die Stadt Criccieth* • the *Isle of* Skye *die Insel Skye*

	western ['westən]	westlich, West-	

north – northern

	north	south	east	west
nouns:	north	south	east	west
adjectives:	northern	southern ⚠ ['sʌðən]	eastern	western

	view (of/over) [vjuː]	Aussicht, Blick (auf/über)	This postcard shows a ~ *of* the beach. From the tower there's a lovely ~ *over* the city.
	huge [hjuːdʒ]	sehr groß, riesig	very large
	(to) **celebrate** ['selɪbreɪt]	feiern	My grandma wants to ~ her 75th birthday in a restaurant. *lat.* celebrare, *frz.* célébrer
p. 13/A6	(to) **be a favourite (with)**	sehr beliebt sein (bei)	Laura is a good pupil. She'*s a ~ with* the teachers.
	railway ['reɪlweɪ]	Eisenbahn	

'Why not' + Infinitiv / 'Why' + Infinitiv

- Mit *'Why not'* + Infinitiv kann man Vorschläge machen:

  I don't know what to do. – *Why not write* to your friends in Germany? (= Why don't you write ...?)
  What shall we do tonight? – *Why not go* to the cinema? (= Why don't we go ...?)

- Mit *'Why'* + Infinitiv kann man ausdrücken, dass man etwas für nicht nötig oder nicht sinnvoll hält:

  Why pay more at other shops? We have the cheapest clothes in town.
  Warum in anderen Geschäften mehr bezahlen? ...
  Why be lonely? Join our club and have fun!
  Warum/Wozu einsam sein? ...

A7	(to) **form** [fɔːm]	(sich) bilden, formen	You ~ the simple past of regular verbs with '-ed'.
	(to) **go on**	(an)dauern; vor sich gehen, im Gange sein	(to) last: How long *has* this *been going* ~? (to) happen: A party *was going* ~ in the next room.
A9	**popular (with)** [⚠ 'pɒpjələ]	beliebt (bei), populär	Swimming is very ~ *with* girls in Wales. *lat.* popularis,e, *frz.* populaire

TIPP

Und jetzt ganz entspannt ...

- Mach es dir gemütlich: Setz oder leg dich mit deinem Englischbuch ungestört hin.
- Wähle etwa 10 neue Vokabeln aus, die du lernen willst.
- Schau dir ein neues englisches Wort, dessen deutsche Entsprechung und das Beispiel in der 3. Spalte an. Dann schließ die Augen und stell dir bildhaft vor, was das Wort bezeichnet (es kann ein Einzelbild oder eine ganze Situation sein). Sprich dir das englische Wort mehrmals laut vor, dann wird sich der Klang des Wortes fest mit deinem Bild verbinden und besser im Gedächtnis bleiben.

P 3	**last** [lɑ:st]	zuletzt, das letzte Mal	He was very ill when I ~ saw him. ▸◂ first
P 7	**billion** [⚠ 'bɪljən]	Milliarde(n)	1,000,000,000
P 8	**conversation** [ˌkɒnvə'seɪʃn]	Gespräch, Unterhaltung	to have a ~ with someone = to talk to someone about something *frz.* la conversation
P 11	**in the open air**	im Freien	
P 12	**tourist board** ['tʊərɪst bɔ:d]	Fremdenverkehrsbüro	
	Dear Sir or Madam [sɜ:], ['mædəm]	Sehr geehrte Damen und Herren	
	(to) **look forward to** sth. [ˌlʊk 'fɔ:wəd]	sich auf etwas freuen	School this week has been boring. I'*m* really *looking ~ to* the weekend. ⚠ Wir *freuen uns darauf*, von Ihnen *zu hören*. = We *look forward to hearing* from you.
	(to) **be born** [bɔ:n]	geboren sein/werden	When *were* you ~? – I *was* ~ on 15th March, 1987. ⚠ Wann *bist* du geboren? = When *were* you born? Never: I ~~am born~~ in 1987.
	No., *pl* **Nos. (= number/s)**	*Abkürzung von „number"*	*Nos.* 1–6: right; *Nos.* 7–12: wrong
	per cent (%) [pə'sent]	Prozent	Two ~ ~ of two hundred is four. *lat.* per centum, *frz.* pour-cent
	transparency [træns'pærənsi]	Folie *(für den Tageslichtprojektor)*	
	at the back (of the book/bus/cinema**)**	hinten (im Buch/Bus/Kino)	There are lists and maps *at the ~ of* the book. ▸◂ at the front (of ...)

p. 18 The Race

article [⚠ 'ɑ:tɪkl]	(Zeitungs-)Artikel	There was an ~ in the newspaper about the race.
(to) **have** sth. **in common** ['kɒmən]	etwas miteinander gemein haben	We're very different – we *have* nothing *in ~*.
even ['i:vn]	sogar, selbst	Everyone helped, ~ the children. I'm very tall, but my sister is ~ taller.
pass [pɑ:s]	Pass, Ballabgabe	
team-mate ['ti:mmeɪt]	Mannschaftskamerad/in	After games my ~*s* and I usually eat something.
16-year-old	16-Jährige(r); 16-jährige(r, s)	*16-year-olds* in Britain are not allowed to drive. *16-year-old* Sue lives here. (= Die 16-jährige Sue ...)
junior ['dʒu:niə]	Junioren-, Jugend-	*frz.* junior
neither (of) ['naɪðə, 'ni:ðə]	keine(r, s) (von beiden)	Who won the race, you or Steve? – Oh, ~ *of* us. Someone from another school won. Which do you like better, the red or the black hat? – *Neither!* I think they're both horrible.

(to) **come (in) third**	als Dritte/r ins Ziel kommen; Dritte/r werden	David *came (in) third* in the race, after Tom and Nathan.
(to) **be ahead (of** sb.**)** [ə'hed]	führen, in Führung liegen (vor jm.); jm. voraus sein	Sometimes David *was ~ of* Aled, sometimes Aled *was ~ of* David.
rival [⚠ 'raɪvl]	Rivale, Rivalin; Konkurrent, Konkurrentin	David and Aled are ~*s* – they both want to win the race. *lat.* rivalis, *frz.* le rival / la rivale
(to) **do so**; (to) **say so**	es/das tun; es/das sagen	Buy now. If you *do ~*, you'll save a lot of money. Mark is lazy. – Who *said ~*?

p. 19 How to take notes

how to do sth.	wie man etwas tun kann/soll	You can ask your teacher or your parents ~ *to do* your homework.
mostly ['məʊstli]	hauptsächlich, größtenteils; meistens	The milk we drink is ~ from cows.
c. (= circa) ['sɜ:kə]	ca. (= zirka)	
programme [⚠ 'prəʊgræm]	(Radio-, Fernseh-) Sendung; Programm	*frz.* le programme
abbreviation [əˌbri:vi'eɪʃn]	Abkürzung	*lat.* abbreviatura, *frz.* l'abréviation *(f)*
mail [meɪl], *(BE auch:)* **post** [pəʊst]	Post(sendung)	The ~ always comes in the morning. ⚠ zur Post gehen = *(to) go to the post office*
if [ɪf]	ob	Ann wants to know ~ you need help. ⚠ *if* = **1.** wenn, falls; **2.** ob

TIPP

Das Vokabelpuzzle

- Du brauchst einen Bogen weißen Karton (DIN A4), ein Lineal, eine Schere, Schreibzeug.
- Unterteile den Karton mit Lineal und Bleistift wie im Beispiel rechts in Drei- und Vierecke.
- Trage jetzt – wie im Beispiel rechts – die Vokabeln und ihre Übersetzung ein.
- Schneide nun die einzelnen Puzzleteile aus. Beim Puzzeln helfen dir die Form der Teile und deine Vokabelkenntnisse.

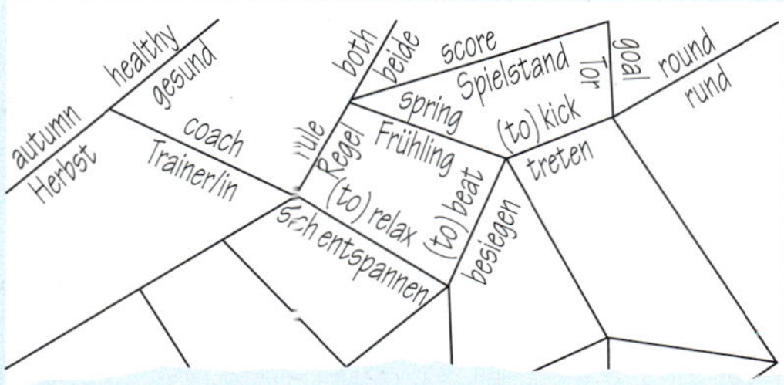

Am besten, du arbeitest mit einem Partner/einer Partnerin, dann könnt ihr eure Puzzles tauschen.

Unit 2: London

pp. 22/23 **bank** [bæŋk] | (Fluss-)Ufer

⚠ *(Sitz-)Bank = bench*

theatre [⚠ 'θɪətə] | Theater | *lat.* theatrum, *frz.* le théâtre

(to) **learn about** sth. | etwas über/von etwas erfahren, etwas über etwas herausfinden | When *did* you ~ *about* their plans? Come to 'Water World' and ~ *about* dolphins and sea lions!

violent ['vaɪələnt] | gewalttätig, gewaltsam | Some pupils become ~ and hit other pupils.

(to) **mention** ['menʃn] | erwähnen, nennen | They'll help you if you ~ my name. *frz.* mentionner

Some places and sights in London

Big Ben die Glocke der Turmuhr des Parlamentsgebäudes (umgangssprachlich auch für Turm und Uhr des Parlamentsgebäudes gebraucht)

Buckingham Palace [ˌbʌkɪŋəm 'pæləs] Londoner Wohnsitz der Königin/des Königs

Chinatown ['tʃaɪnətaʊn] Straßenviertel im Stadtteil Soho mit vielen chinesischen Läden und Restaurants

Covent Garden [ˌkɒvnt 'gɑːdn] ehemaliger Obst-, Blumen- und Gemüsegroßmarkt, jetzt bunter Treffpunkt mit Straßencafés, Verkaufsständen, Straßentheater, Straßenmusikern usw.

the **Globe Theatre** [ˌgləʊb 'θɪətə] Nachbau des Theaters, in dem Anfang des 17. Jahrhunderts Shakespeares berühmteste Stücke uraufgeführt wurden (*globe* = Globus)

the **Houses of Parliament** das Parlamentsgebäude

Leicester Square [⚠ ˌlestə 'skweə] bes. bei Touristen beliebter autofreier Platz im Zentrum Londons

the **London Aquarium** [ə'kweəriəm] das Londoner Aquarium (mit ca. 3.000 verschiedenen Arten von Meerestieren u. -pflanzen)

the **London Dungeon** ['dʌndʒən] Stadtmuseum nahe der London Bridge (*dungeon* = Kerker, Verlies)

the **London Eye** im Jahr 2000 eröffnetes, 135 m hohes Riesenrad am Themseufer

Madame Tussaud's [ˌmædəm tə'sɔːdz] Madame Tussauds Wachsfigurenkabinett

the **Millennium Bridge** [mɪ'leniəm] im Jahr 2000 eröffnete, 325 m lange Fußgängerbrücke über die Themse (*millennium* = Jahrtausend[wende])

the **Monument** ['mɒnjumənt] Säule zum Gedenken an das „Große Feuer" in London (1666)

Nelson's Column [ˌnelsnz 'kɒləm] die Nelson-Säule (auf dem Trafalgar Square)

Piccadilly Circus [ˌpɪkədɪli 'sɜːkəs] Platz im West End mit berühmter Eros-Statue (*Statue of Eros* ['ɪərɒs]), Touristentreffpunkt

St Paul's (Cathedral) [sənt 'pɔːlz] die St. Pauls-Kathedrale (im Zentrum Londons)

the **(River) Thames** [temz] die Themse

the **Tate Modern** Gemäldegalerie am Südufer der Themse

the **Tower (of London)** mittelalterliche Festung, heute Aufbewahrungsort der Kronjuwelen

Tower Bridge Klappbrücke beim Tower

Trafalgar Square [trəˌfælgə 'skweə] Platz im West End mit Nelson-Säule

the **West End** [ˌwest‿'end] Stadtteil im Zentrum mit zahlreichen Einkaufsstraßen, Hotels, Kinos, Diskotheken und Theatern

Westminster Abbey [ˌwestmɪnstər‿'æbi] die Westminster-Abtei (Krönungskirche der englischen Könige und Königinnen)

avenue ['ævənjuː] Allee, Boulevard
circus ['sɜːkəs] (runder) Platz *(in einer Stadt)*
column ['kɒləm] Säule
palace ['pæləs] Palast, Schloss
square [skweə] Platz *(in einer Stadt)*
statue ['stætʃuː] Statue

p. 24/A1	(to) **get off** **(-tt-)** [ˌget_ˈɒf]	aussteigen	This is Oxford Circus. We have to ~ *off* here.

German 'einsteigen' – 'aussteigen'

(to) **get on** / (to) **get off** – **a bus**, **a train**, **a plane**, **a bike**

She *got on* the bus at 2.30.
He *got off* the train at Euston Station.
We *got in(to)* the car and drove away.
The driver helped me to *get out of* the taxi.

(to) **get in(to)** / (to) **get out of** – **a car**, **a taxi**

	nervous [⚠ ˈnɜːvəs]	nervös, aufgeregt	Do you feel frightened before tests? – No, just a bit ~.
	the underground *(no pl)* [ˈʌndəgraʊnd]	die U-Bahn	Take *the underground / the tube* to Oxford Street. There's an *underground* station / a *tube* station at Oxford Circus.
	the tube *(no pl)* [tjuːb] *(infml)*	die U-Bahn *(in London) (eigentlich:* Rohr, Röhre*)*	⚠ Wann fährt die nächste *U-Bahn* nach …? = When's the next *(underground) train* to …?
	(to) **walk off** [ˌwɔːk_ˈɒf]	weggehen	When I try to talk to him, he just *~s off*.
A2	**line** [laɪn]	(U-Bahn-)Linie	What's the best *route* from Queensway to Piccadilly Circus? – Take the Central *Line* to Oxford Circus. Then *change* to the Bakerloo *Line*.
	route [ruːt]	Route, Strecke	
	(to) **change** (trains)	umsteigen	
p. 25/A4	**wax figure** [ˈwæks ˌfɪgə]	Wachsfigur	At Madame Tussaud's you can see ~ *figures* of a lot of famous people.

Time phrases with 'for'

Present perfect + *for*

The people at Madame Tussaud's *have made* wax figures *for more than 200 years*.
… machen schon seit über 200 Jahren Wachsfiguren.

Etwas hat in der Vergangenheit begonnen und **dauert heute/jetzt noch an.**
(Deutsch: Präsens + „seit …")

Simple past + *for*

Marie Tussaud *made* wax figures *for more than 20 years* in the 18th century.
Im 18. Jahrhundert machte Marie Tussaud mehr als 20 Jahre lang Wachsfiguren.

Etwas dauerte einen bestimmten Zeitraum in der Vergangenheit an, **ist aber beendet.**
(Deutsch: Präteritum + „… lang")

	owner [ˈəʊnə]	Besitzer/in	Who's the ~ of that car outside? Is it the Scott's car?
	mask [mɑːsk]	Maske	*masks* 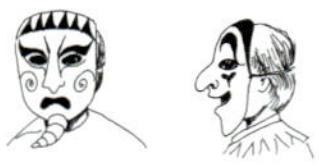 *frz.* la masque
	revolution [ˌrevəˈluːʃn]	Revolution	*frz.* la révolution
	successful [səkˈsesfl]	erfolgreich	Madonna is a very ~ pop singer.
	all around the country [ˈɔːl_əˌraʊnd]	überall im Land	People play football ~ ~ *the world*.
	known as [ˈnəʊn_əz]	bekannt als	His name is Marshall Mathers, but he is ~ ~ Eminem.
	(to) **execute** [ˈeksɪkjuːt]	hinrichten	*frz.* exécuter
	natural [⚠ ˈnætʃrəl]	natürlich, Natur-	It is ~ for parents to love their children. *lat.* naturalis,e *frz.* naturel,le
	earthquake [ˈɜːθkweɪk]	Erdbeben	The ~ destroyed a lot of buildings and killed hundreds of people.
	live *(adj; adv)* [laɪv]	live, direkt, Live-	Listening to ~ music is more exciting than listening to CDs.
	event [ɪˈvent]	Ereignis; Veranstaltung	The first day at school is a big ~ in a child's life.
	scientific [ˌsaɪənˈtɪfɪk]	(natur)wissenschaftlich	adjective: *scientific* – nouns: *science, scientist* *frz.* scientifique
	scientist [ˈsaɪəntɪst]	(Natur-)Wissenschaftler/in	
	discovery [dɪˈskʌvəri]	Entdeckung	The ~ of penicillin [ˌpenɪˈsɪlɪn] has saved many lives.
	(to) **discover** [dɪˈskʌvə]	entdecken; herausfinden, feststellen	Alexander Fleming *~ed* penicillin in 1928. Yesterday I *~ed* that there's a new café in Elm Street.
A5	(to) **be made of …**	aus … (gemacht) sein	*Is* the bottle ~ *of* plastic or glass?
p. 26/A7	(to) **pick** sb./sth. **up** [ˌpɪk_ˈʌp]	jn./etwas abholen, mitnehmen; etwas *(vom Boden)* aufheben	You can come with me, my mother is going to drive me. We'*ll* ~ you *up* at 8.20. OK? Who dropped this paper on the floor? Come and ~ it *up*.

	by	von; durch	The song 'We are the champions' was written ~ *Queen*. Our house was destroyed ~ fire.
	(to) **hold** [həʊld], **held, held** [held]	veranstalten, abhalten	Where *do* they ~ the Changing of the Guard ceremony? In front of Buckingham Palace?
	pigeon [⚠ 'pɪdʒɪn]	Taube	*frz.* le pigeon
	(to) **chase** sb. **(away)** [tʃeɪs]	jn. (weg-/ver)jagen	The dog *is chasing* the cat. 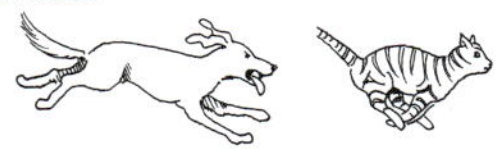
	pocket ['pɒkɪt]	Tasche *(an einem Kleidungsstück)*	 pockets  bags
	(to) **rob (-bb-)** [rɒb]	berauben, ausrauben	⚠ • People *steal* things *from* a place or person: A man *stole* £50 *from* Mr Harold. *(stehlen, rauben)* • People *rob* a bank, a post office, etc. or a person: The men *robbed* the bank. *(ausrauben)* A woman *robbed* me on my way home. *(berauben)*
	hero ['hɪərəʊ], *pl* **heroes** ['hɪərəʊz]	Held, Heldin; Idol, Vorbild	Batman and Superwoman are famous comic ~*es*. When I was a little boy, my grandpa was my ~. *lat.* heros, *frz.* le héros
p. 27/A10	**homelessness** ['həʊmləsnəs]	Obdachlosigkeit	
	homeless ['həʊmləs]	obdachlos	A person without a home is a ~ person.
	(to) **sell** [sel], **sold, sold** [səʊld]	verkaufen	▸◂ (to) buy
	issue ['ɪʃuː]	(Streit-)Frage, Thema, Angelegenheit	Homelessness is one of the big ~*s* of our time.
	off [ɒf]	von (… herunter/ hinunter)	We must help homeless people to get ~ the streets. The boy fell ~ the roof and broke his leg.
A11	how he **might** answer [maɪt]	wie er (vielleicht) antworten könnte	Where could they be? – I don't know. They ~ be at home. (= Vielleicht sind sie zu Hause.)
A12	**rest (of)** [rest]	Rest	After lunch we spent the ~ *of* the day at the beach.
A13	**e.g.** [ˌiː 'dʒiː] *(from Latin 'exempli gratia')*	z. B. (zum Beispiel)	Some English words are the same in German, *e.g.* (= for example) 'quiz' or 'computer'.
	transport *(no pl)* ['trænspɔːt]	Verkehrsmittel	Buses, trains and cars are all forms of ~.
p. 28/A14	**celebration** [ˌselɪ'breɪʃn]	(Gedenk-)Feier	Mum will be 40 next week. We're going to have a ~. *lat.* celebratio, *frz.* la célébration
	community [kə'mjuːnəti]	Gemeinde, Gemeinschaft	a group of people who live in the same place *lat.* communitas, *frz.* la communauté
	mayor [⚠ meə]	Bürgermeister/in	the head of a town or city
	(to) **take part (in)**	teilnehmen (an), mitmachen (bei)	80 people *took* ~ *in* the race. (= 80 people ran.)
	colourful ['kʌləfl]	bunt, farbenfroh, farbenprächtig	I don't like ~ clothes. I always wear black.
	(to) **watch out**	aufpassen	*Watch* ~. There's a lot of traffic on this road.
	thief [θiːf], *pl* **thieves** [θiːvz]	Dieb/in	
	(to) **be about** [ə'baʊt]	unterwegs sein	It was late at night, so there *weren't* many people ~.
	purse [pɜːs]	Portmonee, Geldbeutel	Don't leave the money on the table, put it in your ~ or your pocket.
	any ['eni]	jede(r/s) (beliebige)	It's so easy, ~ child could do it.

'any' in positive sentences

You can come *any* day you like.	… an *irgendeinem* Tag / an *jedem beliebigen* Tag
You're just as good as *anybody/anyone* else.	… wie *jeder* andere / wie *irgendein* anderer
You can have *anything* you like for Christmas.	… *(alles,) was* du willst
There are more tourists here than *anywhere* else.	… als *irgendwo* sonst, als an *jedem* anderen Ort

any/anybody etc. is often used after *if*: If *anybody* has *any* questions, I'll do my best to answer them.
Wenn jemand irgendwelche Fragen hat, …

	exactly *(adv)* [ɪɡ'zæktli]	genau	Sue and John are ~ the same size. *lat.* exactus,a,um
	exact *(adj)* [ɪɡ'zækt]	genau	What's the ~ size of Germany? *frz.* exact,e
	fault [fɔːlt]	Schuld; Fehler	You didn't wake me up this morning. It's your ~ that I'm late for school. *frz.* la faute
	wherever [weər'evə]	wohin (auch) immer; wo (auch) immer	I'll come with you, ~ you go. We'll find you, ~ you are.

wherever, whenever, whoever, whatever

Wherever you go, I'll come with you.	*Wo auch immer* du hingehst, …
Visit me *whenever* you like.	…, *wann immer* du willst.
I won't open the door, *whoever* you are.	…, *wer immer* Sie *auch* sind.
I'll help you *whatever* happens.	…, *was immer auch* geschieht.

P 1 **Adverb oder Adjektiv nach bestimmten Verben?**

- **verb + adverb:**
  Wie du weißt, werden nach Verben **Adverbien der Art und Weise** verwendet, um zu sagen, **wie jemand etwas tut**.
  Mr Martin waited nervously.
  Mr Martin wartete nervös.
  (Wie wartete er? – Nervös.)
- **verb + adjective:**
  Es gibt auch Verben, die nicht Tätigkeiten beschreiben, sondern **Zustände oder Eigenschaften (wie jemand oder etwas ist)**. Nach diesen Verben stehen **Adjektive**.
  to smell to taste to seem to become
  – Mr Martin felt *nervous*.
  Mr Martin fühlte sich nervös / war nervös.
  (Wie fühlte er sich? Wie war er? – Nervös.)
  – The choir sang a song. It sounded *beautiful*.
  Der Chor sang ein Lied. Es klang wunderschön.

Vergleiche: (1) Debbie looked *angrily* at Nick. *Debbie sah Nick wütend an.* (Tätigkeit)
(2) Debbie looked *angry*. *Debbie sah wütend aus.* (Zustand)

P 5	(to) **design** [dɪ'zaɪn]	entwerfen, konstruieren	Jill's parents *~ed* and built their own house.
	bell [bel]	Glocke, Klingel	*bells* 
P 7	**prince** [prɪns]	Prinz	*lat.* princeps, *frz.* le prince
	rich [rɪtʃ]	reich	Someone who has a lot of money is ~. ⧓ poor
P 9	(to) **welcome** sb. **(to)** ['welkəm]	jn. willkommen heißen (in)	When Liz and Pete arrived, Sue *~d* them.  ⚠ *(to) welcome* is a regular verb: *welcome – welcomed – welcomed*
	headteacher [ˌhed'tiːtʃə], **Head** *(BE)*	Schulleiter/in	The person who runs the school is called the ~.
P 11	**suggestion** [sə'dʒestʃn]	Vorschlag	verb: (to) suggest – noun: *suggestion*
P 12	(to) **get** sb. **into trouble**	jn. in Schwierigkeiten bringen	You*'ll* ~ me *into* ~ if you take my father's bike.
	mystery *(n; adj)* ['mɪstri]	Rätsel; rätselhafte(r, s)	How the car got in the swimming-pool is a ~. She's got a ~ illness. Nobody knows what it is.

Save the Crown Jewels

p. 33	**maze** [meɪz]	Irrgarten, Labyrinth	
	enough [ɪ'nʌf]	genug	I wanted to go to the beach but it wasn't warm ~.
	total *(n)* [⚠ 'təʊtl]	Gesamtbetrag, Summe	I've got 20p and you've got 50p. We've got a ~ of 70p.
	(to) **be alive** [ə'laɪv]	leben, am Leben sein	⧓ (to) be dead ⚠ Pronunciation: *alive* [ə'laɪv] – *(to) live* [lɪv]
	pipe [paɪp]	Pfeife	*frz.* la pipe 

	(to) **smoke** [sməʊk]	rauchen	When you see this sign, you mustn't ~. 
	(to) **pass** [pɑːs]	vergehen, vorübergehen *(Zeit)*	The lesson was so interesting that the time ~*ed* really quickly. *frz.* passer
	directions *(pl)* [də'rekʃnz]	Anweisung(en)	
	(to) **catch a train/bus** [kætʃ], **caught, caught** [kɔːt]	einen Zug/Bus nehmen, erreichen	We don't have to walk, we can ~ *a bus*. We had to run to ~ *the bus*.
p. 34	(to) **hide** [haɪd], **hid** [hɪd], **hidden** ['hɪdn]	(sich) verstecken	Let's ~ behind that tree. They won't see us there.
	platform ['plætfɔːm]	Bahnsteig, Gleis	The train to London leaves from ~ 3.
	invention [ɪn'venʃn]	Erfindung	*lat.* inventio, *frz.* l'invention *(f)*
	(to) **invent** [ɪn'vent]	erfinden	Alexander Graham Bell ~*ed* the telephone in 1876. *lat.* invenire, *frz.* inventer
p. 35	**until** [ən'tɪl]	bis	till
	gun [gʌn]	Schusswaffe	The police officer pulled out his ~ and shouted, 'Stop!'
	(to) **scan** **(-nn-)** [skæn]	*(einen Text)* überfliegen *(um bestimmte Informationen zu finden)*	
	specific [spə'sɪfɪk]	bestimmte(r, s), spezifische(r, s)	*frz.* spécifique specific – spezifisch
	past *(prep; adv)* [pɑːst]	vorbei, vorüber (an)	We drove ~ houses, farms and factories. I was waiting at the bus stop when Julia's mother drove ~. ⚠ She walked *past* me. = She passed me.
	technique [⚠ tek'niːk]	(Arbeits-)Verfahren, Technik, Methode	How do you learn new words? Do you have a special ~? *frz.* la technique
	edge [edʒ]	Rand, Kante	Put your cup in the middle of the table, not on the ~.
p. 36	(to) **make sure** [ʃʊə]	sich vergewissern; darauf achten/dafür sorgen (, dass)	Please *make* ~ that you turn off the lights when you leave the room.
	character [⚠ 'kærəktə]	Charakter; Person, Figur *(in Roman, Film usw.)*	*frz.* le caractère
	(to) **let** sb. **in (-tt-), let, let** [let]	jn. hereinlassen	The front door is locked. Can you ~ me *in*, please?
	useful ['juːsfəl]	nützlich	A boat with a hole in the bottom is not very ~.
	He/she won't take 'no' for an answer.	Er/sie will ein „Nein" nicht akzeptieren.	
	I'm afraid ... [ə'freɪd]	Leider ...	I have to go now, *I'm* ~. *or:* *I'm* ~ I have to go now. (= Sorry, but I can't stay.)

TIPP

So unregelmäßig sind die unregelmäßigen Verben gar nicht!

Wenn du dir die Liste der unregelmäßigen Verben (S. 202/203) einmal genauer ansiehst, wirst du feststellen, dass man Gruppen bilden kann, die sich viel leichter lernen lassen.

- Gruppe 1: **A** **A** **A**
  cost cost cost
  let let let
  …
- Gruppe 2: **A** **B** **A**
  become became become
  run ran run
  …
- Gruppe 3: **A** **B** **B**
  hold held held
  sell sold sold
  …
- Gruppe 4: **A** **B** **C**
  hide hid hidden
  take took taken
  …

Welche der unregelmäßigen Verben, die dir bekannt sind, passen in welche Gruppe?

How to find and use information

p. 37	**site** [saɪt]	Stätte; Stelle, Standort	
	(to) **explore** [ɪk'splɔː]	erforschen, erkunden	You really need a car to ~ the countryside. *lat.* explorare, *frz.* explorer
	interpretation [⚠ ɪnˌtɜːprɪ'teɪʃn]	Interpretation, Deutung	*lat.* interpretatio, *frz.* l'interpretation *(f)*
	(to) **run**	verlaufen, sich erstrecken *(Grenze, Straße)*	The Berlin Wall *ran* through the German city of Berlin.
	conference [⚠ 'kɒnfrəns]	Konferenz, Kongress, Tagung	*frz.* la conférence
	(to) **underline** [ˌʌndə'laɪn]	unterstreichen	Go through the text and ~ all the verbs.
	(to) **mark** [mɑːk]	markieren, kennzeichnen	
	source [sɔːs]	*(Informations-, Text-)* Quelle	The Internet can be a useful ~ of information. *frz.* la source
	statistics *(pl)* [stə'tɪstɪks]	Statistik(en)	*Statistics* show that women live longer than men. *frz.* la statistique

Unit 3: When the Romans Ruled Britannia

p. 40	**bath** [bɑːθ]	Bad	⚠ *(in der Wanne)* baden, ein Bad nehmen = *(to) take a bath, (to) have a bath*
	70 **AD** [ˌeɪ'diː]	70 n. Chr.	70 *AD* = 70 years after the birth of Christ [kraɪst]
	70 **BC** [ˌbiː'siː]	70 v. Chr.	70 *BC* = 70 years before the birth of Christ ⚠ Wortstellung: *70 **AD*** or ***AD** 70*; but only: *70 **BC***
	comb [⚠ kəʊm]	Kamm	a *comb* 
	(to) **comb**	kämmen	⚠ Vergiss nicht, dich *zu kämmen*. = Don't forget *to comb your hair*.
	spoon [spuːn]	Löffel	*knife and fork* 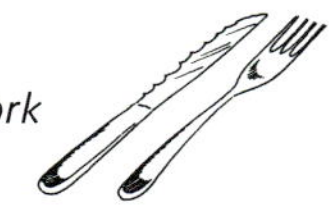 *spoons* 
	fork [fɔːk]	Gabel	
	oil-lamp ['ɔɪllæmp]	Öllampe	The Romans didn't have electric lights. They used ~-~*s*.
	coin [kɔɪn]	Münze	I tried to make a phone call, but it was one of those old phone boxes where you still need ~*s*.
	(to) **belong to** [bɪ'lɒŋ]	gehören (zu)	Who *does* this book ~ *to*? – I think it's Julia's.
	(to) **light** [laɪt], **lit, lit** [lɪt]	anzünden; beleuchten, erhellen	*(to) light* a firework 
	(to) **keep** [kiːp], **kept, kept** [kept]	aufbewahren, aufheben	Where *do* you ~ all your photos? – In my album. You should ~ your notes, you might need them again.
p. 41/A1	(to) **run out**	knapp werden, zu Ende gehen, ausgehen	There's only five more minutes before the match finishes – time *is running* ~.
	I'**ve run out of** money.	Mir ist das Geld ausgegangen.	

(to) run

John can't *run* very fast.	*laufen, rennen*	We*'ve been running* cycling holidays for 25 years.	*durchführen, veranstalten*
Till 1989, the Berlin Wall *ran* along this street.	*verlaufen, sich erstrecken*	I'm afraid we*'ve run out of* coffee. Would you like tea?	*ausgehen, knapp werden*
Catherine's parents *run* a hotel by the sea.	*betreiben, leiten*		

(to) **dig (up)** **(-gg-)** [dɪg], **dug, dug** [dʌg]	(aus-, um)graben	Last week archaeologists *dug* ~ a Roman comb.
(to) **return** [rɪ'tɜːn]	zurückkehren; zurücksenden, -bringen	I left London on 3rd May and ~*ed* on 14th May. I have to ~ my library books tomorrow. *frz.* retourner
unfortunately [ʌn'fɔːtʃnətli]	leider, unglücklicherweise	Jane is giving a party on Saturday, but ~ I can't go. ⧓ fortunately
valuable ['væljuəbl]	wertvoll	This oil-lamp is Roman. It's very ~.

one/ones

Im Deutschen können Adjektive und Artikel auch allein, ohne folgendes Nomen stehen:	Die rote Jacke steht dir gut, aber die **schwarze** ist billiger. Die Boutiquen hier sind nicht so gut wie **die** in Ashton.
Im Englischen musst du in solchen Fällen *one* (Singular) bzw. *ones* (Plural) verwenden:	The red jacket looks good on you, but the **black one** is cheaper. The boutiques here are not as good as **the ones** in Ashton.

That **may** be your idea of … [meɪ]	Das ist vielleicht deine Vorstellung von …	

möglich – wahrscheinlich – sicherlich

My parents	**may** **might** **could** **should** **must**	be at home now.	Meine Eltern	sind jetzt *vielleicht* zu Hause. *könnten* jetzt *vielleicht* zu Hause sein. *könnten* jetzt zu Hause sein. *sollten/müssten eigentlich* jetzt zu Hause sein. *müssen* jetzt zu Hause sein.

	fence [fens]	Zaun	a *fence* 
	painted ['peɪntɪd]	bemalt; farbig	
	(to) **paint** [peɪnt]	malen, anstreichen	Picasso *~ed* all his girlfriends. *lat.* pingere, *frz.* peindre The kids want to ~ their bedroom pink.
	painting ['peɪntɪŋ]	Gemälde, Bild; Malerei	a *painting* of his mother 
p. 42/A5	**modern** [⚠ 'mɒdən]	modern	*frz.* moderne
	while *(conj)* [waɪl]	während	I can learn some new words ~ I'm waiting. ⚠ 'False friends': *while* = während • weil = *because*
	empire ['empaɪə]	Reich, Weltreich	*lat.* imperium, *frz.* l'empire *(m)*
	soldier ['səʊldʒə]	Soldat, Soldatin	*frz.* le soldat
	(to) **last** [lɑːst]	halten, nicht kaputtgehen *(Dinge, Obst, Ehe usw.)*	It's a very cheap radio. It *won't* ~ very long.
	pot [pɒt]	Topf, Kochtopf	*frz.* le pot
	(to) **bake** [beɪk]	backen	Many Roman families *~d* their own bread.
	oven [⚠ 'ʌvn]	Backofen	
	olive [⚠ 'ɒlɪv]	Olive; Oliven-	*lat.* oliva, *frz.* l'olive *(f)*
	skin [skɪn]	Haut	Do 'white' people really have white ~?
p. 43/A6	**car park** *(BE)*	Parkplatz	 a *car park*  a *parking space*
	god, goddess [gɒd, 'gɒdes]	Gott, Göttin	⚠ *God* (= christlicher Gott) wird großgeschrieben.
	wine [waɪn]	Wein	*lat.* vinum, *frz.* le vin
	comfortable [⚠ 'kʌmftəbl]	bequem, komfortabel, angenehm	◂▸ uncomfortable *frz.* confortable
	central heating [ˌsentrəl 'hiːtɪŋ]	Zentralheizung	Most homes in Britain have *central ~*.
	bowl [⚠ bəʊl]	Schüssel, Schale	a *bowl* 
	mosaic [⚠ məʊ'zeɪɪk]	Mosaik	*lat.* mosaicus, *frz.* la mosaïque
p. 44/A10	(to) **reply (to** sb./sth.**)** [rɪ'plaɪ]	erwidern; (jm.) antworten; (auf etwas) antworten	(to) answer *lat.* replicare 'Some cake?' asked Scott. – 'Yes, please,' Sue *replied.* Please ~ *to* this letter before the end of the month.
	more and more expensive	immer teurer	⚠ immer teurer = *more and more expensive* immer billiger = *cheaper and cheaper*
A12	(to) **thank** sb. [θæŋk]	jm. danken, sich bei jm. bedanken	(to) say 'thank you'
	(to) **get married (to** sb.**)** [ˌget 'mærɪd]	(jn.) heiraten, (sich ver)heiraten (mit jm.)	Ann is married now. She *got* ~ to Tom Dean last year.
	(to) **marry** (sb.) ['mæri]	(jn.) heiraten	Ann *married* Tom Dean last year. *frz.* se marier avec qn

	Bad luck.	Pech (gehabt)!	
	anyway ['eniweɪ]	trotzdem; sowieso	

anyway

It was raining, but they went out *anyway*. – …, aber sie gingen *trotzdem* raus.
It was raining, but we didn't want to go out *anyway*. – …, aber wir wollten *sowieso* nicht rausgehen.

	(to) **be good at** sth.	gut in etwas sein; etwas gut können	My sister likes maths – she's really *good* ~ it. And she's *good* ~ writing poems. ⧓ (to) be bad at sth.
	sum [sʌm]	Rechenaufgabe; Summe	I hate maths. I hate doing ~s. ⚠ *(to) do sums* = rechnen *lat.* summa, *frz.* la somme
	straight *(adj; adv)* [streɪt]	gerade; gerade(wegs), direkt	a ~ line ——— When I saw how late it was, I went ~ home.
P 2	(to) **be interested (in)** ['ɪntrəstɪd]	interessiert sein (an), sich interessieren (für)	David is a sports freak. He *is* very *interested* ~ sports. ⚠ (to) be *interested* (in) = *interessiert* (an); an *interesting* book = ein *interessantes* Buch
P 8	(to) **grow** [grəʊ], **grew** [gru:], **grown** [grəʊn]	wachsen	Orange trees ~ only in hot countries. I've ~*n* a lot. I'm almost as tall as my father now.
P 11	**religion** [⚠ rɪ'lɪdʒn]	Religion	*lat.* religio, *frz.* la religion
	art [ɑ:t]	Kunst	⚠ 'False friends': *art* = Kunst • Art, Sorte = *sort, type* *lat.* ars, *frz.* l'art *(m)*
P 12	**prefix** ['pri:fɪks]	Vorsilbe, Präfix	*frz.* le préfixe
P 13	(to) **replace** sth. **(with)** [rɪ'pleɪs]	etwas ersetzen (durch)	We had to ~ the underlined nouns *with* pronouns. ⚠ ersetzen durch = *(to) replace with*
P 14	**planet** [⚠ 'plænɪt]	Planet	*lat.* planeta, *frz.* la planète
	Invaders		
p. 49	(to) **invade (a country)** [ɪn'veɪd]	einmarschieren (in ein Land), (ein Land) überfallen	The Romans ~*d* Britain in 43 AD. *lat.* invadere
	invasion (of) [⚠ ɪn'veɪʒn]	Invasion, Einmarsch, Einfall (in)	1066 was the year of the Norman ~ *of* Britain. *lat.* invasio, *frz.* l'invasion *(f)*
	The Britons		
	peaceful ['pi:sfl]	friedlich, friedfertig	adjective: *peaceful* – adverb: *peacefully* ⧓ violent
	peace [pi:s]	Friede(n)	*lat.* pax, *frz.* la paix
	(to) **fight (against)** sb./sth. [faɪt], **fought, fought** [fɔ:t]	jn./etwas bekämpfen, gegen jn./etwas kämpfen	Look, those two dogs *are* ~*ing* again.
	fight *(n)* [faɪt]	Kampf, Schlägerei	
	nature [⚠ 'neɪtʃə]	Natur	⚠ No article: *Nature* is the mother of life. *lat.* natura, *frz.* la nature
	feeling ['fi:lɪŋ]	Gefühl	I feel funny. I've got a funny ~ in my head. verb: (to) feel – noun: *feeling*
	(to) **get rid of** sb./sth. [rɪd]	jn./etwas loswerden	I don't want to see him. Can't you *get* ~ *of* him? I never wear this pullover. I'm going to *get* ~ *of* it.
	The Romans		
	Latin [⚠ 'lætɪn]	Latein	
	(to) **do well**	erfolgreich sein, gut zurechtkommen	I'*m doing* ~ in English. In my last test I got a '1'.
	army [⚠ 'ɑ:mi]	Armee, Heer	*frz.* l'armée *(f)*
	goods *(pl)* [gʊdz]	Waren, Güter	The Romans made ~ and sold them all over Europe.
p. 50	**The Anglo-Saxons**		
	(to) **push** [pʊʃ]	drücken, schieben, stoßen	
	(to) **be left**	übrig sein	The dog has eaten all the cake. There's nothing ~.
	common ['kɒmən]	häufig, weit verbreitet	Red buses are very ~ in London. *lat.* communis,e

	except [ɪk'sept]	außer	They have invited everybody ~ me. Homework is OK, ~ maths. *lat.* exceptus,a,um *frz.* excepté

The Vikings

> **as = 'wie'**
>
> *As* you know, Chester is a town in England.
> *Wie ihr wisst, ist Chester eine Stadt in England.*
> Traffic is a problem here, *as* in all big cities.
> *…, wie in allen großen Städten.*
>
> **as = 'als'**
>
> 'Hi,' he said *as* (= when) she opened the door.
> *„Hi", sagte er, als sie die Tür öffnete.*
> My uncle works *as* a taxi driver.
> *Mein Onkel arbeitet als Taxifahrer.*

	(to) **smell** [smel]	riechen	I could ~ the cake that my mum was making. 'Mmmm, that ~s good,' I said.
p. 51	**The Normans**		
	battle ['bætl]	Schlacht, Kampf	How many soldiers were killed in the ~? *frz.* la bataille
	(to) **order** sth. ['ɔːdə]	etwas befehlen, anordnen	⚠ *(to) order* = **1.** bestellen *(im Restaurant)*; **2.** befehlen, anordnen
	survey (of) ['sɜːveɪ]	Umfrage, Untersuchung (über/von)	We did a ~ *of* people's favourite sports at our school. Most people liked football best.
	detail [⚠ 'diːteɪl]	Detail, Einzelheit	I know the story, but I can't remember the ~*s*.
	people	Volk	⚠ *the people* = **1.** die Leute/Menschen; **2.** das Volk *the peoples* = die Völker *lat.* populus, *frz.* le peuple
	influence (on) ['ɪnfluəns]	Einfluss (auf)	*frz.* l'influence *(f)*
p. 52	**extract (from)** [⚠ 'ekstrækt]	Auszug (aus *einem Buch, Text, Film usw.*)	In our test, we had to answer questions on an ~ *from* a book.
	mainly ['meɪnli]	hauptsächlich, vorwiegend	The tourists were ~ from Germany, but there were some from other countries, too.
	main [meɪn]	Haupt-	the ~ question = the most important question There's always a lot of traffic on ~ roads.
	however [haʊ'evə]	jedoch, aber	Our team played well. *However*, we lost the game. ⚠ *however* ist förmlicher als *but*. Es steht mit Komma.
	(to) **stay behind**	dableiben, zurückbleiben	When we went away on holiday, our dog had to *stay* ~.
	direct speech [⚠ ˌdaɪrekt 'spiːtʃ]	wörtliche Rede, direkte Rede	
p. 53	**How to listen for information**		
	changing room	Umkleideraum	

Welcome to the USA

pp. 56/57	**crime** [kraɪm]	Verbrechen; Kriminalität	⚠ **1.** *crime, pl crimes* = Verbrechen **2.** *crime (no pl)* = Kriminalität *lat.* crimen, *frz.* le crime
	high school ['haɪ skuːl]	(US) *Gesamtschule mit den Klassen 7–12 für 13- bis 18-Jährige*	
	(to) **prefer** sth. **(to)** (-rr-) [prɪ'fɜː]	etwas lieber haben/tun (als), etwas *(einer anderen Sache)* vorziehen	What do you like better, milk or cola? – I ~ milk. *Do* you really ~ milk to cola? *lat.* praeferre, I ~ drinking tea. (= I ~ to drink tea.) *frz.* préferer qc (à)

> **German 'gern' and 'lieber'**
>
> | | |
> |---|---|
> | Ich lese *gern* im Bett. | I *like* reading in bed. |
> | Ich würde/möchte *gern* ihren Namen wissen. | I'*d like to* know her name (= I *would like to* …). |
> | Willst du meinen neuen Computer sehen? | Do you want to see my new computer? |
> | – Oh ja, sehr *gern*. | – Oh yes, I'*d love to* (= I *would love to*). |
> | Was magst du *lieber* – Cola oder Orangensaft? | What do you like *better* – cola or orange juice? |
> | Ich würde *lieber* zu Hause bleiben. | I'*d prefer to* stay at home (= I *would prefer to* …). |

	how they feel about …	was sie über … denken / was sie von … halten	

TIPP

Do-it-yourself-Vokabelrätsel

Selbst gestaltete Vokabelrätsel eignen sich prima zum Wiederholen von Vokabeln in Partner- oder Gruppenarbeit – hier sind zwei Vorschläge:

- ***Versteckte Wörter:***
  1) Zeichne ein Rätselgitter mit 10 mal 10 Feldern.
  2) Wähle einen Oberbegriff, z.B. *clothes*, und suche 8 bis 10 Unterbegriffe dazu *(shirt, trousers, socks, …)*.
  3) Trage die Unterbegriffe in das Gitter ein – waagerecht, senkrecht oder diagonal, vorwärts oder rückwärts.
  4) Ergänze die noch leeren Felder mit beliebig gewählten Buchstaben. (Achtung, es dürfen keine neuen Wörter entstehen!)

  Nun tausche dein Rätsel mit einem Partner/einer Partnerin – wer findet am schnellsten die versteckten Wörter? (Im Beispiel rechts sind die Lösungen hervorgehoben.)

clothes

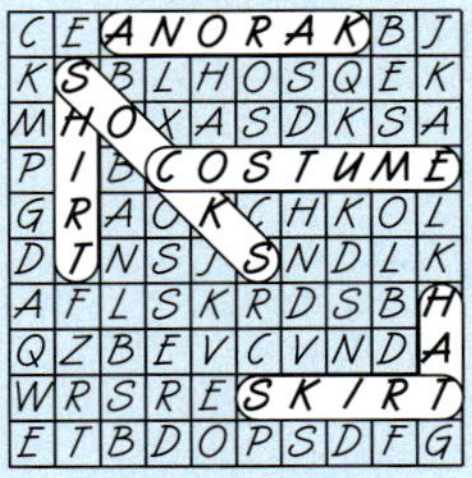

- ***Kammrätsel:***
  1) Zeichne einen „Kamm" wie im Beispiel rechts und lege ein Lösungswort mit 8 bis 10 Buchstaben fest, z.B. *breakfast*.
  2) Suche Wörter, die mit dem 2., 4., 6. und 8. Buchstaben deines Lösungsworts beginnen. Diese Wörter sollten alle gleich viele Buchstaben haben, damit das Rätsel die Form eines Kamms bekommt, z.B. ***r**oad; **a**unt; **f**ast; **s**hop*.
  3) Gib deinem Partner/deiner Partnerin Hinweise, welche senkrechten Wörter gesucht sind, z.B.
     2: *another word for 'street'* 4: *your mother's or your father's sister*
     6: *not slow, but …* 8: *Here you can buy things.*
  4) Gib deinem Partner/deiner Partnerin einen Hinweis auf dein Lösungswort, z.B.
     _ _ _ _ _ _ _ _ _ *is the first meal of the day.*

  Kann dein Partner/deine Partnerin dein Lösungswort finden?

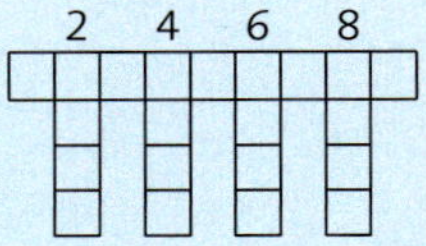

Unit 4: Florida, Space and Sunshine State

p. 58	**sunshine** ['sʌnʃaɪn]	Sonnenschein	
	during *(prep)* ['djʊərɪŋ]	während	We met for a day ~ the summer holidays.

German 'während'

Before a noun:	**during** *(preposition)*	Ann phoned *during* lunch. *Ann rief während des Mittagessens an.*
Before a clause:	**while** *(conjunction)*	Ann phoned *while* we were eating. *Ann rief an, während wir aßen.*

experience [ɪk'spɪəriəns]	Erlebnis, Erfahrung	How was your holiday? – It was a wonderful ~. Bob didn't get the job because he hasn't got enough ~. ⚠ Sie *hat* heute eine neue Erfahrung *gemacht*. = She *had* (nicht: ~~made~~) a new experience today.
mission [⚠ 'mɪʃn]	Einsatz, Mission	The first US ~ into space was in 1964. *frz.* la mission
crew [kru:]	Crew, Besatzung, Mannschaft *(eines Schiffs, Flugzeugs)*	
briefing ['bri:fɪŋ]	Instruktionen, Anweisungen; Einsatzbesprechung	I don't know much about the project. Can you give me a quick ~, please?

	critical (of) ['krɪtɪkl]	entscheidend; kritisch (gegenüber)	very important: The next three weeks will be ~. My parents are always very ~ *of* my choices.
	repair [rɪ'peə]	Reparatur	I've got to do some ~ on my bike tomorrow.
	(to) **repair** [rɪ'peə]	reparieren	The video recorder doesn't work. Do you think you can ~ it? *lat.* reparare, *frz.* réparer
	(to) **drop** sth. **off** **(-pp-)** [ˌdrɒp_'ɒf]	etwas abliefern, etwas vorbeibringen	Can you ~ my books *off* at the library?
	supplies *(pl)* [sə'plaɪz]	Vorräte	The astronauts dropped off ~ at the space station.
	infinite ['ɪnfɪnət]	unendlich	*lat.* infinitus,a,um, *frz.* infini,e
	(to) **book** [bʊk]	buchen, reservieren	I'd like to ~ a table for three for 7 o'clock, please.
p. 59	**program** [⚠ 'prəʊgræm] *(AE)*	Programm	= *BE* programme
	(to) **fall in love (with** sb./sth.**)**	sich verlieben (in jn./etwas)	My best friend *has fallen in* ~ with my brother.
	alligator [⚠ 'ælɪgeɪtə]	Alligator	*frz.* l'alligator *(m)*
	(to) **produce** [prə'djuːs]	produzieren, erzeugen, herstellen	Charles Rolls and Henry Royce ~*d* their first car in 1904. *lat.* producere, *frz.* produire
	grapefruit, *pl* **grapefruit** ['greɪpfruːt]	Grapefruit	
	(to) **offer** ['ɒfə]	bieten, anbieten	She ~*ed* me $50 for my bike. *lat.* offere, *frz.* offrir The language school ~s French and Italian classes.
	Hispanic *(n; adj)* [hɪ'spænɪk]	Hispano-Amerikaner/in *(Einwanderer aus Lateinamerika und dessen/deren Nachkommen)*; hispanisch	
	technical [⚠ 'teknɪkl]	technisch	
	attraction [⚠ ə'trækʃn]	Attraktion, Anziehungspunkt	*frz.* l'attraction *(f)*
p. 60/A1	**ever since** she could remember	seit sie sich erinnern konnte	
	(to) **come true**	wahr werden, sich bewahrheiten	I hope your dreams ~ *true* one day.
	scholarship ['skɒləʃɪp]	Stipendium	(to) win a ~ (= ein Stipendium bekommen)
	elevator ['elɪveɪtə] *(AE)*, **lift** [lɪft] *(BE)*	Fahrstuhl, Aufzug	
	too bad *(infml)*	schade	It's *too* ~ you couldn't come to the party. It was fun.
	whether ['weðə]	ob	He asked me ~ I was coming to his party. ⚠ *whether (conj)* = ob – *weather (n)* = Wetter
p. 61/A4	**pretty** *(adv)* ['prɪti] *(infml)*	ziemlich	⚠ *pretty* = **1.** *(adj)* hübsch – a very *pretty* village **2.** *(adv)* ziemlich – The party was *pretty* good.
	your **loved ones**	deine/eure Lieben	In difficult situations, people often ask their ~ ~ for help.
	(to) **let** sb. **do** sth. **(-tt-), let, let** [let]	jn. etwas tun lassen; jm. erlauben, etwas zu tun	What a big bag! *Let* me *carry* it for you. *Do* your parents ~ you *watch* late films?
	you **ought to** … ['ɔːt tə]	ihr solltet; ihr müsstet (eigentlich)	You ~ *to* go now. = You should go now.

ought to – should

It's cold outside.	You *ought to* put on a jacket. You *should* put on a jacket.	*Du solltest …*	⚠ *ought to* und *should* sind oft austauschbar. *should* wird häufiger verwendet.
We left early.	We *ought to* have enough time. We *should* have enough time.	*Wir müssten (eigentlich) …*	

	leader ['liːdə]	Anführer/in	
	(to) **lead** [liːd], **led, led** [led]	führen, leiten	This road ~*s* to the next village. You ~ and we'll follow.
	(to) **make** sb. **do** sth.	jn. dazu bringen, etwas zu tun; jn. zwingen, etwas zu tun	Our teacher ~*s* us *speak* English in our lessons. I like cartoons. They ~ me *laugh* and they ~ me *feel good*.

(to) let sb. do sth. – (to) make sb. do sth.

He's *letting him drive*.
Er lässt ihn fahren. / Er erlaubt ihm zu fahren.

He's *making him drive* to the airport.
Er bringt ihn dazu / zwingt ihn dazu, zum Flughafen zu fahren.

	access ['ækses]	Zugang	We're disabled. Does the cinema have wheelchair ~? *lat.* accessus, *frz.* l'accès *(m)*
	(to) **need to do** sth.	etwas tun müssen	(to) have to do sth.

'need' – Hilfsverb und Vollverb

Hilfsverb

You *needn't* go now.
Need she go now? *(fml)*

Du brauchst jetzt nicht zu gehen.
Muss sie jetzt gehen?
Musste er abreisen?

Vollverb

You *don't need to* go now.
Does she *need to* go now?
Did he *need to* leave?

⚠ • Fragen und Verneinungen werden ohne *do* gebildet.
• Der folgende Infinitiv steht ohne *to*.

Das Hilfsverb *need(n't)* wird nur im *simple present* verwendet, und zwar hauptsächlich in verneinten Sätzen, seltener auch in Fragen.
Es kommt im britischen Englisch häufiger vor als im amerikanischen Englisch.

⚠ • Fragen und Verneinungen werden mit einer Form von *do* gebildet.
• Der folgende Infinitiv steht mit *to*.

Das Vollverb *(to) need* kann in allen Zeiten verwendet werden.
Es kommt auch in bejahten Sätzen vor:
He *needs to* talk to his mother.

	anyway ['eniweɪ]	außerdem; und überhaupt	No, you can't go out now. And ~, didn't you want to wash the dishes?
	real nice *(adv)* ['ri:əl] *(AE, infml)*	wirklich nett, echt nett	= *BE* really
p. 62/A8	**VIP** [ˌvi:_aɪ 'pi:]	*Abkürzung für „very important person"*	Factory workers are not allowed to use this bathroom. It's for our ~ visitors only.
	out of this world *(infml)*	fantastisch, spitze	This is the best cake I've ever had. It's *out of this* ~.
	(to) **launch** [lɔ:ntʃ]	starten, ins All schießen	(to) ~ a space shuttle = (to) send it into space
	launch	Start, Abschuss	
	satellite [⚠ 'sætəlaɪt]	Satellit	*frz.* le satellite
	especially [ɪ'speʃli]	besonders, insbesondere	I love chocolate, ~ chocolate from Switzerland and Belgium.
	rice [raɪs]	Reis	In China people eat a lot of ~. *lat.* oryza, *frz.* le riz
	(to) **wonder** [⚠ 'wʌndə]	sich fragen, gern wissen wollen	(to) ask yourself I don't know that boy over there. I ~ who he is.
A9	**perception** [pə'sepʃn]	Wahrnehmung	*frz.* la perception
P 8	(to) **enter** ['entə]	betreten; einreisen in	When the new teacher *~ed* the room, everyone stopped talking. Do you need a passport when you ~ Britain? *frz.* entrer
	(to) **catch** [kætʃ], **caught**, **caught** [kɔ:t]	fangen, einfangen	You throw the ball, and *I'll* ~ it. The assistant *caught* the thief and called the police.
	crowd [kraʊd]	(Menschen-)Menge	
	orchestra [⚠ 'ɔ:kɪstrə]	Orchester	a large group of people who play music together
P 9	**line** [laɪn]	(Telefon-)Leitung	⚠ *line* = **1.** Linie; **2.** Zeile; **3.** (Telefon-)Leitung
P 10	**cool** [ku:l]	kühl	
P 12	**instruction** [⚠ ɪn'strʌkʃn]	Anweisung, Anleitung	Read the *~s* carefully before you use the CD player. *frz.* l'instruction *(f)*
P 15	**foot** [fʊt], *pl* **feet** [fi:t]	Fuß *(Längenmaß; 1 Fuß = ca. 30,5 cm)*	My dad is 6 *ft* (= 6 *feet*) tall.

AE pronunciation – BE pronunciation

	American English	British English
ask, last, dance	[æ] [æsk, læst, dæns]	[ɑː] [ɑːsk, lɑːst, dɑːns]
new, Tuesday, stupid	[uː] [nuː, 'tuːzdi, 'stuːpɪd]	[juː] [njuː, 'tjuːzdi, 'stjuːpɪd]
bottle, hot, forgot	[ɑː] ['bɑːtl, hɑːt, fər'gɑːt]	[ɒ] ['bɒtl, hɒt, fə'gɒt]

- In American English you can usually hear the **'r'** in words like ***here***, ***more***, ***shirt***, ***farm***.
- The **'t'** in words like *city*, *better*, *motor* sounds more like a **'d'** in American English.

AE spelling – BE spelling

American English: '-ter'	British English: '-tre'	American English: '-or'	British English: '-our'
cen**ter**	cen**tre**	col**or**	col**our**
me**ter**, kilome**ter**	me**tre**, kilome**tre**	fav**or**ite	fav**our**ite
thea**ter**	thea**tre**	harb**or**	harb**our**

AE: progra**m** – **BE:** progra**mme**
AE: gr**a**y – **BE:** gr**e**y
AE: trave**l**ed, trave**l**ing – **BE:** trave**ll**ed, trave**ll**ing

Little Miss Astronaut

p. 68	(to) **get time off**	frei bekommen, Urlaub bekommen	Mr Jones *got time* ~ when his daughter was born.
	like [laɪk] *(conj, infml)*	als ob	He looked ~ something was wrong. ⚠ *like* („als ob“) is informal. Most people use 'as if', especially in written English: He looked *as if* something was wrong.
	gate [geɪt]	Tor, Pforte, Gatter	Close the ~ so the dog can't get out of the garden.
	fall [fɔːl] *(AE)*	Herbst	= *BE* autumn
	talk [tɔːk]	Vortrag, Referat, Rede; Gespräch	verb: (to) talk – noun: *talk* ⚠ *einen Vortrag/eine Rede (über etwas) halten = (to) give a talk (on sth.)*
	guys *(pl)* [gaɪz] *(besonders AE, infml)*	Leute	⚠ Americans use the plural *guys* (= „Leute“) for women and girls, too:

	recess ['riːses, rɪ'ses] *(AE)*	Pause *(zwischen Schulstunden)*	= *BE* break At ~ I stayed in the classroom.
	proud (of sb./sth.**)** [praʊd]	stolz (auf jn./etwas)	Our daughter is the best pupil in her class. We're ~ *of* her.
p. 69	**Ms** Morrison [mɪz, məz]	Frau Morrison	⚠ Some women prefer the form *Ms* because it doesn't show if they are married or not. Others are happy with *Mrs* (= married) or *Miss* (= unmarried).
	not (...) any more	nicht mehr	I don't need this dictionary ~ ~. Do you want it?
	(to) **call** sb. **(stupid) names**	jn. verspotten, jn. beschimpfen	
	clique [⚠ kliːk]	Clique, Freundeskreis	*frz.* la clique
	jealous (of) ['dʒeləs]	neidisch (auf); eifersüchtig (auf)	John is ~ *of* his sister because she's good at school. Sue is ~ when her boyfriend goes out with other girls. *lat.* zelosus,a,um, *frz.* jaloux,ouse
	block [blɒk]	(Häuser-, Wohn-)Block	*frz.* le bloc
	college ['kɒlɪdʒ]	Hochschule, Fachschule (⚠ *nicht:* ~~Kollege~~)	(to) go to ~; (to) be in ~
	sidewalk ['saɪdwɔːk] *(AE)*	Gehweg, Bürgersteig	= *BE* pavement (⚠ *AE* pavement = Fahrbahn)
	Hang in there! [ˌhæŋ_'ɪn] *(AE, infml)*	Halte durch!	

	glamour *(BE)*/**glamor** *(AE)* ['glæmə] **glamorous** ['glæmərəs]	Glanz glanzvoll	noun: glamour *(BE)* / glamor *(AE)* – adjective: *glamorous (BE, AE)*
	suit [⚠ suːt]	(Herren-)Anzug; (Damen-)Kostüm	*suits*  a space*suit*  ⚠ *suitcase* = Koffer
	neat [niːt] *(AE, infml)*	toll, prima, klasse	= *BE* brilliant, great
	bathroom *(AE)* [*BE:* 'bɑːθruːm, *AE:* 'bæθruːm]	Toilette *(in einem Privathaus)*	= *BE* toilet ['tɔɪlət] ⚠ *restroom* = *AE* for 'öffentliche Toilette'
	(to) **yawn** [jɔːn]	gähnen	 She*'s yawning*.
	(to) look at **each other** [iːtʃ_'ʌðə]	sich (gegenseitig) ansehen, einander ansehen	Paul likes Linda and Linda likes Paul. Linda and Paul like *~ other*.
	(to) **be scared (of; about)** [skeəd]	Angst haben (vor; wegen)	(to) be frightened My little brother *is ~ of* ghosts. What's wrong? – I*'m ~ about* the Maths test.
p. 70	(to) **act** [ækt]	sich verhalten, handeln	Tom *is ~ing* very strangely. What's wrong with him? ⚠ *(to) act* = **1.** spielen, schauspielern; **2.** sich verhalten, handeln
	(to) **stick together** [stɪk], **stuck, stuck** [stʌk]	zusammenhalten	Linda, Rita and their friends always ~ together.
	opinion (of) [ə'pɪnjən]	Meinung (von, zu)	What's your *~ of* this wine? *lat.* opinio ⚠ *In my opinion ...* = Meiner Meinung nach ...

TIPP

Reim dich oder ich fress dich!

Du kannst dir schwierige Wörter, z.B. unregelmäßige Verben, besser merken, wenn du sie in Reimform bringst und dann rhythmisch sprichst – du kannst dabei im Rhythmus klatschen, dann wird daraus so eine Art Rap.
Versuche es mal mit diesen Verben:
drink, fight, let, spend.

lead - led - led sounds like feed - fed - fed
and sell - sold - sold sounds like tell - told - told.
keep - kept - kept sounds like sl... - ...
and grow - grew - grown sounds like ...

In der Liste der unregelmäßigen Verben findest du sicher noch weitere Paare (siehe S. 202/203).

p. 71	**How to tell a story**		
	moon [muːn]	Mond	
	broadcast ['brɔːdkɑːst]	Sendung, Übertragung *(Radio, Fernsehen)*	And now today's news followed by a live ~ from 10 Downing Street.
	oxygen ['ɒksɪdʒən]	Sauerstoff	*frz.* l'oxigène *(m)*
	(to) **explode** [ɪk'spləʊd]	explodieren	Ten people died when a bomb *~d* in a cinema yesterday.
	normal [⚠ 'nɔːml]	normal	usual, ordinary *frz.* normal,e

Stress on the first syllable

alligator	Alligator	**di**alogue	Dialog	**nor**mal	normal	**pro**gram(me)	Programm
alphabet	Alphabet	**in**teresting	interessant	**ner**vous	nervös	**res**taurant	Restaurant
article	Artikel	**mis**sion	Mission, Einsatz	**or**chestra	Orchester	**sa**tellite	Satellit
conference	Konferenz			**pa**radise	Paradies	**sym**bol	Symbol
detail	Detail, Einzelheit	**mo**dern	modern	**per**fect	perfekt	**sys**tem	System
		nature	Natur	**pla**net	Planet	**the**atre	Theater

	controls *(pl)* [kən'trəʊlz]	Steuerpult, Schalttafel; Kontrollinstrumente	
	(to) **join** sb. [dʒɔɪn]	sich jm. anschließen; mitmachen	We're going to the cinema. Do you want to ~ us? *(to) join* = **1.** beitreten, eintreten in *(einen Klub usw.)*; **2.** sich anschließen; mitmachen
	atmosphere [⚠ 'ætməsfɪə]	Atmosphäre	*frz.* l'atmosphère *(f)*
	linking word	Bindewort	Words like *and, but, or, when, because,* etc. are sometimes called '*~ words*'.

Unit 5: Alaska – the Great Land

pp. 74/75	**range** [reɪndʒ]	(Berg-, Felsen-)Kette	The Himalayas is the highest mountain ~ in the world.
p. 76/A1	**whaling** ['weɪlɪŋ]	Walfang	In spring, Amy went ~ in Alaska.
	whale [weɪl]	Wal(fisch)	a *whale* 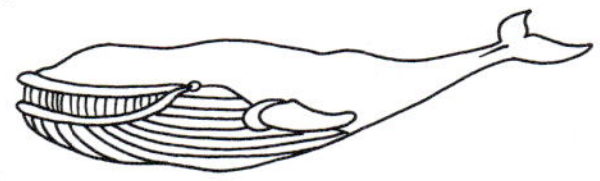
	probably ['prɒbəbli]	wahrscheinlich	Are you going to Steve's party? – *Probably*, but I'm not sure yet. *lat.* probabiliter
	(to) **cover** [⚠ 'kʌvə]	beziehen, überziehen; bedecken, zudecken	That old sofa looks terrible. I'm going to ~ it in red. She *~ed* the piece of paper with her hand so I couldn't read what was on it.
	tent [tent]	Zelt	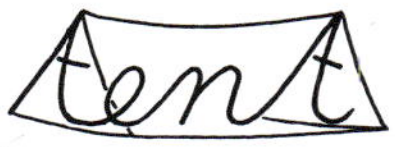 *lat.* tentorium, *frz.* la tente
	in order to do sth. ['ɔːdə]	um etwas zu tun	I went early *in ~ to* get a good seat. ⚠ No comma before *in order to*.
	climate [⚠ 'klaɪmət]	Klima	*frz.* le climat
A2	**introduction (to)** [ˌɪntrə'dʌkʃn]	Einleitung, Einführung (in)	This little book is a good ~ *to* geography. *frz.* l'introduction *(f)*
	(to) **pin (-nn-)** [pɪn]	(an)heften, (an)stecken	
	shocked [ʃɒkt]	schockiert	When I heard that she had died, I was really ~.
	argument [⚠ 'ɑːgjumənt]	Argument, Begründung; Streit	Prepare your *~s* before you start the discussion. Mum and Dad had an ~ last night. Dad shouted a lot.
	(to) **argue (about** sth.) ['ɑːgjuː]	argumentieren, behaupten; sich streiten, zanken (über/wegen etwas)	'I cooked lunch, so you should wash the dishes,' she *~d*. We often ~ *about* which videos we should watch. Don't ~ with me. Just do what I say! *lat.* arguere, verb: *(to) argue* – noun: *argument* *frz.* arguer
	conclusion [kən'kluːʒn]	Schluss(folgerung), Abschluss	At the end of their report they presented their main *~s*. *lat.* conclusio, *frz.* la conclusion
	outline ['aʊtlaɪn]	Gliederung, Entwurf	
p. 77/A3	**versus** ['vɜːsəs]	gegen, gegenüber	Johnson ~ Walker = Johnson against Walker
	the day (that) her article appeared	der Tag, an dem ihr Artikel erschien	I'll never forget ~ ~ we met.
	microwave ['maɪkrəweɪv]	Mikrowelle, Mikrowellengerät	a *microwave* 
	supper ['sʌpə]	(warmes) Abendessen	the last meal of the day
	butcher [⚠ 'bʊtʃə]	Metzger/in, Fleischer/in	⚠ I must go to the *butcher's* (= zum Metzger, in die Metzgerei).
	fresh [freʃ]	frisch; neu	Is this milk ~? – No, it's four days old. Let's make a ~ start. fresh – frisch
	(to) **combine** [kəm'baɪn]	kombinieren, verbinden	On our trip we tried to ~ work with fun. *lat.* combinare, *frz.* combiner
	(to) **complain (to** sb. **about** sth.) [kəm'pleɪn]	sich (bei jm. über etwas) beschweren, beklagen	The food isn't very good. – If you don't like it, you should ~ *to* the waiter.
	(to) **make fun of** sb./sth.	sich über jn./etwas lustig machen	The children *made ~ of* Julie's hair after her sister had cut it.
	(to) **practice** ['præktɪs] *(AE)*	üben, trainieren	= *BE* (to) practise *lat.* practicare, *frz.* pratiquer
	at least [ət 'liːst]	wenigstens, mindestens; zumindest	These shoes aren't cool, but *at ~* they're warm! You have to be *at ~* 16 to be allowed to see that film.
	useless ['juːsləs]	nutzlos, zu nichts nütze	◄► useful

German 'man'

you – *You* should brush *your* teeth three times a day. **one** – *One* should brush *one's* teeth three times a day.	▶	*Man (= Jeder)* sollte ... *seine* Zähne putzen.
they – *They* say Inupiaq is a difficult language. **people** – *People* say Inupiaq is a difficult language.	▶	*Man* sagt *(= Die Leute* sagen), Inupiaq sei eine schwierige Sprache.
(the passive) – This colour *isn't worn* any more.		Diese Farbe trägt *man* nicht mehr.

One is used mainly in formal English. In informal English *you* is more usual.

A4	(to) **disagree (with)** [ˌdɪsəˈgriː]	nicht übereinstimmen (mit); anderer Meinung sein (als)	▸◂ (to) agree
	(to) **react (to)** [riːˈækt]	reagieren (auf)	How *did* your parents ~ *to* your holiday plans?
A5	**distance** [⚠ ˈdɪstəns]	Entfernung, Abstand; Ferne	What's the ~ between London and Chester? – About 190 miles. Here's a photo of our house. In the ~ you can see the sea. *lat.* distantia, *frz.* la distance
p. 78/A6	(to) **date** sb. [deɪt] *(besonders AE)*	mit jm. (aus)gehen	Didn't you know? Ann and Tom *have been dating* each other for two months now.
	You think so?	Glaubst du?	'I'm sure you'll like your new school.' – *'You think ~?'*
	I think so.	Ich glaube (ja).	'Is Fiona Scottish?' – *'I think ~*, but I'm not quite sure.'
	I don't think so.	Das finde/glaube ich nicht.	'Manchester will lose the match.' – *I don't think ~*. They're a very good team.'
	cute [kjuːt] *(infml)*	niedlich, süß	Mum doesn't like Orlando Bloom, but I think he's ~.
	(to) **embarrass** sb. [ɪmˈbærəs]	jn. in Verlegenheit bringen, jn. verlegen machen	My dad asked my girlfriend a lot of questions about her parents. He really *~ed* me.
	embarrassed [ɪmˈbærɪst]	verlegen, peinlich berührt	I had forgotten where I had left my car. I was so ~.
	weird [⚠ wɪəd] *(infml)*	verrückt, seltsam	strange
p. 79/A10	(to) **exchange** [ɪksˈtʃeɪndʒ]	aus-, umtauschen; *(Geld)* wechseln	At the end of the holiday we *~d* addresses. I'd like to ~ some euros into dollars. *frz.* échanger

German 'weit'

Questions and negative statements: ***far***		**Positive statements:** ***a long way***
Is it *far* to the town centre?	–	Yes, it's *a long way*.
How *far* did you walk?	–	We walked *a long way*.
I do*n't* live *far* from here.		But my cousins live *a long way* away.
We did*n't* travel *far* on the first day.		But on the next day we went *a long way*.

deer, *pl* **deer** [dɪə]	Reh, Hirsch	
herd [hɜːd]	Herde *(z.B. Kühe)*, Herden-	A group of cows is called a ~.
plant [plɑːnt]	Pflanze	 *a plant* *frz.* la plante
sick [sɪk]	krank	⚠ • (to) be/feel/look <u>ill</u> *(BE)* – (to) be/feel/look <u>sick</u> *(AE)* *(BE)* You look *ill*. Do you feel *ill*? *(AE)* You look *sick*. Do you feel *sick*? • *sick* + noun *(BE and AE)*: a *sick* animal, a very *sick* man
wolf [⚠ wʊlf], *pl* **wolves** [⚠ wʊlvz]	Wolf	⚠ one *wolf* [wʊlf] – two *wol<u>ves</u>* [wʊlvz] (Remember: *life, lives / shelf, shelves / thief, thieves*)
weak [wiːk]	schwach	This tea is very ~. It's like water.
(to) **support** [səˈpɔːt]	*(Familie usw.)* ernähren, unterhalten, unterstützen	She has to ~ a husband and four children, so she works at weekends too. *frz.* supporter

p. 120

a lot (adv): 'viel', 'oft', 'sehr'

Wow! You *eat a lot*. That's your third piece of cake.
Look at those cars! – Yes, they're great. But they *cost a lot*.
Glen and Amy *argue a lot*.
I *see* Barbara *a lot*. We're good friends.
Denali *has changed a lot* in the last 30 years.
Kelly *liked* Amy's article *a lot*.
I *missed* my family *a lot* when I was abroad.

(to) **eat a lot**	viel essen
(to) **cost a lot**	viel kosten
(to) **argue a lot**	viel/oft streiten
(to) **see sb. a lot**	jn. oft sehen
(to) **change a lot**	sich sehr verändern
(to) **like sth. a lot**	etwas sehr mögen
(to) **miss sb. a lot**	jn. sehr vermissen

	(to) **protect** sb. **(from** sth.**)** [prə'tekt]	jn. (be)schützen (vor etwas)	Trees can ~ you *from* the sun. *lat.* protegere, *frz.* protéger
	(to) **hunt (for)** [hʌnt]	jagen (nach); Jagd machen (auf), suchen	Do you think that people still ~ lions in Africa? I've *~ed* everywhere *for* my keys, but I can't find them.
P 1	**sled** [sled] *(AE)*, **sledge** [sledʒ] *(BE)*	Schlitten	*a sled (AE) / sledge (BE)* 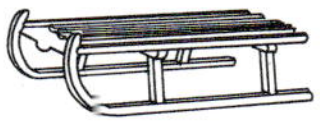
P 2	he should find out **for himself** [hɪm'self]	er sollte es selbst herausfinden	
	manual ['mænjuəl]	Handbuch	Read the ~ before you turn on your new computer.
P 3	**construction** [⚠ kən'strʌkʃn]	Konstruktion	*lat.* constructio, *frz.* la construction
P 4	**outside** *(prep)* [ˌaʊt'saɪd]	vor; außerhalb (von)	You can park your car ~ our house. Megan lives ~ the city, on a farm. ▸◂ inside
	student [⚠ 'stju:dənt]	Student/in; *(besonders AE auch:)* Schüler/in	
	cellphone ['selfəʊn] *(besonders AE)*	Handy	= *BE* mobile (phone)
	Congratulations! *(pl)* [kənˌɡrætʃu'leɪʃnz]	Herzlichen Glückwunsch!	 a speech bubble
P 5	**speech bubble** ['spi:tʃ ˌbʌbl]	Sprechblase	The things people say in comics are shown in ~ ~s.
	complete *(adj)* [kəm'pli:t]; **completely** *(adv)* [kəm'pli:tli]	vollständig, komplett; völlig, vollkommen	verb: (to) complete – adjective: *complete* – adverb: *completely* I'm sorry. I *~ly* forgot that it's your birthday today.
P 6	(to) **tie** sb./sth. **up** [ˌtaɪ‿'ʌp]	jn./etwas festbinden	Let's ~ the dog *up* so that it can't run away. ⚠ -ing form: *tying*
	(to) **tie** [taɪ]	(zusammen)binden, (zusammen)schnüren	
	bear [beə]	Bär	**bear – Bär**
P 8	**death** [deθ]	Tod; Todesfall	verb: (to) die – adjective: dead – noun: *death*
P 9	**60° F (= 60 degrees Fahrenheit)** [dɪˌgri:z 'færənhaɪt]	60 Grad Fahrenheit	⚠ You write: *134° F* You say: *134 degrees Fahrenheit*
	schedule [*BE:* 'ʃedju:l, *AE:* 'skedʒəl]	Zeitplan; *(AE auch:)* Stundenplan, Fahrplan	= *BE* timetable
P 10	(to) **be over** ['əʊvə]	vorbei sein, zu Ende sein	At 5.30 the match *was* ~. Everyone went home.
P 11	(to) **organize** [⚠ 'ɔ:gənaɪz]	organisieren, veranstalten	to plan something and get ready for it *frz.* organiser

Alone on the North Slope

p. 84	**slope** [sləʊp]	Hang	
	nice and warm/dry/...	schön warm/trocken/...	It's ~ ~ *warm* by the fire.
	(to) **hurt** [hɜ:t]	schaden, schädigen	Bikes *don't* ~ the environment, but cars do.
	(oil) well [wel]	Ölquelle	
	(to) **grow up** [ˌgrəʊ‿'ʌp]	aufwachsen; erwachsen werden	When Grandma *was ~ing up*, she didn't have a TV. Dave is 12. When he *~s up*, he wants to be a doctor.
	native ['neɪtɪv] *(n; adj)*	Ur(einwohner/in); eingeboren, einheimisch	The ~ peoples of Australia have lived there for 20,000 years.
	regional [⚠ 'ri:dʒənl]	regional	There are ~ differences in the way people speak. *frz.* régional,e
	company [⚠ 'kʌmpəni]	Firma, Gesellschaft	Steve works for an oil ~ in Scotland. *frz.* la compagnie
	at (the age of) 39	mit 39, im Alter von 39 Jahren	
	president [⚠ 'prezɪdənt]	Präsident/in	*frz.* le président, la présidente

	meanwhile ['mi:nwaɪl]	inzwischen, währenddessen	I went to bed at 10 pm. *Meanwhile*, in Japan, people were getting up.
	(to) **joke** [dʒəʊk]	witzeln, scherzen	noun: joke – verb: *(to) joke*
	equipment *(no pl)* [ɪ'kwɪpmənt]	Ausrüstung	⚠ *Without 'a/an':* I need new sports *equipment*. (… <u>*eine*</u> neue Sport*ausrüstung*.)
	(to) **teach** sb. **a lesson**	jm. eine Lektion erteilen	If you do that again, you won't get any birthday presents. That *will ~ you a lesson*.
	(to) **matter** ['mætə]	von Bedeutung sein, etwas ausmachen	Sorry, I forgot the potatoes. – It *doesn't ~*. We can have bread instead.
	cold *(n)* [kəʊld]	Kälte; Erkältung	adjective: cold – noun: *cold* ⚠ Ich *bin (schwer) erkältet*. = *I've got a (bad) cold*.
	(to) **rise** [raɪz], **rose** [rəʊz], **risen** ['rɪzn]	aufgehen *(Sonne, Mond)*; (an-, auf)steigen	The sun *~s* in the east. Prices *have risen* by 10%.
p. 85	**leaf** [li:f], *pl* **leaves** [li:vz]	Blatt *(an Pflanzen)*	In the autumn, the *leaves* fall to the ground. ⚠ ein *Blatt* Papier = a *piece of* paper
	(to) **pour** [⚠ pɔ:]	gießen, schütten; einschenken	 *(to) pour*
	flat (-tt-) *(adj)* [flæt]	flach, eben	The countryside is very ~. There are no mountains. ⚠ *flat* = **1.** *(n)* Wohnung; **2.** *(adj)* flach, eben
	frozen ['frəʊzn]	zugefroren; tiefgefroren	They only sell ~ food or food in tins here.
	(to) **freeze** [fri:z], **froze** [frəʊz], **frozen** ['frəʊzn]	(ge)frieren; einfrieren	Rivers and lakes sometimes ~ in winter. It's *freezing* outside. (= It's very cold outside.)
	(to) **melt** [melt]	schmelzen	The sun came out and the snow began to ~. (to) **melt** – sch**mel**zen ▸◂ (to) freeze
	(to) **hang** [hæŋ], **hung** [hʌŋ], **hung**	hängen, aufhängen	Please ~ your jacket over the chair. A photo of Alaska *hung* on the wall.
	(to) **tear** sth. **(off)** [teə], **tore** [tɔ:], **torn** [tɔ:n]	etwas (ab)reißen; etwas zerreißen	Fill in your new address at the bottom of this page. *Tear* that part ~ and send it back to us. The dog *tore* the newspaper into little pieces.
	strong [strɒŋ]	stark	Only a very ~ person could move that sofa.
	tool [tu:l]	Werkzeug	
	flame [fleɪm]	Flamme	*lat.* flamma, *frz.* la flamme a *flame* 
	thirst [θɜ:st]	Durst	adjective: thirsty – noun: *thirst* ⚠ Ich *habe Durst*. = *I'm thirsty*.
	(to) **survive** [sə'vaɪv]	überleben	Three people *~d* the accident, two people died.
	track [træk]	Spur, Fährte	Look at those *~s* in the snow. I think that was a bear.
	brain [breɪn]	Gehirn	Your ~ is inside your head. You think with it.
	movement ['mu:vmənt]	Bewegung	I think my leg is broken. Every ~ hurts. verb: (to) move – noun: *movement* *frz.* le mouvement
p. 86	(to) **rewrite** [ˌri:'raɪt]	neu schreiben, noch einmal schreiben	(to) write again, (to) write with different words
	education [ˌedʒu'keɪʃn]	(Schul-, Aus-)Bildung; Erziehung	My school ~ started when I was 5 and finished when I was 16. *lat.* educatio, *frz.* l'éducation *(f)*

AE vocabulary – BE vocabulary

AE	BE	
bathroom / restroom	**toilet**	Toilette
bathroom	bathroom	Bad(ezimmer)
(to) **date** sb. / **go out with** sb.	(to) **go out with** sb.	mit jm. (aus-)gehen
elevator	**lift**	Fahrstuhl, Aufzug
fall	**autumn**	Herbst
(French) fries	**chips**	Pommes frites
mom	**mum**	Mama, Mutti

AE	BE	
movie, film	**film, movie**	Film
movie theater	**cinema**	Kino
neat	**brilliant, great**	toll, klasse
sidewalk	**pavement**	Gehweg, Bürgersteig
sled	**sledge**	Schlitten
student	**pupil, student**	Schüler/in
student	student	Student/in
vacation	**holiday(s)**	Ferien, Urlaub
Z [zi:]	**Z** [zed]	Z *(Buchstabe)*

How to use a dictionary – Part 1

p. 87	(to) **look** sth. **up** [,lʊk‿'ʌp]	etwas nachschlagen, etwas heraussuchen	If you don't know a word, *look* it ~ in a dictionary. Can you *look* ~ John's new phone number for me?
	task [tɑ:sk]	Aufgabe	a piece of work that has to be done
	entry ['entri]	Eintrag, Eintragung *(in einem Wörterbuch/ Tagebuch)*	I've bought a new dictionary. It has 200,000 *entries*. There's no ~ in Jane's diary for 12th June. *frz.* l'entrée *(f)*
	headword ['hedwɜ:d]	Stichwort	
	(to) **pronounce** [prə'naʊns]	aussprechen	(to) say *frz.* prononcer How do you ~ this word? ⚠ verb: *(to) pronounce* – noun: pronunciation
	(to) **study** ['stʌdi]	studieren; lernen; sorgfältig durchlesen	She's a professor now, but she had to ~ for a long time. There's a test tomorrow so I have to ~ tonight. My father *studies* the sports page every morning. *lat.* studere
	in italics *(pl)* [ɪ'tælɪks]	in Kursivschrift, kursiv	*These words are written in ~.* *frz.* en italique

TIPP

Nun aber fix ...

Folgende Wortschatzspiele könnt ihr in der Gruppe nach Zeit spielen:

- Eine/r von euch gibt einen *Oberbegriff* vor, die anderen müssen in der vorgegebenen Zeit – probiert es mal mit 2 oder 3 Minuten – so viele *Unterbegriffe* aufschreiben wie möglich. Beispiel:
  family*: mother, father, sister, uncle, ...*
- Eine/r von euch gibt einen *Anfangsbuchstaben* vor, die anderen müssen in der vorgegebenen Zeit so viele Wörter mit diesem Anfangsbuchstaben aufschreiben wie möglich. Beispiel:
  „c"*: clean, clothes, cold, colour, come, ...*
- Eine/r von euch gibt ein *langes Wort* vor, die anderen müssen in der vorgegebenen Zeit so viele Wörter aus den Buchstaben des vorgegebenen Wortes bilden wie möglich. Beispiel:
  breakfast*: a, as, are, eat, sea, tea, best, east, fast, rest, break, ...*

Unit 6: Dreamland California

pp. 90/91	(to) **shut (-tt-), shut, shut** [ʃʌt]	schließen, zumachen	(to) close
p. 92/A1	**desert** [⚠ 'dezət]	Wüste	*lat.* deserta, *frz.* le désert
	temperature [⚠ 'temprətʃə]	Temperatur	*frz.* la température
	54° C (= 54 degrees Celsius) [dɪ,gri:z 'selsiəs]	54 Grad Celsius	⚠ You write: *54° C* You say: *54 degrees Celsius* Water freezes at 0° C (= at zero degrees Celsius)
	twice **an** hour	zweimal pro Stunde, zweimal in der Stunde	I get £5 pocket money *a* week.
	inch [ɪntʃ]	Zoll *(= 2,54 cm)*	about two and a half centimetres
	deep [di:p]	tief	How ~ is the water at this end of the pool? – 3 metres.
	forest ['fɒrɪst]	Wald	There are lots of different trees in this ~.
	awesome ['ɔ:səm] *(AE, infml)*	großartig, klasse	very good, great, fantastic
	spider ['spaɪdə]	Spinne	
	Enjoy yourself ... [ɪn'dʒɔɪ jə,self]	Amüsier dich ... / Vergnüg dich ...	I'm going to the theatre tonight. – Well, ~ *yourself*! (= Viel Spaß! / Amüsier dich gut!)
	nowhere ['nəʊweə]	nirgendwo, nirgendwohin	You can find this animal in Australia, and ~ else. Where are you going? – *Nowhere*. ◄► somewhere
A3	**historic** [hɪ'stɒrɪk]	historisch	When the Berlin Wall fell in 1989, it was a(n) ~ event for Germany and the world. *lat.* historicus,a,um, *frz.* historique

German 'groß'

large – big:	*large* is mainly used for things; *big* is used for things and people.	We've got a *big/large* house near Ashton. Lord Nelson was not a very *big* man.
tall:	*tall* (groß, hoch) is used to talk about the height[1] of people and things. [1]height [haɪt] *Größe, Höhe*	Is Janet *taller* than Karen? How *tall* is Nelson's Column?
huge:	sehr groß, riesig	Have you seen their new house? It's *huge*!
great:	**1.** großartig, toll	*Great*! No homework today. We had a *great* time at the party. The music was *great*.
	2. groß, beträchtlich	The children were in *great* danger. A *great* number of people arrived late.
	3. groß, bedeutend, wichtig	Do you know the CD '*Greatest* Rap Hits'? Who do you think was the world's *greatest* sailor?

p. 121 Bodie **was left to itself.** [ɪt'self] — Bodie wurde sich selbst überlassen.

Reflexive pronouns (Reflexivpronomen)

I've hurt **myself**.	Ich habe *mir* wehgetan / *mich* verletzt.		
You've hurt **yourself**.	Du hast *dir* wehgetan / *dich* verletzt.		
He has hurt **himself**.	Er hat *sich* wehgetan / *sich* verletzt.		
She has hurt **herself**.	Sie hat *sich* wehgetan / *sich* verletzt.		
It has hurt **itself**.	Es hat *sich* wehgetan / *sich* verletzt.		
We've hurt **ourselves**.	Wir haben *uns* wehgetan / *uns* verletzt.		
You've hurt **yourselves**.	Ihr habt *euch* wehgetan / *euch* verletzt.		
They've hurt **themselves**.	Sie haben *sich* wehgetan / *sich* verletzt.		

⚠ **Pronunciation and stress:**

-self [-'self]

-selves [-'selvz]

p. 93/A4	**actor** ['æktə]	Schauspieler	a man who acts in a film or play	*frz.* l'acteur
	actress ['æktrəs]	Schauspielerin	a woman who acts in a film or play	*frz.* l'actrice
	success [sək'ses]	Erfolg	I tried but I didn't have much ~. noun: *success* – adjective: successful	*lat.* successio, *frz.* le succès
	documentary [ˌdɒkju'mentri]	Dokumentar-, dokumentarisch	*frz.* documentaire	
	iron [⚠ 'aɪən]	Eisen		
	(to) **make** sb. sth.	jn. zu etwas machen	Her second film *made* her a star.	
	politics [⚠ 'pɒlətɪks]	(die) Politik	⚠ No article, singular verb: *Politics* is interesting.	
	political [pə'lɪtɪkl]	politisch	noun: *politics* – adjective: *political*	
	legend [⚠ 'ledʒənd]	Legende	*lat.* legenda, *frz.* la légende	
	(to) **elect** sb. (sth.) [ɪ'lekt]	jn. (zu etwas) wählen	The club members ~*ed* her president for two years.	
	governor [⚠ 'gʌvənə]	Gouverneur/in	the 'boss' of a state	
	nail polish ['neɪl ˌpɒlɪʃ] *(AE)*, **nail varnish** ['neɪl ˌvɑːnɪʃ] *(BE)*	Nagellack	⚠ *nail polish* ['pɒlɪʃ] – *Polish* ['pəʊlɪʃ] („polnisch")	
	she made some **herself**	sie machte selbst/selber welchen	Where did Sally buy that dress? – She made it ~!	
	(to) **borrow** sth. ['bɒrəʊ]	sich etwas (aus)leihen, etwas entleihen	Can I ~ your dictionary, please? You'll get it back in a minute.	
	studies *(pl)* ['stʌdiz]	Studien, Studium	noun: *studies* – verb: (to) study	
	the two of them	die beiden; alle beide	Hannah and Tony met after school, and then *the ~ of ~* went shopping.	
	search engine ['sɜːtʃ‿ˌendʒɪn]	Suchmaschine	'Yahoo' and 'Google' are famous ~ *engines*.	
p. 94/A7	**war** [wɔː]	Krieg		
	hardly ['hɑːdli]	kaum	⚠ She *hardly* works. = Sie arbeitet *kaum*. She works *hard*. = Sie arbeitet *hart*.	

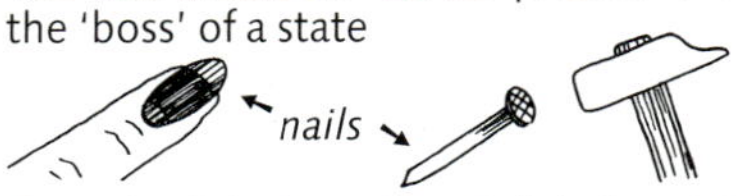

	(to) **move (to)** [muːv]	(um)ziehen (nach, in)	Later we *~d* to London. We *~d* to a small flat in Camden Town. – When did you ~ in? ⚠ *(to) move* = **1.** (sich) bewegen; **2.** (um)ziehen
	laundry [ˈlɔːndri]	Wäscherei	The nurses' uniforms are washed in the hospital ~.
	immigrant [ˈɪmɪɡrənt]	Einwanderer/Einwanderin, Immigrant/in	Every year thousands of *~s* start new lives in the USA. *frz.* l'immigré
	(to) **work full-time** [ˌfʊl ˈtaɪm]	ganztags arbeiten, als Vollzeitkraft beschäftigt sein	
p. 95/A9	**apartment** [əˈpɑːtmənt] *(AE)*	Wohnung	= *BE* flat *frz.* l'appartement *(m)*
	siren [⚠ ˈsaɪrən]	Sirene	After the accident we heard the ~ of an ambulance.
	explosion [⚠ ɪkˈspləʊʒn]	Explosion	There was an ~, and then somebody screamed for help.
	holiday	Feiertag, freier Tag	Christmas Day is a ~ in most countries.
	Buddhist [⚠ ˈbʊdɪst]	Buddhist, Buddhistin	
	rude (to sb.**)** [ruːd]	unhöflich, grob (zu jm.)	She was ~ *to* me: she called me stupid and silly.
	pastry [ˈpeɪstri]	(Mürbe-, Blätter-)Teig	
	envelope [ˈenvələʊp]	(Brief-)Umschlag	I want to send this birthday card to my cousin, but I haven't got a big enough ~. *frz.* l'enveloppe *(f)*
	good luck [lʌk]	(viel) Glück	Good ~ with your test tomorrow!
A10	**generation** [⚠ ˌdʒenəˈreɪʃn]	Generation	Not many people of my parents' ~ like techno music. *lat.* generatio, *frz.* la génération
P 2	**entrance** [ˈentrəns]	Eingang	Let's meet at the main ~ to the disco.
P 3	**as soon as** *(conj)* [əz ˈsuːn_əz]	sobald	I'll phone you *as ~ as* I know the date of the meeting.
	cookie [ˈkʊki] *(besonders AE)*	Keks	= *BE* biscuit
P 4	**although** [ɔːlˈðəʊ]	obwohl	*Although* I studied hard, I got a bad mark.

Reflexive in German – not reflexive in English

⚠ The following verbs are **reflexive in German**, but **not reflexive in English** – you don't need a reflexive pronoun in English:

(to) **change**	sich (ver)ändern; sich umziehen	(to) **open**	sich öffnen
(to) **complain**	sich beschweren, sich beklagen	(to) **prepare for**	sich vorbereiten auf
(to) **decide**	sich entscheiden	(to) **refer to**	sich beziehen auf
(to) **feel**	sich fühlen	(to) **relax**	sich entspannen
(to) **hide**	sich verstecken	(to) **remember**	sich erinnern (an)
(to) **imagine** sth.	sich etwas vorstellen	(to) **rhyme**	sich reimen
(to) **listen to** sth.	sich etwas anhören	(to) **sit down**	sich (hin)setzen
(to) **make/take notes**	sich Notizen machen	(to) **turn (around)**	sich umdrehen
(to) **meet**	sich treffen (mit)	(to) **watch** sth.	sich etwas ansehen
(to) **move**	sich bewegen	(to) **worry**	sich Sorgen machen

P 8	**frequency** [⚠ ˈfriːkwənsi]	Häufigkeit	There is a very high ~ of traffic accidents in this area.
	manner [ˈmænə]	Art und Weise	I don't like it when you speak to me in that ~.
	bug [bʌɡ] *(besonders AE)*	Insekt, Käfer	
P 10	(to) **be around** *(infml)*	in der Nähe sein, da sein	My dad is always at work. He's never ~.
P 13	**fridge** [frɪdʒ]	Kühlschrank	Food and drinks stay cold in the ~.
	(to) **take** sth. **round to** sb.	jm. etwas bringen	Can you *take* this cake ~ *to* Grandma, please?
P 14	(to) **border (on)** [ˈbɔːdə]	(an)grenzen (an)	
P 17	**bacon** [ˈbeɪkən]	Schinkenspeck	We had ~ and eggs for breakfast.

fridge

Next Month ... Hollywood

p. 102	**talent** [⚠ ˈtælənt]	Talent, Begabung	*frz.* le talent
	relationship [rɪˈleɪʃnʃɪp]	Beziehung	Do you have a good ~ with your mother? *frz.* la relation
	background [ˈbækɡraʊnd]	Hintergrund	Here's a photo of Madonna. In the ~ you can see part of her house.
	(to) **sign up (for** sth.) [saɪn]	sich (für etwas) einschreiben	
	(to) **sign**	unterschreiben	Please don't forget to ~ the letter. *frz.* signer

	totally *(adv)* [⚠ 'təʊtəli]	völlig, total	I'm not ~ happy with the situation. *lat.* totaliter, *frz.* totalement
	actually ['æktʃuəli]	wirklich, tatsächlich, eigentlich	*Actually*, 'Eminem' is not his real name. It's Mathers – Marshall Mathers.
	anyway ['eniweɪ]	wie dem auch sei	*Anyway*, let's forget about that for the moment.
	Why the hell not? *(infml)*	*etwa:* Warum denn nicht, verdammt nochmal?	
	hell [hel]	Hölle	
	(to) **breathe (in/out)** [bri:ð]	(ein-/aus)atmen	*B~ in* through your nose and *out* through your mouth.
p. 103	**idiot** [⚠ 'ɪdiət] *(infml)*	Idiot/in	*lat.* idiota, *frz.* l'idiot,e
	(to) **see** sb.	mit jm. zusammensein; sich mit jm. treffen	John *has been ~ing* Alison for half a year. (She's been his girlfriend for half a year.)
	reliable [rɪ'laɪəbl]	zuverlässig, verlässlich	Tom's car is not very ~. There's always something wrong with it.
	in sight [saɪt]	in Sicht(weite)	I looked around but there was no one *in ~*.
	neck [nek]	Hals, Nacken, Genick	
	(to) **lift** [lɪft]	(an-, hoch)heben	
	in fact [ɪn 'fækt]	eigentlich, genau gesagt; in Wirklichkeit	I think she's fifteen. *In ~* I know she is. Ken said he lives in Chester, but *in ~* he lives in Cardiff.
	act [ækt]	Nummer, Akt *(Show, Theater)*	
	outfit ['aʊtfɪt]	Outfit, Kleidung	
	(to) **introduce** sth./sb. **(to** sb.**)** [ˌɪntrə'dju:s]	(jm.) etwas/jn. vorstellen	You don't know him? Let me ~ you *to* him.
	audience ['ɔ:dɪəns]	Zuschauer/innen, Zuhörer/innen, Publikum	the people who are watching a show, film, play, TV programme, or listening to a radio programme
	violin [ˌvaɪə'lɪn]	Violine, Geige	*frz.* le violon
p. 104	**stage** [steɪdʒ]	Bühne	At 9 o'clock the band came on ~ and started to play.
	(to) **make it** *(infml)*	es schaffen, Erfolg haben	Cathy *will* never *~ it* as a singer. She has no talent.
	cable ['keɪbl]	Kabel	 *frz.* le câble
	stomach ['stʌmək]	Magen, Bauch	*lat.* stomachus, *frz.* l'estomac *(m)*
	What's the matter? ['mætə]	Was ist denn (los)?	What's wrong?
	So?	Na und?	
p. 105	**How to use a dictionary – Part 2**		
	style [staɪl]	Stil	If you like jackets, that shop has lots of different *~s*.
	possible ['pɒsəbl]	möglich	I'll send some money as soon as ~. ◂▸ impossible *lat.* possibilis,e, *frz.* possible

TIPP

Englisch und andere Fremdsprachen

Manche Wörter sind im Englischen, Französischen und Lateinischen sehr ähnlich. Wenn du also ein unbekanntes Wort siehst, überleg erst einmal, ob du das Wort vielleicht schon aus einer anderen Sprache kennst.

⚠ Aber Vorsicht bei der Schreibung, z.B. engl. ex<u>a</u>mple – frz. ex<u>e</u>mple.

English	*French*	*Latin*
animal	**animal**	**animal**
(to) **celebrate**	**célébrer**	**celebrare**
community	**communauté**	**communitas**
(to) **complete**	**compléter**	**complere**
colour	**couleur**	**color**
difficult	**difficile**	**difficilis**
example	**exemple**	**exemplum**
family	**famille**	**familia**
hour	**heure**	**hora**
language	**langage**	**lingua**
(to) **offer**	**offrir**	**offerre**
opinion	**opinion**	**opinio**
(to) **protect**	**protéger**	**protegere**

Working with a dictionary

Dieses ***DICTIONARY*** enthält den Wortschatz der Bände 1 bis 3 in alphabetischer Reihenfolge. Wenn du einmal nicht weißt, wie ein Wort geschrieben wird, was es bedeutet oder wie man es ausspricht, kannst du hier nachschlagen.

In diesem ***DICTIONARY*** werden folgende **Abkürzungen** und **Symbole** verwendet:

sb.	= somebody *(jemand)*	*pl*	= *plural*	*AE*	= *American English*
sth.	= something *(etwas)*	*no pl*	= *no plural*	*BE*	= *British English*
jm.	= jemandem	*Part. Perf.*	= *Partizip Perfekt*	*infml*	= *informal* (umgangssprachlich, informell)
jn.	= jemanden	*si. past*	= *simple past (form)*		

° – Mit diesem Kringel sind Wörter markiert, die nicht zum Lernwortschatz gehören.

* – Dieser Stern kennzeichnet unregelmäßige Verben (vgl. List of irregular verbs, S. 202–203).

Fundstellenangaben (Ziffern in Klammern bezeichnen Seitenzahlen; Wörter und Wendungen ohne Fundstellenangabe stammen aus Band 1 oder 2)

2 Li	= Unit 2, LEAD IN	5 A 3 (163)	= Unit 5, A-Abschnitt 3, Seite 163 (im VOCABULARY)
3 A 5	= Unit 3, A-Abschnitt 5	UK Call (6)	= UK Calling, Seite 6
1 P 3	= Unit 1, P-Abschnitt, Übung 3	Welc (56)	= Welcome to the USA, Seite 56
2 T (33)	= Unit 2, TEXT, Seite 33	Rev 3 (112)	= Revision-Abschnitt, Übung 3, Seite 112
4 How (71)	= Unit 4, HOW TO ...-Seite 71		

A

a, an [ə, ən] **1.** ein, eine • **a bit** ein bisschen, etwas • **a few** ein paar, einige • **a little** ein bisschen, ein wenig • **a lot** *(adv)* viel, oft, sehr 5 A 10 (165) • **a lot (of)** eine Menge, viel, viele **2. twice an hour** zweimal pro Stunde/in der Stunde 6 A 1

abbreviation [əˌbriːviˈeɪʃn] Abkürzung 1 How (19)

able [ˈeɪbl]: **be able to do sth.** etwas tun können; fähig sein / in der Lage sein, etwas zu tun

about [əˈbaʊt] **1.** über • **a question about your book** eine Frage über dein Buch / zu deinem Buch **this book is about ...** dieses Buch handelt von ... • **It's about Mrs McCann.** Es ist wegen Mrs McCann. • **the worst thing about ... is ...** das Schlimmste an ... ist ... **What was funny about ...?** Was war komisch an ...? • **What about a calendar?** Wie wärs mit einem Kalender? • **What about Jenny?** Was ist mit Jenny? / Und Jenny? • **What are they talking about?** Worüber reden sie? **how they feel about ...** was sie über ... denken / was sie von ... halten Welc (57) • **hear/know about sth.** von etwas hören/wissen • **learn sth. about ...** etwas über/von ... erfahren, etwas über ... herausfinden 2 Li **2.** ungefähr; **3. be about** unterwegs sein 2 A 14

above [əˈbʌv] **1.** *(adv)* oben; **2.** *(prep)* über, oberhalb (von)

abroad [əˈbrɔːd] im/ins Ausland

accent [ˈæksənt] Akzent; Betonung, Aussprache UK Call (7)

access [ˈækses] Zugang 4 A 4

accident [ˈæksɪdənt] Unfall

acid rain [ˌæsɪd ˈreɪn] saurer Regen

across [əˈkrɒs] **1.** *(prep)* (quer) über, durch; **2.** *(adv)* hinüber, herüber

act [ækt] **1.** sich verhalten, handeln 4 T (70); **2.** spielen, schauspielern **Act the dialogue.** Spiel(t) den Dialog. • **act out** vorspielen **3.** Nummer, Akt *(Show, Theater)* 6 T (103)

action [ˈækʃn] Handlung, Tat

active [ˈæktɪv] aktiv, tätig

activity [ækˈtɪvəti] Aktivität, Tätigkeit

actor [ˈæktə] Schauspieler 6 A 4

actress [ˈæktrəs] Schauspielerin 6 A 4 (168)

actually [ˈæktʃuəli] wirklich, tatsächlich, eigentlich 6 T (102)

AD [ˌeɪˈdiː]: **70 AD** 70 n. Chr. 3 Li

ad [æd] *(infml für:* **advert***)* Reklame, Anzeige, Annonce 6 T (103)

add [æd] hinzufügen, ergänzen

address [əˈdres] Adresse, Anschrift

admiral [ˈædmərəl] Admiral 2 A 7

adopt [əˈdɒpt] adoptieren, die Patenschaft übernehmen für

adventure [ədˈventʃə] Abenteuer

advert [ˈædvɜːt] Reklame, Anzeige, Annonce

aerobics [eəˈrəʊbɪks] Aerobic 1 Li (145)

afraid [əˈfreɪd]: **I'm afraid ...** Leider ... 2 T (36)

after [ˈɑːftə] **1.** *(prep)* nach *(zeitlich)* • **after that** danach **2.** *(conj)* nachdem

afternoon [ˌɑːftəˈnuːn] Nachmittag • **Good afternoon.** Guten Tag. *(nachmittags)* • **in the afternoon(s)** am Nachmittag, nachmittags • **this afternoon** heute Nachmittag

again [əˈgen] noch einmal, wieder

age [eɪdʒ] Alter • **at the age of 39** mit 39, im Alter von 39 Jahren 5 T (84)

against [əˈgenst] gegen

agent [ˈeɪdʒənt] Agent/in 2 T (33)

ago [əˈgəʊ]: **a year ago** vor einem Jahr • **a long time ago** vor langer Zeit

agree [əˈgriː] zustimmen • **agree on sth.** etwas vereinbaren, sich auf etwas einigen 1 A 6 • **agree with** übereinstimmen mit

ahead [əˈhed]: **be ahead (of sb.)** führen, in Führung liegen (vor jm.); jm. voraus sein 1 T (18)

air [eə] Luft • **in the open air** im Freien 1 P 11

airline [ˈeəlaɪn] Fluggesellschaft

airport [ˈeəpɔːt] Flughafen

album [ˈælbəm] Album UK Call (6)

alcohol [ˈælkəhɒl] Alkohol 2 P 7

°**alien** ['eɪliən] Außerirdische(r) 3 P 14
alive [ə'laɪv]: **be alive** leben, am Leben sein 2 T (33)
all [ɔːl] alle; alles • **all in all** alles in allem 4 P 13 • **all wet** ganz nass, völlig nass • **all day/morning/summer** den ganzen Tag/ Morgen/Sommer (lang) • **all day long** den ganzen Tag lang 3 A 1 **all around the country** überall im Land 2 A 4 • °**all of Europe** ganz Europa 3 T (50) • **all over the world** auf der ganzen Welt, überall auf der Welt • **all right** gut, (alles) in Ordnung • **all the kids** alle Kinder • **all the time/money** die ganze Zeit (lang)/das ganze Geld • **at all times** immer, jederzeit 2 A 14 • **of all time** aller Zeiten 6 A 1
°**all hands gallery** ['gæləri] *interaktive Ausstellung zum Anfassen und Ausprobieren* 2 How (37)
°**all-terrain vehicle (ATV)** [ˌɔːltəˌreɪn 'viːəkl] Geländewagen 5 A 1
alligator ['ælɪgeɪtə] Alligator 4 Li
allowed [ə'laʊd]: **be allowed to do sth.** etwas tun dürfen
almost ['ɔːlməʊst] fast, beinahe
alone [ə'ləʊn] allein
along [ə'lɒŋ]: **1.** *(prep)* **along the street** entlang der Straße, die Straße entlang; **2. come along** vorbeikommen 5 P 4
alphabet ['ælfəbet] Alphabet
already [ɔːl'redi] schon, bereits
also ['ɔːlsəʊ] auch
alternative *(n; adj)* [ɔːl'tɜːnətɪv] **1.** Alternative; **2.** Alternativ-
although [ɔːl'ðəʊ] obwohl 6 P 4
always ['ɔːlweɪz] immer
... am [ˌeɪ_'em] ... Uhr morgens/ vormittags
ambulance ['æmbjələns] Krankenwagen
American *(n; adj)* [ə'merɪkən] **1.** Amerikaner/in • **Native American** amerikanische(r) Ureinwohner/in, „Indianer/in" **2.** amerikanisch • **American football** Football 1 Li (145)
°**amphora** ['æmfərə] Amphore *(Krug mit Henkeln)* 3 Li
an [ən] **1.** ein, eine; **2. twice an hour** zweimal pro Stunde, zweimal in der Stunde 6 A 1
and [ənd, *betont:* ænd] und • **and so on** und so weiter • **more and more expensive** immer teurer 3 A 10 • **nice and warm/dry/...** schön warm/trocken/... 5 T (84)
°**Angles** ['æŋglz]: **the Angles** die Angeln *(Angehörige des Volksstammes der Angeln)* 3 T (50)
°**Anglo: the Anglo-Saxons** [ˌæŋgləʊ 'sæksnz] die Angelsachsen 3 T (50)
angrily *(adv)* ['æŋgrəli] zornig, wütend
angry (with/about) ['æŋgri] böse, zornig, wütend (auf/über)
animal ['ænɪml] Tier
anorak ['ænəræk] Anorak
annoy [ə'nɔɪ] ärgern, belästigen
another [ə'nʌðə] ein(e) andere(r, s); noch ein(e) • **one another** einander, sich (gegenseitig) 6 (138)
answer *(n; v)* ['ɑːnsə] **1.** Antwort; **2.** antworten; beantworten **answer the phone** ans Telefon gehen
answering machine ['ɑːnsərɪŋ məˌʃiːn] Anrufbeantworter
anticlockwise [ˌænti'klɒkwaɪz] entgegen dem Uhrzeigersinn
any ['eni] jede(r/s) (beliebige); irgendein(e) beliebige(r/s) 2 A 14 **any?** (irgend)welche? • **not any** kein(e) • **not (...) any more** nicht mehr 4 T (69)
anybody jede(r) (Beliebige); (irgend)jemand 2 A 14 (151) • **anybody else** sonst (noch) jemand 1 A 3 (146) • **not ... anybody** niemand
anyone jede(r) (Beliebige); (irgend)jemand 2 A 14 (151) • **anyone else** sonst (noch) jemand 1 A 3 (146) • **not ... anyone** niemand
anything (irgend)etwas (X-Beliebiges); alles 2 A 14 (151) • **anything else** sonst (noch) etwas 1 A 3 (146) **not ... anything** nichts
anyway ['eniweɪ] **1.** trotzdem; sowieso 3 A 12; **2.** außerdem; und überhaupt 4 A 4; **3.** wie dem auch sei 6 T (102)
anywhere irgendwo; irgendwohin 2 A 14 (151) • **anywhere else** sonst (noch) irgendwo(hin) 1 A 3 (146) • **not ... anywhere** nirgendwo; nirgendwohin
apartment [ə'pɑːtmənt] *(AE)* Wohnung 6 A 9
appear [ə'pɪə] erscheinen, auftauchen
apple ['æpl] Apfel
April ['eɪprəl] April
°**archaeological** [ˌɑːkiə'lɒdʒɪkl] archäologisch 3 A 6 • °**archaeologist** [ˌɑːki'ɒlədʒɪst] Archäologe/Archäologin 3 Li
are [ə, *betont:* ɑː] bist; seid; sind **Here you are.** Hier bitte. / Bitte sehr. • **How are you?** Wie geht es dir/euch? • **How much are ...?** Was kosten ...?/Wie viel kosten ...? • **there are** es sind (vorhanden); es gibt
area ['eəriə] Bereich; Gebiet, Gegend
argue ['ɑːgjuː] **1.** argumentieren, behaupten 5 A 2 (163); **2. argue (about)** sich streiten, zanken (über/wegen) 5 A 2 (163) • **argument** ['ɑːgjumənt] **1.** Argument, Begründung 5 A 2; **2.** Streit 5 A 2
arm [ɑːm] Arm
army ['ɑːmi] Armee, Heer 3 T (49)
around [ə'raʊnd] um ... herum, in ... umher • **around 430** um das Jahr 430 herum 3 T (50) • **around Ashton** in Ashton umher, durch Ashton • **all around the country** überall im Land 2 A 4 • **be around** *(infml)* in der Nähe sein, da sein 6 P 10 • **Look around (you).** Sieh dich um. • **run around** herumrennen, umherrennen • **stand around** herumstehen
arrange [ə'reɪndʒ] (an)ordnen
arrive [ə'raɪv] ankommen, eintreffen
art [ɑːt] Kunst 3 P 11
article ['ɑːtɪkl] (Zeitungs-)Artikel 1 T (18)
as [əz, *betont:* æz] **1.** *(conj)* als, während • **as if** als ob 4 T (161) **as soon as** sobald 6 P 3 **2.** *(conj)* wie 3 T (50) • **as you know** wie du weißt, wie ihr wisst 3 T (157) **3.** *(prep)* **as a child** als Kind **known as** bekannt als 2 A 4 **4.** *(adv)* **as quick as** so schnell wie
ask [ɑːsk] fragen • **ask sb. about sth.** jn. zu/über etwas befragen **ask sb. to do sth.** jn. bitten, etwas zu tun 2 T (35) • **ask for** bitten um, fragen nach • **ask for help** um Hilfe bitten • **ask questions** Fragen stellen • **ask the way** nach dem Weg fragen
°**asleep** [ə'sliːp]: **fall asleep** einschlafen Rev 7 (113)
assembly [ə'sembli] Schulversammlung *(oft mit Andacht)*
assistant [ə'sɪstənt] Verkäufer/in
astronaut ['æstrənɔːt] Astronaut/in
at [ət, *betont:* æt] an, bei • **at (the age of) 39** mit 39, im Alter von 39 Jahren 5 T (84) • **at all times** immer, jederzeit 2 A 14 • **at first** zuerst, anfangs, am Anfang • **at home** zu Hause, daheim • **at Kingsway High School** an/auf der Kingsway High School • **at last** schließlich, endlich • **at least** wenigstens, mindestens; zumindest 5 A 3 • **at lunch** beim Mittagessen • **at night** in der Nacht, nachts • **at once** sofort, (so)gleich • **Open your books at**

page 5. Schlagt Seite 5 auf. • **at school** in der Schule • **at sea** auf See • **at six** um sechs • **at the back (of the book/bus/cinema)** hinten (im Buch/Bus/Kino) 1 P 12 • **at the door** an der Tür • **at the end** am Ende, am Schluss • **at the front** vorn **at the moment** im Moment, gerade, zurzeit • **at the restaurant** im Restaurant • **at the same time** zur selben Zeit • **at the weekend** am Wochenende • **at this time of year** in/zu dieser Jahreszeit 5 A 10 • **at weekends** an Wochenenden • **at work** bei der Arbeit, am Arbeitsplatz

ate [et, eɪt] *si. past von „eat"*

athletics [æθ'letɪks] Leichtathletik 1 Li (145)

Atlantic: the Atlantic Ocean [ət,læntɪk_'əʊʃn] der Atlantische Ozean UK Call (7)

atlas ['ætləs] Atlas

atmosphere ['ætməsfɪə] Atmosphäre 4 How (71)

attack *(v; n)* [ə'tæk] **1.** angreifen UK Call (7); **2.** Angriff UK Call (144)

attitude (towards) ['ætɪtju:d] Haltung (gegenüber), Einstellung (zu) 1 Li (118)

attraction [ə'trækʃn] Attraktion, Anziehungspunkt 4 Li

au pair [,əʊ 'peə] Aupairmädchen, -junge

audience ['ɔ:dɪəns] Zuschauer/innen, Zuhörer/innen, Publikum 6 T (103)

audio tours ['ɔ:diəʊ] Audiotour *(Führung mit Erläuterung über Kopfhörer)* 3 How (53)

August ['ɔ:gəst] August

aunt [ɑ:nt] Tante • **auntie** ['ɑ:nti] *(infml)* Tante 4 P 13

authentic [ɔ:'θentɪk] authentisch

autumn ['ɔ:təm] Herbst 1 A 6 (146)

avenue ['ævənju:] Allee, Boulevard 2 Li (149)

°**aviation** [,eɪvi'eɪʃn] Luftfahrt 5 P 3

away [ə'weɪ] weg, fort; entfernt

awesome ['ɔ:səm] *(AE, infml)* großartig, klasse 6 A 1

B

back *(adv; n)* [bæk] **1.** zurück **back in Chester** daheim in Chester **2.** Rücken; **3.** Rückseite 1 Li • **at the back (of the book/bus/cinema)** hinten (im Buch/Bus/Kino) 1 P 12

background ['bækgraʊnd] Hintergrund 6 T (102)

bacon ['beɪkən] Schinkenspeck 6 P 17

bad [bæd] schlecht, schlimm **Bad luck.** Pech (gehabt)! 3 A 12 **be bad at sth.** schlecht in etwas sein; etwas schlecht können 3 A 12 (156) • **too bad** *(infml)* schade 4 A 1

badminton ['bædmɪntən] Badminton, Federball

bag [bæg] Tasche, Beutel, Tüte; Sack

bake [beɪk] backen 3 A 5

°**bald eagle** [,bɔ:ld_'i:gl] Weißkopf-Seeadler 4 P 1

ball [bɔ:l] Ball

banana [bə'nɑ:nə] Banane

bang [bæŋ] Knall

bank [bæŋk] **1.** Bank, Sparkasse **bottle bank** Altglascontainer **2.** (Fluss-)Ufer 2 Li

barbecue ['bɑ:bɪkju:] Grillparty

baseball ['beɪsbɔ:l] Baseball 1 Li (145)

basket ['bɑ:skɪt] Korb

basketball ['bɑ:skɪtbɔ:l] Basketball

bath [bɑ:θ] Bad 3 Li • **have/take a bath** *(in der Wanne)* baden, ein Bad nehmen 3 Li (154)

bathroom [*BE:* 'bɑ:θru:m, *AE:* 'bæθru:m] **1.** Badezimmer; **2.** *(AE)* Toilette *(in einem Privathaus)* 4 T (69)

battle ['bætl] Schlacht, Kampf 3 T (51)

bay [beɪ] Bucht UK Call (7)

BC [,bi:'si:]**: 70 BC** 70 v. Chr. 3 Li (154)

be* [bi, *betont:* bi:] sein • **be able to do sth.** etwas tun können; fähig sein / in der Lage sein, etwas zu tun • **be allowed to do sth.** etwas tun dürfen • **be born** geboren sein/werden 1 P 12 • **be called** heißen, genannt werden **be cold** frieren • **be in trouble** in Schwierigkeiten sein; Ärger kriegen • **be late** zu spät sein/kommen • **be late for school** zu spät zur Schule kommen • **be missing** fehlen • **be out** weg sein, nicht da sein • **be pleased (with)** sich freuen (über), zufrieden sein (mit) • **be right** Recht haben • **be special** etwas Besonderes sein

beach [bi:tʃ] Strand • **on the beach** am Strand

bear [beə] Bär 5 P 6

beat* [bi:t] **1.** schlagen; besiegen 1 A 3; **2.** *si. past von „beat"* 1 A 3

beaten ['bi:tn] *Part. Perf. von „beat"* 1 A 3

beautiful ['bju:tɪfl] (wunder)schön

became [bɪ'keɪm] *si. past von „become"*

because [bɪ'kɒz] weil • **that's because** das kommt daher, weil 5 A 6

become* [bɪ'kʌm] **1.** werden; **2.** *Part. Perf. von „become"*

bed [bed] Bett

bedroom ['bedru:m] Schlafzimmer

been [bi:n, bɪn] *Part. Perf. von „be"*

beep [bi:p] Piepton 4 P 11

before [bɪ'fɔ:] **1.** *(prep)* vor *(zeitlich)* • **the day before yesterday** vorgestern 6 P 4 **2** *(conj)* bevor; **3.** *(adv)* vorher schon mal • **than before** als vorher/als früher • **the day/week before** am Tag zuvor / in der Woche zuvor

began [bɪ'gæn] *si. past von „begin"*

begin* **(-nn-)** [bɪ'gɪn] beginnen, anfangen (mit) • **beginning** [bɪ'gɪnɪŋ] Anfang, Beginn • **at the beginning** am Anfang

begun [bɪ'gʌn] *Part. Perf. von „begin"*

behind [bɪ'haɪnd] hinter • **stay behind** dableiben, zurückbleiben 3 T (52)

believe [bɪ'li:v] glauben

bell [bel] Glocke, Klingel 2 P 5

belong to [bɪ'lɒŋ] gehören (zu) 3 Li

below [bɪ'ləʊ] **1.** *(adv)* unten; **2.** *(prep)* unter, unterhalb (von)

bench [bentʃ] Bank *(zum Sitzen)*

best [best] **1.** am besten • **Which ending do you like best?** Welches Ende magst du am liebsten? **2. the best ...** der/die/das beste ... ; die besten ...

bet* **(-tt-)** [bet] **1.** wetten; **2.** *si. past von „bet"*; **3.** *Part. Perf. von „bet"*

better ['betə] besser • **better than** besser als • **like sth. better** etwas lieber mögen Welc (157)

between [bɪ'twi:n] zwischen • **in between** [,ɪn bɪ'twi:n] dazwischen 1 Li

beyond [bɪ'jɒnd] über ... hinaus, jenseits (von)

bicycle ['baɪsɪkl] Fahrrad

big [bɪg] groß

bike [baɪk] Fahrrad • **ride a bike** Rad fahren • **Let's ride our bikes to school.** Lass uns mit dem Rad zur Schule fahren. • **bike ride** Radfahrt, Radtour • **biking** *(das)* Radfahren 1 Li (145)

bikini [bɪ'ki:ni] Bikini

billion ['bɪljən] Milliarde(n) 1 P 7

bin [bɪn] Papierkorb, Mülleimer

bingo ['bɪŋgəʊ] Bingo

bird [bɜ:d] Vogel

biro ['baɪrəʊ] Kugelschreiber

birthday ['bɜ:θdeɪ] Geburtstag **Happy birthday!** Herzlichen Glückwunsch zum Geburtstag! **It's my birthday next week.** Ich habe nächste Woche Geburtstag. **When's your birthday?** Wann

hast du Geburtstag? • **birthday card** Geburtstagskarte
biscuit ['bɪskɪt] Keks, Plätzchen
bit [bɪt]: **a bit** ein bisschen, etwas
°**bitch** [bɪtʃ] *(infml)* dumme Kuh, Miststück *(wörtlich:* Hündin) 6 T (102)
black [blæk] schwarz
blew [blu:] *si. past von „blow"*
block [blɒk] (Häuser-, Wohn-) Block 4 T (69)
blouse [blaʊz] Bluse
blow* [bləʊ] wehen, blasen
blown [bləʊn] *Part. Perf. von „blow"*
°**blubber** ['blʌbə] (Walfisch-)Speck 5 A 1
blue [blu:] blau
board [bɔ:d] **1.** Brett 1 P 8; **2.** Spielbrett • **board game** Brettspiel 3 Li
3. (Wand-)Tafel • **notice board** Anschlagtafel, schwarzes Brett
4. tourist board ['tʊərɪst bɔ:d] Fremdenverkehrsbüro 1 P 12
5. on board (the ship) an Bord (des Schiffes)
6. board a plane/ship an Bord eines Flugzeugs/Schiffes gehen
boat [bəʊt] Boot, Schiff
body ['bɒdi] Körper • **bodybuilding** Bodybuilding *(Training zum Muskelaufbau)* 6 A 4
bold print [ˌbəʊld 'prɪnt] Fettdruck
bomb [bɒm] Bombe 2 T (33)
bone [bəʊn] Knochen
book *(n; v)* [bʊk] **1.** Buch; **2.** buchen, reservieren 4 Li
bookshelf ['bʊkʃelf], *pl* **bookshelves** ['bʊkʃelvz] Bücherregal
border (on) ['bɔ:də] (an)grenzen (an) 6 P 14
boring ['bɔ:rɪŋ] langweilig
born [bɔ:n]: **be born** geboren sein/werden 1 P 12
borrow sth. ['bɒrəʊ] sich etwas (aus)leihen, etwas entleihen 6 A 4
boss [bɒs] *(infml)* Boss, Chef/in 2 T (33)
both [bəʊθ] beide, beides
bottle ['bɒtl] Flasche • **a bottle of ...** eine Flasche ... • **bottle bank** Altglascontainer
bottom ['bɒtəm] Boden *(eines Gefäßes usw.)*; unteres Ende • **at the bottom of the page** am Fuß der Seite • **bottom row** [ˌbɒtəm 'rəʊ] untere Reihe
bought [bɔ:t] **1.** *si. past von „buy"*; **2.** *Part. Perf. von „buy"*
boutique [bu:'ti:k] Boutique
bowl [bəʊl] Schüssel, Schale 3 A 6
bowling ['bəʊlɪŋ] Bowling
box [bɒks] Kasten, Kiste • **a box of chocolates** eine Schachtel Pralinen
boy [bɔɪ] Junge
boyfriend ['bɔɪfrend] (fester) Freund
bracket ['brækɪt] Klammer *(in Texten)*
brain [breɪn] Gehirn 5 T (85)
bread *(no pl)* [bred] Brot
break [breɪk] Pause • **have a break** (eine) Pause machen 4 P 7
break* [breɪk] (zer)brechen; kaputtmachen; kaputtgehen
breakfast ['brekfəst] Frühstück **have breakfast** frühstücken
breathe (in/out) [bri:ð] (ein-/aus-) atmen 6 T (102)
bridge [brɪdʒ] Brücke
briefing ['bri:fɪŋ] Instruktionen, Anweisungen; Einsatzbesprechung 4 Li
brigade: fire brigade ['faɪə brɪˌgeɪd] Feuerwehr
bright [braɪt] leuchtend, hell
brightness ['braɪtnəs] Helligkeit, *(das)* Leuchten 2 P 12
brilliant ['brɪliənt] toll, glänzend, großartig
bring* [brɪŋ] bringen, mitbringen
°**bring to life** lebendig machen, zum Leben erwecken 2 A 4
British ['brɪtɪʃ] britisch • **He's/She's British.** Er ist Brite./Sie ist Britin.
°**Briton** ['brɪtn] Britannier *(keltische Urbevölkerung Großbritanniens)* 3 A 5
broadcast ['brɔ:dkɑ:st] Sendung, Übertragung *(Radio, Fernsehen)* 4 How (71)
brochure ['brəʊʃə] Prospekt, Broschüre
broke [brəʊk] *si. past von „break"*
broken ['brəʊkən] **1.** *Part. Perf. von „break"*; **2.** gebrochen; zerbrochen
brother ['brʌðə] Bruder
brought [brɔ:t] **1.** *si. past von „bring"*; **2.** *Part. Perf. von „bring"*
brown [braʊn] braun
brush *(n; v)* [brʌʃ] **1.** (Haar-)Bürste; **2.** bürsten • **brush your teeth** sich die Zähne putzen
bubble: speech bubble ['spi:tʃ ˌbʌbl] Sprechblase 5 P 5
Buddhist ['bʊdɪst] Buddhist/in 6 A 9
budgie ['bʌdʒi] Wellensittich
bug [bʌg] *(besonders AE)* Insekt, Käfer 6 P 8
build* [bɪld] bauen
building ['bɪldɪŋ] Gebäude
built [bɪlt] **1.** *si. past von „build"*; **2.** *Part. Perf. von „build"*
°**bull** [bʊl] Bulle, Stier 5 A 10
bulldozer ['bʊldəʊzə] Planierraupe, Bulldozer 3 A 1
burn [bɜ:n] (ver)brennen; anbrennen lassen
bus [bʌs] Bus • **on the bus** im Bus • **bus stop** Bushaltestelle
business ['bɪznəs] Unternehmen, Geschäft(e)
busy ['bɪzi] beschäftigt; belebt, verkehrsreich, hektisch
but [bət, *betont:* bʌt] aber
butcher ['bʊtʃə] Metzger/in, Fleischer/in 5 A 3 • **to the butcher's** zum Metzger, in die Metzgerei 5 A 3 (163)
butter ['bʌtə] Butter
buy* [baɪ] kaufen
by [baɪ] **1.** an, neben; (nahe) bei; **2.** von; durch 2 A 7; **3. by bike/car/...** mit dem Rad/Auto/... **4. by 7.20** bis (spätestens) 7.20 1 A 3
Bye bye! [baɪ 'baɪ] Tschüs! / Servus!

C

c. (= circa) ['sɜ:kə] ca. (= zirka) 1 How (19)
cable ['keɪbl] Kabel 6 T (104)
café ['kæfeɪ] *(kleines)* Restaurant, Imbissstube; Café
cage [keɪdʒ] Käfig
cake [keɪk] Kuchen, Torte
calendar ['kælɪndə] Kalender
call *(v; n)* [kɔ:l] **1.** nennen; rufen **called** mit (dem) Namen 1 Li **be called** heißen, genannt werden • **call sb. (stupid) names** jn. verspotten, jn. beschimpfen 4 T (69) • °**UK calling** *etwa:* Hier spricht das Vereinigte Königreich. UK Call (7)
2. anrufen • **caller** Anrufer/in **3.** aufrufen *(Flug)*; **4.** Anruf • **give sb. a call** jn. anrufen 5 P 4
camcorder ['kæmkɔ:də] Camcorder
came [keɪm] *si. past von „come"*
camera ['kæmərə] Kamera, Fotoapparat
camp [kæmp] (Trainings-, Zelt-) Lager 4 A 1
campaign [kæm'peɪn] Kampagne, (Werbe-)Feldzug
camping ['kæmpɪŋ] Camping, Zelten 5 T (84)
campsite ['kæmpsaɪt] Campingplatz, Zeltplatz
can [kæn] Dose, Büchse
can [kən, *betont:* kæn] **1.** können; **2.** dürfen • **you can't** [kɑ:nt] **(= you cannot)** ['kænɒt] **1.** du kannst nicht; **2.** du darfst nicht
candle ['kændl] Kerze
°**candy** ['kændi] *(AE)* Bonbon; Süßigkeiten 6 A 4
canteen [kæn'ti:n] Kantine, Schulmensa
canyon ['kænjən] Cañon, Schlucht

capital (city) [ˈkæpɪtl] Hauptstadt
captain [ˈkæptɪn] Kapitän/in
caption [ˈkæpʃn] Bildunterschrift
car [kɑː] Auto • **car park** *(BE)* Parkplatz 3 A 6
caravan [ˈkærəvæn] *(BE)* Wohnwagen 1 A 6
card [kɑːd] Karte
cardboard [ˈkɑːdbɔːd] Pappe, Karton
care [keə]: **1. I don't care.** Das/Es ist mir egal. • **Nobody cared.** Niemanden interessierte das/es. 3 A 12 • **Who cares?** Wen interessiert das? / Ist doch egal! 1 Li
2. take care of sb./sth. sich um jn./etwas kümmern 1 A 6
careful *(adj)* [ˈkeəfl] **1.** vorsichtig; **2.** sorgfältig
carefully *(adv)* [ˈkeəfəli] **1.** vorsichtig; **2.** sorgfältig
°**caribou** [ˈkærɪbuː], *pl* **caribou** *or* **caribous** Karibu *(nordamerikanische Rentierart)* 5 A 10
carry [ˈkæri] **1.** tragen; **2.** befördern, transportieren
carton [ˈkɑːtn] Karton, (Milch-, Saft-)Packung
cartoon [kɑːˈtuːn] Cartoon, Bilderwitz 4 A 3
cassette [kəˈset] Cassette
castle [ˈkɑːsl] Burg, Schloss
cat [kæt] Katze
catch* [kætʃ] fangen, einfangen 4 P 8 • **catch a train/bus** einen Zug/Bus nehmen, erreichen 2 T (33)
cathedral [kəˈθiːdrəl] Kathedrale, Dom
caught [kɔːt] **1.** *si. past von „catch"* 2 T (33) / 4 P 8; **2.** *Part. Perf. von „catch"* 2 T (33) / 4 P 8
cause [kɔːz] verursachen
CD [ˌsiːˈdiː] CD • **CD-ROM** [ˌsiː diː ˈrɒm] **(= compact disc read-only memory)** CD-ROM
ceiling [ˈsiːlɪŋ] Decke *(eines Zimmers)*
celebrate [ˈselɪbreɪt] feiern 1 A 6
celebration [ˌselɪˈbreɪʃn] (Gedenk-)Feier 2 A 14
cello [ˈtʃeləʊ], *pl* **cellos** (Violin-)Cello 6 T (103)
cellphone [ˈselfəʊn] *(besonders AE)* Handy 5 P 4
Celsius: 54° C (= 54 degrees Celsius) [dɪˌgriːz ˈselsiəs] 54 Grad Celsius 6 A 1
°**Celt** [kelt] Kelte, Keltin 3 T (49)
°**Celtic** [ˈkeltɪk] keltisch; Keltisch 1 A 6 / 3 A 5
cent (¢) [sent] Cent *(kleinste amerikanische Münze)*
central [ˈsentrəl] Zentral-, Mittel- 3 A 6 (155) • **central heating** Zentralheizung 3 A 6
centre [ˈsentə] Zentrum; Mitte
century [ˈsentʃəri] Jahrhundert
ceremony [*BE:* ˈserəməni, *AE:* ˈserəməʊni] Zeremonie; Feier(lichkeit)
chain [tʃeɪn] Kette
chair [tʃeə] Stuhl
champion [ˈtʃæmpiən] Champion, Meister/in, Wettkampfsieger/in
championship [ˈtʃæmpiənʃɪp] Meisterschaft 1 A 1
chance [tʃɑːns] Chance, Gelegenheit 1 A 3
change *(n; v)* [tʃeɪndʒ] **1.** (Ver-)Änderung, Wechsel; **2.** (sich) ändern, (sich) verändern, umwandeln **change into** sich verändern in; werden zu • **change (trains)** umsteigen 2 A 2 • °**Changing of the Guard** Wachablösung *(vor dem Buckingham Palace)* 2 A 7
3. *(Geld)* wechseln, umtauschen; **4.** sich umziehen • **changing room** Umkleideraum 3 How (53)
channel [ˈtʃænl] Kanal • **Channel Tunnel** [ˌtʃænl ˈtʌnl] Kanaltunnel *(Tunnel zwischen England und Frankreich)*
character [ˈkærəktə] Charakter; Person, Figur *(in Roman, Film usw.)* 2 T (36)
°**charcoal** [ˈtʃɑːkəʊl] Holzkohle 3 A 5
chart [tʃɑːt] Tabelle
chase sb. (away) [tʃeɪs] jn. (weg-/ver)jagen 2 A 7
cheap [tʃiːp] billig, preiswert
check [tʃek] überprüfen, kontrollieren • **check in** [ˌtʃek‿ˈɪn] **1.** einchecken *(Flughafen)*; **2.** sich anmelden, sich eintragen *(Hotel)*
°**checkpoint** [ˈtʃekpɔɪnt] Kontrollpunkt 1 T (18)
cheer [tʃɪə] jubeln, Beifall klatschen
cheese [tʃiːz] Käse
chess [tʃes] Schach
chicken [ˈtʃɪkɪn] Huhn; (Brat-)Hähnchen
child [tʃaɪld], *pl* **children** [ˈtʃɪldrən] Kind
chips *(pl)* [tʃɪps] Pommes frites
chocolate [ˈtʃɒklət] **1.** Schokolade; **2.** Praline
choice [tʃɔɪs] (Aus-)Wahl
choir [ˈkwaɪə] Chor UK Call (7)
choose* [tʃuːz] aussuchen, (aus-)wählen
chose [tʃəʊz] *si. past von „choose"*
chosen [ˈtʃəʊzn] *Part. Perf. von „choose"*
Christ [kraɪst] Christus 3 Li (154)
Christmas [ˈkrɪsməs] Weihnachten
church [tʃɜːtʃ] Kirche
chute: water chute [ˈwɔːtə ʃuːt] Wasserrutsche
cinema [ˈsɪnəmə] Kino
circa (c.) [ˈsɜːkə] zirka (ca.) 1 How (19)
circus [ˈsɜːkəs] **1.** Zirkus; **2.** (runder) Platz *(in einer Stadt)* 2 Li (149)
city [ˈsɪti] Stadt, Großstadt
clap (-pp-) [klæp] klatschen **Clap your hands.** Klatsch(t) in die Hände.
class [klɑːs] **1.** *(deutsche)* (Schul-)Klasse; **2.** Klasse, Kurs
classical [ˈklæsɪkl] klassisch
classmate [ˈklɑːsmeɪt] Klassenkamerad/in, Mitschüler/in
classroom [ˈklɑːsruːm] Klassenzimmer • **classroom phrases** [ˌklɑːsruːm ˈfreɪzɪz] *Redewendungen für das Klassenzimmer; Unterrichtssprache*
clause [klɔːz] Teilsatz, Gliedsatz **main clause** Hauptsatz • **sub-clause** Nebensatz
clean *(v; adj)* [kliːn] **1.** sauber machen; **2.** sauber • **cleaner** Reinigungskraft
clear *(adj)* [klɪə] klar, deutlich **clearly** *(adv)* [ˈklɪəli] eindeutig, klar
clever [ˈklevə] schlau, klug **cleverness** [ˈklevənəs] Klugheit, Cleverness 2 P 12
click [klɪk] klicken
cliff [klɪf] Klippe
climate [ˈklaɪmət] Klima 5 A 1
climb [klaɪm] klettern; hinaufklettern (auf)
clique [kliːk] Clique, Freundeskreis 4 T (69)
clockwise [ˈklɒkwaɪz] im Uhrzeigersinn
close [kləʊz] schließen, zumachen
close (to) [kləʊs] nahe (bei, an)
clothes *(pl)* [kləʊðz, kləʊz] Kleidung, „Klamotten"
cloud [klaʊd] Wolke • **cloudy** [ˈklaʊdi] bewölkt, wolkig
clown [klaʊn] Clown
club [klʌb] Klub; Verein • **club sports** Vereinssportarten 1 A 9
clue [kluː] Hinweis, Anhaltspunkt
coach [kəʊtʃ] **1.** Reisebus; **2.** Trainer/in 1 A 3
coast [kəʊst] Küste • **on the coast** an der Küste
code [kəʊd] (Geheim-)Kode 2 T (33)
coffee [ˈkɒfi] Kaffee
coin [kɔɪn] Münze 3 Li
cola [ˈkəʊlə] Cola
cold *(adj; n)* [kəʊld] **1.** kalt • **be cold** frieren
2. Kälte; Erkältung 5 T (84) • **I've got a (bad) cold.** Ich bin (schwer) erkältet. 5 T (166)
collage [ˈkɒlɑːʒ] Collage
collect [kəˈlekt] **1.** sammeln; **2.** einsammeln

collection [kə'lekʃn] Sammlung
college ['kɒlɪdʒ] Hochschule, Fachschule 4 T (69)
colour *(n; v)* ['kʌlə] **1.** Farbe **What colour is it?** Welche Farbe hat es (er, sie)? • **colourful** bunt, farbenfroh, farbenprächtig 2 A 14 **2.** bunt anmalen
column ['kɒləm] Säule 2 Li (149)
comb *(n; v)* [kəʊm] **1.** Kamm 3 Li; **2.** kämmen 3 Li (154) • **Comb your hair.** Kämm dich. 3 Li (154)
combine [kəm'baɪn] kombinieren, verbinden 5 A 3
come* [kʌm] **1.** kommen • **come along** vorbeikommen 5 P 4 **come in** hereinkommen • **come (in) third** als Dritter ins Ziel kommen; Dritter werden 1 T (18) **Come on.** Los, komm! / Komm schon! • **come over** herüberkommen • **come true** wahr werden, sich bewahrheiten 4 A 1 **2.** *Part. Perf. von „come"*
comfortable ['kʌmftəbl] bequem, komfortabel, angenehm 3 A 6
comic ['kɒmɪk] Comic-Heft
common ['kɒmən] **1.** häufig, weit verbreitet 3 T (50); **2. have sth. in common** etwas miteinander gemein haben 1 T (18)
community [kə'mju:nəti] Gemeinde, Gemeinschaft 2 A 14
company ['kʌmpəni] Firma, Gesellschaft 5 T (84) • **start a company** eine Firma gründen 6 A 4
compare (to/with) [kəm'peə] vergleichen (mit)
comparison [kəm'pærɪsn] Vergleich **make comparisons** Vergleiche anstellen, vergleichen
competition [ˌkɒmpə'tɪʃn] Wettbewerb, Wettkampf
complain (to sb. about sth.) [kəm'pleɪn] sich (bei jm. über etwas) beschweren, beklagen 5 A 3
complete *(v; adj)* [kəm'pli:t] **1.** vervollständigen; **2.** vollständig, komplett 5 P 5 • **completely** *(adv)* völlig, vollkommen 5 P 5 (165)
compound noun ['kɒmpaʊnd] zusammengesetztes Nomen, Kompositum
computer [kəm'pju:tə] Computer, Rechner • **computer science** Informatik 6 A 7
concert ['kɒnsət] Konzert
conclusion [kən'klu:ʒn] Schluss(folgerung), Abschluss 5 A 2
conference ['kɒnfrəns] Konferenz, Kongress, Tagung 2 How (37)
Congratulations! *(pl)* [kənˌgrætʃu'leɪʃnz] Herzlichen Glückwunsch! 5 P 4

°**conqueror** ['kɒŋkərə] Eroberer/Eroberin 3 T (51)
construction [kən'strʌkʃn] Konstruktion 5 P 3
context ['kɒntekst] Zusammenhang, Kontext
continue [kən'tɪnju:] weitergehen/-reden/-machen, weiter (tun) 2 A 10
controls *(pl)* [kən'trəʊlz] Steuerpult, Schalttafel; Kontrollinstrumente 4 How (71)
conversation [ˌkɒnvə'seɪʃn] Gespräch, Unterhaltung 1 P 8
°**conversion** [kən'vɜ:ʃn] *(Rugby)* „Platztritt" *(2 Extrapunkte, erzielt durch Schuss des ruhenden Balles über die gegnerische Querlatte nach einem „Versuch" (try))* 1 A 1
cook *(n; v)* [kʊk] **1.** Koch, Köchin; **2.** kochen, zubereiten • **cooking** *(das)* Kochen 3 P 11 • °**What's cooking?** *(infml)* Was liegt an? / Was ist los? 3 A 5
cookie ['kʊki] *(besonders AE)* Keks 6 P 3
cool [ku:l] **1.** cool, scharf, stark; **2.** kühl 4 P 10
copy *(v; n)* ['kɒpi] **1.** kopieren, übertragen, abschreiben; **2. copy (of)** Kopie (von)
corner ['kɔ:nə] Ecke • **on the corner** an der Ecke
cornflakes ['kɔ:nfleɪks] Cornflakes
°**corny** ['kɔ:ni]: **a corny joke** *(infml)* ein abgedroschener Witz 4 A 8
°**corporation** [ˌkɔ:pə'reɪʃn] Verwaltung 5 T (84)
correct *(v; adj)* [kə'rekt] **1.** verbessern, korrigieren; **2.** korrekt, richtig
correction [kə'rekʃn] Korrektur
cosmonaut ['kɒzmənɔ:t] Kosmonaut/in 4 P 6
cost* *(v; n)* [kɒst] **1.** kosten; **2.** *si. past von „cost"*; **3.** *Part. Perf. von „cost"*; **4.** Kosten
costume ['kɒstju:m] Kostüm, Verkleidung
°**couch potato** [ˌkaʊtʃ pə'teɪtəʊ] *(infml)* „Dauerglotzer" *(wörtlich: Sofakartoffel)* 1 Li
could [kəd, *betont:* kʊd] **1.** konnte(n); **2.** könnte(n)
count [kaʊnt] zählen
counter ['kaʊntə] Spielstein
country ['kʌntri] Land • **in the country** auf dem Land
countryside ['kʌntrɪsaɪd] Landschaft; (ländliche) Gegend 1 A 6
course: of course [əv 'kɔ:s] natürlich, selbstverständlich
cousin ['kʌzn] Cousin, Cousine
cover ['kʌvə] beziehen, überziehen; bedecken, zudecken 5 A 1
cow [kaʊ] Kuh

crash [kræʃ] **1.** abstürzen *(Computer)*; **2. crash (into)** zusammenstoßen (mit), hineinfahren (in)
crazy ['kreɪzi] verrückt • **crazy about sb./sth.** verrückt nach jm./etwas 4 A 1 • °**the audience goes crazy** das Publikum tobt, das Publikum rast 6 T (103)
°**credit** ['kredɪt] Punkt(e) *(für den High School- oder College-Abschluss)* 4 T (68)
°**creepy-crawly** [ˌkri:pi 'krɔ:li] *(infml)* Krabbeltier 2 A 4
crew [kru:] Crew, Besatzung, Mannschaft *(eines Schiffs, Flugzeugs)* 4 Li
cricket ['krɪkɪt] Kricket 1 Li (145)
crime [kraɪm] **1.** Verbrechen Welc (56); **2.** Kriminalität Welc (56)
crisps *(pl)* [krɪsps] Kartoffelchips
critical ['krɪtɪkl] **1.** entscheidend 4 Li; **2. critical (of)** kritisch (gegenüber) 4 Li
°**crofter** ['krɒftə] *(BE, besonders in Schottland)* Bauer/Bäuerin UK Call (7)
cross [krɒs] überqueren; (sich) kreuzen
°**crossbar** ['krɒsbɑ:] Querlatte 1 A 1
crowd [kraʊd] (Menschen-)Menge 4 P 8
°**Crown Jewels** *(pl)* [ˌkraʊn 'dʒu:əlz] Kronjuwelen 2 Li
cry [kraɪ] weinen; schreien
culture ['kʌltʃə] Kultur UK Call (7)
cup [kʌp] **1.** Tasse • **a cup of tea** eine Tasse Tee **2.** Cup, Pokal 1 P 4
cupboard ['kʌbəd] Schrank
customer ['kʌstəmə] Kunde, Kundin
cut* **(-tt-)** [kʌt] **1.** schneiden **cut out** ausschneiden • **cut up** zerschneiden, in Stücke schneiden 5 A 1 **2.** *si. past von „cut"*; **3.** *Part. Perf. von „cut"*
cute [kju:t] *(infml)* niedlich, süß 5 A 6
cycle ['saɪkl] Rad fahren 1 A 6 **cycle lane / cycle track** ['saɪkl leɪn, 'saɪkl træk] Radweg • **cycling** *(das)* Radfahren 1 Li (145) **cyclist** ['saɪklɪst] Radfahrer/in

D

dad [dæd] Vati, Papa; Vater
°**Damn.** [dæm] *(infml)* Verdammt. 6 T (104)
dance *(v; n)* [dɑ:ns] **1.** tanzen **dancer** ['dɑ:nsə] Tänzer/in **dancing** *(das)* Tanzen 1 Li (145) **2.** Tanz 5 A 6

danger ['deɪndʒə] Gefahr • **dangerous** ['deɪndʒərəs] gefährlich
dark *(n; adj)* [dɑːk] **1.** Dunkelheit; **2.** dunkel • **darkness** ['dɑːknəs] Dunkelheit 2 P 12
date *(n; v)* [deɪt] **1.** Datum **What's the date?** Welches Datum haben wir? **2.** Verabredung; Termin; **3. date sb.** *(besonders AE)* mit jm. (aus)gehen 5 A 6
daughter ['dɔːtə] Tochter
day [deɪ] Tag • **day of the week** Wochentag • **day trip** Tagesausflug • **in the old days** in alten Zeiten, früher 5 P 1 • **the day (that) her article appeared** der Tag, an dem ihr Artikel erschien 5 A 3 • **the day before** der Tag zuvor, am Tag zuvor 5 (137) **the day before yesterday** vorgestern 6 P 4 • **to this day** bis heute, bis zum heutigen Tag
dead [ded] tot
dear *(n; adj)* [dɪə] **1.** Liebling, Schatz; **2. Dear Katrin and Julia** Liebe Katrin, liebe Julia • **Dear Sir or Madam** Sehr geehrte Damen und Herren 1 P 12
death [deθ] Tod; Todesfall 5 P 8
December [dɪ'sembə] Dezember
decide (on) [dɪ'saɪd] sich entscheiden (für), beschließen
decision [dɪ'sɪʒn]**: make a decision** eine Entscheidung treffen, fällen
deep [diːp] tief 6 A 1
deer, *pl* **deer** [dɪə] Reh, Hirsch 5 A 10
definition [ˌdefɪ'nɪʃn] Definition
°**defuse** [diː'fjuːz] entschärfen 2 T (33)
degree [dɪˌgriː] Grad 5 P 9 (165) **54° C (= 54 degrees Celsius)** [dɪˌgriːz 'selsiəs] 54 Grad Celsius 6 A 1 • **60° F (= 60 degrees Fahrenheit)** [dɪˌgriːz 'færənhaɪt] 60 Grad Fahrenheit 5 P 9
delay [dɪ'leɪ] Verzögerung, Verspätung
delicious [dɪ'lɪʃəs] lecker, köstlich
department store [dɪ'pɑːtmənt stɔː] Kaufhaus
demonstration [ˌdemən'streɪʃn] Demonstration 3 A 10
departure [dɪ'pɑːtʃə] Abfahrt, Abreise
describe [dɪ'skraɪb] beschreiben **description** [dɪ'skrɪpʃn] Beschreibung
desert ['dezət] Wüste 6 A 1
design *(v; n)* [dɪ'zaɪn] **1.** entwerfen, konstruieren 2 P 5; **2.** Design, Gestaltung
desk [desk] Schreibtisch, Schülertisch
destroy [dɪ'strɔɪ] zerstören, vernichten
detail ['diːteɪl] Detail, Einzelheit 3 T (51)
detective [dɪ'tektɪv] Detektiv/in
dialogue ['daɪəlɒg] Dialog
diary ['daɪəri] Tagebuch; Terminkalender
dice, *pl* **dice** [daɪs] Würfel **throw the dice** würfeln
dictionary ['dɪkʃənri] Wörterbuch, *(alphabetisches)* Wörterverzeichnis
did [dɪd] *si. past von „do"*
die (of) [daɪ] sterben (an)
difference ['dɪfrəns] Unterschied **different** ['dɪfrənt] unterschiedlich, verschieden; anders; andere(r, s) • **different from** anders als 1 A 2
difficult ['dɪfɪkəlt] schwierig, schwer
dig* (up) **(-gg-)** [dɪg] (aus-, um-) graben 3 A 1
dime [daɪm] Zehncentmünze *(USA)*
dining-room ['daɪnɪŋruːm] Esszimmer
dinner ['dɪnə] Abendessen, Abendbrot • **have dinner** Abendbrot essen
°**dinosaur** ['daɪnəsɔː] Dinosaurier 2 A 4
direct speech [ˌdaɪrekt 'spiːtʃ] wörtliche Rede, direkte Rede 3 T (52)
directions *(pl)* [də'rekʃnz] Anweisung(en) 2 T (33)
dirty ['dɜːti] schmutzig
disabled [dɪs'eɪbld] (körper)behindert
disagree (with) [ˌdɪsə'griː] nicht übereinstimmen (mit); anderer Meinung sein (als) 5 A 4
disappear [ˌdɪsə'pɪə] verschwinden
disc [dɪsk] Scheibe 4 P 8
disc jockey ['dɪsk dʒɒki] Diskjockey
disco ['dɪskəʊ] Disko
discover [dɪ'skʌvə] entdecken; feststellen, herausfinden 2 A 4 (150) **discovery** [dɪ'skʌvəri] Entdeckung 2 A 4
discuss sth. [dɪ'skʌs] über etwas diskutieren, etwas besprechen **discussion** [dɪ'skʌʃn] Diskussion
dishes *(pl)* ['dɪʃɪz] Geschirr **wash the dishes** das Geschirr abwaschen
°**display** [dɪ'spleɪ] Display, Auslage, Ausstellung(sstück) 2 A 4
distance ['dɪstəns] Entfernung, Abstand; Ferne 5 A 5
divorced [dɪ'vɔːst] geschieden
DJ [ˌdiː'dʒeɪ], **disc jockey** ['dɪsk dʒɒki] Diskjockey
do* [duː] tun, machen • **do homework** die Hausaufgabe(n) machen • **do jobs** Arbeiten/Aufträge erledigen • **do so** es/das tun 1 T (18) • **do sums** rechnen 3 A 12 (156) • **do well** erfolgreich sein, gut zurechtkommen 3 T (49) **do the shopping** Einkäufe machen/erledigen, einkaufen **Don't do that.** Tu das nicht. / Lass das. • **I don't know.** Ich weiß (es) nicht.
dock [dɒk] Dock, Anlegestelle
doctor ['dɒktə] Arzt, Ärztin
documentary [ˌdɒkju'mentri] Dokumentar-, dokumentarisch 6 A 4
dog [dɒg] Hund
dollar ($) ['dɒlə] Dollar *(amerikanische Währung)* • **a 30-dollar ticket** eine 30-Dollar-Karte, eine Karte für 30 Dollar
dolphin ['dɒlfɪn] Delphin
done [dʌn] *Part. Perf. von „do"*
door [dɔː] Tür • **at the door** an der Tür • **front door** Wohnungstür, Haustür
down [daʊn] hinunter, herunter, nach unten • **down the tree** den Baum hinunter • **up and down** auf und ab 6 T (103) • **put down** hinstellen, hinlegen • **sit down** sich hinsetzen • **write down** aufschreiben
download [ˌdaʊn'ləʊd] herunterladen, downloaden
downstairs [ˌdaʊn'steəz] nach unten; unten
drama ['drɑːmə] Drama, Schauspiel
drank [dræŋk] *si. past von „drink"*
draw* [drɔː] zeichnen • **draw in** einzeichnen • **drawing** ['drɔːɪŋ] Zeichnung
drawn [drɔːn] *Part. Perf. von „draw"*
dream *(n; v)* [driːm] **1.** Traum; **2. dream (about)** träumen (von) **dream house** Traumhaus **dreamland** Traumland 6 Li **dreamy** verträumt
dress [dres] Kleid
drew [druː] *si. past von „draw"*
drink* *(v; n)* [drɪŋk] **1.** trinken; **2.** Getränk
drive* *(v; n)* [draɪv] **1.** *(ein Auto, einen Bus)* fahren • **drive off** wegfahren • **driver** Fahrer/in °**2.** treiben; antreiben 3 T (52) **3.** (Auto-)Fahrt
driven ['drɪvn] *Part. Perf. von „drive"*
drop **(-pp-)** [drɒp] **1.** fallen lassen; **2. drop sth. off** etwas abliefern, etwas vorbeibringen 4 Li; °**3. drop goal** *(Rugby) 3 Punkte, erzielt durch Schuss des Balles über die gegnerische Querlatte per „Sprungtritt" (drop-kick)* 1 A 1; °**4. drop-kick** *(v)* *(Rugby)* „einen Sprungtritt machen" *(den Ball aus*

dem Lauf heraus schießen, gerade nachdem er auf den Boden aufgesprungen ist) 1 A 1
drove [drəʊv] *si. past von „drive"*
drum [drʌm] Trommel • **play the drums** Schlagzeug spielen
drunk [drʌŋk] *Part. Perf. von „drink"*
dry [draɪ] trocken
duck [dʌk] Ente
dug [dʌg] **1.** *si. past von „dig"* 3 A 1; **2.** *Part. Perf. von „dig"* 3 A 1
°**dump** [dʌmp]: **(rubbish) dump** Müllhalde, Müllkippe 3 A 1
during *(prep)* ['djʊərɪŋ] während 4 Li
DVD [ˌdiː viː 'diː] DVD • **DVD-player** DVD-Spieler

E

each [iːtʃ]: **from each group** aus jeder *(einzelnen)* Gruppe • **look at each other** [iːtʃ_'ʌðə] sich (gegenseitig) ansehen, einander ansehen 4 T (69)
ear [ɪə] Ohr
early ['ɜːli] früh; zu früh
earth [ɜːθ] Erde • **on earth** auf der Erde
earthquake ['ɜːθkweɪk] Erdbeben 2 A 4
east [iːst] östlich; (nach) Osten °**eastbound** ['iːstbaʊnd] Richtung Osten 2 A 2 • **eastern** ['iːstən] östlich, Ost- 1 A 6 (147)
easy ['iːzi] leicht, einfach
eat* [iːt] essen
eaten ['iːtn] *Part. Perf. von „eat"*
edge [edʒ] Rand, Kante 2 T (35)
education [ˌedʒu'keɪʃn] (Schul-, Aus-)Bildung; Erziehung 5 T (86)
e.g. [ˌiː 'dʒiː] *(from Latin 'exempli gratia')* z. B. (zum Beispiel) 2 A 13
egg [eg] Ei • **scrambled egg(s)** [ˌskræmbld_'eg(z)] Rührei, Rühreier
either ['aɪðə, 'iːðə]: **not (...) either** auch nicht; auch kein
elect sb. (sth.) [ɪ'lekt] jn. (zu etwas) wählen 6 A 4
electronic [ɪˌlek'trɒnɪk] elektronisch
elephant ['elɪfənt] Elefant
elevator ['elɪveɪtə] *(AE)* Fahrstuhl, Aufzug 4 A 1
else [els]: **anyone else** sonst (noch) jemand 1 A 3 (146) • **anything else** sonst (noch) etwas 1 A 3 (146) **anywhere else** sonst (noch) irgendwo(hin) 1 A 3 (146) • **everyone else** alle anderen 1 A 3 **everything else** alles andere 1 A 3 **everywhere else** überall sonst 1 A 3 (146) • **someone else** (noch) jemand anderes 1 A 3 (146) **something else** (noch) etwas anderes 1 A 3 (146) • **somewhere else** woanders(hin), sonst irgendwo(hin) 1 A 3 (146) • **what else?** was sonst (noch)? • **who else?** wer sonst (noch)? 1 A 3 (146)
e-mail ['iːmeɪl] E-Mail
embarrass sb. [ɪm'bærəs] jn. in Verlegenheit bringen, jn. verlegen machen 5 A 6 • **embarrassed** [ɪm'bærɪst] verlegen, peinlich berührt 5 A 6 (164)
emergency [i'mɜːdʒənsi] Notfall **emergency services** *(pl)* Notdienst
°**emperor** ['empərə] Kaiser 3 T (49)
empire ['empaɪə] Reich, Weltreich 3 A 5
empty ['empti] leer 1 Li
encyclopedia [ɪnˌsaɪklə'piːdɪə] Enzyklopädie, Lexikon UK Call (6)
end *(n; v)* [end] **1.** Ende, Schluss **at the end** am Ende, am Schluss **in the end** schließlich, am Ende, zum Schluss • **endless** ['endləs] endlos 5 A 1
2. end (in) enden (auf)
ending ['endɪŋ] **1.** Endung; **2.** Ende, Schluss • **happy ending** Happyend
endless ['endləs] endlos 5 A 1
enemy ['enəmi] Feind/in UK Call (7)
energy ['enədʒi] Energie • **solar energy** Sonnenenergie, Solarenergie • **wind energy** Windenergie
engine ['endʒɪn] Motor, Maschine
England ['ɪŋglənd] England
English ['ɪŋglɪʃ] **1.** englisch; **2.** Englisch • **We speak English.** Wir sprechen Englisch.
enjoy [ɪn'dʒɔɪ] genießen • **Enjoy yourself ...** Amüsier dich ... / Vergnüg dich ... 6 A 1
enough [ɪ'nʌf] genug 2 T (33)
enter ['entə] betreten; einreisen in 4 P 8
entrance ['entrəns] Eingang 6 P 2
entry ['entri] **1.** Beitrag, Einsendung; **2.** Eintrag, Eintragung *(in einem Wörterbuch/Tagebuch)* 5 How (87)
envelope ['envələʊp] (Brief-)Umschlag 6 A 9
environment [ɪn'vaɪrənmənt] Umwelt, Umgebung • **environment-friendly** umweltfreundlich
equipment *(no pl)* [ɪ'kwɪpmənt] Ausrüstung 5 T (84)
Eskimo ['eskɪməʊ] Eskimo 5 A 1
especially [ɪ'speʃli] besonders, insbesondere 4 A 8
etc. **(= et cetera)** [et 'setərə] usw.
euro (€) ['jʊərəʊ] Euro
Europe ['jʊərəp] Europa
even ['iːvn] sogar, selbst 1 T (18) **even taller/better/...** (sogar) noch größer/besser/... 1 T (148) **even if** selbst wenn, sogar wenn 3 A 6
evening ['iːvnɪŋ] Abend • **Good evening.** Guten Abend. • **in the evening(s)** am Abend, abends **on Monday evening** am Montagabend • **on Monday evenings** montagabends, montags abends **this evening** heute Abend
event [ɪ'vent] Ereignis; Veranstaltung 2 A 4
ever ['evə] je, jemals, schon mal **ever since she could remember** seit sie sich erinnern konnte 4 A 1
every ['evri] jede, jeder, jedes **every ten years** alle zehn Jahre 6 A 1
everybody ['evribɒdɪ] jeder, alle **everybody else** alle anderen 1 A 3
everyday *(adj)* ['evrideɪ] Alltags-; alltäglich 3 Li
everyone ['evriwʌn] jeder, alle **everyone else** alle anderen 1 A 3
everything ['evriθɪŋ] alles **everything else** alles andere 1 A 3
everywhere ['evriweə] überall; überallhin • **everywhere else** überall sonst 1 Li (146)
°**evil spirits** [ˌiːvl 'spɪrɪts] böse Geister 6 A 9
exact *(adj)* [ɪg'zækt] genau 2 A 14 (152) • **exactly** *(adv)* [ɪg'zæktli] genau 2 A 14
example [ɪg'zɑːmpl] Beispiel • **for example** zum Beispiel
except [ɪk'sept] außer 3 T (50)
exchange [ɪks'tʃeɪndʒ] aus-, umtauschen; *(Geld)* wechseln 5 A 10
excited (about) [ɪk'saɪtɪd] aufgeregt (wegen, über) • **exciting** [ɪk'saɪtɪŋ] aufregend, spannend
excuse *(n; v)* **1.** [ɪk'skjuːs] Ausrede, Entschuldigung; **2. Excuse me.** [ɪk'skjuːz] Entschuldigung. / Entschuldigen Sie.
execute ['eksɪkjuːt] hinrichten 2 A 4
exercise ['eksəsaɪz] **1.** Übung **exercise book** Übungsheft, Schulheft
2. (körperliche) Bewegung, Training, Gymnastik 1 Li (118)
expect [ɪk'spekt] erwarten; annehmen, vermuten
expensive [ɪk'spensɪv] teuer
experience [ɪk'spɪərɪəns] Erlebnis, Erfahrung 4 Li
experiment [ɪk'sperɪmənt] Experiment
expert (on) ['ekspɜːt] Experte/Expertin, Fachmann/Fachfrau (für)
explain sth. to sb. [ɪk'spleɪn] jm. etwas erklären, erläutern • **explanation** [ˌeksplə'neɪʃn] Erklärung

explode [ɪk'spləʊd] explodieren 4 How (71) • **explosion** [ɪk'spləʊʒn] Explosion 6 A 9
explore [ɪk'splɔː] erforschen, erkunden 2 How (37) • **explorer** Forscher/in, Forschungsreisende(r) 2 How (37)
explosion [ɪk'spləʊʒn] Explosion 6 A 9
express [ɪk'spres] ausdrücken, äußern • **expression** [ɪk'spreʃn] Ausdruck
extra ['ekstrə] zusätzlich, Extra- 4 A 1
extract (from) ['ekstrækt] Auszug (aus *einem Buch, Text, Film usw.*) 3 T (52)
eye [aɪ] Auge

F

face [feɪs] Gesicht
fact [fækt] Tatsache, Fakt • **in fact** eigentlich, genau gesagt; in Wirklichkeit 6 T (103)
factory ['fæktri] Fabrik
Fahrenheit: **60° F (= 60 degrees Fahrenheit)** [dɪ,griːz 'færənhaɪt] 60 Grad Fahrenheit 5 P 9
fair [feə] fair, gerecht
fall [fɔːl] *(AE)* Herbst 4 T (68)
fall* [fɔːl] fallen • **°fall asleep** einschlafen Rev 7 (113) • **fall in love (with)** sich verlieben (in) 4 Li
fallen ['fɔːlən] *Part. Perf. von „fall"*
false [fɔːls] falsch, unecht
family ['fæməli] Familie • **family member** Familienangehörige(r), Familienmitglied • **family name** Familienname, Nachname • **start a family** eine Familie gründen 6 P 15
famous (for) ['feɪməs] berühmt (für, wegen)
fan [fæn] Fan
fancy-dress party [,fænsi'dres] Kostümfest
fantastic [fæn'tæstɪk] fantastisch, toll
far [fɑː] weit (entfernt) • **farther** ['fɑːðə] weiter (entfernt) • **farthest** ['fɑːðɪst] am weitesten (entfernt)
farm *(n; v)* [fɑːm] **1.** Bauernhof, Farm; **2.** Landwirtschaft betreiben; *(Land)* bebauen; *(Vieh)* halten, züchten 3 T (49) • **farmer** Bauer/Bäuerin UK Call (7) • **farmhouse** Bauernhaus, -hof 3 T (49)
fashion ['fæʃn] Mode
fast [fɑːst] **1.** *(adj)* schnell; **2.** *(adv)* schnell
father ['fɑːðə] Vater
fault [fɔːlt] Schuld; Fehler 2 A 14
favourite ['feɪvərɪt] **1.** Lieblings-; **2.** Favorit/in 1 T (18) • **be a favourite (with)** sehr beliebt sein (bei) 1 A 6
fax [fæks] (Tele-)Fax 4 P 3
February ['februəri] Februar
fed [fed] **1.** *si. past von „feed"*; **2.** *Part. Perf. von „feed"* • **be fed up (with)** satt haben, die Nase voll haben (von) 5 P 2 • **get fed up (with)** satt haben/bekommen; die Nase voll haben (von)
feed* [fiːd] füttern • **feeding times** Fütterungszeiten
feel* [fiːl] fühlen; sich fühlen **how they feel about ...** was sie über ... denken / was sie von ... halten Welc (57) • **feel sorry for sb.** jn. bedauern • **feeling** ['fiːlɪŋ] Gefühl 3 T (49)
feet [fiːt] *pl von „foot"*
fell [fel] *si. past von „fall"*
felt [felt] **1.** *si. past von „feel"*; **2.** *Part. Perf. von „feel"*
felt-tip ['felttɪp] Filzstift
fence [fens] Zaun 3 A 1
ferry ['feri] Fähre
festival ['festɪvl] Fest, Festival
fetch (from) [fetʃ] holen, abholen (von)
few [fjuː] wenige • **a few** ein paar, einige
field [fiːld] Feld, Wiese, Weide **in the fields** auf den Feldern
fight* *(v; n)* [faɪt] **1.** (sich) streiten 5 P 11; **2. fight (against) sb./sth.** jn./etwas bekämpfen, gegen jn./etwas kämpfen 3 T (49); **3.** Kampf, Schlägerei 3 T (156)
figure ['fɪgə] Gestalt, Figur 2 A 4 (150)
fill (with) [fɪl] füllen (mit) 2 A 14 **fill in** [,fɪl_'ɪn] **1.** ausfüllen; **2.** einsetzen
film *(n; v)* [fɪlm] **1.** Film; **2.** filmen
find* [faɪnd] finden • **find out** herausfinden • **he should find out for himself** er sollte es selbst herausfinden 5 P 2
fine [faɪn] gut, fein, schön • **I'm fine.** Mir gehts gut. / Es geht mir gut.
finger ['fɪŋgə] Finger
finish ['fɪnɪʃ] **1.** beenden, zu Ende machen; enden • **finished** fertig, vollendet °**2.** Ziel; Finish 1 T (18)
fire ['faɪə] Feuer, Brand • **on fire** in Brand 3 P 10 • **fire brigade** ['faɪə brɪ,geɪd] Feuerwehr • **°firecracker** ['faɪəkrækə] Knallkörper 6 A 9 • **firework** ['faɪəwɜːk] Feuerwerkskörper • **fireworks** *(pl)* Feuerwerk
first [fɜːst] **1.** erste(r, s); **2.** erstens, zuerst, als Erstes; **3.** das erste Mal, zum ersten Mal • **at first** zuerst, anfangs, am Anfang
fish *(n; v)* [fɪʃ] **1.** *(pl* **fish***)* Fisch; **2.** fischen, angeln 5 T (84) **fishing** *(das)* Angeln • **fishing village** Fischerdorf
fit (-tt-) [fɪt] *(in der Größe)* passen
fitness ['fɪtnəs] Fitness 1 Li
flag [flæg] Flagge, Fahne UK Call (6)
flame [fleɪm] Flamme 5 T (85)
flash [flæʃ] aufleuchten, blinken
flat [flæt] Wohnung
flat (-tt-) [flæt] flach, eben 5 T (85)
°**fleet** [fliːt] Flotte 3 A 1
flew [fluː] *si. past von „fly"*
flight [flaɪt] Flug
float [fləʊt] *(auf dem Wasser)* schwimmen, treiben
floor [flɔː] Fußboden
flown [fləʊn] *Part. Perf. von „fly"*
fly* [flaɪ] fliegen
focus on words ['fəʊkəs] *etwa:* Blickpunkt „Wörter" (5)
follow ['fɒləʊ] folgen; verfolgen **the following words** die folgenden Wörter
food [fuːd] Essen; Lebensmittel; Futter
foot [fʊt], *pl* **feet** [fiːt] **1.** Fuß; **2.** Fuß *(Längenmaß; 1 Fuß = ca. 30,5 cm)* 4 P 15
football ['fʊtbɔːl] Fußball • **American football** Football 1 Li (145)
for [fə, *betont:* fɔː] **1.** für; **2.** seit **for 10 years** seit 10 Jahren 1 A 3 **for a long time** lange Zeit • **for an hour** eine Stunde lang, seit einer Stunde • **for hours** stundenlang • **for breakfast/lunch/dinner** zum Frühstück/Mittagessen/Abendbrot • **for example** zum Beispiel • **for weeks** wochenlang
forecast ['fɔːkɑːst] Vorhersage, Voraussage
foreign ['fɒrən] fremd • **foreign language** Fremdsprache • **foreigner** ['fɒrənə] Fremde(r), Ausländer/in 3 T (52)
forest ['fɒrɪst] Wald 6 A 1
forget* (-tt-) [fə'get] vergessen **Forget about ...** Vergiss ...
forgot [fə'gɒt] *si. past von „forget"*
forgotten [fə'gɒtn] *Part. Perf. von „forget"*
fork [fɔːk] Gabel 3 Li (154)
form *(n; v)* [fɔːm] **1.** *(englische)* (Schul-)Klasse; **2.** Form; **3.** (sich) bilden, formen 1 A 7
fort [fɔːt] Fort 3 P 12
fortunately ['fɔːtʃnətli] glücklicherweise 3 A 1 (154)

forward(s) ['fɔːwəd(z)] vorwärts, nach vorn 1 A 1 • **look forward to sth.** sich auf etwas freuen 1 P 12
fought [fɔːt] **1.** *si. past von „fight"* 3 T (49); **2.** *Part. Perf. von „fight"* 3 T (49)
foul [faʊl] Foul, Regelverstoß 1 A 1
found [faʊnd] **1.** *si. past von „find";* **2.** *Part. Perf. von „find"*
°**freak** [friːk] Freak, Fanatiker/in 1 Li
free [friː] **1.** frei • **free time** Freizeit **2.** kostenlos
freeze* [friːz] (ge)frieren; einfrieren 5 T (85) • °**freeze-dried** ['friːzdraɪd] gefriergetrocknet 4 T (69)
French *(n; adj)* [frentʃ] **1.** Französisch; **2.** französisch
frequency ['friːkwənsi] Häufigkeit 6 P 8
fresh [freʃ] frisch; neu 5 A 3
Friday ['fraɪdeɪ, 'fraɪdi] Freitag
fridge [frɪdʒ] Kühlschrank 6 P 13
friend [frend] Freund/in • **make friends** Freunde finden 1 A 6
friendliness ['frendlɪnəs] Freundlichkeit 2 P 12 • **friendly** ['frendli] freundlich, nett
fries *(pl)* [fraɪz] *(AE)* Pommes frites
frightened ['fraɪtnd] verängstigt **be frightened (of)** Angst haben (vor), sich fürchten (vor)
from [frəm, *betont:* frɒm] **1.** aus **I'm from ...** Ich bin aus ... / Ich komme aus ... • **Where are you from?** Wo kommst du her? **2.** von • **from Monday to Friday** von Montag bis Freitag
front [frʌnt]**: at the front** vorn **in front of** vor • **front door** Wohnungs-, Haustür
froze [frəʊz] *si. past von „freeze"* 5 T (166)
frozen ['frəʊzn] **1.** *Part. Perf. von „freeze"* 5 T (166); **2.** zugefroren; tiefgefroren 5 T (85)
fruit [fruːt] Obst, Früchte; Frucht
full [fʊl] voll • **work full-time** ganztags arbeiten, als Vollzeitkraft beschäftigt sein 6 A 7
fun [fʌn] Spaß • **have fun** Spaß haben, sich amüsieren • **Have fun!** Viel Spaß! • **It's great fun!** Es/Das macht Spaß! • **Shopping is (great) fun.** Einkaufen macht (viel) Spaß. • **make fun of sb./sth.** sich über jn./etwas lustig machen 5 A 3
funny ['fʌni] **1.** witzig, komisch; **2.** merkwürdig
°**furnace** ['fɜːnɪs] Ofen, Heizung 3 How (53)
future ['fjuːtʃə] **1.** Zukunft; **2.** Zukunfts-, zukünftig

G

°**Gaelic** ['geɪlɪk] gälisch; Gälisch UK Call (7)
°**gallery** ['gæləri] Galerie 2 A 4
game [geɪm] Spiel
gang [gæŋ] Bande, Gang 4 T (69)
garage ['gærɪdʒ] Garage
garden ['gɑːdn] Garten
gate [geɪt] **1.** Tor, Pforte, Gatter 4 T (68); **2.** Flugsteig
gave [geɪv] *si. past von „give"*
°**Gee, ...** [dʒiː] *(besonders AE)* Mensch, ...! *(Ausruf)* 6 A 7
general ['dʒenrəl] General/in 6 A 1
generation [ˌdʒenə'reɪʃn] Generation 6 A 10
gentlemen: Ladies and Gentlemen [ˌleɪdiz‿ən 'dʒentlmən] Sehr geehrte Damen und Herren 6 T (103)
°**genuine** ['dʒenjuɪn] echt 3 A 1
Geography [dʒi'ɒgrəfi] Geographie, Erdkunde
German ['dʒɜːmən] **1.** deutsch; **2.** Deutsch; Deutsche(r)
°**Germanic** [dʒɜː'mænɪk] germanisch 3 T (52)
Germany ['dʒɜːməni] Deutschland
get* **(-tt-)** [get] **1.** bekommen, kriegen • **get an unfriendly welcome** unfreundlich empfangen werden 3 P 12 • **get sb. into trouble** jn. in Schwierigkeiten bringen 2 P 12 • **get time off** frei bekommen, Urlaub bekommen 4 T (68) • °**get a good night's sleep** sich (richtig) ausschlafen 3 A 6
2. holen, besorgen
3. gelangen, (hin)kommen • **get in** einsteigen • **get in(to) a car/taxi** in ein Auto/Taxi einsteigen 2 A 1 (150) • **get off** aussteigen 2 A 1 • **get off a bike** von einem Fahrrad absteigen 2 A 1 (150) **get off a bus/train** aus einem Bus/Zug aussteigen 2 A 1 (150) **get on a bike** auf ein Fahrrad aufsteigen 2 A 1 (150) • **get on a bus/train** in einen Bus/Zug einsteigen 2 A 1 (150) • **get out of a car/taxi** aus einem Auto/Taxi aussteigen 2 A 1 (150) • **get through (to sb.)** durchkommen (zu jm.) 4 P 12 • **get up** aufstehen
4. get angry, cold, ... wütend, kalt, ... werden • **get fed up (with sth.)** etwas satt haben/bekommen; die Nase voll haben (von etwas) • **get married (to sb.)** (jn.) heiraten, (sich ver)heiraten (mit jm.) 3 A 12 • **get ready** sich bereitmachen, sich fertig machen 1 A 1 • **get rid of sb./sth.** jn./etwas loswerden 3 T (49)
ghost [gəʊst] Geist, Gespenst **ghost town** Geisterstadt 6 A 3
giant ['dʒaɪənt] riesig, gigantisch
giraffe [dʒə'rɑːf] Giraffe
girl [gɜːl] Mädchen
girlfriend ['gɜːlfrend] (feste) Freundin
give* [gɪv] geben • **give sb. a call** jn. anrufen 5 P 4 • **give a talk (on sth.)** einen Vortrag/eine Rede (über etwas) halten 4 T (161) **give sb. $3.00 off** jm. eine Ermäßigung von 3 Dollar geben • **Give Susan my love.** Grüß Susan von mir. • **give out** verteilen, austeilen • **give sth. up** etwas aufgeben 1 A 1
given ['gɪvn] *Part. Perf. von „give"*
°**glacier** [*BE:* 'glæsiə, *AE:* 'gleɪʃə] Gletscher 5 P 3
glad [glæd]**: be glad (about)** froh sein, sich freuen (über) 1 A 6
glamour ['glæmə] Glanz 4 T (69) **glamorous** ['glæmərəs] glanzvoll 4 T (162)
glass [glɑːs] Glas
global warming [ˌgləʊbl 'wɔːmɪŋ] Erwärmung der Erdatmosphäre, globaler Temperaturanstieg
glue [gluː] Klebstoff
go* [gəʊ] **1.** gehen; fahren • **go to** fahren nach • **Let's go.** Auf gehts! • **go for a ride** eine Spazierfahrt machen; herumfahren 5 T (84) • °**go for the try** *etwa:* versuchen Punkte zu erzielen *(Rugby)* 1 A 1 • **go on 1.** (an-) dauern; vor sich gehen, im Gange sein 1 A 7; **2.** fortfahren, weiterreden; weitermachen; **3.** weitergehen *(Geschichte, Erzählung)* **go on a trip** einen Ausflug/eine Reise machen • **go on board** an Bord gehen • **go out 1.** ausgehen, weggehen; **2.** ausfahren, auslaufen *(Schiff)*; **3.** ausgehen *(Licht)* 4 P 5 • **go over (to)** hinübergehen/-fahren (zu/nach) 3 A 1 **go shopping / go to the shops** einkaufen gehen • **go surfing** wellenreiten gehen, surfen gehen **go to sleep** einschlafen • **go under** untergehen • **go up** steigen, in die Höhe gehen • **go whaling** auf Walfang gehen 5 A 1 (163) • °**go a long way** viel erreichen, viel bewirken 2 A 10 °**the audience goes crazy/wild** das Publikum tobt, das Publikum rast 6 T (103)
2. *(irgendwohin)* gehören, kommen • **go together** zusammenpassen, -gehören 2 How (37) • **go with** passen zu
3. I'm going to cook. Ich werde kochen. / Ich habe vor zu kochen.

goal [gəʊl] Tor *(im Sport)* • °**goal-line** Torlinie 1 A 1 • °**goalpost** Torpfosten 1 A 1
°**goblin** ['gɒblɪn] Kobold 6 A 1
god [gɒd] Gott 3 A 6 • **goddess** ['gɒdes] Göttin 3 A 6
gold [gəʊld] Gold • **golden** ['gəʊldən] golden • **goldfish**, *pl* **goldfish** Goldfisch • °**gold rush** Goldrausch 6 A 3 • °**gold-mining town** Goldgräberstadt 6 A 3
golf [gɒlf] Golf
gone [gɒn] *Part. Perf. von „go"*
good [gʊd] gut • **be good at sth.** gut in etwas sein; etwas gut können 3 A 12 • **Good afternoon.** Guten Tag. *(nachmittags)* • **Good evening.** Guten Abend. • **Good morning.** Guten Morgen. / Guten Tag. / Grüß Gott. • **Good night.** Gute Nacht. • **good luck** (viel) Glück 6 A 9 • **Good luck (with ...)!** Viel Glück (bei ...)! 6 A 9 (169)
Goodbye. [ˌgʊd'baɪ] Auf Wiedersehen. / Servus. • **say goodbye (to sb.)** sich (von jm.) verabschieden 4 A 10
goods *(pl)* [gʊdz] Waren, Güter 3 T (49)
got [gɒt] **1.** *si. past von „get"*; **2.** *Part. Perf. von „get"*; **3. have got** haben, besitzen
°**gotta** ['gɒtə]: **you gotta** *(infml; besonders AE) = you've got to* 6 T (104)
governor ['gʌvənə] Gouverneur/in 6 A 4
grade [greɪd] *(besonders AE)* (Schul-)Note, Zensur
grammar school ['græmə sku:l] (GB) *heute eher seltene, etwa dem Gymnasium entsprechende Schulform* UK Call (7)
grand- ['græn-]: **grandchild** Enkel, Enkelin, Enkelkind 4 How (71) **grandfather** Großvater • **grandma** Oma • **grandmother** Großmutter • **grandpa** Opa • **grandparents** Großeltern
grapefruit, *pl* **grapefruit** ['greɪpfru:t] Grapefruit 4 Li
°**grave** [greɪv] Grab 3 A 1
°**gravity** ['grævəti] Schwerkraft 4 T (69)
gray [greɪ] *(AE)* grau 4 P 15
great [greɪt] **1.** großartig, toll; **2.** groß, beträchtlich 6 A 3 (168); **3.** groß, bedeutend, wichtig 6 A 3 (168)
green [gri:n] grün
grew [gru:] *si. past von „grow"* 3 P 8
grey [greɪ] grau
grim (-mm-) *(adj)* [grɪm] grimmig • **grimly** *(adv)* ['grɪmli] grimmig
°**grizzly bear** ['grɪzli beə] Grislibär 5 A 10
ground [graʊnd] (Erd-)Boden °**grounds** *(pl)* Gelände 3 T (50)
group [gru:p] Gruppe
grow* [grəʊ] wachsen 3 P 8 **grow up** aufwachsen; erwachsen werden 5 T (84)
grown [grəʊn] *Part. Perf. von „grow"* 3 P 8
guess [ges] raten, erraten
guest [gest] Gast
guide [gaɪd] (Fremden-)Führer/in
gun [gʌn] Schusswaffe 2 T (35)
guy [gaɪ] *(infml)* Typ, Kerl • **guys** *(pl) (besonders AE, infml)* Leute 4 T (68)
gym [dʒɪm] Sporthalle, Turnhalle
gymnastics [dʒɪm'næstɪks] Gymnastik, Turnen 1 Li (145)

H

had [hæd] **1.** *si. past von „have" und „have got"*; **2.** *Part. Perf. von „have" und „have got"*
hair [heə] Haar, Haare • °**hairpin** ['heəpɪn] Haarnadel 3 Li
half [hɑ:f], *pl* **halves** [hɑ:vz] Hälfte **half an hour** eine halbe Stunde **the first half** die erste Halbzeit **half-time** Halbzeitpause • **half past eight** halb neun (8.30/ 20.30)
hall [hɔ:l] **1.** Flur, Diele; **2.** Halle, Saal • **town hall** Rathaus
hamburger ['hæmbɜ:gə] Hamburger
hamster ['hæmstə] Hamster
hand [hænd] Hand • **hand signal** Handzeichen
hang* [hæŋ] hängen, aufhängen 5 T (85) • **Hang in there!** *(AE, infml)* Halte durch! 4 T (69)
happen (to) ['hæpən] *jm.* geschehen, passieren • **What's happening?** Was ist los? / Was geht hier vor?
happy ['hæpi] glücklich, froh **Happy birthday!** Herzlichen Glückwunsch zum Geburtstag! **happy ending** Happyend **happiness** Glück 2 P 12
harbour ['hɑ:bə] Hafen
hard [hɑ:d] **1.** *(adj)* hart; schwer, schwierig; **2.** *(adv)* heftig, kräftig, sehr; hart *(arbeiten)* • **try hard** sich sehr bemühen, sich anstrengen
hardly ['hɑ:dli] kaum 6 A 7
°**harpoon** [hɑ:'pu:n] Harpune 5 A 1
hat [hæt] Hut
hate [heɪt] hassen, gar nicht mögen • **hate shopping** gar nicht gern einkaufen gehen

have* [hæv] **1.** haben • **have a bath** *(in der Wanne)* baden, ein Bad nehmen 3 Li (154) • **have a break** (eine) Pause machen 4 P 7 **have a cola/a hamburger** eine Cola trinken/einen Hamburger essen • **have a good time** Spaß haben, sich amüsieren • **have a look at** einen Blick werfen auf, ansehen 1 A 6 • **Have a nice weekend.** Schönes Wochenende. **have a party** eine Party veranstalten, feiern • **have a shower** (sich) duschen • **have breakfast/ lunch/dinner** frühstücken/Mittag essen/Abendbrot essen • **have fun** Spaß haben, sich amüsieren **Have fun!** Viel Spaß! • **have sth. in common** etwas miteinander gemein haben 1 T (18)
2. have got to do sth. etwas tun müssen
3. have to do sth. etwas tun müssen
have got* [həv 'gɒt, *betont:* hæv 'gɒt] **1.** haben, besitzen; **2. have got to do sth.** etwas tun müssen
he [hi, *betont:* hi:] er
head [hed] Kopf • **Head** *(BE)* Schulleiter/in 2 P 9 • **headless** kopflos, ohne Kopf 5 P 10
headache ['hedeɪk] Kopfschmerz(en)
heading ['hedɪŋ] Überschrift
headless kopflos, ohne Kopf 5 P 10
headteacher [ˌhed'ti:tʃə], **Head** *(BE)* Schulleiter/in 2 P 9
headword ['hedwɜ:d] Stichwort 5 How (87)
healthy ['helθɪ] gesund 1 Li (118)
hear* [hɪə] hören • **hear about sth.** von etwas hören
heard [hɜ:d] **1.** *si. past von „hear"*; **2.** *Part. Perf. von „hear"*
heating ['hi:tɪŋ] Heizung 3 A 6 (155)
held [held] **1.** *si. past von „hold"*; **2.** *Part. Perf. von „hold"*
hell [hel] Hölle 6 T (102) • **Why the hell not?** *(infml) etwa:* Warum denn nicht, verdammt noch mal? 6 T (102)
Hello. [hə'ləʊ] Hallo. / Guten Tag. / Grüß Gott. • **Say hello to ... from me.** Grüß ... von mir. • **They all say hello.** Sie lassen alle grüßen.
helmet ['helmɪt] Helm
help *(v; n)* [help] **1.** helfen • **May I help you?** Sie wünschen? **Help yourself.** Greif zu! / Bedien dich! 6 (138)
2. Hilfe
her [hə, *betont:* hɜ:] **1.** ihr, ihre; **2.** sie; ihr
herd [hɜ:d] Herde *(z.B. Kühe)*, Herden- 5 A 10

here [hɪə] hier; hierher • **Here you are.** Hier bitte. / Bitte sehr.
hero ['hɪərəʊ], *pl* **heroes** ['hɪərəʊz] Held, Heldin; Idol, Vorbild 2 A 7
herself [hə'self, *betont:* hɜː'self] sich (selbst); selbst, selber 6 A 3 (168) **she made some herself** sie machte selbst/selber welchen 6 A 4
Hi. [haɪ] *(infml)* Hallo. • **Hi there.** Hallo. • **Say hi to … from me.** Grüß … von mir.
hid [hɪd] *si. past von „hide"* 2 T (34)
hidden ['hɪdn] *Part. Perf. von „hide"* 2 T (34)
hide* [haɪd] (sich) verstecken 2 T (34)
high [haɪ] **1.** hoch; **2.** Höchststand, Höchsttemperatur, Hoch 5 P 9 **high school** ['haɪ skuːl] (US) *Gesamtschule mit den Klassen 7–12 für 13- bis 18-Jährige* Welc (57)
highlight ['haɪlaɪt] Höhepunkt 1 A 3
hill [hɪl] Hügel, Berg
him [hɪm] ihn; ihm
himself [hɪm'self] sich (selbst); selbst, selber 6 A 3 (168) • **he should find out for himself** er sollte es selbst herausfinden 5 P 2
hip hop ['hɪp hɒp] Hip-Hop
his [hɪz] sein, seine
Hispanic *(n; adj)* [hɪ'spænɪk] **1.** Hispano-Amerikaner/in *(Einwanderer aus Lateinamerika und dessen/deren Nachkommen)* 4 Li; **2.** hispanisch 4 Li
history ['hɪstri] Geschichte, Vergangenheit • **historic** [hɪ'stɒrɪk] historisch 6 A 3
hit* **(-tt-)** [hɪt]: **1. hit sb./sth.** jn./etwas schlagen, treffen; gegen jn./etwas stoßen; jn./etwas anfahren **hit the rocks** auf/gegen die Felsen laufen *(Schiff)* 5 P 8
2. *si. past von „hit"*; **3.** *Part. Perf. von „hit"*
hit [hɪt] Hit
hobby ['hɒbi] Hobby
hockey ['hɒki] Hockey
hold* [həʊld] **1.** halten; festhalten; **2.** veranstalten, abhalten 2 A 7 **hold hands** Händchen halten **hold up** hochhalten 4 P 15
hole [həʊl] Loch
holiday ['hɒlədeɪ] **1.** Feiertag, freier Tag 6 A 9; **2. holiday(s)** Ferien, Urlaub • **be/go on holiday** in Urlaub sein/fahren; Ferien haben/machen • **holidaymaker** Urlauber/in
°**hologram** ['hɒləgræm] Hologramm *(mithilfe eines Lasers erzeugtes dreidimensionales Bild)* 2 T (34)
home [həʊm] **1.** Heim, Zuhause; **2.** nach Hause • **at home** zu Hause, daheim • **We're home.** Wir sind (wieder) zu Hause.
homeless obdachlos 2 A 10 **homelessness** Obdachlosigkeit 2 A 10
homepage ['həʊmpeɪdʒ] Homepage
homework *(no pl)* ['həʊmwɜːk] Hausaufgabe(n) • **do homework** die Hausaufgabe(n) machen
honey ['hʌni] Honig UK Call (7)
hope *(v; n)* [həʊp] **1.** hoffen; **2.** Hoffnung 5 P 10 • **hopeless** hoffnungslos, aussichtslos 5 P 10
horrible ['hɒrəbl] scheußlich, grauenhaft, furchtbar
horse [hɔːs] Pferd • **horse riding** *(das)* Reiten UK Call (7)
hospital ['hɒspɪtl] Krankenhaus
hot [hɒt] heiß • **hot dog** ['hɒt dɒg] Hot dog
hotel [həʊ'tel] Hotel • **stay at a hotel** in einem Hotel übernachten
hour ['aʊə] Stunde • **an 8-hour flight** ein 8-stündiger Flug, ein 8-Stunden-Flug • **a 24-hour supermarket** ein Supermarkt, der 24 Stunden geöffnet ist • **for an hour** eine Stunde lang • **for hours** stundenlang • **half an hour** eine halbe Stunde • **opening hours** Öffnungszeiten
house [haʊs] Haus
how [haʊ] wie • **How are you?** Wie geht es dir/euch? • **How did they like …?** Wie gefiel ihnen …? Wie fanden sie …? • **How many?** Wie viele? • **How much?** Wie viel? • **How much is/are …?** Was kostet/kosten …? / Wie viel kostet/kosten …? • **how to do sth.** wie man etwas tun kann/soll 1 How (19)
however [haʊ'evə] jedoch, aber 3 T (52)
huge [hjuːdʒ] sehr groß, riesig 1 A 6
hundred ['hʌndrəd]: **a hundred** einhundert • **hundreds (of)** Hunderte (von)
hung [hʌŋ] **1.** *si. past von „hang"* 5 T (85); **2.** *Part. Perf. von „hang"* 5 T (85)
hungry ['hʌŋgri] hungrig • **be hungry** hungrig sein, Hunger haben
hunt (for) [hʌnt] jagen (nach); Jagd machen (auf), suchen 5 A 10
hurricane ['hʌrɪkən] Hurrikan, Orkan
hurry ['hʌri]: **be in a hurry** in Eile sein, es eilig haben
hurt* [hɜːt] **1.** verletzen; wehtun; **2.** schaden, schädigen 5 T (84); **3.** *si. past von „hurt"*; **4.** *Part. Perf. von „hurt"* • **She wasn't hurt.** Sie war/wurde nicht verletzt.
husband ['hʌzbənd] Ehemann
hybrid car ['haɪbrɪd] Auto mit Elektro- und Verbrennungsmotor
hyphen ['haɪfn] Bindestrich

I

I [aɪ] ich • **I'm fine.** Mir gehts gut. / Es geht mir gut. • **I'm sorry.** Entschuldigung. / Tut mir Leid.
ice [aɪs] Eis • **ice-cream** [ˌaɪs'kriːm] (Speise-)Eis • **ice-hockey** Eishockey 1 Li (145) • **ice skating** *(das)* Eislaufen 1 Li (145)
idea [aɪ'dɪə] Idee, Einfall; Vorstellung
idiot ['ɪdiət] *(infml)* Idiot, Idiotin 6 T (103)
if [ɪf] **1.** ob 1 How (19) • **as if** als ob 4 T (161)
2. wenn, falls • **if I were you** wenn ich du wäre 3 (129) • **even if** selbst wenn, sogar wenn 3 A 6
ill [ɪl] krank • **illness** ['ɪlnəs] Krankheit 2 P 12
°**imaginary** [ɪ'mædʒɪnəri] imaginär *(nur in der Vorstellung vorhanden, nicht wirklich)* 5 Li
imagination [ɪˌmædʒɪ'neɪʃn] Fantasie, Vorstellungskraft
imagine [ɪ'mædʒɪn] sich *etwas* vorstellen
immigrant ['ɪmɪgrənt] Einwanderer/Einwanderin, Immigrant/in 6 A 7
important [ɪm'pɔːtnt] wichtig
impossible [ɪm'pɒsəbl] unmöglich 6 How (170)
improve [ɪm'pruːv] (sich) verbessern; besser machen/werden
in [ɪn] in • **in 1645** (im Jahre) 1645 • **in between** dazwischen 1 Li • **in English** auf Englisch **in fact** eigentlich, genau gesagt; in Wirklichkeit 6 T (103) • **in front of** vor • **in my opinion** meiner Meinung nach 4 T (162) **in November** im November • **in order to do sth.** um etwas zu tun 5 A 1 • **in our own way** auf unsere Art und Weise; so, wie wir wollen • **in sight** in Sicht(weite) 6 T (103) • **in (the) summer** im Sommer • **in the afternoon(s)** am Nachmittag, nachmittags • **in the country** auf dem Land • **in the end** schließlich, am Ende, zum Schluss • **in the evening(s)** am Abend, abends • **in the fields** auf den Feldern • **in the morning(s)** am Morgen, morgens • **in the old days** in alten Zeiten, früher 5 P 1 • **in the open air** im Freien 1 P 11 • **in the photo/picture** auf dem Foto/Bild • **in**

the right places an den richtigen Stellen 5 P 3 • **in the sky** am Himmel • **in the street** auf der Straße • **in the world** auf der Welt • **in there** dort drinnen; dort hinein • **in this weather** bei diesem Wetter 5 P 10 • **in town** in der Stadt • **come in** hereinkommen • **draw in** einzeichnen • **fill in** **1.** einsetzen; **2.** ausfüllen • **get in** einsteigen 2 A 1 (150) • **go in** hineingehen **put in** einsetzen

inch [ɪntʃ] Zoll *(= 2,54 cm)* 6 A 1

Indian *(adj; n)* ['ɪndiən] **1.** indisch; Inder/in; **2.** indianisch; Indianer/in

indirect speech [ˌɪndərekt 'spiːtʃ, ˌɪndaɪrekt 'spiːtʃ] indirekte Rede, nicht wörtliche Rede 5 A 7

infinite ['ɪnfɪnət] unendlich 4 Li

influence (on) ['ɪnfluəns] Einfluss (auf) 3 T (51)

inform [ɪn'fɔːm] informieren, benachrichtigen • **information** *(no pl)* [ˌɪnfə'meɪʃn] Information(en); Auskunft, Auskünfte • **information desk** Informationsschalter

injury ['ɪndʒəri] Verletzung

in-line skating [ˌɪnlaɪn 'skeɪtɪŋ] *(das)* Inline-Skaten 1 Li (145)

inside [ˌɪn'saɪd] **1.** *(adv)* drinnen; nach drinnen, hinein; **2.** *(prep)* innerhalb, im Innern (von); **3.** *(n)* **on the inside** im Innern, innerlich 6 T (103)

inspector [ɪn'spektə] *etwa:* Polizeiinspektor/in

instead [ɪn'sted] stattdessen, dafür

instruction [ɪn'strʌkʃn] Anweisung, Anleitung 4 P 12

interactive [ˌɪntər'æktɪv] interaktiv 2 A 4

interested ['ɪntrəstɪd]: **be interested (in)** interessiert sein (an), sich interessieren (für) 3 P 2

interesting ['ɪntrəstɪŋ] interessant

international [ˌɪntə'næʃnəl] international

Internet ['ɪntənet] Internet • **on the Internet** im Internet

interpretation [ɪnˌtɜːprɪ'teɪʃn] Interpretation, Deutung 2 How (37)

interrupt [ˌɪntə'rʌpt] unterbrechen

interview *(n; v)* ['ɪntəvjuː] **1.** Interview; **2.** interviewen, befragen 6 A 7

into ['ɪntə, *betont:* 'ɪntuː] in (... hinein) • **into your exercise book** in dein Übungsheft

introduce sth./sb. (to sb.) [ˌɪntrə'djuːs] (jm.) etwas/jn. vorstellen 6 T (103) • **introduction (to)** [ˌɪntrə'dʌkʃn] Einleitung, Einführung (in) 5 A 2

°Inuit ['ɪnuɪt, 'ɪnjuɪt], *pl* **Inuit** *or* **Inuits** Inuit, Eskimo 5 A 1

°Inupiaq [ɪ'nuːpiæk] *Sprache der Inupiat* 5 A 1

°Inupiat [ɪ'nuːpiæt] *im Norden und Nordwesten Alaskas lebendes Inuit-Volk* 5 A 1

invade (a country) [ɪn'veɪd] einmarschieren (in ein Land), (ein Land) überfallen 3 T (49) • **°invader** Eindringling, Invasor/in 3 T (49) **invasion (of)** [ɪn'veɪʒn] Invasion, Einmarsch, Einfall (in) 3 T (156)

invent [ɪn'vent] erfinden 2 T (153) **invention** [ɪn'venʃn] Erfindung 2 T (34)

invitation [ˌɪnvɪ'teɪʃn] Einladung

invite [ɪn'vaɪt] *(Gäste)* einladen

iron ['aɪən] Eisen 6 A 4 • **°pump iron** *(infml)* Gewichte stemmen 6 A 4

irregular [ɪ'regjələ] unregelmäßig

is [ɪz] ist • **How much is ...?** Was kostet ...? / Wie viel kostet ...? • **the felt-tip is £1** der Filzstift kostet £1 • **there's = there is** es ist (vorhanden); es gibt

island ['aɪlənd] Insel

isle [aɪl] Insel, Eiland UK Call (6)

issue ['ɪʃuː] (Streit-)Frage, Thema, Angelegenheit 2 A 10

it [ɪt] es *(bei Sachen und Tieren auch:* er/sie) • **it's** es ist *(bei Sachen und Tieren auch:* er/sie ist) **It's me – Sita.** Ich bin es – Sita.

italics [ɪ'tælɪks]: **in italics** *(pl)* in Kursivschrift, kursiv 5 How (87)

its [ɪts] sein, seine *(bei Sachen und Tieren auch:* ihr, ihre)

itself [ɪt'self] sich (selbst); selbst, selber 6 A 3 (168) • **Bodie was left to itself.** Bodie wurde sich selbst überlassen. 6 A 3

J

jacket ['dʒækɪt] Jacke; Jackett, Sakko

jam: **traffic jam** ['træfɪk dʒæm] (Verkehrs-)Stau

January ['dʒænjuəri] Januar

jar [dʒɑː] Glas, Topf

jazz [dʒæz] Jazz

jealous (of) ['dʒeləs] neidisch (auf); eifersüchtig (auf) 4 T (69)

jeans *(pl)* [dʒiːnz] Jeans

°jerk [dʒɜːk] *(infml)* Blödmann, Trottel 4 T (69)

job [dʒɒb] **1.** Beruf, Arbeit, Job; **2.** Aufgabe, Auftrag • **do jobs** Arbeiten/Aufträge erledigen **jobless** arbeitslos 5 P 10

jogging ['dʒɒgɪŋ] *(das)* Joggen, Jogging 1 Li (145)

join [dʒɔɪn] **1.** beitreten, eintreten in *(einen Klub)*; **2. join sb.** sich jm. anschließen; mitmachen 4 How (71)

joke *(n; v)* [dʒəʊk] **1.** Witz; **2.** scherzen, witzeln 5 T (84)

journey ['dʒɜːni] Reise, Fahrt, Weg

judo ['dʒuːdəʊ] Judo

juice [dʒuːs] Saft

July [dʒu'laɪ] Juli

jump [dʒʌmp] springen

June [dʒuːn] Juni

junior ['dʒuːniə] Junioren-, Jugend- T (18)

°Jurassic [dʒu'ræsɪk] jurassisch, Jura- *(aus der Jurazeit vor ca. 180 Millionen Jahren)* 6 A 1

just [dʒʌst] **1.** nur, bloß • **I'm just looking.** Ich sehe mich nur (mal) um. • **Just a moment!** Einen Moment mal (eben)! **2.** gerade (eben), soeben • **just before ...** kurz bevor ... 4 How (71) **3. He just drove off.** Er fuhr einfach davon. **4. just like** genau wie • **just right** genau richtig 3 A 6

°Jutes [dʒuːts]: **the Jutes** die Jüten 3 T (52)

K

karaoke [ˌkærə'əʊkeɪ] Karaoke

keep* [kiːp] **1.** (be)halten; **2.** aufbewahren, aufheben 3 Li • **keep away (from)** weg-, fernbleiben (von) 1 Li • **keep sb./sth. away (from)** jn./etwas fern halten (von)

kept [kept] **1.** *si. past von „keep"*; **2.** *Part. Perf. von „keep"*

ketchup ['ketʃəp] Ketschup

key [kiː] Schlüssel

°keypal ['kiːpæl] (E-Mail-)Brieffreund/in Rev 1 (112)

kick [kɪk] treten (gegen) 1 A 1

kid [kɪd] Kind, Jugendliche(r)

kill [kɪl] töten

kilo ['kiːləʊ] Kilo(gramm) • **two kilos of oranges** zwei Kilo Orangen

kilometre ['kɪləmiːtə] Kilometer

kind [kaɪnd] freundlich, nett, gütig

kindergarten ['kɪndəgɑːtn] Kindergarten; Vorschule

king [kɪŋ] König

kiss [kɪs] küssen

kitchen ['kɪtʃɪn] Küche

kite [kaɪt] Drachen

knew [njuː] *si. past von „know"*

knife [naɪf], *pl* **knives** [naɪvz] Messer

know* [nəʊ] **1.** wissen • **know about sth.** von etwas wissen **you know** weißt du; nämlich **2.** kennen • **known as** bekannt als 2 A 4

known [nəʊn] *Part. Perf. von „know"*

L

ladder ['lædə] *(die)* Leiter
Ladies and Gentlemen [,leɪdiz‿ən 'dʒentlmən] Sehr geehrte Damen und Herren 6 T (103)
lake [leɪk] (Binnen-)See • **on Lake Superior** am Lake Superior
lamb [læm] Lamm
lamp [læmp] Lampe 3 Li (154)
land *(n; v)* [lænd] **1.** Land, Grund und Boden; **2.** landen *(Flugzeug)*, anlegen *(Schiff)*
lane [leɪn] (schmale Land-)Straße; Gasse 1 Li
language ['læŋgwɪdʒ] Sprache **foreign language** Fremdsprache
laptop ['læptɒp] Laptop
large [lɑ:dʒ] groß
laser ['leɪzə] Laser
last [lɑ:st] **1.** (an-, fort)dauern 1 A 1; **2.** halten, nicht kaputtgehen *(Ehe, Obst, Gegenstände usw.)* 3 A 5
last [lɑ:st] **1.** letzte(r, s) • **last night/week/year** letzte Nacht/ letzte Woche/letztes Jahr **2.** zuletzt, das letzte Mal 1 P 3 **at last** schließlich, endlich
late [leɪt] (zu) spät • **be late** zu spät sein, zu spät kommen • **be late for school** zu spät zur Schule kommen • **I'm late for school.** Ich komme zu spät zur Schule. **sleep late** lange schlafen • **later** später
Latin ['lætɪn] Latein 3 T (49)
laugh (at) [lɑ:f] lachen (über); *jn.* auslachen
launch *(v; n)* [lɔ:ntʃ] **1.** starten, ins All schießen 4 A 8; **2.** Start, Abschuss 4 A 8 (160)
laundry ['lɔ:ndri] Wäscherei 6 A 7
lazy ['leɪzi] faul, träge
lead* [li:d] führen, leiten 4 A 4 (159) **leader** ['li:də] Anführer/in 4 A 4
leaf [li:f], *pl* **leaves** [li:vz] Blatt *(an Pflanzen)* 5 T (85)
league [li:g] Liga 1 A 3
learn [lɜ:n] lernen • **learn about sth.** etwas über/von etwas erfahren, etwas über etwas herausfinden 2 Li
least: **at least** [ət 'li:st] wenigstens, mindestens; zumindest 5 A 3
leave* [li:v] **1.** abfahren, weggehen **leave for** abfahren, abreisen nach **2.** verlassen • **leave school** von der Schule abgehen **3.** zurücklassen • **leave a message** eine Nachricht hinterlassen • **leave sth. out** etwas auslassen
led [led] **1.** *si. past von „lead"* 4 A 4 (159); **2.** *Part. Perf. von „lead"* 4 A 4 (159)
°**leek** [li:k] Lauch, Porree Rev 7 (113)
left [left] **1.** *si. past von „leave"*; **2.** *Part. Perf. von „leave"* • **be left** übrig sein 3 T (50)
left [left] (nach) links • **on the left** links, auf der linken Seite **to the left** links, auf der linken Seite, zur Linken 4 P 10
leg [leg] Bein
legend ['ledʒənd] Legende 6 A 4
lemonade [,lemə'neɪd] Limonade
less [les] weniger 1 Li (118)
lesson ['lesn] Unterrichtsstunde **lessons** *(pl)* Unterricht • **teach sb. a lesson** jm. eine Lektion erteilen 5 T (84)
let* **(-tt-)** [let] **1. Let's ...** Lass(t) uns ... • **Let's go.** Auf gehts! **let sb. do sth.** jn. etwas tun lassen; jm. erlauben, etwas zu tun 4 A 4 • **let sb. in** jn. hereinlassen 2 T (36) **2.** *si. past von „let"* 2 T (36) / 4 A 4; **3.** *Part. Perf. von „let"* 2 T (36) / 4 A 4
letter ['letə] **1.** Buchstabe; **2. letter (to)** Brief (an)
lettuce ['letɪs] (Kopf-)Salat
librarian [laɪ'breəriən] Bibliothekar, Bibliothekarin
library ['laɪbrəri] Bibliothek, Bücherei
life [laɪf], *pl* **lives** [laɪvz] (das) Leben • **lifeless** leblos 5 P 10
lift *(v; n)* [lɪft] **1.** (an-, hoch)heben 6 T (103); **2.** *(BE)* Fahrstuhl, Aufzug 4 A 1 (159)
°**liftoff** ['lɪftɒf] Start; *(das)* Abheben 4 Li • °**We have liftoff.** Der Start ist erfolgt. 4 Li
light* *(v; n)* [laɪt] **1.** anzünden; beleuchten, erhellen 3 Li; **2.** Licht, Lampe • **traffic lights** *(pl)* Verkehrsampel
°**lighthouse** ['laɪthaʊs] Leuchtturm 3 T (50) / 6 P 2
like [laɪk] **1.** wie • **You can start like this** So kannst du beginnen **like that** so • **What was ... like?** Wie war ...? • **What was it like?** Wie war es? **2.** *(conj, infml)* als ob 4 T (68)
like [laɪk] mögen, gern haben **like shopping** gern einkaufen gehen • **How did they like ...?** Wie gefiel ihnen ...? / Wie fanden sie ...? • **like sth. better** etwas lieber mögen Welc (157) • **Which ending do you like best?** Welches Ende magst du am liebsten? **I'd like a ... (= I would like a ...)** Ich hätte gern ein/e ... / Ich möchte gern ein/e ... • **I'd like to do it. (= I would like to do it.)** Ich würde es gern tun/möchte es tun. • **What would you like to do?** Was würdest/möchtest du gern machen?
line [laɪn] **1.** Linie; **2.** (U-Bahn-) Linie 2 A 2; **3.** Zeile; **4.** (Telefon-) Leitung 4 P 9
°**line** [laɪn]: **the streets are lined with tourists** Touristen säumen die Straßen 2 A 14
link *(v; n)* [lɪŋk] **1.** verbinden; **2.** Verbindung • **linking word** Bindewort 4 How (71)
lion ['laɪən] Löwe
list [lɪst] Liste
listen (to) ['lɪsn] *jm.* zuhören; sich *etwas* anhören; horchen • **listen for** horchen auf • **listener** ['lɪsnə] Zuhörer/in
lit [lɪt] **1.** *si. past von „light"*; **2.** *Part. Perf. von „light"*
litre ['li:tə] Liter • **2 litres of juice** 2 Liter Saft
little ['lɪtl] **1.** klein, jung; **2. a little** ein bisschen, ein wenig
live [lɪv] leben, wohnen
live *(adj; adv)* [laɪv] live, direkt, Live- 2 A 4 • °**live interpretation** Vorführung/Erläuterung von Ausstellungsstücken *(im Museum)* 2 A 4
lives [laɪvz] *pl von „life"*
living-room ['lɪvɪŋru:m] Wohnzimmer
load [ləʊd] (auf-, ein)laden; beladen
local ['ləʊkl] örtlich; Lokal-; am/ vom Ort
lock [lɒk] **1.** abschließen, zuschließen; **2.** einschließen • **locked** abgeschlossen
lonely ['ləʊnli] einsam • **loneliness** Einsamkeit 2 P 12
long [lɒŋ] lang • **all day long** den ganzen Tag (lang) 3 A 1 • **a long way** ein weiter Weg; weit (entfernt) 5 A 10 (164)
look *(v; n)* [lʊk] **1.** schauen, sehen **I'm just looking.** Ich sehe mich nur (mal) um. • **Look around (you).** Sieh dich um. • **look at** anschauen, ansehen • **Look at the board.** Sieh an die Tafel. **Look at the pictures.** Schau dir die Bilder an. • **look for** suchen **look forward to sth.** sich auf etwas freuen 1 P 12 • **Look out!** Pass auf! / Vorsicht! • **look round (for)** sich umsehen (nach) • **look sth. up** etwas nachschlagen, etwas heraussuchen 5 How (87) **2.** aussehen • **look great** toll aussehen • **Does this shirt look good on me?** Steht mir dieses Hemd? • **look like** aussehen wie **3.** (Gesichts-)Ausdruck **4. have a look at** einen Blick werfen auf, ansehen 1 A 6
Lord [lɔ:d] Lord *(engl. Adelstitel)* 2 A 7

lose* [lu:z] verlieren • **I lost my way.** Ich verirrte mich. • **loser** Verlierer/in

lost [lɒst] **1.** *si. past von „lose"*; **2.** *Part. Perf. von „lose"*; **3.** verloren

lot: a lot *(adv)* [ə 'lɒt] viel, oft, sehr 5 A 10 (165) • **a lot (of)** eine Menge, viel, viele • **lots (of)** ['lɒts_əv] eine Menge, viel, viele

loud [laʊd] laut

love *(v; n)* [lʌv] **1.** lieben, sehr mögen • **love shopping** sehr gern einkaufen gehen • **your loved ones** deine/eure Lieben 4 A 4 **lover** Liebhaber/in 4 Li
2. Liebe • **fall in love (with)** sich verlieben (in) 4 Li • **Give Susan my love.** Grüß Susan von mir. **Love, …** Viele liebe Grüße … *(Briefschluss)*

love [lʌv] null *(Tennis)*

lovely ['lʌvli] schön, herrlich, hübsch

luck [lʌk]: **Bad luck.** Pech (gehabt)! 3 A 12 • **good luck** (viel) Glück 6 A 9 • **Good luck (with …)!** Viel Glück (bei …)! 6 A 9 (169) **You're lucky.** ['lʌki] Du hast Glück. / Du bist gut dran. • **lucky day** Glückstag

lunch [lʌntʃ] Mittagessen • **at lunch** beim Mittagessen • **at lunch-time** mittags, zur Mittagszeit • **have lunch** Mittag essen

M

machine [mə'ʃi:n] Maschine, Gerät

Madam ['mædəm]: **Dear Sir or Madam** Sehr geehrte Damen und Herren 1 P 12

made [meɪd] **1.** *si. past von „make"*; **2.** *Part. Perf. von „make"* • **be made of …** aus … (gemacht) sein 2 A 5

magazine [,mægə'zi:n] Zeitschrift

magic *(n; adj)* ['mædʒɪk] **1.** Magie, Zauberkunst; **2.** magisch, Zauber-

mail [meɪl] Post(sendung) 1 How (19)

main [meɪn] Haupt- 3 T (157) **main clause** [,meɪn 'klɔ:z] Hauptsatz • **mainly** ['meɪnli] hauptsächlich, vorwiegend 3 T (52)

make* [meɪk] bilden, machen; zubereiten; bauen • **What makes a good poster?** Was macht ein gutes Poster aus? / Was gehört zu einem guten Poster? • **make it** *(infml)* es schaffen, Erfolg haben 6 T (104) • **be made of …** aus … (gemacht) sein 2 A 5 • **make sb. do sth.** jn. dazu bringen, etwas zu tun; jn. zwingen, etwas zu tun 4 A 4 • **make sb. sth.** jn. zu etwas machen 6 A 4 • **make a decision** eine Entscheidung treffen, fällen • **make friends** Freunde finden 1 A 6 • **make fun of sb./sth.** sich über jn./etwas lustig machen 5 A 3 • **make notes** sich Notizen machen **make sure** sich vergewissern; darauf achten/dafür sorgen (, dass) 2 T (36) • **make sth. up** etwas bilden UK Call (6)

mall [mɔ:l]: **(shopping) mall** *(besonders AE)* Einkaufszentrum

man [mæn], *pl* **men** [men] Mann

manager ['mænɪdʒə] Geschäftsführer/in, Manager/in 2 T (36)

manner ['mænə] Art und Weise 6 P 8

manual ['mænjuəl] Handbuch 5 P 2

many ['meni] viele • **How many?** Wie viele?

map [mæp] Landkarte, Stadtplan

March [mɑ:tʃ] März

mark *(v; n)* [mɑ:k] **1.** markieren, kennzeichnen 2 How (37); **2.** *(besonders BE)* (Schul-)Note, Zensur

market ['mɑ:kɪt] Markt 2 P 4

marmalade ['mɑ:məleɪd] (Orangen-)Marmelade

marry (sb.) ['mæri] (jn.) heiraten 3 A 12 (155) • **married to** verheiratet mit 2 T (34) • **get married (to sb.)** (jn.) heiraten, (sich ver-)heiraten (mit jm.) 3 A 12

mask [mɑ:sk] Maske 2 A 4

match [mætʃ] zuordnen • **Match the numbers to the letters.** Ordne die Ziffern den Buchstaben zu.

match [mætʃ] **1.** Spiel, Wettkampf; **2.** Streichholz

mate [meɪt] Kumpel

material [mə'tɪəriəl] Material, Stoff

maths [mæθs] *(BE)*/ **math** [mæθ] *(AE)* Mathematik

matter ['mætə] **1.** von Bedeutung sein, etwas ausmachen 5 T (84); **2. What's the matter?** Was ist denn (los)? 6 T (104)

May [meɪ] Mai

may [meɪ] **1.** dürfen • **May I help you?** Sie wünschen? **2. That may be your idea of …** Das ist vielleicht deine Vorstellung von … 3 A 1

maybe ['meɪbi] vielleicht

mayday ['meɪdeɪ] SOS-Ruf, Maydaysignal

mayonnaise [,meɪə'neɪz] Mayonnaise

mayor [meə] Bürgermeister/in 2 A 14

maze [meɪz] Irrgarten, Labyrinth 2 T (33)

me [mi, *betont:* mi:] mir; mich **It's me – Sita.** Ich bin es – Sita. **Me too.** Ich auch.

meal [mi:l] Mahlzeit, Essen

mean* [mi:n] **1.** bedeuten • **mean something to sb.** jm. etwas bedeuten 2 A 10 • **The name means nothing to me.** Der Name sagt mir nichts. / Ich kenne den Namen nicht. 2 T (34)
2. meinen *(sagen wollen)*

meaning ['mi:nɪŋ] Bedeutung

meant [ment] **1.** *si. past von „mean"*; **2.** *Part. Perf. von „mean"*

meanwhile ['mi:nwaɪl] inzwischen, währenddessen 5 T (84)

meat [mi:t] Fleisch

°**mediation** [,mi:di'eɪʃn] Sprachmittlung, Vermittlung 2 P 14

meet* [mi:t] **1.** *jn.* treffen; sich treffen • **Nice to meet you.** Freut mich, euch (dich/Sie) kennen zu lernen.
2. meet sb. jn. abholen 4 T (68)

meeting ['mi:tɪŋ] Versammlung, Besprechung, Treffen

mega ['megə] mega-; Mega-

melt [melt] schmelzen 5 T (85)

member ['membə] Mitglied

men [men] *pl von „man"*

mention ['menʃn] erwähnen, nennen 2 Li

menu ['menju:] **1.** Speisekarte; **2.** (Computer-)Menü

message ['mesɪdʒ] Nachricht **Can I give him/her a message?** Kann ich ihm/ihr etwas ausrichten? 4 P 11

met [met] **1.** *si. past von „meet"*; **2.** *Part. Perf. von „meet"*

metal ['metl] Metall

metre ['mi:tə] Meter

mice [maɪs] *pl von „mouse"*

microchip ['maɪkrəʊtʃɪp] Mikrochip 2 T (34)

microphone ['maɪkrəfəʊn] Mikrofon

microwave ['maɪkrəweɪv] Mikrowelle, Mikrowellengerät 5 A 3

middle ['mɪdl] Mitte • **middle row** [,mɪdl 'rəʊ] mittlere Reihe

°**Midlands** ['mɪdləndz]: **the Midlands** Mittelengland 3 T (52)

midnight ['mɪdnaɪt] Mitternacht **at midnight** um Mitternacht

might [maɪt]: **how he might answer** wie er (vielleicht) antworten könnte 2 A 11

mile [maɪl] Meile *(= ca. 1,6 km)*

milk [mɪlk] Milch • **milkshake** ['mɪlkʃeɪk] Milk-Shake • **milky** ['mɪlki] milchig

mill [mɪl] Mühle 1 Li

million ['mɪljən]: **a million** eine Million

°**mine** *(n)* [maɪn] Bergwerk 3 P 5

mineral water ['mɪnərəl wɔ:tə] Mineralwasser

minute ['mɪnɪt] Minute • **Wait a minute.** Moment mal!

mirror ['mɪrə] Spiegel
Miss Hunt [ˌmɪs 'hʌnt] Fräulein/Frau Hunt *(Anrede für unverheiratete Frauen)*
miss [mɪs] **1.** vermissen; **2.** verpassen, verfehlen • **be missing** fehlen • **the missing dialogue** der fehlende Dialog
mission ['mɪʃn] Einsatz, Mission 4 Li • °**mission control** Kontrollzentrum 4 P 12
mistake [mɪ'steɪk] Fehler
mix up [ˌmɪks_'ʌp] durcheinander bringen • **mixed up** durcheinander
mobile (phone) [ˌməʊbaɪl 'fəʊn] Mobiltelefon, Handy
°**mockingbird** ['mɒkɪŋbɜːd] Spottdrossel 4 P 1
model ['mɒdl] Modell
modern ['mɒdən] modern 3 A 5
mom [mɒm] *(AE)* Mutti, Mama; Mutter
moment ['məʊmənt]: **at the moment** im Moment, gerade, zurzeit • **Just a moment!** Einen Moment mal (eben)!
Monday ['mʌndeɪ, -di] Montag
money ['mʌni] Geld
monitor ['mɒnɪtə] Bildschirm, Monitor
°**monk** [mʌŋk] Mönch 3 T (52)
monkey ['mʌŋki] Affe
monster ['mɒnstə] Monster, Ungeheuer
month [mʌnθ] Monat
moon [muːn] Mond 4 How (71)
°**moorland** ['mɔːlənd, 'mʊələnd] Sumpfland, Moorland 1 Li
°**moose**, *pl* **moose** [muːs] *(amerikanischer)* Elch 5 A 10
more [mɔː] mehr • **more than** mehr als • **more sentences** weitere Sätze • **one more** noch ein(e), ein(e) weitere(r, s) • **not (...) any more** nicht mehr 4 T (69)
°**Who is more of an optimist?** Wer ist eher ein Optimist? 3 A 11
more expensive (than) teurer (als) • **more and more expensive** immer teurer 3 A 10
morning ['mɔːnɪŋ] Morgen, Vormittag • **Good morning.** Guten Morgen. / Guten Tag. / Grüß Gott.
in the morning(s) am Morgen, morgens • **this morning** heute Morgen
mosaic [məʊ'zeɪɪk] Mosaik 3 A 6
most [məʊst] am meisten • **(the) most important** (der/die/das) wichtigste ...; am wichtigsten
most kids/cars/... die meisten Kinder/Autos/... • **most easily** am leichtesten, am einfachsten
mostly ['məʊstli] hauptsächlich, größtenteils; meistens 1 How (19)
motel [məʊ'tel] Motel 5 P 9
mother ['mʌðə] Mutter
motorbike ['məʊtəbaɪk] Motorrad
motorcyclist ['məʊtəsaɪklɪst] Motorradfahrer/in
mountain ['maʊntən] Berg
mouse [maʊs], *pl* **mice** [maɪs] Maus
mouth [maʊθ] Mund
move [muːv] **1.** (sich) bewegen
Move to the music. Beweg dich zur Musik. • **movement** ['muːvmənt] Bewegung 5 T (85)
2. move (to) (um)ziehen (nach, in) 6 A 7 • **move in** einziehen 6 A 7 (169)
°**3. on the move** unterwegs, auf Achse 1 Li
movie ['muːvi] *(besonders AE)* Film
movie theater ['muːvi ˌθɪətə] *(besonders AE)* Kino • **to the movies** ['muːviz] *(AE)* ins Kino 5 P 7
Mr Snow ['mɪstə] Herr Snow
Mrs Snow ['mɪsɪz] Frau Snow *(Anrede für verheiratete Frauen)*
Ms Morrison [mɪz, məz] Frau Morrison 4 T (69)
much [mʌtʃ] **1.** viel • **How much?** Wie viel? • **How much is/are ...?** Was kostet/kosten ...? / Wie viel kostet/kosten ...?
2. sehr, viel
mum [mʌm] Mutti, Mama; Mutter
museum [mju'ziːəm] Museum
music ['mjuːzɪk] Musik
must [məst, *betont:* mʌst] **1.** müssen • **mustn't** ['mʌsnt] nicht *tun* dürfen
2. ... is a must. *(infml)* ... ist ein Muss.
my [maɪ] mein, meine • **My name is ...** Mein Name ist ... / Ich heiße ...
myself [maɪ'self] mir/mich (selbst); selbst, selber 6 A 3 (168) • °**I'll do it myself.** Ich werde es selbst machen. 3 T (49)
mystery ['mɪstri] **1.** Rätsel 2 P 12; **2.** rätselhafte(r, s) 2 P 12

N

nail [neɪl] Nagel 6 A 4 (168) • **nail polish** ['neɪl ˌpɒlɪʃ] *(AE)* / **nail varnish** ['neɪl ˌvɑːnɪʃ] *(BE)* Nagellack 6 A 4
name [neɪm] Name • **My name is ...** Mein Name ist ... / Ich heiße ... • **What's your name?** Wie heißt du? • **call sb. (stupid) names** jn. verspotten, jn. beschimpfen 4 T (69)
narrow ['nærəʊ] schmal, eng
national ['næʃnəl] national, National- • **national park** Nationalpark
native ['neɪtɪv] **1.** Ur(einwohner/in) 5 T (84); **2.** eingeboren, einheimisch 5 T (84) • **Native American** amerikanische(r) Ureinwohner/in, „Indianer/in"
nature ['neɪtʃə] Natur 3 T (49)
natural ['nætʃrəl] natürlich, Natur- 2 A 4
near [nɪə] in der Nähe von, nahe (bei) • **near to** in der Nähe von, nahe bei
neat [niːt] *(AE, infml)* toll, prima, klasse 4 T (69)
neck [nek] Hals, Nacken, Genick 6 T (103)
need [niːd] brauchen, benötigen • **needn't** ['niːdnt] nicht *tun* müssen, nicht *zu tun* brauchen
need to do sth. etwas tun müssen 4 A 4
negative ['negətɪv] **1.** verneint
negative short forms verneinte Kurzformen
2. negativ 1 How (19)
neighbour ['neɪbə] Nachbar/in
neither (of) ['naɪðə, 'niːðə] keine(r, s) (von beiden) 1 T (18)
nervous ['nɜːvəs] nervös, aufgeregt 2 A 1
net [net] Netz
netball ['netbɔːl] Korbball 1 Li (145)
network ['netwɜːk] (Wörter-)Netz, „Wörterspinne"
never ['nevə] nie, niemals
new [njuː] neu • **New Year** Neujahr 1 A 6
newcomer ['njuːkʌmə] Neuling 3 T (52)
news *(no pl)* [njuːz] Nachricht(en), Neuigkeit(en)
newspaper ['njuːspeɪpə] Zeitung
next [nekst] **1.** nächste(r, s) • **next Monday** (am) nächsten Montag
next week nächste Woche, in der nächsten Woche • **the next day** am nächsten Tag; der nächste Tag
2. als Nächstes
3. next to neben
nice [naɪs] schön, nett • **Nice to meet you.** Freut mich, euch (dich/Sie) kennen zu lernen.
nickel ['nɪkl] Fünfcentmünze *(USA)*
night [naɪt] Nacht, (später) Abend
at night in der Nacht, nachts
Good night. Gute Nacht.
nil [nɪl] null
No., *pl* **Nos. (= number, numbers)** *Abkürzung von „number(s)"* 1 P 12
no [nəʊ] **1.** nein; **2.** kein, keine
no later than nicht später als 5 P 8
no more school keine Schule mehr • **no one** ['nəʊ_wʌn] niemand

nobody ['nəʊbədi] niemand **Nobody cared.** Niemanden interessierte das/es. 3 A 12
noise [nɔɪz] Lärm; Geräusch **noisy** ['nɔɪzi] laut, lärmend
none [nʌn] keine(r, s) 1 Li
°**noodles** ['nuːdlz] Nudeln 6 P 13
normal ['nɔːml] normal 4 How (71)
°**Norman** *(n; adj)* ['nɔːmən] **1.** Normanne 3 T (50); **2.** normannisch 3 T (50)
°**Norse** *(n; adj)* [nɔːs] **1.** Nordisch 3 T (50); **2.** nordisch 3 T (50)
north [nɔːθ] nördlich; (nach) Norden • **north-east** [ˌnɔːθ'iːst] nordöstlich; (nach) Nordosten **northern** ['nɔːðən] nördlich, Nord- 1 A 6 (147) • **north-west** [ˌnɔːθ'west] nordwestlich; (nach) Nordwesten
nose [nəʊz] Nase
not [nɒt] nicht • **I'm not German.** Ich bin kein Deutscher / keine Deutsche. • **not any** kein(e) • **not (...) any more** nicht mehr 4 T (69) • **not ... anyone** niemand • **not ... anything** nichts • **not ... anywhere** nirgendwo(hin) • **not (...) either** ['aɪðə, 'iːðə] auch nicht; auch kein **not (...) yet** [jet] noch nicht
note [nəʊt] Notiz • **make notes** sich Notizen machen • **take notes** sich Notizen machen
nothing ['nʌθɪŋ] nichts
notice board ['nəʊtɪs bɔːd] Anschlagtafel, schwarzes Brett
nought [nɔːt] null
November [nəʊ'vembə] November
now [naʊ] nun, jetzt • **Now what?** Was nun?
nowhere ['nəʊweə] nirgendwo, nirgendwohin 6 A 1
nuclear ['njuːklɪə] nuklear, Kern-, Atom- • **nuclear power station** Atom-, Kernkraftwerk
number *(n; v)* ['nʌmbə] **1.** Zahl, Ziffer; **2.** Anzahl; **3.** nummerieren 1 Li
nurse [nɜːs] Krankenschwester, Krankenpfleger
nylon ['naɪlɒn] Nylon 5 T (85)

O

object ['ɒbdʒɪkt] Gegenstand 2 P 10
ocean ['əʊʃn] Ozean, Meer UK Call (7)
o'clock [ə'klɒk]**: six o'clock** sechs Uhr
October [ɒk'təʊbə] Oktober
Odd word out [ˌɒd wɜːd‿'aʊt] *etwa:* Das unpassende Wort raus
of [əv, *betont:* ɒv] von • **a group of girls** eine Gruppe (von) Mädchen • **a small number of children** eine kleine Anzahl Kinder/von Kindern • **in groups of four** in Vierergruppen • **the name of the street** der Name der Straße • **of all time** aller Zeiten 6 A 1 • **the two of them** die beiden; alle beide 6 A 4
of course [əv 'kɔːs] natürlich, selbstverständlich
off [ɒf] **1.** von (... herunter/hinunter) 2 A 10; **2.** aus(geschaltet) **drive off** wegfahren • **get off** aussteigen 2 A 1 • **get time off** frei bekommen, Urlaub bekommen 4 T (68) • **give sb. $3.00 off** jm. eine Ermäßigung von 3 Dollar geben • **take off 1.** ausziehen *(Kleidung)*; **2.** starten, abfliegen, abheben *(Flugzeug)* • **turn sth. off** etwas ausschalten • **walk off** weggehen 2 A 1
offer ['ɒfə] bieten, anbieten 4 Li
office ['ɒfɪs] Büro • **post office** Postamt
officer ['ɒfɪsə] Offizier/in • **police officer** Polizeibeamte(r)/Polizeibeamtin, Polizist/in
often ['ɒfn] oft
oil [ɔɪl] Öl 3 Li (154) • **oilfield** Ölfeld 5 P 10 • **oil-lamp** Öllampe 3 Li • **oil well** Ölquelle 5 T (84)
old [əʊld] alt • **16-year-old** 16-Jährige(r); 16-jährige(r, s) 1 T (18) **in the old days** in alten Zeiten, früher 5 P 1
oldie ['əʊldi] Oldie
olive ['ɒlɪv] Olive; Oliven- 3 A 5
Olympic Games [əˌlɪmpɪk 'geɪmz] Olympische Spiele
on [ɒn] auf • **report/show/film on** Reportage/Show/Film über **on and on** immer weiter • **on 12th January** am 12. Januar **on board (the ship)** an Bord (des Schiffes) • **on fire** in Brand 3 P 10 **on Lake Superior** am Lake Superior • **on Monday** am Montag **on Mondays** montags, jeden Montag • **on Monday evening** am Montagabend • **on Monday evenings** montagabends, montags abends • **on pages 14 and 15** auf den Seiten 14 und 15 **on the beach** am Strand • **on the bus** im Bus • **on the coast** an der Küste • **on the floor** auf dem Fußboden • **on the inside** innerlich, im Innern 6 T (103) • **on the left** links, auf der linken Seite **on the outside** äußerlich, auf der Außenseite 6 T (103) • **on the phone** am Telefon • **on the plane** im Flugzeug • **on the radio** im Radio • **on the right** rechts, auf der rechten Seite • **on the River Elbe** an der Elbe • **on the team** in der Mannschaft, im Team 4 A 8 • **on the train** im Zug • **on the weekend** *(AE)* am Wochenende • **on top (of sth.)** oben, obendrauf (auf etwas) • **on TV** im Fernsehen • **Does this shirt look good on me?** Steht mir dieses Hemd? • **go on 1.** (an-) dauern; vor sich gehen, im Gange sein 1 A 7; **2.** fortfahren, weiterreden; weitermachen; **3.** weitergehen *(Geschichte, Erzählung)* **put sth. on** etwas anziehen *(Kleidung)* • **straight on** geradeaus weiter • **try on** anprobieren *(Kleidung)* • **turn on** einschalten **walk/drive on** weitergehen/weiterfahren • **write on the board** an die Tafel schreiben
once [wʌns] einmal; einst • **at once** sofort, (so)gleich
one [wʌn] **1.** eins • **one day/morning** eines Tages/Morgens **one more** noch ein(e), ein(e) weitere(r, s) • **one of you** eine(r) von euch • **a yellow one** ein gelber, eine gelbe, ein gelbes **the yellow one** der/die/das gelbe **the yellow ones** die gelben **which one(s)** welche(r,s); welche **your loved ones** deine/eure Lieben 4 A 4
2. man 5 A 3 (164) • **one's** sein/e 5 A 3 (164) • **no one** niemand **one another** einander, sich (gegenseitig) 6 (138)
online [ˌɒn'laɪn, 'ɒnlaɪn] online, Online- 4 P 9
only ['əʊnli] **1.** nur, bloß; erst; **2. the only ...** der/die/das einzige ...; die einzigen ...
onto ['ɒntə, *betont:* 'ɒntuː] auf (... hinauf)
open *(v; adj)* ['əʊpən] **1.** öffnen, aufmachen; sich öffnen • **Open your books at page 5.** Schlagt Seite 5 auf. • **opening hours** Öffnungszeiten **2.** eröffnen; **3.** geöffnet • **in the open air** im Freien 1 P 11
opinion (of) [ə'pɪnjən] Meinung (von, zu) 4 T (70) • **in my opinion** meiner Meinung nach 4 T (162)
opposite ['ɒpəzɪt] gegenüber (von)
optimist ['ɒptɪmɪst] Optimist/in 3 A 11
or [ɔː] oder
orange ['ɒrɪndʒ] Apfelsine, Orange • **orange juice** ['ɒrɪndʒ dʒuːs] Orangensaft
orchestra ['ɔːkɪstrə] Orchester 4 P 8

order *(v; n)* ['ɔːdə] **1.** bestellen; **2.** befehlen, anordnen 3 T (51); **3.** Reihenfolge • **word order** Wortstellung
order ['ɔːdə]**: in order to do sth.** um etwas zu tun 5 A 1
ordinary ['ɔːdnəri] gewöhnlich, normal
organize ['ɔːgənaɪz] organisieren, veranstalten 5 P 11
original [ə'rɪdʒənl] Original-
other ['ʌðə] andere • **other words** andere Wörter
ought: you ought to ... ['ɔːt tə] ihr solltet; ihr müsstet (eigentlich) 4 A 4
our ['aʊə] unser, unsere
ourselves [aʊə'selvz] uns (selbst); selbst, selber 6 A 3 (168)
out [aʊt] hinaus, heraus; draußen **out of ...** aus ... (heraus/hinaus) **out of cardboard** aus Pappe, aus Karton • **out of this world** *(infml)* fantastisch, spitze 4 A 8 **out of work** arbeitslos • **out there** dort draußen • **act out** vorspielen • **be out** weg sein, nicht da sein • **cut out** ausschneiden • **find out** herausfinden • **give out** verteilen, austeilen • **Look out!** Pass auf! / Vorsicht! • **read out** vorlesen • **run out** knapp werden, zu Ende gehen, ausgehen 3 A 1 • **I've run out of money.** Mir ist das Geld ausgegangen. 3 A 1 (154) • **take out** herausnehmen • **Odd word out** *etwa:* Das unpassende Wort raus
outfit ['aʊtfɪt] Outfit, Kleidung 6 T (103)
outline ['aʊtlaɪn] Gliederung, Entwurf 5 A 2
outside [ˌaʊt'saɪd] **1.** *(adv)* draußen; nach draußen; **2.** *(prep)* vor; außerhalb (von) 5 P 4; **3.** *(n)* **on the outside** äußerlich, auf der Außenseite 6 T (103)
oval ['əʊvl] oval 1 A 1
oven ['ʌvn] Backofen 3 A 5
over ['əʊvə] **1.** über • **all over the world** auf der ganzen Welt, überall auf der Welt • **over there** dort drüben, da drüben • **go over (to)** hinübergehen/-fahren (zu/nach) 3 A 1
2. mehr als, über UK Call (7)
3. be over vorbei sein, zu Ende sein 5 P 10
overtake* [ˌəʊvə'teɪk] überholen
overtaken [ˌəʊvə'teɪkən] *Part. Perf. von „overtake"*
overtook [ˌəʊvə'tʊk] *si. past von „overtake"*
overwhelm [ˌəʊvə'welm] überwältigen

own [əʊn]**: your own chart** deine/Ihre/eure eigene Tabelle • **in our own way** auf unsere Art und Weise; so, wie wir wollen
owner ['əʊnə] Besitzer/in 2 A 4
oxygen ['ɒksɪdʒən] Sauerstoff 4 How (71)

P

pack [pæk] **1.** packen; **2.** einpacken
°**pack** [pæk] Rudel *(Wölfe, Hunde)* 5 A 10
packet ['pækɪt] Paket, Päckchen; Packung, Tüte
page [peɪdʒ] Seite
paid [peɪd] **1.** *si. past von „pay"*; **2.** *Part. Perf. von „pay"*
pair (of) [peə] Paar
paint [peɪnt] malen, anstreichen 3 A 1 (155) • **painted** ['peɪntɪd] bemalt; farbig 3 A 1 • **painting** ['peɪntɪŋ] Gemälde, Bild; Malerei 3 A 1 (155)
palace ['pæləs] Palast, Schloss 2 Li (149)
paper ['peɪpə] **1.** Papier • **a piece of paper** ein Stück Papier **2.** Zeitung
parade [pə'reɪd] Parade, Umzug
paradise ['pærədaɪs] Paradies 1 Li
paragraph ['pærəgrɑːf] Absatz, Abschnitt
paramedic [ˌpærə'medɪk] Sanitäter, Sanitäterin
parents ['peərənts] Eltern
park [pɑːk] Park • **car park** *(BE)* Parkplatz 3 A 6
parking space ['pɑːkɪŋ speɪs] Parkplatz, Parklücke 3 A 6 (155)
parliament ['pɑːləmənt] Parlament 2 Li (149)
part [pɑːt] Teil • **take part (in)** teilnehmen (an), mitmachen (bei) 2 A 14 • °**partly** ['pɑːtli] teilweise Rev 6 (113)
partner ['pɑːtnə] Partner, Partnerin
party ['pɑːti] Party • **have a party** eine Party veranstalten, feiern
pass *(v; n)* [pɑːs] **1.** überholen; vorbeigehen, vorbeifahren an; **2.** vergehen, vorübergehen *(Zeit)* 2 T (33); **3.** Pass, Ballabgabe 1 T (18)
passenger ['pæsɪndʒə] Passagier/in, Fahrgast
passport ['pɑːspɔːt] (Reise-)Pass
past [pɑːst] **1.** *(n)* Vergangenheit; **2.** *(prep; adv)* vorbei, vorüber (an) 2 T (35) • **half past eight** halb neun (8.30/20.30) • **quarter past eight** Viertel nach acht (8.15/20.15)
pastry ['peɪstri] (Mürbe-, Blätter-) Teig 6 A 9

pavement ['peɪvmənt] **1.** *(BE)* Gehweg, Fußweg; **2.** *(AE)* Fahrbahn 4 T (161)
pay* (for) [peɪ] bezahlen
PE [ˌpiː‿'iː] **(Physical Education** [ˌfɪzɪkəl‿edʒu'keɪʃn]**)** Turnen, Sport(unterricht) *(in der Regel in der Halle)*
peace [piːs] Friede(n) 3 T (156) **peaceful** ['piːsfl] friedlich, friedfertig 3 T (49)
peanut ['piːnʌt] Erdnuss
pen [pen] Füller, Kugelschreiber
°**penalty goal** ['penəlti] *(Rugby)* Tor *(nach einem Foul)* 1 A 1
pence *(pl)* [pens] Pence *(Mehrzahl von „penny")*
pencil ['pensl] Bleistift
pencil case ['pensl keɪs] Federmäppchen
penfriend ['penfrend] Brieffreund, Brieffreundin
penguin ['peŋgwɪn] Pinguin
peninsula [pə'nɪnsjələ] Halbinsel 1 A 6
penny ['peni] *kleinste britische Münze*
people ['piːpl] **1.** *(pl)* Leute, Menschen; **2.** Volk 3 T (51)
per cent (%) [pə'sent] Prozent 1 P 12
perception [pə'sepʃn] Wahrnehmung 4 A 9
perfect ['pɜːfɪkt] perfekt, einwandfrei, vollkommen; ideal 1 Li
°**perfume** ['pɜːfjuːm] Parfüm 3 A 5
perhaps [pə'hæps] vielleicht
person ['pɜːsn] Person • **personal** ['pɜːsənl] persönlich 3 P 11
pessimist ['pesɪmɪst] Pessimist/in 3 A 11
pet [pet] Haustier
phone *(v; n)* [fəʊn] **1.** anrufen; **2.** Telefon • **answer the phone** ans Telefon gehen • **on the phone** am Telefon • **phone box** Telefonzelle • **phone call** (Telefon-)Anruf • **phone number** Telefonnummer • **mobile phone** [ˌməʊbaɪl 'fəʊn] Mobiltelefon, Handy
photo ['fəʊtəʊ] Foto • **in the photo** auf dem Foto • **take photos** Fotos machen, fotografieren
phrase [freɪz] Wortgruppe, Ausdruck; (Rede-)Wendung
Physical Education [ˌfɪzɪkəl‿edʒu'keɪʃn] Turnen, Sport(unterricht) *(in der Regel in der Halle)*
piano [pi'ænəʊ], *pl* **pianos** Klavier, Piano 6 T (104)
pick sb./sth. up [ˌpɪk‿'ʌp] jn./etwas abholen, mitnehmen; etwas *(vom Boden)* aufheben 2 A 7

°**pickpocket** ['pɪkpɒkɪt] Taschendieb/in 2 A 7
picnic ['pɪknɪk] Picknick
picture ['pɪktʃə] Bild • **in the picture** auf dem Bild
°**pie** [paɪ]: **potato pie** *eine Art Kartoffelauflauf* Rev 7 (113)
piece [pi:s] Stück • **a piece of paper** ein Stück Papier
pig [pɪg] Schwein
pigeon ['pɪdʒɪn] Taube 2 A 7
°**pillage** ['pɪlɪdʒ] plündern, brandschatzen 3 T (50)
pilot ['paɪlət] Pilot, Pilotin
pin (-nn-) [pɪn] (an)heften, (an)stecken 5 A 2
pink [pɪŋk] pink(farben), rosa
pipe [paɪp] Pfeife 2 T (33)
pipeline ['paɪplaɪn] Pipeline *(Rohrleitung für Gas/Erdöl)* 5 T (84)
pizza ['pi:tsə] Pizza
place [pleɪs] Ort, Platz, Stelle • **in the right places** an den richtigen Stellen 5 P 3 • **take place** stattfinden
plan *(n; v)* [plæn] **1.** Plan; **2. (-nn-)** planen
plane [pleɪn] Flugzeug • **on the plane** im Flugzeug
planet ['plænɪt] Planet 3 P 14
plant [plɑ:nt] Pflanze 5 A 10
plastic ['plæstɪk] Plastik, Kunststoff
plate [pleɪt] Teller
platform ['plætfɔ:m] Bahnsteig, Gleis 2 T (34)
play *(v; n)* [pleɪ] **1.** spielen • **play a trick on sb.** jm. einen Streich spielen • **play the drums** Schlagzeug spielen • **player** Spieler/in
2. Theaterstück
playground ['pleɪgraʊnd] Schulhof
please [pli:z] bitte *(in Fragen und Aufforderungen)*
pleased [pli:zd]: **be pleased (with)** sich freuen (über), zufrieden sein (mit)
plug [plʌg] Stecker
plural ['plʊərəl] Plural
... pm [,pi:‿'em] ... Uhr nachmittags/abends
pocket ['pɒkɪt] Tasche *(an einem Kleidungsstück)* 2 A 7 • **pocket money** Taschengeld 2 P 13
poem ['pəʊɪm] Gedicht
point *(n; v)* [pɔɪnt] **1.** Punkt; **2. 11.4 (eleven point four)** 11,4 (elf Komma vier) UK Call (144); **3. point (at/to)** zeigen, deuten (auf) • **point sth. at sb.** etwas auf jn. richten
police *(pl)* [pə'li:s] Polizei • **police officer** Polizeibeamte(r)/-beamtin, Polizist/in • **police station** Polizeiwache, Polizeirevier
political [pə'lɪtɪkl] politisch 6 A 4 **politics** ['pɒlətɪks] (die) Politik 6 A 4
pollute [pə'lu:t] *(die Umwelt)* verschmutzen • **pollution** [pə'lu:ʃn] (Umwelt-)Verschmutzung
poor [pɔ:, pʊə] arm • **poor Trundle** der arme Trundle **Poor things!** Die Armen! 2 T (34)
pop [pɒp] Pop(musik)
popcorn ['pɒpkɔ:n] Popcorn
popular (with) ['pɒpjələ] beliebt (bei), populär 1 A 9
population [,pɒpju'leɪʃn] Bevölkerung, Einwohner(zahl) UK Call (6)
positive ['pɒzətɪv] positiv
possible ['pɒsəbl] möglich 6 How (105)
post [pəʊst] *(BE)* Post(sendung) 1 How (19) • **post office** Postamt **postbox** Briefkasten • **postcard** Postkarte
poster ['pəʊstə] Poster
pot [pɒt] Topf, Kochtopf 3 A 5
potato [pə'teɪtəʊ], *pl* **potatoes** [pə'teɪtəʊz] Kartoffel • °**potato pie** *eine Art Kartoffelauflauf* Rev 7 (113)
pound (£) [paʊnd] Pfund *(britische Währung)*
pour [pɔ:] gießen, schütten; einschenken 5 T (85)
power ['paʊə] Strom, Energie **power station** ['paʊə ,steɪʃn] Kraftwerk
practice *(n; v)* ['præktɪs] **1.** *(no pl)* Praxis, Übung(en); **2.** *(AE)* üben, trainieren 5 A 3
practise ['præktɪs] üben, trainieren
prefer sth. (to) (-rr-) [prɪ'fɜ:] etwas lieber haben/tun (als), etwas *(einer anderen Sache)* vorziehen Welc (57) • **prefer to do sth.** etwas lieber tun Welc (157)
prefix ['pri:fɪks] Vorsilbe, Präfix 3 P 12
prepare (for) [prɪ'peə] (sich) vorbereiten (auf); *(Mahlzeit)* zubereiten 1 Li
present ['preznt] **1.** Geschenk; **2.** Gegenwart 3 A 11
present sth. (to sb.) [prɪ'zent] (jm.) etwas präsentieren, zeigen, vorstellen • **presentation** [,prezn'teɪʃn] Präsentation, Darbietung, Vorstellung • **presenter** [prɪ'zentə] Moderator/in 6 T (103)
president ['prezɪdənt] Präsident/in 5 T (84)
pretty ['prɪti] **1.** *(adj)* hübsch; **2.** *(adv, infml)* ziemlich 4 A 4
price [praɪs] (Kauf-)Preis
°**prime meridian** [,praɪm mə'rɪdiən] Nullmeridian 2 How (37)
prince [prɪns] Prinz 2 P 7
print: **bold print** [,bəʊld 'prɪnt] Fettdruck
prize [praɪz] Preis, Gewinn
probably ['prɒbəbli] wahrscheinlich 5 A 1
problem ['prɒbləm] Problem
produce [prə'dju:s] produzieren, erzeugen, herstellen 4 Li
professor [prə'fesə] Professor/in
program ['prəʊgræm] *(AE)* Programm 4 Li
programme ['prəʊgræm] (Radio-, Fernseh-) Sendung; Programm 1 How (19)
project ['prɒdʒekt] Projekt
pronounce [prə'naʊns] aussprechen 5 How (87) • **pronunciation** [prə,nʌnsi'eɪʃn] Aussprache
properly ['prɒpəli] richtig, ordentlich, sachgemäß
protect sb. (from sth.) [prə'tekt] jn. (be)schützen (vor etwas) 5 A 10
proud (of sb./sth.) [praʊd] stolz (auf jn./etwas) 4 T (68)
pub [pʌb] *(BE)* Kneipe, Lokal 1 A 3
pull [pʊl] ziehen
pullover ['pʊləʊvə] Pullover
°**pump iron** [,pʌmp‿'aɪən] *(infml)* Gewichte stemmen 6 A 4
°**punctuation** [,pʌŋktʃu'eɪʃn] Zeichensetzung Rev 1 (110)
pupil ['pju:pl] Schüler, Schülerin
purse [pɜ:s] Portmonee, Geldbeutel 2 A 14
push [pʊʃ] drücken, schieben, stoßen 3 T (50)
put* (-tt-) [pʊt] **1.** *(etwas wohin)* tun, stellen, legen • **put down** hinstellen, hinlegen • **put in** einsetzen, einfügen, hineintun 2 P 11 **put sth. on** etwas anziehen *(Kleidung)* • **put up** aufstellen, errichten; aufhängen 5 T (85) • °**Put that in your pipe and smoke it.** *(infml) etwa:* Lass dir das gesagt sein. / Schreib dir das hinter die Ohren. 2 T (33)
2. *si. past von „put"*;
3. *Part. Perf. von „put"*

Q

quarter ['kwɔ:tə] 25-Cent-Münze *(USA)*
quarter ['kwɔ:tə]: **quarter past eight** Viertel nach acht (8.15/20.15) • **quarter to nine** Viertel vor neun (8.45/20.45)
°**quarterback** ['kwɔ:təbæk] Quarterback *(American football)* 1 Li
queen [kwi:n] Königin
question ['kwestʃən] Frage • **ask questions** Fragen stellen
questionnaire [,kwestʃə'neə] Fragebogen

quick *(adj)* [kwɪk] schnell
quickly *(adv)* ['kwɪkli] schnell
quiet ['kwaɪət] ruhig, leise, still
quite [kwaɪt] ziemlich; ganz
quite a lifeless place ein ziemlich lebloser/toter Ort 5 P 10
quiz [kwɪz], *pl* **quizzes** ['kwɪzɪz] Quiz, Ratespiel

R

rabbit ['ræbɪt] Kaninchen
race [reɪs] Rennen, (Wett-)Lauf
sailing race Regatta
radio ['reɪdiəʊ] **1.** Radio • **on the radio** im Radio • **radio station** Rundfunksender
2. Funk; Funkgerät
railway ['reɪlweɪ] Eisenbahn 1 A 6
railway station Bahnhof 2 P 2
rain *(v; n)* [reɪn] **1.** regnen; **2.** Regen • **acid rain** [ˌæsɪd 'reɪn] saurer Regen • **rainy** ['reɪni] regnerisch
raise [reɪz] (hoch)heben • **Raise your arms.** Heb deine Arme.
ran [ræn] *si. past von „run"*
rang [ræŋ] *si. past von „ring"*
range [reɪndʒ] (Berg-, Felsen-) Kette 5 Li
rap [ræp] Rap *(rhythmischer Sprechgesang)*
rat [ræt] Ratte
rattle ['rætl] rütteln; klappern
reach [ri:tʃ] erreichen
react (to) [ri:'ækt] reagieren (auf) 5 A 4
read* **1.** [ri:d] lesen • **read out** vorlesen • **Read out loud.** Lies laut vor. • **read to a partner** einem Partner/einer Partnerin vorlesen • **reader** ['ri:də] Leser/in
2. [red] *si. past von „read"*;
3. [red] *Part. Perf. von „read"*
ready ['redi] bereit, fertig • **get ready** sich bereitmachen, sich fertig machen 1 A 1
real *(adj)* [rɪəl] echt, wirklich
real nice *(adv)* ['ri:əl] *(AE, infml)* wirklich nett, echt nett 4 A 4
really *(adv)* ['rɪəli] wirklich
reason (for .../why ...) ['ri:zn] Grund, Begründung (für .../dafür, dass ...)
recess ['ri:ses, rɪ'ses] *(AE)* Pause *(zwischen Schulstunden)* 4 T (68)
record *(n; v)* **1.** ['rekɔ:d] Schallplatte; **2.** [rɪ'kɔ:d] aufnehmen, aufzeichnen *(auf Band/CD)*
recorded message Bandansage 5 P 9
recycle [ˌri:'saɪkl] wieder verwerten, wieder aufbereiten • **recycling** [ˌri:'saɪklɪŋ] Wiederverwertung, Wiederaufbereitung
red [red] rot
°**redwood** ['redwʊd] Mammutbaum 6 A 1
refer to **(-rr-)** [rɪ'fɜ:] sich beziehen auf
regional ['ri:dʒənl] regional 5 T (84)
regular ['regjələ] regelmäßig, regulär
relationship [rɪ'leɪʃnʃɪp] Beziehung 6 T (102)
relax [rɪ'læks] (sich) entspannen, sich ausruhen 1 Li (118)
reliable [rɪ'laɪəbl] zuverlässig, verlässlich 6 T (103)
religion [rɪ'lɪdʒn] Religion 3 P 11
°**remains** *(pl)* [rɪ'meɪnz] (Über-) Reste 3 Li
remember [rɪ'membə] **1.** sich erinnern an; **2. remember sth.** an etwas denken; sich etwas merken
remote [rɪ'məʊt] abgelegen, entlegen, weit entfernt UK Call (7)
repair *(v; n)* [rɪ'peə] **1.** reparieren 4 Li (159); **2.** Reparatur 4 Li
replace sth. (with) [rɪ'pleɪs] etwas ersetzen (durch) 3 P 13
reply [rɪ'plaɪ] erwidern 3 A 10
reply to sb. jm. antworten 3 A 10
reply to sth. auf etwas antworten 3 A 10
report (on) *(v; n)* [rɪ'pɔ:t] **1.** berichten (über) • **reporting verb** die indirekte Rede einleitendes Verb 5 A 7 • **reporter** Reporter/in
2. Bericht, Reportage (über)
request [rɪ'kwest] Bitte, Wunsch
rescue ['reskju:] retten; befreien
reservation [ˌrezə'veɪʃn] Reservation *(den Indianern vorbehaltenes Gebiet)*
rest (of) [rest] Rest 2 A 12
restaurant ['restrɒnt] Restaurant
at the restaurant im Restaurant
restroom ['restru:m] *(AE)* *(öffentliche)* Toilette 4 T (162)
result [rɪ'zʌlt] Ergebnis, Resultat
as a result als Ergebnis, als Resultat; infolgedessen
retell* [ˌri:'tel] nacherzählen
retold [ˌri:'təʊld] **1.** *si. past von „retell"*; **2.** *Part. Perf. von „retell"*
return [rɪ'tɜ:n] zurückkehren; zurücksenden, -bringen 3 A 1
revision [rɪ'vɪʒn] Wiederholung *(des Lernstoffs)*
revolution [ˌrevə'lu:ʃn] Revolution 2 A 4
rewrite* [ˌri:'raɪt] neu schreiben, noch einmal schreiben 5 T (86)
rhyme [raɪm] sich reimen
rice [raɪs] Reis 4 A 8
rich [rɪtʃ] reich 2 P 7
rid [rɪd]**: get rid of sb./sth.** jn./etwas loswerden 3 T (49)
ridden ['rɪdn] *Part. Perf. von „ride"*
ride* *(v; n)* [raɪd] **1.** reiten • **ride a wave** auf einer Welle reiten
rider Reiter/in • **riding** *(das)* Reiten, Reitsport 1 Li (145) • **horse riding** *(das)* Reiten UK Call (7)
2. ride a bike Rad fahren • **Let's ride our bikes to school.** Lass uns mit dem Rad zur Schule fahren.
rider (Rad-)Fahrer/in
3. *(Karussell- usw.)*Fahrt • **go for a ride** eine Spazierfahrt machen; herumfahren 5 T (84) • **bike ride** Radfahrt, Radtour
right [raɪt] **1.** richtig • **Right, Debbie?** Nicht wahr, Debbie?
all right gut, (alles) in Ordnung
be right Recht haben • **That's right.** Das ist richtig. / Das stimmt.
You're right. Du hast Recht. / Stimmt.
2. (nach) rechts • **on the right** rechts, auf der rechten Seite • **to the right** rechts, auf der rechten Seite, zur Rechten 4 P 10
3. *(adv)* direkt, gerade(wegs), genau UK Call (7)
ring* [rɪŋ] klingeln, läuten
rise* [raɪz] aufgehen *(Sonne, Mond)*; (an-, auf)steigen 5 T (84)
risen ['rɪzn] *Part. Perf. von „rise"* 5 T (84)
rival ['raɪvl] Rivale, Rivalin; Konkurrent, Konkurrentin 1 T (18)
river ['rɪvə] Fluss • **on the River Elbe** an der Elbe
road [rəʊd] Straße, Landstraße
road sign Verkehrszeichen
roast [rəʊst] rösten
rob **(-bb-)** [rɒb] berauben, ausrauben 2 A 7
robot ['rəʊbɒt] Roboter
rock [rɒk] **1.** Fels, Felsen;
2. Rock(musik)
rode [rəʊd] *si. past von „ride"*
role [rəʊl] Rolle • **role-play** Rollenspiel
Roman *(adj; n)* ['rəʊmən] **1.** römisch; **2.** Römer, Römerin
romantic [rəʊ'mæntɪk] romantisch 1 A 6
roof [ru:f] Dach
room [ru:m] Zimmer, Raum
rope [rəʊp] Seil
rose [rəʊz] Rose 2 P 11
rose [rəʊz] *si. past von „rise"* 5 T (84)
round [raʊnd] **1.** rund 1 A 1; **2.** um ... (herum) • **look round (for)** sich umsehen (nach) • **take sth. round to sb.** jm. etwas bringen 6 P 13
route [ru:t] Route, Strecke 2 A 2
row [rəʊ] Reihe • **top row / middle row / bottom row** [ˌtɒp / ˌmɪdl / ˌbɒtəm 'rəʊ] obere Reihe / mittlere Reihe / untere Reihe

°**rub** **(-bb-)** [rʌb] reiben, einreiben 3 A 5

rubber ['rʌbə] Radiergummi

rubbish ['rʌbɪʃ] **1.** Abfall, Müll °**rubbish dump** Müllhalde, Müllkippe 3 A 1 **2.** *(infml)* Quatsch, Blödsinn 1 A 1

rucksack ['rʌksæk] Rucksack

rude (to sb.) [ru:d] unhöflich, grob (zu jm.) 6 A 9

rugby ['rʌgbi] Rugby 1 Li (145)

rule [ru:l] **1.** Regel, Vorschrift; °**2.** (be)herrschen, regieren 3 Li

ruler ['ru:lə] Lineal

run* **(-nn-)** [rʌn] **1.** laufen, rennen **run around** herumrennen, umherrennen • °**run for the try** *etwa:* versuchen Punkte zu erzielen *(Rugby)* 1 T (18) • **running** *(das)* Laufen 1 Li (145) **2.** verlaufen, sich erstrecken *(Grenze, Straße)* 2 How (37) **3.** durchführen, veranstalten, betreiben, leiten 1 A 6 **4. run out** knapp werden, zu Ende gehen, ausgehen 3 A 1 • **I've run out of money.** Mir ist das Geld ausgegangen. 3 A 1 (154) **5.** *Part. Perf. von „run"*

rung [rʌŋ] *Part. Perf. von „ring"*

S

sad [sæd] traurig • **sadness** ['sædnəs] Traurigkeit 2 P 12

safe (from) [seɪf] sicher (vor), gefahrlos • **safety** ['seɪfti] Sicherheit

said [sed] **1.** *si. past von „say"*; **2.** *Part. Perf. von „say"*

sail [seɪl] segeln • **sailing** *(das)* Segeln 1 Li (145) • **sailing race** Regatta

sailor ['seɪlə] Seemann, Matrose

salad ['sæləd] Salat *(als Gericht oder Beilage)*

salt [sɔ:lt] Salz • **salty** ['sɔ:lti] salzig, gesalzen

same [seɪm]: **the same** der-/die-/dasselbe, dieselben

sand [sænd] Sand 1 A 6 • **sandy** sandig 1 A 6 (147)

sandal ['sændl] Sandale

sandwich ['sænwɪdʒ] *(zusammengeklapptes)* belegtes Brot, Sandwich

sang [sæŋ] *si. past von „sing"*

sank [sæŋk] *si. past von „sink"*

sat [sæt] **1.** *si. past von „sit"*; **2.** *Part. Perf. von „sit"*

satellite ['sætəlaɪt] Satellit 4 A 8

Saturday ['sætədeɪ, 'sætədi] Samstag, Sonnabend

sauce [sɔ:s] Soße 3 A 5

sauna ['sɔ:nə] Sauna 1 P 8

sausage ['sɒsɪdʒ] (Brat-, Bock-) Würstchen, Wurst

save [seɪv] **1.** sparen; **2. save from** retten vor

saw [sɔ:] *si. past von „see"*

°**Saxons: the Saxons** ['sæksnz] die Sachsen 3 T (50)

say* [seɪ] sagen • **say goodbye (to sb.)** sich (von jm.) verabschieden 4 A 10 • **Say hello/Say hi to ... from me.** Grüß ... von mir. **They all say hello.** Sie lassen alle grüßen. • **say so** es/das sagen 1 T (18)

scan **(-nn-)** [skæn] *(einen Text)* überfliegen *(um bestimmte Informationen zu finden)* 2 T (35)

scare [skeə] erschrecken, Angst machen • **be scared (of; about)** Angst haben (vor; wegen) 4 T (69)

scarf [skɑ:f], *pl* **scarves** [skɑ:vz] Schal

scary ['skeəri] unheimlich, gruselig

scene [si:n] Szene

schedule [*BE:* 'ʃedju:l, *AE:* 'skedʒəl] Zeitplan; *(AE auch:)* Stundenplan, Fahrplan 5 P 9

scholarship ['skɒləʃɪp] Stipendium 4 A 1 • **win a scholarship** ein Stipendium bekommen 4 A 1 (159)

school [sku:l] Schule • **at school** in der Schule • **leave school** von der Schule abgehen • **school day** Schultag • **school subject** Schulfach

science ['saɪəns] (Natur-)Wissenschaft • **computer science** Informatik 6 A 7 • **scientific** [,saɪən'tɪfɪk] (natur)wissenschaftlich 2 A 4 • **scientist** ['saɪəntɪst] (Natur-)Wissenschaftler/in 2 A 4 (150)

scissors *(pl)* ['sɪzəz] *(eine)* Schere

score *(v; n)* [skɔ:] **1.** *(einen Treffer)* erzielen, *(ein Tor)* schießen; **2.** Spielstand, (Spiel-)Ergebnis, Punktestand 1 Li

scrambled egg(s) [,skræmbld_'eg(z)] Rührei, Rühreier

scrapbook ['skræpbʊk] Sammelalbum

scream [skri:m] schreien, kreischen

screen [skri:n] Bildschirm; Leinwand

sea [si:] Meer, *(die)* See • **at sea** auf See

°**seafaring** ['si:,feərɪŋ] Seefahrt 2 How (37)

sea lion ['si: laɪən] Seelöwe

seal [si:l] Robbe, Seehund

°**seashore** ['si:ʃɔ:] (Meeres-)Ufer, Küste 6 P 2

search engine ['sɜ:tʃ_endʒɪn] Suchmaschine 6 A 4

°**seaside town** ['si:saɪd] Stadt am Meer, Küstenstadt 1 A 6

seat [si:t] Sitzplatz • **take a seat** Platz nehmen

second ['sekənd] zweite(r, s)

second ['sekənd] Sekunde

secret *(n; adj)* ['si:krət] **1.** Geheimnis; **2.** geheim • **Secret Service** Geheimdienst 2 T (33)

section ['sekʃn] Abschnitt, Teil 1 A 1

sector ['sektə] Sektor, Bereich

see* [si:] sehen • **see sb. 1.** jn. besuchen, jn. aufsuchen; **2.** mit jm. zusammensein; sich mit jm. treffen 6 T (103) • **I see!** Ich verstehe! / Aha! / Ach so! • **See you.** Servus. / Bis bald. / Bis dann. **See you tomorrow.** Bis morgen. 2 A 7 • **you see** weißt du, nämlich

seem (to be/do) [si:m] (zu sein/tun) scheinen

seen [si:n] *Part. Perf. von „see"*

sell* [sel] verkaufen 2 A 10

send* (to) [send] schicken, senden (an)

sent [sent] **1.** *si. past von „send"*; **2.** *Part. Perf. von „send"*

sentence ['sentəns] Satz

September [sep'tembə] September

°**sequoia** [sɪ'kwɔɪə] Mammutbaum 6 A 1

service ['sɜ:vɪs] Dienst, Service

°**settle** ['setl] sich niederlassen, sesshaft werden 3 T (50)

sexy ['seksi] sexy 6 T (103)

shake* [ʃeɪk] zittern; schütteln

shaken ['ʃeɪkən] *Part. Perf. von „shake"*

Shall I ...? [ʃæl, ʃəl] Soll ich ...?

she [ʃi, *betont:* ʃi:] sie

sheep, *pl* **sheep** [ʃi:p] Schaf

shelf [ʃelf], *pl* **shelves** [ʃelvz] Regal

shelter (from) ['ʃeltə] Schutz (vor)

ship [ʃɪp] Schiff

shirt [ʃɜ:t] (Ober-)Hemd

shocked [ʃɒkt] schockiert 5 A 2

shoe [ʃu:] Schuh

shook [ʃʊk] *si. past von „shake"*

shop *(n; v)* [ʃɒp] **1.** Laden, Geschäft; **2. (-pp-)** einkaufen gehen **shopper** Käufer/in • **shopping** Einkaufen; Einkäufe • **shopping mall** *(besonders AE)* Einkaufszentrum • **do the shopping** Einkäufe machen/erledigen, einkaufen • **go shopping** einkaufen gehen • **go to the shops** einkaufen gehen • **hate shopping** gar nicht gern einkaufen gehen **like shopping** gern einkaufen gehen • **love shopping** sehr gern einkaufen gehen

short [ʃɔ:t] kurz • **short answer** Kurzantwort • **short forms** Kurzformen

shorts *(pl)* [ʃɔːts] Shorts, kurze Hose
should [ʃəd, *betont:* ʃʊd]: **they should ...** sie sollten ...
shout [ʃaʊt] schreien, laut rufen
show* *(v; n)* [ʃəʊ] **1.** zeigen; **2.** Schau, Show; **3.** (Fernseh-, Radio-)Sendung • **on the show** in der Sendung
shower ['ʃaʊə] Dusche; Regenschauer • **have a shower** (sich) duschen
shown [ʃəʊn] *Part. Perf. von „show"*
shut* **(-tt-)** [ʃʌt] **1.** schließen, zumachen 6 Li • **Shut up.** Halt den Mund! **2.** *si. past von „shut"* 6 Li; **3.** *Part. Perf. von „shut"* 6 Li
sick [sɪk] krank 5 A 10
side [saɪd] Seite
sidewalk ['saɪdwɔːk] *(AE)* Gehweg, Bürgersteig 4 T (69)
sight [saɪt] **1.** Sehenswürdigkeit; **2. in sight** in Sicht(weite) 6 T (103)
sign [saɪn] Schild; Zeichen • **road sign** Verkehrszeichen
sign [saɪn] unterschreiben 6 T (102) **sign up (for sth.)** sich (für etwas) einschreiben 6 T (102)
silly ['sɪli] albern, dumm • **silliness** Albernheit, Dummheit 2 P 12
°**simulator** ['sɪmjuleɪtə] Simulator *(Gerät, in dem bestimmte Bedingungen wirklichkeitsgetreu nachgestellt werden)* 4 Li
since [sɪns] seit 1 A 3 • **since four o'clock** seit vier Uhr 1 A 3
sincerely [sɪn'sɪəli]: **Yours sincerely,** Mit freundlichen/herzlichen Grüßen
sing* [sɪŋ] singen • **singer** ['sɪŋə] Sänger/in
sink* [sɪŋk] sinken, untergehen
Sir [sɜː, sə] *engl. Adelstitel* 2 Li **Dear Sir or Madam** Sehr geehrte Damen und Herren 1 P 12
siren ['saɪrən] Sirene 6 A 9
sister ['sɪstə] Schwester
sit* **(-tt-)** [sɪt] sich (hin)setzen; sitzen • **sit down** sich hinsetzen
site [saɪt] **1.** Stätte; Stelle, Standort 2 How (37); **2.** Ausgrabungsstätte 3 A 1
situation [ˌsɪtʃu'eɪʃn] Situation
size [saɪz] Größe • **What size are you?** Welche Größe hast du/haben Sie?
ski [skiː] Ski laufen, Ski fahren **skiing** *(das)* Skilaufen, Skisport 1 Li (145)
skin [skɪn] Haut 3 A 5
skirt [skɜːt] Rock
sky [skaɪ] Himmel • **in the sky** am Himmel
°**slave** [sleɪv] Sklave, Sklavin 3 P 5
sled [sled] *(AE)* Schlitten 5 P 1
sledge [sledʒ] *(BE)* Schlitten 5 P 1 (165)
sleep* *(v; n)* [sliːp] **1.** schlafen **sleep late** lange schlafen **sleeping-bag** Schlafsack 5 T (84) **2.** Schlaf • °**get a good night's sleep** sich (richtig) ausschlafen 3 A 6 • **go to sleep** einschlafen **sleepless** schlaflos 5 P 10 **sleepy** schläfrig, verschlafen
slept [slept] **1.** *si. past von „sleep"*; **2.** *Part. Perf. von „sleep"*
slogan ['sləʊgən] Slogan, Werbespruch
slope [sləʊp] Hang 5 T (84)
slow [sləʊ] langsam
small [smɔːl] klein
smell [smel] riechen 3 T (50)
smile *(n; v)* [smaɪl] **1.** Lächeln 6 A 9; **2. smile (at sb.)** (jn. an)lächeln
smoke [sməʊk] rauchen 2 T (33)
snake [sneɪk] Schlange
snap **(-pp-)** [snæp]: **Snap your fingers.** Schnips mit den Fingern.
snow [snəʊ] Schnee
°**snowmobile** ['snəʊməˌbiːl] Schneemobil 5 A 1
so [səʊ] **1.** deshalb, daher; also **So?** Na und? 6 T (104) **2. so boring** so langweilig; **3. so (that)** sodass, damit; **4. do so** es/das tun 1 T (18) • **say so** es/das sagen 1 T (18) • **I think so.** Ich glaube (ja). 5 A 6 (164) • **I don't think so.** Das finde/glaube ich nicht. 5 A 6 (164) • **You think so?** Glaubst du? 5 A 6 • **Cars can be dangerous. But so can cyclists.** Autos können gefährlich sein. Aber Radfahrer auch.
°**soccer** ['sɒkə] Fußball Rev 1 (112)
sock [sɒk] Socke, Strumpf
sofa ['səʊfə] Sofa
software ['sɒftweə] (Computer-)Software 6 P 15
solar ['səʊlə]: **solar energy** Sonnenenergie, Solarenergie • **solar system** Sonnensystem 4 P 8
sold [səʊld] **1.** *si. past von „sell"* 2 A 10; **2.** *Part. Perf. von „sell"* 2 A 10
soldier ['səʊldʒə] Soldat/in 3 A 5
some [səm, *betont:* sʌm] einige, ein paar; etwas
somebody ['sʌmbədi] jemand **somebody else** (noch) jemand anderes 1 Li (146)
someone ['sʌmwʌn] jemand **someone else** (noch) jemand anderes 1 Li (146)
something ['sʌmθɪŋ] etwas **something else** (noch) etwas anderes 1 Li (146)
sometimes ['sʌmtaɪmz] manchmal
somewhere ['sʌmweə] irgendwo; irgendwohin • **somewhere else** woanders(hin), sonst irgendwo(hin) 1 Li (146)
son [sʌn] Sohn
song [sɒŋ] Lied
soon [suːn] bald • **as soon as** *(conj)* sobald 6 P 3
sorry ['sɒri]: **1. Sorry. / I'm sorry.** Entschuldigung. Tut mir Leid.; **2. Sorry?** Wie bitte?; **3. feel sorry for sb.** jn. bedauern
sort (of) [sɔːt] Art, Sorte
sound *(n; v)* [saʊnd] **1.** Laut; Geräusch, Ton; **2.** klingen, sich *(gut usw.)* anhören
soup [suːp] Suppe
source [sɔːs] *(Informations-, Text-)* Quelle 2 How (37)
south [saʊθ] südlich; (nach) Süden °**southbound** ['saʊθbaʊnd] Richtung Süden 2 A 2 • **south-east** [ˌsaʊθ'iːst] südöstlich; (nach) Südosten • **southern** ['sʌðən] südlich, Süd- 1 A 6 (147) • **south-west** [ˌsaʊθ'west] südwestlich; (nach) Südwesten
souvenir [ˌsuːvə'nɪə] Souvenir, Andenken
space [speɪs] Raum, Platz; (der) Weltraum • **parking space** Parkplatz, Parklücke 3 A 6 (155) **spaceship** Raumschiff • °**space shuttle** Weltraumfähre, Shuttle 4 Li • **space station** Raumstation **spacesuit** ['speɪssuːt] Raumanzug 4 T (69)
Spanish *(n; adj)* ['spænɪʃ] **1.** Spanisch; **2.** spanisch
°**spark** [spɑːk] Funke 5 T (85)
speak* [spiːk] sprechen • **speaker** ['spiːkə] Sprecher/in
special ['speʃl] besondere(r, s), Spezial- • **be special** etwas Besonderes sein
specific [spə'sɪfɪk] bestimmte(r, s), spezifische(r, s) 2 T (35)
speech [spiːtʃ]: **speech bubble** Sprechblase 5 P 5 • **direct speech** wörtliche Rede, direkte Rede 3 T (52) • **indirect speech** indirekte Rede, nicht wörtliche Rede 5 A 7
spell [spel] buchstabieren **spelling** (Recht-)Schreibung, Schreibweise
spend* time/money (on) [spend] Zeit verbringen (mit) / Geld ausgeben (für) 1 Li (118)
spent [spent] **1.** *si. past von „spend"* 1 Li (118); **2.** *Part. Perf. von „spend"* 1 Li (118)
spider ['spaɪdə] Spinne 6 A 1
°**spirit**: **evil spirits** [ˌiːvl 'spɪrɪts] böse Geister 6 A 9
spoke [spəʊk] *si. past von „speak"*
spoken ['spəʊkən] *Part. Perf. von „speak"*

spoon [spu:n] Löffel 3 Li
sport [spɔ:t] Sport, Sportart **sportsman/-woman** Sportler/in 1 P 5
spot **(-tt-)** [spɒt] entdecken **Spot the difference.** Entdecke den Unterschied.
spring [sprɪŋ] Frühling 1 A 6
square [skweə] **1.** Quadrat **square mile** Quadratmeile 5 A 9 **2.** Feld *(auf Brettspiel)*; **3.** Platz *(in einer Stadt)* 2 Li (149)
squash [skwɒʃ] Squash 1 Li (145)
stage [steɪdʒ] Bühne 6 T (104)
stamp [stæmp] Briefmarke
stand* [stænd] stehen; sich (hin-)stellen • **stand around** herumstehen • **stand back (from)** zurücktreten (von); entfernt stehen (von)
star [stɑ:] **1.** (Film-, Pop-)Star; **2.** Stern
start *(v; n)* [stɑ:t] **1.** anfangen, beginnen (mit) • **start a car** ein Auto anlassen, starten • **start a company** eine Firma gründen 6 A 4 • **start a computer** einen Computer starten • **start a family** eine Familie gründen 6 P 15 **2.** Anfang, Beginn
state [steɪt] Staat; (Bundes-)Land
statement ['steɪtmənt] Aussage, Aussagessatz
station ['steɪʃn] **1.** Bahnhof; **2.** Station • **police station** Polizeiwache, Polizeirevier • **power station** Kraftwerk • **radio station** Rundfunksender
statistics *(pl)* [stə'tɪstɪks] Statistik(en) 2 How (37)
statue ['stætʃu:] Statue 2 Li (149)
stay (with) [steɪ] bleiben; übernachten (bei) • **stay at a hotel** in einem Hotel übernachten **stay behind** dableiben, zurückbleiben 3 T (52)
steal* [sti:l] stehlen
step [step] Schritt; Stufe • **step by step** Schritt für Schritt
stick* [stɪk] kleben • **stick together** zusammenhalten 4 T (70) **sticker** ['stɪkə] Sticker, Aufkleber
still [stɪl] **1.** (immer) noch; **2.** trotzdem, dennoch
sting* [stɪŋ] stechen
stole [stəʊl] *si. past von „steal"*
stolen ['stəʊlən] *Past. Perf. von „steal"*
stomach ['stʌmək] Magen, Bauch 6 T (104)
stone [stəʊn] Stein
stood [stʊd] **1.** *si. past von „stand"*; **2.** *Part. Perf. von „stand"*
stop *(v; n)* [stɒp] **1. (-pp-)** anhalten, stoppen; aufhören • **Stop it, Nick!** Hör auf damit, Nick! **2.** Halt; Haltestelle • **bus stop** Bushaltestelle
store [stɔ:] *(besonders AE)* Geschäft, Laden
storm [stɔ:m] Sturm; Gewitter
story ['stɔ:ri] Geschichte, Erzählung
straight [streɪt] **1.** *(adj)* gerade 3 A 12; **2.** *(adv)* gerade(wegs), direkt 3 A 12 • **straight on** geradeaus weiter
strange [streɪndʒ] seltsam, sonderbar
stream [stri:m] Bach
street [stri:t] Straße *(in einer Stadt)* • **in the street** auf der Straße • °**street entertainer** [ˌentə'teɪnə] Straßenkünstler/in 2 A 7 • **streetball** ['stri:tbɔ:l] *eine Art Basketball (wird auf der Straße mit nur einem Korb gespielt)* Welc (57)
stress [stres] Betonung **stressed syllable** [ˌstrest 'sɪləbl] betonte Silbe
string [strɪŋ] Schnur, Bindfaden
strong [strɒŋ] stark 5 T (85)
stuck [stʌk] **1.** *si. past von „stick"*; **2.** *Part. Perf. von „stick"*
student ['stju:dənt] Student/in; *(besonders AE auch:)* Schüler/in 5 P 4
studies *(pl)* ['stʌdiz] Studien, Studium 6 A 4
studio ['stju:diəʊ] Studio
study ['stʌdi] studieren; lernen; sorgfältig durchlesen 5 How (87)
stuff [stʌf] Zeug, Kram
stung [stʌŋ] **1.** *si. past von „sting"*; **2.** *Part. Perf. von „sting"*
stupid ['stju:pɪd] blöd, dämlich
style [staɪl] Stil 6 How (105)
sub-clause ['sʌbklɔ:z] Nebensatz
subject ['sʌbdʒɪkt] (Unterrichts-)Fach
success [sək'ses] Erfolg 6 A 4 **successful** [sək'sesfl] erfolgreich 2 A 4
suddenly ['sʌdnli] plötzlich, auf einmal
suffix ['sʌfɪks] Nachsilbe, Suffix
suggest [sə'dʒest] vorschlagen **suggestion** [sə'dʒestʃn] Vorschlag 2 P 11
suit [su:t] (Herren-)Anzug; (Damen-)Kostüm 4 T (69)
suitcase ['su:tkeɪs] Koffer
suite [swi:t] Suite 6 T (103)
sum [sʌm] Rechenaufgabe; Summe 3 A 12 • **do sums** rechnen 3 A 12 (156)
summer ['sʌmə] Sommer • **in (the) summer** im Sommer
sun [sʌn] Sonne • **sunny** ['sʌni] sonnig • **sunshine** ['sʌnʃaɪn] Sonnenschein 4 Li
Sunday ['sʌndeɪ, 'sʌndi] Sonntag
sung [sʌŋ] *Part. Perf. von „sing"*
sunk [sʌŋk] *Part. Perf. von „sink"*
sunny ['sʌni] sonnig
sunshine ['sʌnʃaɪn] Sonnenschein 4 Li
super ['su:pə] super, toll • **supermarket** ['su:pəmɑ:kɪt] Supermarkt
supper ['sʌpə] (warmes) Abendessen 5 A 3
supplies *(pl)* [sə'plaɪz] Vorräte 4 Li
support [sə'pɔ:t] *(Familie usw.)* ernähren, unterhalten, unterstützen 5 A 10
suppose [sə'pəʊz] annehmen, vermuten
sure [ʃʊə, ʃɔ:] sicher; sicherlich **Sure!** Sicher! Natürlich! Klar! **make sure** sich vergewissern; darauf achten/dafür sorgen (, dass) 2 T (36)
surfing ['sɜ:fɪŋ] *(das)* Wellenreiten, Surfen • **go surfing** wellenreiten gehen, surfen gehen
surprise [sə'praɪz] Überraschung **surprised (at)** überrascht (über) 2 P 12
survey (of) ['sɜ:veɪ] Umfrage, Untersuchung (über/von) 3 T (51)
survive [sə'vaɪv] überleben 5 T (85)
swam [swæm] *si. past von „swim"*
swap **(-pp-)** [swɒp] tauschen
sweatshirt ['swetʃɜ:t] Sweatshirt
swim* **(-mm-)** [swɪm] schwimmen • **swimming** *(das)* Schwimmen • **swimming-pool** ['swɪmɪŋpu:l] Swimmingpool, Schwimmbad • **swimming-trunks** *(pl)* ['swɪmɪŋtrʌŋks] Badehose • **swimsuit** ['swɪmsu:t] Badeanzug
swum [swʌm] *Part. Perf. von „swim"*
syllable ['sɪləbl] Silbe • **stressed syllable** betonte Silbe
symbol ['sɪmbl] Symbol
system ['sɪstəm] System

T

table ['teɪbl] **1.** Tisch; **2.** Tabelle 1 A 4
°**tackle** ['tækl] angreifen; *(beim Rugby)* fassen 1 A 1
°**taco** ['tɑ:kəʊ] *eine Art Pfannkuchen, mit Fleisch oder Gemüse, Käse und Gewürzen gefüllt* 4 A 8
tail [teɪl] Schwanz
take* [teɪk] **1.** nehmen; mitnehmen; (weg-, hin)bringen • **take a bath** *(in der Wanne)* baden, ein Bad nehmen 3 Li (154) • **take a boat trip** eine Bootsfahrt machen 1 A 6 • **take care of sb./sth.** sich um jn./etwas kümmern 1 A 6

Take a little time. Nehmen Sie sich etwas Zeit. 2 A 10 • **take notes** sich Notizen machen
take off **1.** ausziehen *(Kleidung)*; **2.** starten, abfliegen, abheben *(Flugzeug)* • **take part (in)** teilnehmen (an), mitmachen (bei) 2 A 14 • **take photos** Fotos machen, fotografieren • **take place** stattfinden • **take sth. round to sb.** jm. etwas bringen 6 P 13 • **take a seat** Platz nehmen • **take a walk** einen Spaziergang machen, spazieren gehen
He/she won't take 'no' for an answer. Er/sie will ein „Nein" nicht akzeptieren. 2 T (36)
2. dauern, *(Zeit)* brauchen UK Call (7) • **it takes** es dauert
take-off ['teɪk‿ɒf] Start *(Flugzeug)*
taken ['teɪkən] *Part. Perf. von „take"*
talent ['tælənt] Talent, Begabung 6 T (102)
talk *(n; v)* [tɔːk] **1.** Vortrag, Referat, Rede; Gespräch 4 T (68) • **give a talk (on sth.)** einen Vortrag/eine Rede (über etwas) halten 4 T (161)
2. talk (to) reden (mit), sich unterhalten (mit)
tall [tɔːl] groß *(gewachsen)*; hoch *(Bäume, Türme usw.)*
tank [tæŋk] (Fisch-)Becken; Tank
task [tɑːsk] Aufgabe 5 How (87)
taught [tɔːt] **1.** *si. past von „teach"*; **2.** *Part. Perf. von „teach"*
taxi ['tæksi] Taxi
tea [tiː] Tee
teach* [tiːtʃ] unterrichten, lehren
teach sb. a lesson jm. eine Lektion erteilen 5 T (84) • **teacher** ['tiːtʃə] Lehrer, Lehrerin
team [tiːm] Team, Mannschaft
on the team in der Mannschaft, im Team 4 A 8 • **team-mate** ['tiːmmeɪt] Mannschaftskamerad, -kameradin 1 T (18)
tear* sth. (off) [teə] etwas (ab)reißen; etwas zerreißen 5 T (85)
technical ['teknɪkl] technisch 4 Li
technique [tek'niːk] (Arbeits-)Verfahren, Technik, Methode 2 T (35)
techno ['teknəʊ] Techno
teenager ['tiːneɪdʒə] Teenager
teeth [tiːθ] *pl von „tooth"*
telephone *(n; v)* ['telɪfəʊn] **1.** Telefon • **telephone number** Telefonnummer • **(tele)phone box** Telefonzelle
2. anrufen
tell* (about) [tel] erzählen (von), berichten (über) • **tell sb. to do sth.** jn. auffordern, etwas zu tun; jm. sagen, dass er/sie etwas tun soll 6 A 7 • **tell sb. not to do sth.** jn. auffordern, etwas nicht zu tun; jm. sagen, dass er/sie etwas nicht tun soll 6 A 7 • **tell sb. the way (to)** jm. den Weg (zu/nach ...) beschreiben
temperature ['temprətʃə] Temperatur 6 A 1
°**temple** ['templ] Tempel 3 T (49)
tennis ['tenɪs] Tennis
tense [tens] (grammatische) Zeit, Zeitform
tent [tent] Zelt 5 A 1
term [tɜːm] Trimester
terrible ['terəbl] schrecklich, furchtbar
test *(n; v)* [test] **1.** Test, Prüfung, Schulaufgabe; **2.** testen, prüfen 5 How (87)
text [tekst] Text
than [ðən, *betont:* ðæn]**: slower than** langsamer als • **... than before** ... als vorher/als früher
thank sb. [θæŋk] jm. danken, sich bei jm. bedanken 3 A 12 • **Thank you.** Danke (schön). • **thanks** danke • **Thanks a lot.** Danke vielmals./Vielen Dank. • **thanks to Ben and Jenny** dank Ben und Jenny; wegen Ben und Jenny
that [ðət, *betont:* ðæt] **1.** das (dort), jene(r, s) • **That's right.** Das ist richtig. / Das stimmt. • **that day/night** an jenem Tag/in jener Nacht
that's because das kommt daher, weil 5 A 6 • **that's why** deshalb, darum • **after that** danach
like that so
2. dass • **so that** sodass, damit
3. der, die, das; die *(Relativpronomen)* • **the day that her article appeared** der Tag, an dem ihr Artikel erschien 5 A 3
the [ðə] der, die, das; die • **the next day** am nächsten Tag; der nächste Tag • **the same** der-/die-/dasselbe, dieselben
theatre ['θɪətə] Theater 2 Li
their [ðeə] ihr, ihre *(Plural)*
them [ðəm, *betont:* ðem] sie; ihnen
the two of them die beiden; alle beide 6 A 4
°**theme park** ['θiːm pɑːk] *Freizeitpark mit Attraktionen zu einem bestimmten Thema* 4 Li
themselves [ðəm'selvz] sich (selbst); selbst, selber °3 A 5 / 6 A 3 (168)
then [ðen] **1.** dann, danach; **2.** damals, zu der Zeit
there [ðeə] da, dort; dahin, dorthin • **there are** es sind (vorhanden); es gibt • **there's (= there is)** es ist (vorhanden); es gibt
Hi there. Hallo. • **in there** dort drinnen; dort hinein • **out there** dort draußen • **over there** dort drüben, da drüben
these [ðiːz] diese, die (hier)
they [ðeɪ] **1.** sie *(Plural)*; **2.** man 5 A 3 (164)
thick [θɪk] dick
thief [θiːf], *pl* **thieves** [θiːvz] Dieb, Diebin 2 A 14
thing [θɪŋ] Ding, Sache • **Poor things!** Die Armen! 2 T (34)
think* [θɪŋk] denken, meinen, glauben • **I think** Ich glaube / Ich meine / Ich denke • **I think so.** Ich glaube (ja). 5 A 6 (164) • **I don't think so.** Das finde/glaube ich nicht. 5 A 6 (164) • **You think so?** Glaubst du? 5 A 6 • **think (about)** nachdenken (über)
think about/of halten von, denken über • **think of** denken an; sich ausdenken
third [θɜːd] dritte(r, s)
thirst [θɜːst] Durst 5 T (85)
thirsty ['θɜːsti] durstig • **be thirsty** durstig sein, Durst haben
this [ðɪs] das (hier), dies • **this morning/afternoon/evening** heute Morgen/Nachmittag/Abend • **like this** so • **this way** **1.** hier entlang, in diese Richtung; **2.** so, auf diese Weise
those [ðəʊz] die (da), jene (dort)
thought [θɔːt] **1.** *si. past von „think"*; **2.** *Part. Perf. von „think"*
thousand ['θaʊznd]**: a thousand** eintausend
threw [θruː] *si. past von „throw"*
through [θruː] durch
throw* [θrəʊ] werfen • **throw the dice** würfeln • **throw up** sich übergeben
thrown [θrəʊn] *Part. Perf. von „throw"*
Thursday ['θɜːzdeɪ, 'θɜːzdi] Donnerstag
ticket ['tɪkɪt] **1.** Eintrittskarte; **2.** Fahrkarte • **ticket office** (Fahr-)Kartenschalter; Kartenvorverkaufsstelle 2 A 1
tidy *(adj; v)* ['taɪdi] **1.** ordentlich, aufgeräumt; **2. tidy up** aufräumen
tie [taɪ] (zusammen)binden, (zusammen)schnüren 5 P 6 (165)
tie sb./sth. up jn./etwas festbinden 5 P 6
tiger ['taɪgə] Tiger
°**tile** [taɪl] Fliese, Kachel; Ziegel 3 A 1
till [tɪl] bis *(zeitlich)*
time [taɪm] **1.** Zeit • **What time is it?** Wie spät ist es? • **What time is the film?** Wann fängt der Film an? • **a long time ago** vor langer Zeit • **at all times** immer, jederzeit 2 A 14 • **at the same time** zur selben Zeit • **at this time of year** in/zu dieser Jahreszeit 5 A 10 • **of all time** aller

Zeiten 6 A 1 • **get time off** frei bekommen, Urlaub bekommen 4 T (68) • **have a good time** Spaß haben, sich amüsieren • **work full-time** ganztags arbeiten, als Vollzeitkraft beschäftigt sein 6 A 7
feeding times Fütterungszeiten
free time Freizeit • **timeless** zeitlos, ewig 5 A 3
2. time(s) Mal(e); -mal • **five times nought** fünf mal null
timetable ['taɪmteɪbl] Stundenplan
tin [tɪn] Dose, Büchse
tip [tɪp] Tipp
tired ['taɪəd] müde
title ['taɪtl] Titel, Überschrift
to [tə, *betont:* tu:] **1.** zu, nach • **to school** zur Schule, in die Schule
to the butcher's zum Metzger, in die Metzgerei 5 A 3 (163) • **to the left** links, auf der linken Seite, zur Linken 4 P 10 • **to the right** rechts, auf der rechten Seite, zur Rechten 4 P 10 • **We've been to London.** Wir waren (schon mal) in London. / Wir sind (schon) in London gewesen. • **1 to 100** 1 bis 100 • **from Monday to Friday** von Montag bis Freitag
one nil to Kingsway eins zu null für Kingsway • **quarter to nine** Viertel vor neun (8.45/20.45)
to this day bis heute, bis zum heutigen Tag • **Welcome to ...** Willkommen in ...
2. um zu;
3. time to go Zeit zu gehen
today [tə'deɪ] heute • **today's match** das heutige Spiel
together [tə'geðə] zusammen
toilet ['tɔɪlət] Toilette 4 T (162)
told [təʊld] **1.** *si. past von „tell"*; **2.** *Part. Perf. von „tell"*
tomato [tə'mɑ:təʊ], *pl* **tomatoes** [tə'mɑ:təʊz] Tomate
tomorrow [tə'mɒrəʊ] morgen
tomorrow morning/afternoon/evening morgen früh/Nachmittag/Abend
tonight [tə'naɪt] heute Nacht, heute Abend
too [tu:] **1.** auch • **I'm from Bamberg, too.** Ich komme auch aus Bamberg.
2. you're too small du bist zu klein • **too bad** *(infml)* schade 4 A 1
took [tʊk] *si. past von „take"*
tool [tu:l] Werkzeug 5 T (85)
tooth [tu:θ], *pl* **teeth** [ti:θ] Zahn
brush your teeth sich die Zähne putzen
top [tɒp] Spitze, oberes Ende
at the top (of) oben, am oberen Ende, an der Spitze (von) • **on top (of)** oben, obendrauf (auf)
top of the table Tabellenspitze 1 P 4 • **top row** obere Reihe
topic ['tɒpɪk] Thema, Themenbereich
tore [tɔ:] *si. past von „tear"* 5 T (85)
torn [tɔ:n] *Part. Perf. von „tear"* 5 T (85)
tortoise ['tɔ:təs] Schildkröte
total *(n)* ['təʊtl] Gesamtbetrag, Summe 2 T (33)
totally *(adv)* ['təʊtəli] völlig, total 6 T (102)
touch [tʌtʃ] berühren, anfassen
tour *(v; n)* [tʊə] **1.** bereisen, reisen durch; **2. tour (of)** Tour, (Rund-)Reise (durch) • **tour guide** Fremdenführer/in, Reiseleiter/in
tourist ['tʊərɪst] Tourist, Touristin
tourist board ['tʊərɪst bɔ:d] Fremdenverkehrsbüro 1 P 12
towards Mark [tə'wɔ:dz] auf Mark zu, in Marks Richtung
tower ['taʊə] Turm
town [taʊn] Stadt • **in town** in der Stadt • **town hall** [ˌtaʊn 'hɔ:l] Rathaus
toy [tɔɪ] Spielzeug
track [træk] Weg, Pfad UK Call (7); Spur, Fährte 5 T (85)
tradition [trə'dɪʃn] Tradition
traffic ['træfɪk] Verkehr • **traffic jam** ['træfɪk dʒæm] (Verkehrs-)Stau
traffic lights *(pl)* Verkehrsampel
tragedy ['trædʒədi] Tragödie
train [treɪn] Zug • **on the train** im Zug
train [treɪn] trainieren, üben
trainer Trainer/in • **training** Training
translate (into) [træns'leɪt] übersetzen (in) • **translation** [træns'leɪʃn] Übersetzung
transparency [træns'pærənsi] Folie *(für den Tageslichtprojektor)* 1 P 12
transport *(no pl)* ['trænspɔ:t] Verkehrsmittel 2 A 13
travel *(v; n)* ['trævl] **1.** *(BE:* **-ll-***)* reisen; **2.** *(das)* Reisen • **travel agent** ['trævl‿eɪdʒənt] Reisebürokaufmann/-frau • **traveller** Reisende(r) 3 A 6
tree [tri:] Baum
trend [trend] (Mode-)Trend
trendy ['trendi] modisch, schick
°**tribe** [traɪb] Stamm, Volksstamm 3 A 5
trick [trɪk] Streich; Trick • **play a trick on sb.** jm. einen Streich spielen
trip (to) [trɪp] Ausflug, Reise (nach)
go on a trip einen Ausflug/eine Reise machen • **take a boat trip** eine Bootsfahrt machen 1 A 6
trouble ['trʌbl]**: be in trouble** in Schwierigkeiten sein; Ärger kriegen • **get sb. into trouble** jn. in Schwierigkeiten bringen 2 P 12
trousers *(pl)* ['traʊzəz] (lange) Hose
true [tru:] wahr • **come true** wahr werden, sich bewahrheiten 4 A 1
try [traɪ] **1.** versuchen, (aus)probieren • **Try and make sentences.** Versuche, Sätze zu bilden. • **try hard** sich sehr bemühen, sich anstrengen • **try on** anprobieren *(Kleidung)*
°**2.** *(n) (Rugby)* „Versuch" *(5 Punkte, erzielt durch Ablegen des Balles hinter der gegnerischen Torlinie)* 1 A 1 • °**go/run for the try** *etwa:* versuchen Punkte zu erzielen *(Rugby)* 1 A 1 / 1 T (18)
T-shirt ['ti:ʃɜ:t] T-Shirt
tube [tju:b]**: the tube** *(no pl) (infml)* die U-Bahn *(in London) (eigentlich:* Rohr, Röhre*)* 2 A 1
Tuesday ['tju:zdeɪ, 'tju:zdi] Dienstag
°**tundra** ['tʌndrə] Tundra *(baumlose Steppe)* 5 A 1
tunnel ['tʌnl] Tunnel
Turkish *(n; adj)* ['tɜ:kɪʃ] **1.** Türkisch; **2.** türkisch
turn *(v; n)* [tɜ:n] **1.** sich umdrehen
turn around sich umdrehen 4 A 1
turn (a vehicle) (ein Fahrzeug) wenden • **turn right/left (into)** (nach) rechts/links abbiegen (in)
turn to sb. sich jm. zuwenden; sich an jn. wenden
2. turn sth. off etwas ausschalten
turn sth. on etwas einschalten
turn over *(BE)* umschalten *(Fernsehen)* 1 A 3
3. It's my turn (to write/...) Ich bin an der Reihe (zu schreiben/...)
TV [ˌti:'vi:] Fernsehgerät; Fernsehen • **on TV** im Fernsehen
watch TV fernsehen
twice [twaɪs] zweimal
twins [twɪnz] Zwillinge
type (of) [taɪp] Art, Sorte, Typ 1 A 1
typical (of) ['tɪpɪkl] typisch (für)

U

UK [ˌju:'keɪ]**: the UK (the United Kingdom)** [juˌnaɪtɪd 'kɪŋdəm] das Vereinigte Königreich *(Großbritannien und Nordirland)* UK Call (6)
°**umiak** ['u:miæk] *offenes, mit Robbenhaut bespanntes Boot der Inuit* 5 A 1
uncle ['ʌŋkl] Onkel
uncomfortable [ˌʌn'kʌmftəbl] unbequem, unkomfortabel, unangenehm 3 A 6 (155)
under ['ʌndə] unter • **go under** untergehen

underground ['ʌndəgraʊnd]: **the underground** *(no pl)* die U-Bahn 2 A 1
underline [ˌʌndə'laɪn] unterstreichen 2 How (37) • **underlined** unterstrichen
understand* [ˌʌndə'stænd] verstehen, begreifen
understood [ˌʌndə'stʊd] **1.** *si. past von „understand"*; **2.** *Part. Perf. von „understand"*
unfortunately [ʌn'fɔːtʃnətli] leider, unglücklicherweise 3 A 1
unfriendly [ˌʌn'frendli] unfreundlich 3 P 12 • **get an unfriendly welcome** unfreundlich empfangen werden 3 P 12
unhappy [ˌʌn'hæpi] unglücklich, traurig 3 P 12
unhealthy [ˌʌn'helθi] ungesund 3 P 12
uniform ['juːnɪfɔːm] Uniform
unimportant [ˌʌnɪm'pɔːtnt] unwichtig 3 P 12
unit ['juːnɪt] Kapitel, Lektion
united: **the United Kingdom** [juˌnaɪtɪd 'kɪŋdəm] das Vereinigte Königreich *(Großbritannien und Nordirland)* UK Call (6)
°**universe** ['juːnɪvɜːs] Universum 6 A 4
university [ˌjuːnɪ'vɜːsəti] Universität, Hochschule 2 T (33)
unload [ˌʌn'ləʊd] ausladen, abladen 3 P 12
unlucky [ˌʌn'lʌki] unglückselig, Unglücks- 3 P 12
unpack [ˌʌn'pæk] auspacken 3 P 12
untidy [ˌʌn'taɪdi] unordentlich, unaufgeräumt 3 P 12
until [ən'tɪl] bis 2 T (35)
unusual [ʌn'juːʒuəl] ungewöhnlich, außergewöhnlich
up [ʌp] hinauf, herauf, nach oben **up the tree** den Baum hinauf **up and down** auf und ab 6 T (103) **get up** aufstehen • **go up** steigen, in die Höhe gehen • **mix up** durcheinander bringen • **Shut up.** Halt den Mund! • **tidy up** aufräumen
upstairs [ˌʌp'steəz] nach oben; oben
us [əs, *betont:* ʌs] uns
use [juːz] gebrauchen, verwenden, benutzen • **user** Benutzer/in, Anwender/in
useful ['juːsfəl] nützlich 2 T (36)
useless ['juːsləs] nutzlos, zu nichts nütze 5 A 3
usual *(adj)* ['juːʒuəl] gewöhnlich, üblich • **usually** *(adv)* ['juːʒuəli] meistens, gewöhnlich, normalerweise

V

vacation [*BE:* və'keɪʃn, *AE:* veɪ'keɪʃn] *(AE)* Urlaub, Ferien
valley ['væli] Tal 1 Li
valuable ['væljuəbl] wertvoll 3 A 1
van [væn] Lieferwagen
vanilla [və'nɪlə] Vanille
vegetable ['vedʒtəbl] (ein) Gemüse
vegetarian [ˌvedʒə'teəriən] Vegetarier/in
°**veggie burger** ['vedʒi ˌbɜːgə] Gemüseburger 6 T (103)
vehicle ['viːəkl] Fahrzeug
verse [vɜːs] Vers, Strophe
versus ['vɜːsəs] gegen, gegenüber 5 A 3
very ['veri] sehr • **very funny** sehr witzig, sehr komisch
video ['vɪdiəʊ] Video • **video recorder** ['vɪdiəʊ rɪˌkɔːdə] Videorecorder
view (of/over) [vjuː] Aussicht, Blick (auf/über) 1 A 6
°**Viking** ['vaɪkɪŋ] Wikinger/in UK Call (7)
°**villa** ['vɪlə] Landhaus 3 T (49)
village ['vɪlɪdʒ] Dorf
vinegar ['vɪnɪgə] Essig
violent ['vaɪələnt] gewalttätig, gewaltsam 2 Li
violin [ˌvaɪə'lɪn] Violine, Geige 6 T (103)
VIP [ˌviː‿aɪ 'piː] *Abkürzung für „very important person"* 4 A 8
virus ['vaɪrəs] Virus
visit *(n; v)* ['vɪzɪt] **1.** Besuch; **2.** besuchen; besichtigen • **visitor** ['vɪzɪtə] Besucher, Besucherin
vocabulary [və'kæbjələri] **1.** Vokabelverzeichnis, Wörterverzeichnis; **2.** Wortschatz, Vokabular 4 P 15
voice [vɔɪs] Stimme
°**volcano** [vɒl'keɪnəʊ], *pl* **volcanoes** *or* **-os** Vulkan 2 A 4
volleyball ['vɒlibɔːl] Volleyball
volunteer [ˌvɒlən'tɪə] Freiwillige(r) **volunteer work** ehrenamtliche Arbeit *(ohne Bezahlung)* Welc (57)
vote [vəʊt] **1.** abstimmen; **2. vote for sb.** jn. wählen, für jn. stimmen

W

wait (for) [weɪt] warten (auf) **Wait a minute.** Moment mal!
waiter ['weɪtə] Kellner • **waitress** ['weɪtrəs] Kellnerin
wake* [weɪk]: **1. wake sb. (up)** jn. (auf)wecken; **2. wake up** aufwachen
walk *(v; n)* [wɔːk] **1.** (zu Fuß) gehen, laufen • **walk about** herumlaufen • **walk off** weggehen 2 A 1 **walking track** Wanderweg UK Call (7)
2. Spaziergang; Wanderung **take a walk** einen Spaziergang machen, spazieren gehen
walkman ['wɔːkmən] Walkman
wall [wɔːl] Wand; Mauer
want [wɒnt] (haben) wollen • **I want to go.** Ich will/möchte gehen. • **want sb. to do sth.** wollen, dass jd. etwas tut 6 A 9
war [wɔː] Krieg 6 A 7
warm [wɔːm] warm • **global warming** Erwärmung der Erdatmosphäre, globaler Temperaturanstieg
warn sb. (about/of sth.) [wɔːn] jn. (vor etwas) warnen UK Call (7) **warn sb. not to do sth.** jn. davor warnen, etwas zu tun UK Call (144)
was [wəz, *betont:* wɒz]: **I/he/she/it was** *si. past von „be"*
wash [wɒʃ] waschen • **wash the dishes** das Geschirr abwaschen
wasp [wɒsp] Wespe
watch [wɒtʃ] Armbanduhr
watch [wɒtʃ] beobachten, sich *etwas* ansehen; zuschauen • **watch TV** fernsehen • **watch out** aufpassen 2 A 14
water ['wɔːtə] Wasser • **water chute** ['wɔːtə ʃuːt] Wasserrutsche **waterfall** ['wɔːtəfɔːl] Wasserfall °**water polo** ['wɔːtə pəʊləʊ] Wasserball 1 P 8 • **water power** Wasserkraft
wave [weɪv] Welle
°**wavy lines** [ˌweɪvi 'laɪnz] Wellenlinien, Schlangenlinien 2 T (35)
wax [wæks] Wachs 2 A 4 (150) **wax figure** ['wæks ˌfɪgə] Wachsfigur 2 A 4
way [weɪ] **1.** Weg • **ask the way** nach dem Weg fragen • **tell the way (to)** den Weg (zu/nach …) beschreiben • **Can you tell me the way to …?** Können Sie mir sagen, wie ich zu/nach … komme? **a long way** ein weiter Weg; weit (entfernt) 5 A 10 (164)
2. Richtung • **this way** hier entlang, in diese Richtung • **the wrong way** in die falsche Richtung • **the wrong way round** verkehrt herum
3. Art, Weise • **in our own way** auf unsere Art und Weise; so, wie wir wollen • **this way** so, auf diese Weise • **old/new ways** alte/neue Lebensweisen, Denkweisen, Bräuche 5 A 3 • **western ways** *(pl)* westliche Lebensweise/Lebensart 6 A 9
we [wi, *betont:* wiː] wir
weak [wiːk] schwach 5 A 10
wear* [weə] tragen, anhaben *(Kleidung)*

weather ['weðə] Wetter • **in this weather** bei diesem Wetter 5 P 10
web [web]: **the Web** (*kurz für:* **the World Wide Web**) das Netz, das Web • **web site** ['websaɪt] Website (*alle Seiten eines Anbieters im World Wide Web*)
Wednesday ['wenzdeɪ, 'wenzdi] Mittwoch
week [wi:k] Woche • **a two-week holiday** ein zweiwöchiger Urlaub • **day of the week** Wochentag
weekend [,wi:k'end] Wochenende **at the weekend** am Wochenende **at weekends** an Wochenenden **on the weekend** (*AE*) am Wochenende • **Have a nice weekend.** Schönes Wochenende.
weird [wɪəd] (*infml*) verrückt, seltsam 5 A 6
welcome ['welkəm] **1.** willkommen **Welcome to** Willkommen in **2. welcome sb. (to)** jn. willkommen heißen (in) 2 P 9 **3. get an unfriendly welcome** unfreundlich empfangen werden 3 P 12
Well, ... [wel] Nun, ...; Also, ...
well (*adv*) [wel] gut • **You're doing well.** Du machst es gut. **do well** erfolgreich sein, gut zurechtkommen 3 T (49)
well [wel]: **(oil) well** Ölquelle 5 T (84)
Welsh [welʃ] walisisch; Walisisch UK Call (7)
went [went] *si. past von „go“*
were [wə, *betont:* wɜ:]: **we/you/they were** *si. past von „be“*
west [west] westlich; (nach) Westen • °**westbound** ['westbaʊnd] Richtung Westen 2 A 2 **western** ['westən] westlich, West- 1 A 6 • **western ways** (*pl*) westliche Lebensweise/Lebensart 6 A 9
wet **(-tt-)** [wet] nass, feucht
whale [weɪl] Wal(fisch) 5 A 1 **whaling** ['weɪlɪŋ] Walfang 5 A 1 **go whaling** auf Walfang gehen 5 A 1 (163)
what [wɒt] **1.** was; **2.** welche(r, s) **what a ...** was für ein(e) ... **Now what?** Was nun? • **What about a calendar?** Wie wärs mit einem Kalender? • **What about Jenny?** Was ist mit Jenny? / Und Jenny? • **What are they talking about?** Worüber reden sie? **What colour is it?** Welche Farbe hat es (er, sie)? • **What day is 1st January?** Was für ein Tag ist der 1. Januar? • **What do you call ...?** Wie nennt man ...? • **what else** was sonst (noch) • **What time is it?** Wie spät ist es? • **What time is the film?** Wann fängt der Film an? • °**What's cooking?** (*infml*) Was liegt an? / Was ist los? 3 A 5 **What's the date?** Welches Datum haben wir? • **What's the matter?** Was ist denn (los)? 6 T (104) • **What's this in English?** Wie heißt das auf Englisch? **What's wrong, Sita?** Was ist los, Sita? • **What's your name?** Wie heißt du? • **What was ... like?** Wie war ...?
whatever [wɒt'evə] was (auch) immer 2 A 14 (152)
wheelchair ['wi:ltʃeə] Rollstuhl
when [wen] **1.** wann • **When is it?** Wann fängt es an? • **When's your birthday?** Wann hast du Geburtstag? **2.** wenn; **3.** als
whenever [wen'evə] wann (auch) immer 2 A 14 (152)
where [weə] wo; wohin • **Where are you from?** Wo kommst du her?
wherever [weər'evə] wo (auch) immer; wohin (auch) immer 2 A 14
whether ['weðə] ob 4 A 1
which [wɪtʃ] **1.** welche(r, s); **2.** der, die, das; die (*Relativpronomen*)
while (*conj*) [waɪl] während 3 A 5
whisper ['wɪspə] flüstern
whistle ['wɪsl] pfeifen
white [waɪt] weiß
who [hu:] **1.** wer • **who else?** wer sonst (noch)? 1 Li (146) **2.** wen; wem; **3.** der, die, das; die (*Relativpronomen*)
whoever [hu:'evə] wer (auch) immer, wen/wem (auch) immer 2 A 14 (152)
whole [həʊl] ganze(r,s), gesamte(r,s)
whose [hu:z] **1.** wessen • **Whose are these (CDs)?** Wem gehören die (CDs) hier? **2.** deren, dessen (*Relativpronomen*)
why [waɪ] warum • **Why be lonely?** Warum/Wozu einsam sein? 1 A 6 (147) • **Why not ask ...?** Warum fragst du nicht ...? / Warum fragen wir nicht ...? 1 A 6 (147) • **Why the hell not?** (*infml*) *etwa:* Warum denn nicht, verdammt nochmal? 6 T (102) **that's why** deshalb, darum
wife [waɪf], *pl* **wives** [waɪvz] Ehefrau
wild [waɪld] wild • °**the audience goes wild** das Publikum tobt, das Publikum rast 6 T (103) • °**wildly popular** (*infml*) wahnsinnig beliebt 6 A 4
will [wɪl]: **The world will be fantastic.** Die Welt wird fantastisch sein. • **You won't (= will not) find many.** [wəʊnt] Du wirst nicht viele finden.
win* (*v; n*) [wɪn] **1. (-nn-)** gewinnen • **win a scholarship** ein Stipendium bekommen 4 A 1 (159) **winner** ['wɪnə] Gewinner/in **2.** Sieg 1 T (18)
wind [wɪnd] Wind • **wind energy** Windenergie • **windy** ['wɪndi] windig
windsurfing ['wɪndsɜ:fɪŋ] (*das*) Windsurfen 1 Li (145)
window ['wɪndəʊ] Fenster
windy ['wɪndi] windig
wine [waɪn] Wein 3 A 6
winter ['wɪntə] Winter
witch [wɪtʃ] Hexe
with [wɪð] mit; bei
without [wɪ'ðaʊt] ohne
wives [waɪvz] *pl von „wife“*
woke (up) [wəʊk] *si. past von „wake (up)“*
woken (up) ['wəʊkən] *Part. Perf. von „wake (up)“*
wolf [wʊlf], *pl* **wolves** [wʊlvz] Wolf 5 A 10
woman ['wʊmən], *pl* **women** ['wɪmɪn] Frau
won [wɒn] **1.** *si. past von „win“*; **2.** *Part. Perf. von „win“*
wonder ['wʌndə] sich fragen, gern wissen wollen 4 A 8
wonderful ['wʌndəfəl] wunderbar
won't [wəʊnt] **1. You won't find many. (= You will not find many.)** Du wirst nicht viele finden. **2. He/she won't take 'no' for an answer.** Er/sie will ein „Nein“ nicht akzeptieren. 2 T (36) • °**He/she won't go away.** Er/sie will nicht weggehen. 2 T (36)
wood [wʊd] Holz
word [wɜ:d] Wort • **word building** Wortbildung • **word field** Wortfeld • **word group** Wortgruppe • **word link** Wortverbindung • **word order** Wortstellung
wore [wɔ:] *si. past von „wear“*
work (*v; n*) [wɜ:k] **1.** arbeiten **work on sth.** an etwas arbeiten **work full-time** ganztags arbeiten, als Vollzeitkraft beschäftigt sein 6 A 7 • **worker** Arbeiter/in **2.** funktionieren **3.** Arbeit • **at work** bei der Arbeit, am Arbeitsplatz • **out of work** arbeitslos
world [wɜ:ld] Welt • **in the world** auf der Welt • **World Cup** [,wɜ:ld 'kʌp] Weltmeisterschaft °**World Heritage Site** ['herɪtɪdʒ] Weltkulturerbe 2 How (37)
worn [wɔ:n] *Part. Perf. von „wear“*

worried (about) ['wʌrid] beunruhigt (wegen), besorgt (wegen/um) 5 P 10
worry *(v; n)* ['wʌri] **1.** *jn.* beunruhigen, *jm.* Sorgen machen • **worry (about)** sich Sorgen machen (wegen, um)
2. Sorge, Kummer
worse (than) [wɜːs] schlechter, schlimmer (als)
worst [wɜːst]: **(the) worst** (der/die/das) schlechteste ..., schlimmste ...; am schlechtesten, schlimmsten • **the worst thing about ... is/was ...** das Schlimmste an ... ist/war ...
would [wəd, *betont:* wʊd] würde, würdest, würden • **I'd like a ... (= I would like a ...)** Ich hätte gern ein/e ... / Ich möchte gern ein/e ... • **I'd like to do it. (= I would like to do it.)** Ich würde es gern tun/möchte es tun. • **What would you like to do?** Was würdest/möchtest du gern machen?
write* (to) [raɪt] schreiben (an) **write down** aufschreiben **write on the board** an die Tafel schreiben • **writer** Schreiber/in, Schriftsteller/in
written ['rɪtn] *Part. Perf. von „write"*
wrong [rɒŋ] falsch • **be wrong** **1.** sich irren, Unrecht haben; **2.** nicht in Ordnung sein, nicht stimmen • **the wrong way** in die falsche Richtung • **the wrong way round** verkehrt herum **What's wrong, Sita?** Was ist los, Sita?
wrote [rəʊt] *si. past von „write"*

Y

yawn [jɔːn] gähnen 4 T (69)
year [jɪə] Jahr; Jahrgangsstufe **16-year-old** 16-Jährige(r); 16-jährige(r, s) 1 T (18)
yellow ['jeləʊ] gelb
yes [jes] ja • **Yes, I did!** Doch!
yesterday ['jestədeɪ, -di] gestern **the day before yesterday** vorgestern 6 P 4
yet [jet]: **... yet?** ... schon ...? **not (...) yet** noch nicht
you [jʊ, *betont:* juː] **1.** du; ihr; Sie; **2.** dich/dir; euch; Sie/Ihnen; **3.** man • **..., you know** ..., weißt du; nämlich • **you see** weißt du, nämlich • **See you.** Servus. / Bis bald. / Bis dann. • **You're lucky.** Du hast Glück. / Du bist gut dran. **Here you are.** Hier bitte./Bitte sehr. • **How are you?** Wie geht es dir? / Wie geht es euch?
young [jʌŋ] jung • **the young** *(pl)* die Jungen *(eines Tieres)* 5 A 10
your [jɔː] dein, deine; euer, eure; Ihr, Ihre
yours [jɔːz]: **Yours, ...** dein/deine; euer/eure; Ihr/Ihre *(Briefschluss)* **Yours sincerely, ...** [sɪn'sɪəli] Mit freundlichen/herzlichen Grüßen ...
yourself [jə'self, *betont:* jɔː'self] dir/dich (selbst); selbst, selber 6 A 3 (168) • **about yourself** über dich selbst UK Call (7) • **Enjoy yourself ...** Amüsier dich ... / Vergnüg dich ... 6 A 1 • **Help yourself.** Greif zu! / Bedien dich! 6 (138)
yourselves [jə'selvz, *betont:* jɔː'selvz] euch (selbst); selbst, selber 6 A 3 (168)
youth [juːθ] Jugend UK Call (7)
Yuck! [jʌk] Igitt! / Bäh!

Z

zebra ['zebrə] Zebra
zero ['zɪərəʊ] Null, null
zoo [zuː] Zoo, Tierpark

ENGLISH SOUNDS

In den Wörterverzeichnissen steht hinter jedem englischen Wort in eckigen Klammern die Lautschrift. Sie gibt an, wie das Wort ausgesprochen und betont wird.
In der folgenden Übersicht findest du alle Lautzeichen.

Vokale (Vowels)

[iː]	gr**ee**n	[eɪ]	n**a**me
[i]	stor**y**	[aɪ]	m**y**
[ɪ]	**i**n	[ɔɪ]	b**oy**
[e]	y**e**s	[əʊ]	**o**ld
[æ]	bl**a**ck	[aʊ]	n**ow**
[ɑː]	p**ar**tner	[ɪə]	h**ere**
[ɒ]	n**o**t	[eə]	wh**ere**
[ɔː]	m**or**ning	[ʊə]	t**our**
[uː]	bl**ue**		
[ʊ]	b**oo**k		
[ʌ]	m**u**m		
[ɜː]	g**ir**l		
[ə]	**a** rul**er**		

Konsonanten (Consonants)

[p]	**p**en	[j]	**y**ou
[b]	**b**ox	[f]	**f**it
[t]	**t**en	[v]	o**v**er
[d]	**d**a**d**	[s]	**s**i**s**ter
[k]	**c**at	[z]	ha**s**
[g]	**g**ood	[tʃ]	tea**ch**er
[m]	**m**u**m**	[dʒ]	**G**ermany
[n]	**n**o	[θ]	**th**anks
[ŋ]	so**ng**	[ð]	**th**is
[l]	he**ll**o	[ʃ]	**sh**e
[r]	**r**ed	[ʒ]	televi**s**ion
[w]	**w**e	[h]	**h**e

– [ː] zeigt, dass der vorangehende Vokallaut **lang** gesprochen wird.
– ['] und [ˌ] sind Betonungszeichen. Sie stehen immer **vor** der betonten Silbe. ['] zeigt die Hauptbetonung, [ˌ] die Nebenbetonung.
– Der Bindebogen [‿] gibt an, dass zwei Wörter beim Sprechen aneinander gebunden und wie ein Wort gesprochen werden.

Bildquellen

AA Photolibrary, Basingstoke (S. 42 unten); Accent Alaska, Girdwood (S. 88 unten); Action Press/Action Sport, Hamburg (S. 8); Alamy, Abingdon (S. 113 links: Image State, rechts: Kolvenbach); Alaska Department of Environmental Conservation, Juneau (S. 89 unten links); AP; Frankfurt/Main (S. 31); Ardea Ltd., London (S. 120 oben); Avenue Images, Hamburg (S. 90 Obdachloser: Index Stock); John Berthelot, Santa Barbara (S. 57 Bild 1); Best of Camden Ltd., Tunbridge Wells (S. 38 unten rechts: Chris Tucker); Bilderbox, Thening (S. 83); John Birdsall, Nottingham (S. 7); Brian Brown Photography, Dover (S. 41); Britain on View, London (S. 6 Belfast, London; S. 49 oben); British Airways London Eye, London (S. 22 Bild 6); British Museum, London (S. 38 unten links; S. 115 Mitte); CartoonStock Ltd., Bath (S. 98 unten: Werner Wejp-Olsen); J. Allan Cash, London (S. 12 oben; S. 21 rechts); Cinetext, Frankfurt/Main (S. 90 Spiderman); Corbis, Düsseldorf (S. 6 oben: Tim Graham; S. 25 oben: Bill Varie; S. 26 Mitte: Jeremy Horner; S. 57 Bild 6: Ariel Skelley; S. 80: Vince Streano; S. 90 Chinatown: Mark L. Stephenson; S. 91 Google: James Leynse, grape harvester: Jim Sugar, beach: Steve Starr; S. 117: Gerald French); Corel Library (S. 12 unten; S. 15; S. 18; S. 22 Bild 1 u. 2; S. 26; S. 39 unten Mitte u. rechts; S. 59 Alligator; S. 63; S. 66 unten; S. 88 oben u. Mitte; S. 89 oben links, Mitte u. unten rechts; S. 90 Golden Gate Bridge, earthquake, Hollywood sign, black bear; S. 91 surfer, mission, ghost town, Lake Tahoe; S. 96); Roy Corral, Eagle River, AK (S. 58 Glen; S. 78 Portrait); Terry Deary Illustrations © Martin Brown first published by Scholastic Ltd., London (S. 44; S. 49 Cartoons); English Heritage, London (S. 40 Bild 5 u. 6; S. 49 unten, S. 50 Mitte; S. 53); Mary Evans Picture Library, London (S. 20 links; S. 28: Barnaby's Picture Library, London); Exploratorium, San Francisco (S. 107 unten rechts: Lily Rodriguez); Brian Fairlee, Woodland Hills (S. 108 oben); F1 Online, Frankfurt/Main (S. 23 Bild 3); Peter Ferstl, Regensburg (S. 115 Bruckmandl); Angelika Fischer, Berlin (S. 109); Focus, Hamburg (S. 57 Bild 2; S. 91 black youths: Magnum/Paul Fusco); Das Fotoarchiv, Essen (S. 59 Nummernschild); Getty Images, München (S. 56/57: Taxi; S. 58/59 Erdkugel: Stone;); Roz Goodman, Dillingham, AK (S. 78 Eskimos); Dwight Haigh, Flagstaff (S. 57 Bild 3 u. 5); Tim Hetherington, London (S. 27 oben); Historic Royal Palaces Enterprises Ltd., Surrey (S. 23 Bild 4 u. S. 38); Henry P. Huntington, Eagle River, AK (S. 74/75; S. 76 rechts); IFA-Bilderteam, Ottobrunn S. 66 oben: International Stock/Scott Barrow); Impact Photos, London (S. 27 unten); Kennedy Space Center, FL (S. 58 ATX Logo; S. 67 Logo); Kent Archaeological Rescue Unit, Dover (S. 43); Keystone, Hamburg (S. 98 links); London Aquarium (S. 38 Logo); London Dungeon(S. 23 Bild 5); London's Transport Museum (S. 24: Map); Madame Tussaud's, London (S. 25 unten); Mauritius, Berlin (S. 58 Margo u. Nasa Logo; S. 90 Oscar; S. 91 Death Valley; S. 92); Museum of London (S. 40 Bild 7; S. 42 Mitte); Museum of London, Archaeology Service (S. 40 Hintergrund u. Bild 1); NASA, Washington, DC (S. 58 Cockpit u. Astronauten; S. 65; S. 71); National Museum of Wales/Museum of Welsh Life, Cardiff (S. 21 links); National Oceanic and Atmospheric Administration (NOAA), Dept. of Commerce, Washington, DC (S. 72 oben; S. 73); North Slope Borough Public Information Office, Barrow, AK (S. 76 links); Okapia, Frankfurt/Main (S. 39 oben u. unten links; S. 79/120 moose, wolf); PC Magazine, December 15, 1998 (S. 93 unten); Picture-Alliance, Frankfurt/Main (S. 16; S.38 Arsenal Logo: dpa –Sportreport; S. 64: dpa; S. 91 Sequoia: Okapia/John W. Warden; S. 93 oben u. S. 101: dpa; S. 107 oben: AKG; S. 115 Regensburg: dpa); Punch Cartoon Library, London (S. 48; S. 81 unten rechts; S. 111); Redferns, London (S. 108 unten); Michael Reeve, Potters Bar (S. 37); Schapowalow, Hamburg (S. 6 Edinburgh; S. 91 Walk of Fame); Lonnie Schleich, New York (S. 57 Bild 4); Sven Simon, Essen (S. 114); Slim Films, New York (S. 72 unten); South Pacific Pictures, Auckland/ApolloMedia GmbH & Co Filmproduktion KG, Köln (S. 116: Image from Whale Rider used with kind permission of © South Pacific Pictures and ApolloMedia); Space Office of Tourism, Viera (S. 60); The Spectator, London (S. 81 links); Bildarchiv Steffens, Mainz (S. 40 Bild 2: Klaus Hansmann; Bild 3: Helmuth Loose; Bild 4: Bridgeman; S. 47: Pieter Jos von Limberger); Stock Food, München (S. 62); Cristina Taccone, San Francisco (S. 58 Scott; S. 94; S. 95); Vieri Tomaselli, Miami (S. 58 Conchita; S. 59 Seaquarium u. Restaurant; S. 61 links); Tower of London (S. 38 Mitte rechts u. S. 51: JM Massi); Transglobe, Hamburg (S. 90 highway sign; S. 93 Mitte);ullstein bild, Berlin (S. 98 rechts: IT); U.S. Geological Survey (USGS); Reston (S. 106);U.S. Space and Rocket Center, Huntsville (S. 61 rechts); Wales Tourist Board, Cardiff (S. 6/7 Hintergrund; S. 6 Cardiff; S. 9; S. 13); Welsh Language Board, Cardiff (S. 21 unten); White Cliffs Experience, Dover (S. 46); York Archaeological Trust, York (S. 50 unten); Zefa, Düsseldorf (S. 79 oben; S. 79 /S. 120 caribou, grizzly bear)

Titelbild: Corbis, Düsseldorf

Textquellen

S. 31: *The Prince's schoolfriend* from Newsweek, 15, December 1997 © 1997 by Newsweek, Inc., New York; S. 44: *Girls had it harder* und *Roman Maths* adapted from: *The Rotten Romans* by Terry Deary/Martin Brown, Scholastic Children's Books, London; S. 52: Invaders adapted from: *An Illustrated History of Britain* by David McDowall © 1989 by Longman Group UK/Pearson Education, Harlow; S. 73: *Hurricane Survivor* story adapted from: http://bryant.rbe.sk.ca/School/cyber2001/clarke/andrew.html (Januar 2004) © Judge Bryant Elementary School, Regina, CA; S. 73 *Hurricane Night* by Eve C. © Teen Ink, Newton; S. 73: *Windy Nights* by Robert Louis Stevenson taken from *A Child's Garden of Verses*, Simon & Schuster Children's Publishing, Revised edition, 1999; S. 87/105: excerpts taken from *English G 2000 Wörterbuch. Das Wörterbuch zum Lehrwerk. Englisch-Deutsch, Deutsch-Englisch* © 2002 Cornelsen Verlag GmbH & CO. OHG, Berlin und Langenscheidt KG, Berlin/München; S. 102-104: adapted from: *Next Month Hollywood* by Jean Davies Okimoto © 1993 by Jean D. Okimoto, from *Join In*, edited by Donald R. Gallo, Delacorte Press, New York. Reprinted, abridged and adapted by permission of Jean D. Okimoto; S. 116: tapescript/dialogue from the film *Whale Rider* used with kind permission of South Pacific Pictures and ApolloMedia © South Pacific Pictures Limited and ApolloMedia GmbH & Co Filmproduktion KG 2002; S. 116: adapted and abridged from: http://www.cdnn.info/eco/e030109/e030109.html (März 2004) © 2003 Cyber Diver News Network (CDNN), New York.

Liedquellen

S. 16: *We are the Champions* by Freddie Mercury © by Queen Music Ltd. D/A/CH/Osteuropäische Länder: EMI Music Publishing Germany GmbH Hamburg; S. 28: *Maybe it's because I'm a Londoner* by Hubert Gregg © 1947 by Francis, Day & Hunter Ltd., London. Für D/A/CH/ost-europäische Länder: EMI Music Publishing Germany GmbH Hamburg; S. 108: *Do you know the way to San Jose?* by Hal David © by New-Hidden-Valley-Music Company/Casa David, Melodie der Welt J. Michel KG Musikverlag, Frankfurt/Main; S. 108: *Don't be denied* by Neil Young © Silver Fiddle, Global Musikverlag, München; S. 109: *You've got a friend* by Carole King © 1971 by Screen Gems-EMI Music Inc. Für D/A/CH/osteuropäische Länder: EMI Music Publishing Germany GmbH, Hamburg; S. 109: *I miss you* by Björk Gudmundsdottir und Howard Simon Bernstein © Universal Music Publishing GmbH/ Sony/ATV Music Publishing (Germany GmbH), Berlin.

Nicht alle Copyrightinhaber konnten ermittelt werden; deren Urheberrechte werden hiermit vorsorglich und ausdrücklich anerkannt.

Summary-Abschnitt			
U2: 1	**active** ['æktɪv]	Aktiv	*A fire **destroyed** the house.*
	adjective ['ædʒɪktɪv]	Adjektiv	*good, new, red, funny, boring*
	adverb ['ædvɜ:b]	Adverb	*always, badly, here, really, today*
U6: 4	**adverb of frequency** ['fri:kwənsi]	Häufigkeitsadverb	*always, usually, often, sometimes, never*
U6: 4	**adverb of indefinite time** [ɪn,defɪnət 'taɪm]	Adverb der unbestimmten Zeit	*already, always, before, ever, just, never, often, yet, not … yet*
U6: 4	**adverb of manner** ['mænə]	Adverb der Art und Weise	*badly, nicely, happily, terribly, electronically, fast, hard, well*
	article ['ɑ:tɪkl]	Artikel	*the, a/an*
U6: 3	**auxiliary** [ɔ:g'zɪliəri]	Hilfsverb	
U5: 2 / U6: 5	**backshift of tenses** ['bækʃɪft]	Verschiebung der Zeiten *(in der indirekten Rede)*	*Ann: 'I **am** sorry.' → Ann said she **was** sorry.*
	comparison [kəm'pærɪsn]	Steigerung; Vergleich	*tall – taller – tallest; boring – more boring – most boring* *easily – more easily – most easily*
U3: 2	**conditional sentence** [kən,dɪʃənl 'sentəns]	Bedingungssatz	*If it rains, we'll stay at home.* *I'd fly to Spain if I had the money.*
	conjunction [kən'dʒʌŋkʃn]	Konjunktion	*Let's play **when** you come home.* *Wash your hands **before** we eat.*
	contact clause ['kɒntækt klɔ:z]	Relativsatz ohne Relativpronomen	*That's the man **we met** last week.* *The bike **I got** is great.*
U2: 2	**countable noun** [,kaʊntəbl 'naʊn]	zählbares Nomen	*girl – girls, ruler – rulers*
	definite article [,defɪnət_'ɑ:tɪkl]	bestimmter Artikel	*the*
U5: 2 / U6: 5	**direct speech** [,daɪrekt 'spi:tʃ]	direkte Rede, wörtliche Rede	*Ann said, **'I'm sorry.'***
U6: 2	**emphasizing pronoun** [,emfəsaɪzɪŋ 'prəʊnaʊn]	verstärkendes Pronomen	*I made this dress **myself.***
	future ['fju:tʃə]	Futur, Zukunft	
U1: 1	***going to*-future**	Futur mit *going to*	***I'm going to watch** TV tonight.* *Careful! You**'re going to fall**.*
U3: 2	***if*-clause** ['ɪf klɔ:z]	Nebensatz mit „if", „if"-Satz	***If it rains,** we'll stay at home.*
	imperative [ɪm'perətɪv]	Imperativ (Befehlsform)	***Open** your books. **Don't talk.***
	indefinite article [ɪn,defɪnət_'ɑ:tɪkl]	unbestimmter Artikel	*a/an*
U5: 2 / U6: 5	**indirect speech** [,ɪndɪrekt 'spi:tʃ]	indirekte Rede, nicht wörtliche Rede	*Ann said **(that) she was sorry.***
U5: 1 / U6: 6	**infinitive** [ɪn'fɪnətɪv]	Infinitiv	*(to) open, (to) see, (to) hear*
	irregular verb [ɪ,regjələ 'vɜ:b]	unregelmäßiges Verb	*go – went – gone*
U3: 2	**main clause** [,meɪn 'klɔ:z]	Hauptsatz	*If it rains, **we'll stay at home.***
U4: 3	**modal auxiliary** [,məʊdl_ɔ:g'zɪliəri]	modales Hilfsverb, Modalverb	*can, could, may, might, must, needn't, ought to, should, would*
	negative statement [,negətɪv 'steɪtmənt]	verneinter Aussagesatz	*I'm not ten. I haven't got a sister. I don't like techno.*
	noun [naʊn]	Nomen, Substantiv	*Glen, Amy, girl, brother, time*
	object ['ɒbdʒɪkt]	Objekt	*Amy is cleaning **the kitchen**.*
U6: 3	**object question**	Objektfrage, Frage nach dem Objekt	*Who do they help? What did you eat?*
U2: 1	**passive** ['pæsɪv]	Passiv	*The house **was destroyed** by fire.*
	past [pɑ:st]	Vergangenheit	
	past participle [,pɑ:st 'pɑ:tɪsɪpl]	Partizip Perfekt	*climbed, saved, stopped, tidied, bought, fallen, gone, written*
U4: 1	**past perfect** [,pɑ:st 'pɜ:fɪkt]	Plusquamperfekt, Vorvergangenheit	*Mike was late because he **had missed** the bus.*
U4: 2	**past perfect progressive** [,pɑ:st ,pɜ:fɪkt prə'gresɪv]	Verlaufsform des *past perfect*	*Liz **had been waiting** for two hours when Pete arrived.*
U1: 1	**past progressive** [,pɑ:st prə'gresɪv]	Verlaufsform der Vergangenheit	*What **were** you **doing** at 8 o'clock yesterday evening?*
	personal pronoun [,pɜ:snəl 'prəʊnaʊn]	Personalpronomen (persönliches Fürwort)	*I, you, he, she, it, we, they, me, him, her, us, them*
	plural ['plʊərəl]	Plural	
	positive statement [,pɒzətɪv 'steɪtmənt]	bejahter Aussagesatz	*I'm ten. I've got a sister. I like techno.*
	possessive determiner [pə,zesɪv dɪ'tɜ:mɪnə]	Possessivbegleiter (besitzanzeigender Begleiter)	*my, your, his, her, its, our, their*

GRAMMATICAL TERMS *(Grammatische Fachbegriffe)*

Summary-Abschnitt			
	prefix ['pri:fɪks]	Vorsilbe, Präfix	*in-, im-, un-*
	preposition [ˌprepəˈzɪʃn]	Präposition	*after, at, in, next to, on, to, under*
	present ['preznt]	Präsens, Gegenwart	
U1: 1–2	**present perfect** [ˌpreznt 'pɜ:fɪkt]	*present perfect* (Perfekt)	*I**'ve packed** my bag. **Have** you **packed** your bag? – Yes, I **have**. Liz **has known** Pete for years.*
U1: 3	**present perfect progressive** [ˌpreznt ˌpɜ:fɪkt prə'gresɪv]	Verlaufsform des *present perfect*	*Liz **has been waiting** for two hours.*
U1: 1	**present progressive** [ˌpreznt prə'gresɪv]	Verlaufsform der Gegenwart	*Conchita **is reading** a book. I**'m leaving** England tomorrow.*
	pronoun ['prəʊnaʊn]	Pronomen	
U3: 1	**prop-word** ['prɒpwɜ:d]	Stützwort	*I've got three dogs, a black **one** and two brown **ones**.*
U2: 2	**quantifier** ['kwɒntɪfaɪə]	Mengenbezeichnung	*some, any; much, many, a little, a few*
	question tag ['kwestʃən tæg]	Frageanhängsel	*Ann lives in Chester, **doesn't she?** But she isn't British, **is she?***
	question word ['kwestʃən wɜ:d]	Fragewort	*who?, what?, when?, where?, why?, how?*
U6: 1	**reflexive pronoun** [rɪˌfleksɪv 'prəʊnaʊn]	Reflexivpronomen	*myself, yourself, himself, herself, itself, ourselves, yourselves, themselves*
	regular verb [ˌregjələ 'vɜ:b]	regelmäßiges Verb	*help – helped – helped*
	relative clause [ˌrelətɪv 'klɔ:z]	Relativsatz	*That's the girl **who helped me**. We need a plan **that really works**.*
	relative pronoun [ˌrelətɪv 'prəʊnaʊn]	Relativpronomen	*who, that, which, whose*
U5: 2 / U6: 5	**reporting verb** [rɪˌpɔ:tɪŋ 'vɜ:b]	Verb des Berichtens *(zur Einleitung der indirekten Rede)*	*say, tell, think, explain, write, ask*
	***s*-genitive** ['es ˌdʒenətɪv]	*s*-Genitiv	*Sue**'s** brother; my sister**'s** room*
U1: 1	**simple past** [ˌsɪmpl 'pɑ:st]	einfache Form der Vergangenheit	*I **didn't go** to school yesterday. I **stayed** at home. **Did** you **go**?*
U1: 1	**simple present** [ˌsɪmpl 'preznt]	einfache Form der Gegenwart	*I **start** school at 8.45 every day. When **do** you **start** school? Our train **leaves** in 10 minutes.*
	singular ['sɪŋgjələ]	Singular	
	sub-clause ['sʌbklɔ:z], **subordinate clause** [səˌbɔ:dɪnət 'klɔ:z]	Nebensatz	***If it rains,** we'll stay at home. I can't come **because I'm ill**.*
	subject ['sʌbdʒɪkt]	Subjekt	***My dog** is black. **His name** is Tim.*
U6: 3	**subject question**	Subjektfrage, Frage nach dem Subjekt	*Who helped you? What woke you up?*
	suffix ['sʌfɪks]	Nachsilbe, Suffix	*-er, -ion, -less, -ly, -ness*
U1: 1	**tense** [tens]	(grammatische) Zeitform, Tempus	
U2: 2	**uncountable noun** [ʌnˌkaʊntəbl 'naʊn]	nicht zählbares Nomen	*music, water, butter, money, homework, information*
	verb [vɜ:b]	Verb	*count, hear, open, rain, see*
U4: 4	**verb of perception** [pə'sepʃn]	Verb der Wahrnehmung	*see, hear, feel*
U1: 1	***will*-future**	Futur mit *will*	*I**'ll be** 13 next week. I'm thirsty. – I**'ll get** you a drink.*
U6: 4	**word order** ['wɜ:d_ɔ:də]	Wortstellung	
U6: 3	**yes/no question**	Entscheidungsfrage	*Are you eleven? Have you got a sister? Do you like techno?*

Infinitive	*Simple past*	*Past participle*	
(to) **be**	**was/were**	**been**	sein
(to) **beat**	**beat**	**beaten**	schlagen; besiegen
(to) **become**	**became**	**become**	werden
(to) **begin**	**began**	**begun**	beginnen, anfangen (mit)
(to) **bet**	**bet**	**bet**	wetten
(to) **blow**	**blew**	**blown**	wehen, blasen
(to) **break** [eɪ]	**broke**	**broken**	(zer)brechen; kaputtgehen
(to) **bring**	**brought**	**brought**	(mit-, her-)bringen
(to) **build**	**built**	**built**	bauen
(to) **buy**	**bought**	**bought**	kaufen
(to) **catch**	**caught**	**caught**	(ein)fangen; *(Zug, Bus)* nehmen, erreichen
(to) **choose** [uː]	**chose** [əʊ]	**chosen** [əʊ]	(aus)wählen, aussuchen
(to) **come**	**came**	**come**	kommen
(to) **cost**	**cost**	**cost**	kosten
(to) **cut**	**cut**	**cut**	schneiden
(to) **dig**	**dug**	**dug**	graben
(to) **do**	**did**	**done** [ʌ]	tun, machen
(to) **draw**	**drew**	**drawn**	zeichnen
(to) **drink**	**drank**	**drunk**	trinken
(to) **drive** [aɪ]	**drove**	**driven** [ɪ]	*(ein Auto, einen Bus usw.)* fahren
(to) **eat**	**ate** [et, eɪt]	**eaten**	essen
(to) **fall**	**fell**	**fallen**	(hin)fallen
(to) **feed**	**fed**	**fed**	füttern
(to) **feel**	**felt**	**felt**	fühlen; sich fühlen
(to) **fight**	**fought**	**fought**	(be)kämpfen
(to) **find**	**found**	**found**	finden
(to) **fly**	**flew**	**flown**	fliegen
(to) **forget**	**forgot**	**forgotten**	vergessen
(to) **freeze**	**froze**	**frozen**	(ge)frieren; einfrieren
(to) **get**	**got**	**got**	bekommen; holen, besorgen; gelangen, hinkommen; werden
(to) **give**	**gave**	**given**	geben
(to) **go**	**went**	**gone** [ɒ]	gehen; fahren
(to) **grow**	**grew**	**grown**	wachsen
(to) **hang**	**hung**	**hung**	hängen, aufhängen
(to) **have (have got)**	**had**	**had**	haben
(to) **hear** [ɪə]	**heard** [ɜː]	**heard** [ɜː]	hören
(to) **hide**	**hid**	**hidden**	(sich) verstecken
(to) **hit**	**hit**	**hit**	schlagen, treffen; anfahren
(to) **hold**	**held**	**held**	(fest)halten; veranstalten
(to) **hurt**	**hurt**	**hurt**	verletzen; wehtun; schädigen
(to) **keep**	**kept**	**kept**	(be)halten; aufbewahren
(to) **know** [nəʊ]	**knew** [njuː]	**known** [nəʊn]	wissen; kennen
(to) **lead**	**led**	**led**	führen, leiten
(to) **leave**	**left**	**left**	verlassen; weggehen, abfahren
(to) **let**	**let**	**let**	(zu)lassen, erlauben
(to) **light**	**lit**	**lit**	anzünden; beleuchten
(to) **lose** [uː]	**lost** [ɒ]	**lost** [ɒ]	verlieren
(to) **make**	**made**	**made**	machen; bilden; zubereiten
(to) **mean** [iː]	**meant** [e]	**meant** [e]	bedeuten; meinen, sagen wollen
(to) **meet**	**met**	**met**	(sich) treffen
(to) **overtake**	**overtook**	**overtaken**	überholen
(to) **pay**	**paid**	**paid**	bezahlen
(to) **put**	**put**	**put**	legen, stellen, *(wohin)* tun
(to) **read** [iː]	**read** [e]	**read** [e]	lesen
(to) **retell**	**retold**	**retold**	nacherzählen
(to) **ride**	**rode**	**ridden**	reiten; *(Rad)* fahren
(to) **ring**	**rang**	**rung**	klingeln, läuten
(to) **rise** [aɪ]	**rose**	**risen** [ɪ]	(an-, auf)steigen; aufgehen *(Sonne)*
(to) **run**	**ran**	**run**	rennen, laufen; durchführen; leiten; verlaufen *(Straße, Grenze)*
(to) **say** [eɪ]	**said** [e]	**said** [e]	sagen
(to) **see**	**saw**	**seen**	sehen; besuchen
(to) **sell**	**sold**	**sold**	verkaufen

Infinitive	*Simple past*	*Past participle*	
(to) **send**	**sent**	**sent**	schicken, senden
(to) **shake**	**shook**	**shaken**	zittern; schütteln
(to) **show** [əʊ]	**showed** [əʊ]	**shown** [əʊ]	zeigen
(to) **shut**	**shut**	**shut**	schließen, zumachen
(to) **sing**	**sang**	**sung**	singen
(to) **sink**	**sank**	**sunk**	sinken, untergehen
(to) **sit**	**sat**	**sat**	sitzen; sich setzen
(to) **sleep**	**slept**	**slept**	schlafen
(to) **speak**	**spoke**	**spoken**	sprechen
(to) **spend**	**spent**	**spent**	*(Zeit)* verbringen; *(Geld)* ausgeben
(to) **stand**	**stood**	**stood**	stehen; sich (hin)stellen
(to) **steal**	**stole**	**stolen**	stehlen
(to) **stick**	**stuck**	**stuck**	kleben
(to) **sting**	**stung**	**stung**	stechen
(to) **swim**	**swam**	**swum**	schwimmen
(to) **take**	**took**	**taken**	(mit)nehmen; (weg)bringen; dauern, *(Zeit)* brauchen
(to) **teach**	**taught**	**taught**	unterrichten, lehren
(to) **tear** [eə]	**tore**	**torn**	reißen; zerreißen
(to) **tell**	**told**	**told**	erzählen, berichten
(to) **think**	**thought**	**thought**	(nach)denken; glauben, meinen
(to) **throw**	**threw**	**thrown**	werfen
(to) **understand**	**understood**	**understood**	verstehen, begreifen
(to) **wake up**	**woke up**	**woken up**	aufwachen; (auf)wecken
(to) **wear** [eə]	**wore**	**worn**	tragen, anhaben
(to) **win**	**won** [ʌ]	**won** [ʌ]	gewinnen
(to) **write**	**wrote**	**written**	schreiben

'A virus ate my homework.'

First names

Aled ['æled]
Alison ['ælɪsən]
Amy ['eɪmi]
Andrew ['ændru:]
Antonio [æn'təʊniəʊ]
Arthur ['ɑ:θə]
Bede [bi:d]
Brian ['braɪən]
Catherine ['kæθrɪn]
Cher [ʃeə]
Cheryl ['ʃerəl]
Chrissie ['krɪsi]
Christine ['krɪsti:n]
Christopher ['krɪstəfə]
Clive [klaɪv]
Colin ['kɒlɪn]
Conchita [kən'tʃi:tə, kɒn'tʃi:tə]
Craig [kreɪg]
David ['deɪvɪd]
Deleisha [də'li:ʃə]
Dina ['daɪnə]
Dionne [,di:'ɒn]
Drew [dru:]
Emma ['emə]
Fiona [fi'əʊnə]
Ginny ['dʒɪni]
Gordon ['gɔ:dn]
Gwenllian ['gwenhliən]
Hoa [hwʌ]
Ivy ['aɪvi]
Jake [dʒeɪk]
James [dʒeɪmz]
Jane [dʒeɪn]
Jean [dʒi:n]
Jenna ['dʒenə]
Jennifer ['dʒenɪfə]
Jerry ['dʒeri]
José [həʊ'zeɪ]
Joseph ['dʒəʊzɪf, 'dʒəʊsɪf]
Julia ['dʒu:liə]
Keith [ki:θ]
Lance [lɑ:ns, læns]
Lavell [lə'vel]
Lester ['lestə]
Linda ['lɪndə]
Lisa ['li:sə, 'li:zə]
Louis ['lu:i, 'lu:ɪs]
Margo ['mɑ:gəʊ]
María [mə'ri:ə]
Marie [mə'ri:]
Max [mæks]
Megan ['megən]
Melissa [mə'lɪsə]
Morgan ['mɔ:gən]
Natalie ['nætəli]
Nathan ['neɪθən]
Neil [ni:l]
Nguyen Duc [,ŋwiən 'dʌk]
Paco ['pɑ:kəʊ]
Pedro ['pedrəʊ, 'peɪdrəʊ]
Phuong ['fʌəŋ]
Rita ['ri:tə]
Robert ['rɒbət]
Rodney ['rɒdni]
Samantha [sə'mænθə]
Sandra ['sændrə]
Shane [ʃeɪn]
Sharon ['ʃærən]
Sheree ['ʃeri]
Sherlock ['ʃɜ:lɒk]
Shirley ['ʃɜ:li]
Stephen, Steven ['sti:vn]
Susan ['su:zn]
Suzanne [su'zæn]
Suzy ['su:zi]
Thomas ['tɒməs]
Tina ['ti:nə]
Todd [tɒd]
Trisha ['trɪʃə]
William ['wɪljəm]

Family names

Armstrong ['ɑ:mstrɒŋ]
Banderas [bæn'derəs]
Blair [bleə]
Boleyn [bə'lɪn]
Butcher ['bʊtʃə]
Columbus [kə'lʌmbəs]
Croaker ['krəʊkə]
Darwin ['dɑ:wɪn]
Dean [di:n]
Donovan ['dɒnəvən]
Evans ['evnz]
Filo ['faɪləʊ]
Gladstone ['glædstən]
Gonzales [gɒn'zɑ:lez, gən'zɑ:ləs]
Harold ['hærəld]
Holmes [həʊmz]
Hughes [hju:z]
Jenkins ['dʒeŋkɪnz]
Johnson ['dʒɒnsn]
Jordan ['dʒɔ:dən]
Marshall ['mɑ:ʃl]
Masters ['mɑ:stəz]
Mohajer [məʊ'heɪdʒə]
Morrison ['mɒrɪsən]
Muramoto [,mu:rə'məʊtəʊ]
Okimoto [,əʊki'məʊtəʊ]
Oktollik [ɒk'tɒlɪk]
Omori [ə'mɔ:ri]
Porter ['pɔ:tə]
Ramos ['rɑ:mɒs, 'reɪmɒs]
Redding ['redɪŋ]
Rosser ['rɒsə]
Sawyer ['sɔ:jə]
Seles ['selez]
Serkoak ['sɜ:kəʊ,æk]
Seward ['si:wəd, 'sju:əd]
Shakespeare ['ʃeɪkspɪə]
Sherman ['ʃɜ:mən]
Smith [smɪθ]
Stevenson ['sti:vnsən]
Strauss [straʊs]
Suyama [su'jɑ:mə]
Swenson ['swensn]
Thomas ['tɒməs]
Truong ['tʃʌəŋ]
Tussaud ['tu:səʊ]
Tyler ['taɪlə]
Wade [weɪd]
Warwick ['wɒrɪk, 'wɔ:wɪk]
Watson ['wɒtsn]
Watts [wɒts]
Whyte [waɪt]
Willis ['wɪlɪs]
Wren [ren]
Yang [jæŋ]

Place names

(siehe auch S. 149: Some places and sights in London)

Aberaeron [,æbər'aɪrən]
A.J. Dimond High School [,eɪ ,dʒeɪ 'daɪmənd]
the **Alps** [ælps] *die Alpen*
Angel Island [,eɪndʒəl_'aɪlənd]
Anchorage ['æŋkərɪdʒ]
the **Aquadome** ['ækwədəʊm]
Atqasuk ['ætkəsʊk]
the **Augustan Way** [ɔ:,gʌstn 'weɪ]
the **Avon** ['ævn]
Bangor ['bæŋgə]
Barmouth ['bɑ:məθ]
Barrow ['bærəʊ]
Bavaria [bə'veəriə] *Bayern*
Bayswater ['beɪzwɔ:tə]
Belfast [,bel'fɑ:st]
Ben Nevis [,ben 'nevɪs]
Berlin [bɜ:'lɪn]
Big Sur [,bɪg 'sɜ:]
Blackfriars [,blæk'fraɪəz]
Bodie ['bəʊdi]
Boston ['bɒstən]
the **Brecon Beacons** [,brekən 'bi:kənz]
the **Brooks Range** [,brʊks 'reɪndʒ]
Caistor Grammar School [,keɪstə 'græmə sku:l]
Camden Town [,kæmdən 'taʊn]
Cardiff ['kɑ:dɪf]
Carlisle [kɑ:'laɪl]
the **Chabot Space and Science Center** ['tʃæbət]
Chelsea ['tʃelsi]
Chicago [ʃɪ'kɑ:gəʊ]
the **Chugach Mountains** [,tʃu:gætʃ 'maʊntɪnz]
Chysauster [,tʃaɪ'sɔ:stə]
Cilcain [kɪl'keɪn]
Cirencester ['saɪrən,sestə]
Cocoa Beach [,kəʊkəʊ 'bi:tʃ]
Colwyn Bay [,kɒlwɪn 'beɪ]
the **Corinium Museum** [kə,rɪniəm mju:'zi:əm]
Cornwall ['kɔ:nwɔ:l]
Cumbria ['kʌmbriə]
Denali [də'nɑ:li]
Denver ['denvə]
Dover ['dəʊvə]
Durham ['dʌrəm]
Edinburgh ['edɪnbərə]
Euston ['ju:stən]
the **Everglades** ['evəgleɪdz]
Franklin High School ['fræŋklɪn]
the **Gower** ['gaʊə]
Greenland ['gri:nlənd]
Greenwich ['grenɪtʃ]
Hadrian's Wall [,heɪdrɪənz 'wɔ:l]
Hastings ['heɪstɪŋz]
Hearst Castle [,hɜ:st 'kɑ:sl]
the **Himalayas** [,hɪmə'leɪəz]
Hungerford ['hʌŋgəfəd]
Huntsville ['hʌntsvɪl]
Iditarod [aɪ'dɪtərɒd]
Jacksonville ['dʒæksənvɪl]
the **Jorvik Viking Centre** [,jɔ:vɪk 'vaɪkɪŋ ,sentə]
Juneau ['dʒu:nəʊ]
Kennedy Space Center [,kenədi 'speɪs ,sentə]
Laid [leɪd]
Lambeth ['læmbəθ]
Leeds [li:dz]
Lincoln Wolds [,lɪŋkən 'wəʊldz]
Liverpool Street ['lɪvəpu:l stri:t]
Llandysul [hlæn'dɪsɪl]
London ['lʌndən]
Los Angeles (L.A.) [lɒs_'ændʒəli:z, -lɪs]
Louisville ['lu:ɪvɪl]
the **Madison Center** ['mædɪsən ,sentə]
Magilligan Strand [mə,gɪlɪgən 'strænd]
Mallorca [mə'jɔ:kə]
the **Mersey** ['mɜ:zi]
Miami [maɪ'æmi]
the **Millennium Pier** [mɪ,leniəm 'pɪə]
Milwaukee [mɪl'wɔ:ki]
Monterey [,mɒntə'reɪ]
Moscow ['mɒskəʊ, 'mɒskaʊ] *Moskau*
Mount McKinley [,maʊnt mə'kɪnli]
Mount Whitney [,maʊnt 'wɪtni]
the **National Maritime Museum** [,næʃnəl ,mærɪtaɪm mju'zi:əm]
Nepenthe [nɪ'penθi]
Nome [nəʊm]

Northumberland [nɔ:'θʌmbələnd]
O'Hare Airport [əʊ'heə]
Orlando [ɔ:'lændəʊ]
Oxford ['ɒksfəd]
Paddington ['pædɪŋtən]
Paris ['pærɪs]
Pembrokeshire ['pembrʊkʃə]
Phoenix ['fi:nɪks]
Point Reyes [,pɔɪnt 'reɪjez]
Portage Glacier [,pɔ:tɪdʒ 'glæsiə, 'gleɪʃə]
Prudhoe Bay [,pru:dəʊ 'beɪ]
Ramsey Island [,ræmzi_'aɪlənd]
Richborough ['rɪtʃbərə]
Roberto Clemente High School [rə,bɜ:təʊ klɪ'menti]
Rome [rəʊm] *Rom*
the **Royal Observatory** [,rɔɪəl_əb'zɜ:vətri]
St Mary-in-Castro [sn ,meəri_ɪn 'kæstrəʊ]
St Peter and St Paul's Church [sn ,pi:tər_ən sn ,pɔ:lz 'tʃɜ:tʃ]
San Francisco [,sæn frən'sɪskəʊ]
San Jose [,sæn həʊ'zeɪ]
Scafell Pike [,skɔ:fel 'paɪk]
Scandinavia [,skændɪ'neɪviə]
Seattle [si'ætl]
the **Severn** ['sevn]
Silicon Valley [,sɪlɪkən 'væli]
Sitka ['sɪtkə]
Slieve Donard [,sli:v 'dɒnəd]
Snowdon ['snəʊdn]
Snowdonia [snəʊ'dəʊniə]
Soho ['səʊhəʊ]
Southwark ['sʌðək]
the **Sperrin Mountains** [,sperɪn 'maʊntɪnz]
Stanford ['stænfəd]
Stewart Island [,stju:ət_'aɪlənd]
Stonehenge [,stəʊn'hendʒ]
Strumble Head [,strʌmbl 'hed]
Sydney ['sɪdni]
Tallahassee [,tælə'hæsi]
Tokyo ['təʊkiəʊ]
Tomales Point [tə,mɑ:lez 'pɔɪnt]
Universal Studios [,ju:nɪvɜ:sl 'stju:diəʊz]
Valdez [væl'di:z]
Vauxhall ['vɒksɔ:l]
Venice Beach [,venɪs 'bi:tʃ]
Waterloo [,wɔ:tə'lu:]
Westminster Pier [,westmɪnstə 'pɪə]
Whistling Sands [,wɪslɪŋ 'sændz]
the **Wye Valley** [,waɪ 'væli]
York [jɔ:k]
Yorkshire ['jɔ:kʃə]

Other names

Arsenal Football Club [,ɑ:snəl 'fʊtbɔ:l klʌb]
the **Atlantic Ocean** [ət,læntɪk_'əʊʃn]
Bacchus ['bækəs]
the **Bakerloo Line** [,beɪkə'lu:]
the **BBC** [,bi: bi: 'si:] (British Broadcasting Corporation)
Britannia [brɪ'tæniə]
Caesar ['si:zə]
the **Circle Line** ['sɜ:kl]
Classis Britannica [,klæsɪs brɪ'tænɪkə]
the **Cutty Sark** [,kʌti 'sɑ:k]
Daedalus ['di:dələs]
the **Danube River** ['dænju:b] *die Donau*
the **Domesday Book** ['du:mzdeɪ ,bʊk]
Epcot ['epkɒt] (Experimental Prototype City of Tomorrow)
Ferrari [fə'rɑ:ri]
Godzilla [gɒd'zɪlə]
Henry VIII [,henri ði_eɪtθ]
Igaramkin [ɪ'gæræmkən]
the **Jubilee Line** ['dʒu:bɪli:]
Jupiter ['dʒu:pɪtə]
Madog ['mædɒg]
the **Metropolitan Line** [,metrə'pɒlɪtn]
the **Missouri River** [mɪ'zʊəri]
Miwok ['mi:wɒk]
Nalukataq [næ'lu:kæ,tek]
NASA ['næsə]
Owain ['əʊaɪn]
the **Pacific Ocean** [pə,sɪfɪk_'əʊʃn]
Prince Charles [,prɪns 'tʃɑ:lz]
the **San Andreas Fault** [,sæn_æn,dreɪəs 'fɔ:lt]
Tomesha [tɒ'mi:ʃə]
the **Union Jack** [,ju:niən 'dʒæk] *(die britische Flagge)*
the **Victoria Line** [vɪk'tɔ:riə]
Voyager ['vɔɪədʒə]
William I [,wɪljəm ðə 'fɜ:st]
William the Conqueror [,wɪljəm ðə 'kɒŋkərə]

The United States of America

Alabama (AL) [,ælə'bæmə]
Alaska (AK) [ə'læskə]
Arizona (AZ) [,ærɪ'zəʊnə]
Arkansas (AR) ['ɑ:kənsɔ:]
California (CA) [,kælə'fɔ:niə]
Colorado (CO) [,kɒlə'rɑ:dəʊ]
Connecticut (CT) [kə'netɪkət]
Delaware (DE) ['deləweə]
Florida (FL) ['flɒrɪdə]
Georgia (GA) ['dʒɔ:dʒə]
Hawaii (HI) [hə'waɪi]
Idaho (ID) ['aɪdəhəʊ]
Illinois (IL) [,ɪlə'nɔɪ]
Indiana (IN) [,ɪndi'ænə]
Iowa (IA) ['aɪəwə]
Kansas (KS) ['kænzəs]
Kentucky (KY) [ken'tʌki]
Louisiana (LA) [lu,i:zi'ænə]
Maine (ME) [meɪn]
Maryland (MD) ['meərilənd]
Massachusetts (MA) [,mæsə'tʃu:sɪts]
Michigan (MI) ['mɪʃɪgən]
Minnesota (MN) [,mɪnɪ'səʊtə]
Mississippi (MS) [,mɪsɪ'sɪpi]
Missouri (MO) [mɪ'zʊəri]
Montana (MT) [mɒn'tænə]
Nebraska (NE) [nə'bræskə]
Nevada (NV) [nə'vɑ:də]
New Hampshire (NH) [,nju: 'hæmpʃə]
New Jersey (NJ) [,nju: 'dʒɜ:zi]
New Mexico (NM) [,nju: 'meksɪkəʊ]
New York (NY) [,nju: 'jɔ:k]
North Carolina (NC) [,nɔ:θ kærə'laɪnə]
North Dakota (ND) [,nɔ:θ də'kəʊtə]
Ohio (OH) [əʊ'haɪəʊ]
Oklahoma (OK) [,əʊklə'həʊmə]
Oregon (OR) ['ɒrɪgən]
Pennsylvania (PA) [,pensl'veɪniə]
Rhode Island (RI) [,rəʊd_'aɪlənd]
South Carolina (SC) [,saʊθ kærə'laɪnə]
South Dakota (SD) [,saʊθ də'kəʊtə]
Tennessee (TN) [,tenə'si:]
Texas (TX) ['teksəs]
Utah (UT) ['ju:tɑ:]
Vermont (VT) [və'mɒnt]
Virginia (VA) [və'dʒɪniə]
Washington (WA) ['wɒʃɪŋtən]
West Virginia (WV) [,west və'dʒɪniə]
Wisconsin (WI) [wɪs'kɒnsɪn]
Wyoming (WY) [waɪ'əʊmɪŋ]

District of Columbia (DC) [,dɪstrɪkt_əv kə'lʌmbiə]

Country/Continent	***Adjective* • *Person(s)* ***
Africa ['æfrɪkə] *Afrika*	African ['æfrɪkən]
America [ə'merɪkə] *Amerika*	American [ə'merɪkən]
Asia ['eɪʃə, 'eɪʒə] *Asien*	Asian ['eɪʃn, 'eɪʒn]
Australia [ɒ'streɪliə] *Australien*	Australian [ɒ'streɪliən]
Austria ['ɒstriə] *Österreich*	Austrian ['ɒstriən]
Belgium ['beldʒəm] *Belgien*	Belgian ['beldʒən]
Bosnia-Herzegovina [ˌbɒzniə ˌhɜːtsəgə'viːnə] *Bosnien-Herzegowina*	Bosnian ['bɒzniən]
Bulgaria [bʌl'geəriə] *Bulgarien*	Bulgarian [bʌl'geəriən]
(Great) Britain ['brɪtn] *Großbritannien*	British ['brɪtɪʃ] • a Briton ['brɪtn], *pl* the British
Canada ['kænədə] *Kanada*	Canadian [kə'neɪdiən]
China ['tʃaɪnə] *China*	Chinese [ˌtʃaɪ'niːz] • a Chinese, *pl* the Chinese
Croatia [krəʊ'eɪʃə] *Kroatien*	Croatian [krəʊ'eɪʃən]
the **Czech Republic** [ˌtʃek rɪ'pʌblɪk] *Tschechien, die Tschechische Republik*	Czech [tʃek]
Denmark ['denmɑːk] *Dänemark*	Danish ['deɪnɪʃ] • a Dane [deɪn], *pl* -s
England ['ɪŋglənd] *England*	English ['ɪŋglɪʃ] • an Englishman/-woman, *pl* the English
Estonia [es'təʊniə] *Estland*	Estonian [es'təʊniən]
Europe ['jʊərəp] *Europa*	European [ˌjʊərə'piːən]
Finland ['fɪnlənd] *Finnland*	Finnish ['fɪnɪʃ] • a Finn [fɪn], *pl* -s
France [frɑːns] *Frankreich*	French [frentʃ] • a Frenchman/-woman, *pl* the French
Germany ['dʒɜːməni] *Deutschland*	German ['dʒɜːmən]
Greece [griːs] *Griechenland*	Greek [griːk]
Holland ['hɒlənd] *Holland*	Dutch [dʌtʃ] • a Dutchman/-woman, *pl* the Dutch
Hungary ['hʌŋgəri] *Ungarn*	Hungarian [hʌŋ'geəriən]
Iceland ['aɪslənd] *Island*	Icelandic [aɪs'lændɪk]
India ['ɪndiə] *Indien*	Indian ['ɪndiən]
Ireland ['aɪələnd] *Irland*	Irish ['aɪrɪʃ] • an Irishman/-woman, *pl* the Irish
Italy ['ɪtəli] *Italien*	Italian [ɪ'tæliən]
Japan [dʒə'pæn] *Japan*	Japanese [ˌdʒæpə'niːz] • a Japanese, *pl* the Japanese
Latvia ['lætviə] *Lettland*	Latvian ['lætviən]
Lithuania [ˌlɪθju'eɪniə] *Litauen*	Lithuanian [ˌlɪθju'eɪniən]
Mexico ['meksɪkəʊ] *Mexiko*	Mexican ['meksɪkən]
the **Netherlands** ['neðələndz] *die Niederlande*	Dutch [dʌtʃ] • a Dutchman/-woman, *pl* the Dutch
New Zealand [ˌnjuː 'ziːlənd] *Neuseeland*	New Zealand • a New Zealander [ˌnjuː 'ziːləndə], *pl* -s
Norway ['nɔːweɪ] *Norwegen*	Norwegian [nɔː'wiːdʒən]
Pakistan [ˌpɑːkɪ'stɑːn] *Pakistan*	Pakistani [ˌpɑːkɪ'stɑːni]
the **Philippines** ['fɪlɪpiːnz] *die Philippinen*	Philippine ['fɪlɪpiːn] • a Filipino/-na [ˌfɪlɪ'piːnəʊ, -nə], *pl* -s
Poland ['pəʊlənd] *Polen*	Polish ['pəʊlɪʃ] • a Pole [pəʊl], *pl* -s
Portugal ['pɔːtʃʊgl] *Portugal*	Portuguese [ˌpɔːtʃu'giːz] • a Portuguese, *pl* the Portuguese
Romania [ru'meɪniə] *Rumänien*	Romanian [ru'meɪniən]
Russia ['rʌʃə] *Russland*	Russian ['rʌʃn]
Scotland ['skɒtlənd] *Schottland*	Scottish ['skɒtɪʃ] • a Scotsman/-woman *or* a Scot [skɒt], *pl* the Scottish *or* the Scots
Slovakia [sləʊ'vɑːkiə, sləʊ'vækiə] *die Slowakei*	Slovak ['sləʊvæk]
Slovenia [sləʊ'viːniə] *Slowenien*	Slovene ['sləʊviːn] *or* Slovenian [sləʊ'viːniən]
Spain [speɪn] *Spanien*	Spanish ['spænɪʃ] • a Spaniard ['spænɪəd], *pl* -s
Sweden ['swiːdn] *Schweden*	Swedish ['swiːdɪʃ] • a Swede [swiːd], *pl* -s
Switzerland ['swɪtsələnd] *die Schweiz*	Swiss [swɪs] • a Swiss, *pl* the Swiss
Turkey ['tɜːki] *die Türkei*	Turkish ['tɜːkɪʃ] • a Turk [tɜːk], *pl* -s
the **United Kingdom (**the **UK)** [juˌnaɪtɪd 'kɪŋdəm, juː'keɪ] *das Vereinigte Königreich*	British ['brɪtɪʃ] • a Briton ['brɪtn], *pl* the British
the **United States of America (**the **USA)** [juˌnaɪtɪd ˌsteɪts‿əv‿ə'merɪkə, juː‿es‿'eɪ] *die Vereinigten Staaten von Amerika*	American [ə'merɪkən] *or* US [ˌjuː‿'es] • an American, *pl* -s
Vietnam [ˌviət'næm, ˌviət'nɑːm] *Vietnam*	Vietnamese [ˌviətnə'miːz] • a Vietnamese, *pl* the Vietnamese
Wales [weɪlz] *Wales*	Welsh [welʃ] • a Welshman/-woman, *pl* the Welsh
Yugoslavia [ˌjuːgəʊ'slɑːviə] *Jugoslavien*	Yugoslavian [ˌjuːgəʊ'slɑːviən] • a Yugoslav ['juːgəʊslɑːv], *pl* -s

* Wenn nur ein Wort in dieser Spalte steht, bedeutet das, dass Adjektiv und Personenbezeichnung identisch sind: *Naples is an **Italian** city. / I met an **Italian** called Marco.* Der Plural endet auf *-s*: *The **Italians** invented pizza.*

What you can say to the teacher

Sorry, I don't understand ...
What's ... in English/in German, please?
What does ... mean?
How do you spell ...?
Could you repeat[1] it, please?
Could you explain it again, please?
Could you write it on the board, please?
I can't see the board/transparency.
Could you move over, please?
Can you push the transparency up/down/to the right/ to the left?
Can you focus[2] the overhead projector[3], please?
Can you speak louder, please?
Can you turn the volume[4] up/down, please?
Can we ...
- act out the story, please?
- listen to the CD again?
- work with a partner, please?
- do this in group work, please?
- play the game/sing the song on page ...?

What's for homework?
Will this be in the next test?
When's the next test?

What you can say to other pupils

What are we going to do?
Why don't we do this together?
Let's make a list/a poster/a wall display[5].
I think we should ...
Why don't we write .../ask ...?
Whose turn is it?
It's my/your turn now.
Can you look that word up in the dictionary?

What your teacher says

Who hasn't finished yet?
Could somebody ...
- plug in the video recorder/CD player, please?
- get some chalk[6], please?
- collect the exercise books, please?

Act out the conversation/the scene/...
Who would like to play the part of ...?
Work with a partner/in a group.

Swap your exercise books/notes/...
Make a wall display[5]/poster/...
Make/Take notes on ...
Read your poem/story/... out to the class.

Was du zur Lehrerin/zum Lehrer sagen kannst

Entschuldigung, aber ... verstehe ich nicht.
Was heißt ... auf Englisch/Deutsch?
Was bedeutet ...?
Wie buchstabiert man ...?
Könnten Sie das bitte wiederholen?
Könnten Sie das bitte noch einmal erklären?
Könnten Sie das bitte an die Tafel schreiben?
Ich kann die Tafel/die Folie nicht sehen.
Könnten Sie bitte ein Stück zur Seite rücken?
Können Sie die Folie nach oben/unten/rechts/links schieben?
Können Sie den Overheadprojektor bitte scharf stellen?
Können Sie bitte etwas lauter sprechen?
Können Sie bitte den Ton etwas lauter/leiser stellen?
Können wir ...
- die Geschichte vorspielen, bitte?
- die CD noch einmal hören?
- bitte mit einem Partner/einer Partnerin arbeiten?
- das bitte in der Gruppe machen?
- das Spiel spielen/das Lied auf Seite ... singen?

Was haben wir als Hausaufgabe auf?
Kommt das in der nächsten Schulaufgabe dran?
Wann schreiben wir die nächste Schulaufgabe?

Was du zu anderen Schülerinnen und Schülern sagen kannst

Was wollen wir machen?
Wollen wir das nicht zusammen machen?
Machen wir eine Liste/ein Poster/ein Wandbild.
Ich finde, wir sollten ...
Warum schreiben wir nicht .../fragen wir nicht ...?
Wer ist an der Reihe?
Ich bin/Du bist jetzt an der Reihe.
Kannst du das Wort im Wörterbuch nachschlagen?

Was deine Lehrerin/dein Lehrer sagt

Wer ist noch nicht fertig?
Könnte jemand bitte ...
- den Stecker vom Videorecorder/CD-Spieler in die Steckdose stecken?
- Kreide holen?
- die Hefte einsammeln?

Spielt das Gespräch/die Szene/... vor.
Wer möchte die Rolle des/der ... spielen?
Arbeitet mit einem Partner oder einer Partnerin/ in der Gruppe.
Tauscht eure Hefte/Notizen/... aus.
Macht ein Wandbild/ein Poster/...
Macht euch Notizen zu ...
Lies dein Gedicht/deine Geschichte/... laut vor.

[1] (to) repeat [rɪ'pi:t] [2] (to) focus ['fəʊkəs] [3] overhead projector [ˌəʊvəhed prə'dʒektə] [4] volume ['vɒlju:m]
[5] wall display ['wɔ:l dɪˌspleɪ] [6] chalk [tʃɔ:k]